DATE DUE
D0936948

NONLOCAL PROBLEMS OF THE THEORY OF OSCILLATIONS

V. A. PLISS
LENINGRAD STATE UNIVERSITY
LENINGRAD, U.S.S.R.

Translated by SCRIPTA TECHNICA, INC.

Translation Edited by
HARRY HERMAN
DEPARTMENT OF MECHANICAL ENGINEERING
NEWARK COLLEGE OF ENGINEERING
NEWARK, NEW JERSEY

1966

ACADEMIC PRESS New York and London

Copyright © 1966, by Academic Press Inc.
ALL RIGHTS RESERVED.
NO PART OF THIS BOOK MAY BE REPRODUCED IN ANY FORM, BY PHOTOSTAT, MICROFILM, OR ANY OTHER MEANS, WITHOUT WRITTEN PERMISSION FROM THE PUBLISHERS.

ACADEMIC PRESS INC.
111 Fifth Avenue, New York, New York 10003

United Kingdom Edition published by
ACADEMIC PRESS INC. (LONDON) LTD.
Berkeley Square House, London W.1

Library of Congress Catalog Card Number: *65-27553*

Originally published as:
"Nelokal'nyye Problemy Teorii Kolebaniy"
Nauka Press, Moscow-Leningrad, 1964

PRINTED IN THE UNITED STATES OF AMERICA

JOINT UNIVERSITY
LIBRARIES
NASHVILLE, TENN.
PHYSICS

628911
Science
QA
871
.P813
1966

Translation Editor's Preface

Continued progress both permits and requires increasingly accurate mathematical models of physical phenomena, taking into account nonlinear and dissipative behavior of systems. This has spurred an increase of interest in mathematical theory dealing with the behavior of such systems.

In view of the rising proliferation of publications, the researcher's task of locating pertinent information is becoming increasingly difficult. Hence, Prof. Pliss' fine work collecting and extending recent developments pertaining to stability in the large of nonlinear systems, especially dissipative systems, represents a significant contribution, and I am happy to have shared in the effort to make this work available to English reading audiences.

NEW YORK, MARCH 1966 HARRY HERMAN

Preface

Recently, efforts of many specialists in the theory of differential equations have been addressed to the study of so-called nonlocal problems. A very important position in this group of problems is occupied by problems on the existence of periodic solutions and their stability in the large. It is this group of problems that is the subject of the present monograph. The book considers two broad classes of systems: Systems whose right sides are periodic functions of time and autonomous systems.

The book consists of three chapters. Basically, the first chapter is devoted to multidimensional periodic systems. Section 1 is introductory, and considers the most general autonomous and periodic systems. Fundamental definitions are stated, and general theorems on the behavior of solutions of periodic and autonomous systems are proved. These theorems are important to the sequel.

Section 2 deals with the general properties of dissipative systems, i.e., systems for which, after a sufficiently long time, every solution enters a fixed region. Conditions which are necessary and sufficient, in order that a system be dissipative, are given in terms of the existence of certain generalized forms of classical Lyapunov functions. Existence is proved for a bounded set S of entire solutions such that all solutions of a dissipative system approach S as time increases without bound.

The next three sections (Sections 3-5) present conditions that are sufficient in order that certain specific systems of differential equations be dissipative. The general theorems proved in Section 2 are used to prove dissipativity.

Section 6 is devoted to the study of multidimensional nondissipative periodic systems. The existence of periodic solutions with the same period as the right sides is proved under various assumptions.

Sections 7 and 8 study systems with convergence, by which we mean systems with a periodic solution that is stable in the large. In investigating systems with convergence, the periodic solutions are usually unknown, so that it is natural to consider the problem of approximation of solutions in general. For this reason, we introduce in Section 7, functions that depend on two points in a space and vanish when the two points coincide. Conditions which are necessary and sufficient for the existence of convergence are stated in terms of the existence of such functions. In the sequel, these conditions are used to establish the existence of convergence for certain specific multidimensional and two-dimensional systems.

Chapter 2 is devoted to the study of first- and second-order periodic systems. Proofs of the theorems presented here depend essentially on the fact that we are dealing with systems of these particular types, and the majority of these theorems do not generalize to systems of order greater than two.

In Section 9, we consider first-order equations, and state several general theorems on the locations of the solution curves of these equations. A large part of the section is devoted to the study of equations with polynomial right sides, and there is a detailed study of the possible number of periodic solutions for such equations. Here we give a number of conditions sufficient to guarantee that the number of periodic solutions will be no greater than the degree of the polynomial in the right side.

In Sections 10 and 11, we consider first-order equations whose right sides are periodic with respect to both arguments. It is natural to discuss such equations on a torus, and in Section 10 the general behavior of trajectories on a torus is studied. In Section 11, we consider the relationship between the behavior of solutions and the parameters in the right side of an equation. The relationship between the turning number and the parameters of the problem is studied, and conditions necessary and sufficient for coarseness are given.

The remaining Sections (Sections 12-17) of Chapter 2 are devoted to the study of second-order periodic systems.

In Section 12, we prove general theorems on the behavior of the solution curves of a periodic system of two differential equations. In particular, we prove the fundamental theorem of Massera on the existence of periodic solutions for second-order systems. There is a detailed study of the behavior of a dissipative second-order system, and the possible structure of the set S for such a system is investigated.

The next two sections (Sections 13 and 14), deal with the problem of the existence of toroidal invariant surfaces. A system is assumed to have a toroidal solution surface with certain definite properties, and we show that all systems "close" to it have such a solution surface. Sections 13 and 14 also contain various propositions about the behavior of solutions on the invariant surfaces of initial systems. The methods which are used in these two sections to prove the existence of solution surfaces differ. In Section 13, we introduce a space of closed curves whose transformation into itself is associated with the system and we prove that this transformation has a stationary point. In Section 14, the argument is based on the well-known first method of Lyapunov.

In Section 15, we present an example of a dissipative second-order system with a very complex set S. In particular, we show that the intersection between this set and a plane in which the arguments of the system are constant is a region whose boundary is not a Jordan curve.

Sections 16 and 17 are devoted to the study of concrete second-order systems. Here we show that, under certain assumptions, there exist periodic solutions with period equal to an integral multiple of the period of the right side.

Chapter 3 deals with autonomous systems.

In Section 18, we prove several general theorems on periodic solutions of autonomous systems and prove the well-known principle of the torus. Sufficient conditions for the existence and uniqueness of periodic solutions in some region of phase space are given.

Section 19 deals with a concrete system; the principle of the torus is used to prove the existence of a periodic solution.

The next three sections of the book consider a third-order equation with a nonlinearity satisfying a so-called generalized Hurwitz criterion.

In Section 20, we prove several theorems on the location of the trajectories of this equation.

Section 21 deals with sufficient conditions for all solutions of the equation in question to be bounded. Assuming the preceding conditions to be satisfied, we conduct a detailed qualitative study of the location of the trajectories. In particular, we show that if the equation has no periodic solutions, all of its solutions approach an equilibrium state.

Finally, in Section 22, we state conditions that are sufficient for the existence of periodic solutions.

No pretense is made to a complete exposition of all methods in the nonlocal theory of oscillations; only some of the theory's most important developments are discussed. Specialists will, of course, find that in addition to having left out individual, highly important results which have a direct bearing on the topics under consideration, we have omitted entire branches of the subject. For example, there is absolutely no mention of two-dimensional autonomous systems (the theory of such systems was exhaustively discussed in [90]).

The bibliography is also incomplete, including only work that is referred to in the course of the exposition. The reader may find additional bibliographic information in any of the many surveys that have recently appeared (e.g., [91, 92]).

I would like to express my deep gratitude to Academician V. I. Smirnov, who reviewed the manuscript and made a number of important suggestions that were incorporated into the final version of the book.

V. A. Pliss

Contents

1

Multidimensional Periodic Systems

1. GENERAL CONCEPTS CONCERNING PERIODIC AND AUTONOMOUS SYSTEMS

Forced oscillations of mechanical systems with a finite number of degrees of freedom are frequently described by vector differential equations in the form

$$\frac{dX}{dt} = F(X, t), \tag{1.1}$$

where the right sides are periodic functions of t.

In subsequent investigations, (1.1) will be considered subject to the following assumptions: $X = \{x_1, \ldots, x_n\}$ is an n-dimensional vector; the vector function $F = \{f_1, \ldots, f_n\}$ is defined and continuous on all real X and t, satisfies the necessary condition in order that the solution of system (1.1) be unique for all X and t, and has the period ω with respect to t, i.e., $F(X, t + \omega) \equiv F(X, t)$.

In the case of free oscillations, the right side of Eq. (1.1) does not explicitly depend on time, and we will have a system of the form

$$\frac{dX}{dt} = F(X). \tag{1.2}$$

Here again we will assume that the n-dimensional vector function F is defined and continuous on all real n-dimensional vectors X and satisfies the necessary condition in order that the solution of Eq. (1.2) be unique for all X.

Since the right side of system (1.1) is periodic with respect to time, it is desirable to study this system in a toroidal space in which all points of the form $(X, t + k\omega)$, where $k = 0, \pm 1, \pm 2, \ldots$ are coincident. By adjoining the equation $d\theta/dt = 1$ to system (1.1), we obtain the system

$$\left.\begin{aligned} \frac{dX}{dt} &= F(X, \theta), \\ \frac{d\theta}{dt} &= 1. \end{aligned}\right\} \tag{1.3}$$

The right sides of this system do not depend explicitly on time, i.e., this system is of the form (1.2). The previously described toroidal space (X, θ) represents the phase space of system (1.3) in which points of the form $(X, \theta + k\omega)$, $k = 0, \pm 1, \pm 2, \ldots$, are coincident.

1. If all solutions of system (1.2) can be extended to any t, $-\infty < t < +\infty$ (and this, as we know, is easily done by simple substitution of the variable t [1]), then the solution of (1.2) will represent the dynamical system in the appropriate phase space. In our case, this space will be the Euclidean space $\{X\}$ [for system (1.2)] or the toroidal space described above [for system (1.3)].

The behavior of dynamical systems has been thoroughly studied (see [1, 2]). Here we will present only those results that are particularly important for future use.

Let $X = \Phi(p, t)$ be the solution of system (1.2) with the initial data $t = 0$, $X = p$, i.e., $\Phi(p, 0) = p$. Since the solution $X = \Phi(p, t)$ is, by hypothesis, unique, the following theorem holds [3]: For all $T > 0$ and $\varepsilon > 0$ there exists a $\delta > 0$, such that if $\rho(p, q) < \delta$, then

$$\rho[\Phi(p, t), \Phi(q, t)] < \varepsilon \tag{1.4}$$

for $|t| \leqslant T$, where $\rho(\alpha, \beta)$ is the distance between the points α and β. This theorem will hereafter be referred to as the theorem on integral continuity.

Since the right sides of system (1.2) do not depend explicitly on time, the following relation (group property of the dynamical system) holds:

$$\Phi(p, t_1 + t) = \Phi(\Phi(p, t_1), t). \tag{1.5}$$

Let $T_1 < t < T_2$ be the largest interval in which the solution $\Phi(p, t)$ is defined, i.e., the solution $X = \Phi(p, t)$ is not defined for $t = T_i$ $(i = 1, 2)$, (X may be singular at one or both of the points T_1 and T_2). We will call the set of points $\Phi(p, t)$, $T_1 < t < T_2$ the trajectory of system (1.2) and denote it by $\Phi(p, I_0)$. The set of points $\Phi(p, t)$, $0 \leqslant t \leqslant T_2$ will be called the positive half-trajectory, the negative half-trajectory being defined similarly.

If a point p is such that $F(p) = 0$, it is clear that $X = \Phi(p, t) = p$ for all $t \in (-\infty, +\infty)$. Such points are called equilibrium states.

Let a point p be such that there exists a $\tau > 0$ such that $\Phi(p, \tau) = p$ and $\Phi(p, t) \neq p$ for $0 < t < \tau$. Then, by virtue of (1.5), we have

$$\Phi(p, t + \tau) = \Phi(\Phi(p, \tau), t) = \Phi(p, t). \tag{1.6}$$

Thus, $\Phi(p, t)$ is a periodic vector function with period τ, and the trajectory $\Phi(p, t)$, $(-\infty < t < +\infty)$ is a closed curve.

Let M be a set of points in phase space, and let $\Phi(M, t)$ denote the set of points $\Phi(p, t)$ for which $p \in M$. The set M is said to be invariant if

$$\Phi(M, t) = M \tag{1.7}$$

for all t. It follows from the definition of invariant sets that an invariant set consists of entire trajectories and, conversely, a set consisting of entire trajectories is invariant.

It follows from the theorem on integral continuity that the closure of an invariant set is invariant.

A very important role in the theory of dynamical systems is played by the concept of limit points. Consider the positive half-trajectory $\Phi(p, t)$, $0 \leqslant t < +\infty$. If there exists a sequence

$$0 \leqslant t_1 < t_2 < t_3 < \ldots \to +\infty, \tag{1.8}$$

such that

$$\lim_{k\to\infty} \Phi(p, t_k) = q,$$

then the point q is said to be a limit point of the positive half-trajectory $\Phi(p, t)$, $0 \leqslant t < +\infty$ and an ω-limit point of the trajectory $\Phi(p, t)$. Limit points for the negative half-trajectory $\Phi(p, t)$, $0 \geqslant t > -\infty$ are defined analogously. A limit point of the negative half-trajectory $\Phi(p, t)$, $0 \geqslant t > -\infty$ is called an α-limit point of the trajectory $\Phi(p, t)$.

Theorem 1.1. The set of limit points of any half-trajectory is invariant and closed.

We will prove the theorem for the positive half-trajectory $\Phi(p, t)$, $0 \leqslant t < +\infty$. Let q be a limit point of this trajectory. Then there exists a sequence $t_1 < t_2 < \ldots \to +\infty$ such that

$$\lim_{k\to\infty} \Phi(p, t_k) = q. \tag{1.9}$$

Consider a point $\Phi(q, \tau)$ on the trajectory passing through the point q. By the theorem on integral continuity, for all $\varepsilon > 0$ and $T = |\tau|$ there exists a $\delta > 0$ such that if $\rho(\Phi(p, t_k), q) < \delta$ then $\rho(\Phi(p, t_k + \tau), \Phi(q, \tau)) < \varepsilon$. It follows from (1.9) that the first of these two inequalities is satisfied for sufficiently large k; consequently, for sufficiently large k the second is also satisfied, and this, in turn, means that

$$\lim_{k\to\infty} \Phi(p, t_k + \tau) = \Phi(q, \tau)$$

i.e., the point $\Phi(q, \tau)$ is a limit point of the half-trajectory $\Phi(p, t)$, $0 \leqslant t < +\infty$. Therefore, the set of limit points of this half-trajectory is invariant.

We will now show that it is also closed. Let the points q_1, q_2, q_3, ... be limit points of the half-trajectory, and assume that

$$\lim_{k \to \infty} q_k = q. \tag{1.10}$$

We will show that the point q is a limit point of the half-trajectory $\Phi(p, t)$, $0 \leqslant t < +\infty$. Take an arbitrary $\varepsilon > 0$. By virtue of (1.10), for this ε there exists a q_k such that $\rho(q_k, q) < \varepsilon/2$. Since q_k is a limit point of $\Phi(p, t)$, there exists an arbitrarily large $\bar{t}$ such that $\rho(\Phi(p, \bar{t}), q_k) < \varepsilon/2$. It follows that $\rho(\Phi(p, \bar{t}), q) < \varepsilon$; this shows that the point q is a limit point of the half-trajectory.

Hereafter, we will naturally be most interested in bounded solutions. The trajectories corresponding to such solutions have a special name:

Definition 1.1. A bounded half-trajectory is said to be Lagrange-stable. A motion is said to be positive (negative) Lagrange-stable is its positive (negative) half-trajectory is Lagrange-stable. A motion that is both positive and negative Lagrange-stable is said to be Lagrange-stable.

It follows from the Bolzano-Weierstrass theorem that the set of limit points of a Lagrange-stable half-trajectory is nonempty.

Theorem 1.2. If a half-trajectory is Lagrange-stable, then its set of limit points is connected.

Proof. Let the positive half-trajectory $\Phi(p, t)$, $0 \leqslant t < +\infty$ be Lagrange-stable. Contrary to the assertion of the theorem, assume that its set Ω of limit points is not connected. Then the set Ω splits into two nonempty closed subsets: $\Omega = \Omega_1 + \Omega_2$ and $\Omega_1 \cdot \Omega_2 = 0$. Since the half-trajectory under discussion is bounded, the set Ω is also bounded; consequently, the separability theorem gives us $\rho(\Omega_1, \Omega_2) = d > 0$.

Since $\Omega_1 \subset \Omega$ and $\Omega_2 \subset \Omega$, there exist arbitrarily large t'_k such that

$$\rho(\Phi(p, t'_k), \Omega_1) < \frac{d}{3} \tag{1.11}$$

and arbitrarily large t''_k such that

$$\rho(\Phi(p, t''_k), \Omega_2) < \frac{d}{3}. \tag{1.12}$$

It is possible to chose a sequence of t'_k and t''_k so that the inequalities

$$0 < t'_1 < t''_1 < t'_2 < t''_2 < \ldots < t'_k < t''_k < \ldots$$

will be satisfied. Since $\rho(\Phi(p, t), \Omega_1)$ is a continuous function of t and satisfies the inequalities

$$\rho(\Phi(p, t'_k), \Omega_1) < \frac{d}{3},$$

$$\rho(\Phi(p, t''_k), \Omega_1) \geqslant \rho(\Omega_1, \Omega_2) - \rho(\Phi(p, t''_k), \Omega_2) \geqslant \frac{2}{3} d,$$

there exists a $\tau_k (t'_k < \tau_k < t''_k)$ such that

$$\rho(\Phi(p, \tau_k), \Omega_1) = \frac{d}{2}.$$

Since the half-trajectory $\Phi(p, t)$ is bounded, the sequence $\Phi(p, \tau_k)$ contains a subsequence converging to a point q. The point q will be a limit point for the half-trajectory $\Phi(p, t)$, $0 \leqslant t < +\infty$ while, on the other hand, $\rho(q, \Omega_1) = d/2$; as a result, q belongs to neither Ω_1 nor Ω_2.

We have obtained a contradiction, thus proving the theorem.

2. In what follows we will need the concept of minimal sets.

Definition 1.2. A set Σ of points in phase space is said to be minimal if it is nonempty, closed, invariant, and has no proper subset with these properties.

Equilibrium states and trajectories of periodic motion are clearly minimal sets.

Bounded minimal sets are of great interest. The following theorem can be stated about the existence of such sets.

Theorem 1.3. A bounded closed invariant set contains a minimal set.

Proof. Let M be an invariant, closed, and bounded set of points in phase space. If it has no proper subset with these properties, then M is a minimal set and the theorem is proved. Assume that there exists a set M_1 such that $M_1 \subset M, M_1 \neq M$ and M_1 is closed and invariant. If M_1 does not contain a proper subset that is closed and invariant, it is minimal. Assume that there exists a closed invariant set $M_2 \subset M_1$ and $M_2 \neq M_1$, etc., continuing this process. If no minimal set appears at any step, then there exists a sequence of closed invariant sets

$$M \supset M_1 \supset M_2 \supset \ldots . \qquad (1.13)$$

The intersection of these sets, M_ω, is closed, bounded, and nonempty. We will show that it is also invariant. Indeed, let $p \in M_\omega$. As a result, $p \in M_k$ for all k. All of the M_k are invariant, so for any t and k we have $\Phi(p, t) \in M_k$. It follows that $\Phi(p, t) \in M_\omega$ for all t, which proves that M_ω is invariant.

If M_ω is not minimal, then we select a closed invariant set $M_{\omega+1} \subset M_\omega (M_{\omega+1} \neq M_\omega)$, etc. If β is a limit number and an M_α has been constructed for all $\alpha < \beta$, we set $M_\beta = \prod_{\alpha<\beta} M_\alpha$. Clearly, M_β will be closed and invariant.

We thus obtain a transfinite sequence of imbedded sets

$$M \supset M_1 \supset \ldots \supset M_k \supset \ldots \supset M_\omega \supset \ldots \supset M_\beta \supset \ldots.$$

By Baire's theorem (see, for example [4]), there exists a transfinite number β of the second class with the property that $M_\beta = M_{\beta+1}$, i.e., the set M_β has no closed and invariant proper subset. As a result, M_β is a minimal set.

The theorem is proved.

Corollary 1.1. If a half-trajectory is Lagrange-stable, then its set of limit points contains a minimal set.

We introduce the following notation. Denote the set of points $\Phi(p, t)$ for $\Phi(p, t_0, t_1)$ by $t_0 \leqslant t \leqslant t_1$. Let M be a set of points in phase space; we denote the ε-neighborhood of this set, i.e., the set of points p such that $\rho(M, p) < \varepsilon$ by $U(M, \varepsilon)$.

Definition 1.3. A solution $\Phi(p, t)$ is said to be positive Poisson-stable (P^+-stable) if, for any $\varepsilon > 0$ and $T > 0$, there exists a $t > T$ such that $\rho(\Phi(p, t), p) < \varepsilon$. Similarly, if there exists a $t < -T$ such that $\rho(\Phi(p, t), p) < \varepsilon$ then the solution $\Phi(p, t)$ is said to be negative Poisson-stable (P^--stable).

A solution that is both positive and negative Poisson-stable is said to be Poisson-stable.

Definition 1.4. A solution $\Phi(p, t)$ is said to be recurrent if for all $\varepsilon > 0$ there exists a $T(\varepsilon)$ such that the entire trajectory of motion is approximated within ε accuracy by any arc whose length corresponds to the time interval $T(\varepsilon)$, i.e., for any $\varepsilon > 0$ there exists a T such that the relation

$$\Phi(p, I_0) \subset U(\Phi(p, t_0, t_0 + T), \varepsilon) \tag{1.14}$$

is satisfied for all t_0.

It not difficult to see that any recurrent motion is Poisson-stable. Indeed, for any $\varepsilon > 0$ and $t_0 > 0$ there exists points t_1 and t_2, $t_1 \in [t_0, t_0 + T]$, $t_2 \in [-t_0 - T, -t_0]$, such that $\rho(p, \Phi(p, t_k)) < \varepsilon\ (k = 1, 2)$ which proves that $\Phi(p, t)$ is Poisson-stable.

It turns out that minimal sets consists entirely of recurrent trajectories. Then, we have

Theorem 1.4. Any trajectory in a bounded minimal set is recurrent.

Proof. Let p be a point in a bounded minimal set Σ. Assume, contrary to the statement of the theorem, that the motion $\Phi(p, t)$ is not recurrent. This means that there exists a number α and a sequence of infinitely increasing time intervals $[t_\nu - T_\nu, t_\nu + T_\nu]$ $T_\nu \to +\infty$, such that the distance between each of the arcs $\Phi(p, t_\nu - T_\nu, t_\nu + T_\nu)$ and $q_\nu = \Phi(p, \tau_\nu)$ is at least α. Because the set Σ is bounded, we can assume that the sequences q_ν and $p_\nu = \Phi(p, t_\nu)$ are convergent (otherwise we would transfer the argument to convergent subsequences). Let

$$\lim_{\nu\to\infty} q_\nu = q, \quad \lim_{\nu\to\infty} p_\nu = p'. \tag{1.15}$$

Since Σ is closed, we have $q \in \Sigma$ and $p' \in \Sigma$. Choose an arbitrary $T > 0$ and consider the arc $\Phi(p, -T, T)$. From the theorem on integral continuity, there exists a δ such that if $\rho(p', r) < \delta$, then $\rho(\Phi(p', t), \Phi(r, t)) < \alpha/3$ for $|t| \leqslant T$. It follows from (1.15) that the inequalities

$$T_\nu > T, \ \rho(p', p_\nu) < \delta, \ \rho(q_\nu, q) < \frac{\alpha}{3} \tag{1.16}$$

are satisfied for sufficiently large ν. The inequality

$$\rho(\Phi(p', t), \Phi(p_\nu, t)) < \frac{\alpha}{3}, \tag{1.17}$$

will then hold for any t in the interval $-T \leqslant t \leqslant T$. Because $|t| < T < T_\nu$, we can, by the proper choice of the points q_ν, write

$$\rho(\Phi(p_\nu, t), q_\nu) = \rho(\Phi(p, t_\nu + t), q_\nu) \geqslant \alpha. \tag{1.18}$$

It follows from inequalities (1.16)-(1.18) that the inequality

$$\rho(\Phi(p', t), q) > \frac{\alpha}{3} \tag{1.19}$$

holds for all $|t| \leqslant T$. Since the number T is absolutely arbitrary, the last inequality is satisfied for all t between $-\infty$ and $+\infty$, i.e., $\rho(\Phi(p', I_0), q) \geqslant \alpha/3$.

As we have already noted, $p' \in \Sigma$. The invariance of Σ implies that

$$\Phi(p', I_0) \subset \Sigma. \tag{1.20}$$

As usual, let $\overline{\Phi(p', I_0)}$ denote the closure of the set $\Phi(p', I_0)$. It is clear that $\rho(\overline{\Phi(p', I_0)}, q) \geqslant \alpha/3$, i.e., q is not a member of $\overline{\Phi(p', I_0)}$. Thus, the set $\overline{\Phi(p', I_0)}$ is a proper subset of the set Σ.. But the closure of an invariant set is invariant and closed. Thus, the set Σ contains an invariant closed set, $\overline{\Phi(p', I_0)}$, as a proper subset, and, therefore, is not minimal.

We have obtained a contradiction, which proves the theorem.

Corollary 1.2. If a half-trajectory is Lagrange-stable, then its set of limit points contains a recurrent trajectory.

This corollary follows from Corollary 1.1 and Theorem 1.4.

Theorem 1.4 admits the following converse.

Theorem 1.5. If a motion $\Phi(p, t)$ is recurrent, then the closure $\overline{\Phi(p, I_0)}$ of its trajectory is a bounded minimal set.

Proof. We will first prove that the trajectory $\Phi(p, I_0)$ is bounded. Set $\varepsilon = 1$; for this ε, in virtue of the definition of recurrent motion, there exists a T such that for all t

$$\Phi(p, t) \in U(\Phi(p, -T, T), 1).$$

But the arc $\Phi(p, -T, T)$ is clearly a bounded set. It thus follows that the set $\Phi(p, I_0)$ is bounded.

It remains to be proved that the set $\overline{\Phi(p, I_0)} = \Sigma$ is minimal. Assume that this is not so. Then there exists a closed invariant set M that is a proper subset of Σ, and p is not a member of M, for otherwise we would have $M = \overline{\Phi(p, I_0)} = \Sigma$. Since M is bounded and closed, we have $\rho(M, p) = d > 0$. Set $\varepsilon = d/3$ and $T(\varepsilon)$ to conform with the definition of recurrent trajectories. Now, consider any point $q \in M$. By virtue of the theorem on integral continuity, for the numbers ε and T that have been chosen, there exists a $\delta > 0$ such that if $\rho(q, r) < \delta$, then for all $|t| \leqslant T$

$$\rho(\Phi(q, t), \quad \Phi(r, t)) < \delta.$$

The point $q \in M \subset \overline{\Phi(p, I_0)}$. Consequently, there exists a t_1 such that

$$\rho(\Phi(p, t_1), q) < \delta.$$

Hence, by the choice of δ, the inequality

$$\rho(\Phi(q, t), \quad \Phi(p, t_1 + t)) < \varepsilon \tag{1.21}$$

is satisfied for all $|t| \leqslant T$.

Since the set M is invariant, $\Phi(q, t) \in M$ for all t, which, together with inequality (1.21), implies

$$\rho(M, \Phi(p, t_1 + t)) < \varepsilon$$

for $|t| \leqslant T$. As a result, for $|t| \leqslant T$ we have

$$\rho(p, \Phi(p, t_1 + t)) > d - \varepsilon = \frac{2d}{3} > \varepsilon.$$

This inequality shows that the point p does not belong to the ε-neighborhood of the arc of the trajectory $\Phi(p, t)$ corresponding to a time interval 2T with the center at the point $\Phi(p, t_1)$, which contradicts the choice of T. Q.E.D.

3. Recurrent motion, as its very definition implies, is a type of oscillatory process in a system of nonlinear oscillations. It is relatively simple to prove the existence of such processes: It is only necessary to establish the presence of a bounded motion. Among recurrent motions, the most interesting are the "pure" oscillations, i.e., periodic solutions. We will now turn to the study of such solutions.

First, let us establish a test for the existence of periodic solutions for the dynamical system (1.2).

Theorem 1.6. A positive Poisson-stable motion $\Phi(p, t)$ *of system (1.2) will be periodic if there exists a continuous function* $\alpha(t)$, $\alpha(t)\to 0$ *as* $t\to+\infty$, *that is positive for* $t\geqslant 0$ *and which has the property that for any* $\varkappa>0$ *one can find an* $\varepsilon>0$ *such that if* $\rho(q, p)\leqslant\varepsilon$, *then there exists an* $h(q)$ $(|h(q)|<\varkappa)$ *satisfying the relation*

$$\rho(\Phi(p, t+h(q)), \quad \Phi(q, t))<\alpha(t)$$

for $t\geqslant 0$.

Proof. The theorem is obvious if p is an equilibrium state. In what follows, therefore, we will assume that p is not an equilibrium state of (1.2). Through the point p we pass an $(n-1)$-dimensional hyperplane L normal to the direction field vector p. Let U be a sufficiently small neighborhood of the point p so that the closure S of its intersection with the hyperplane L has no contact with the direction field of system (1.2).

It is not difficult to see that there exists an $H>0$ such that if the point r belongs to $\bar{S}$, then the trajectory $\Phi(r, t)$ does not meet S when $-4H\leqslant t\leqslant 4H$.

By hypothesis, there exists for this H an $\varepsilon>0$ such that if $\rho(p, q)\leqslant\varepsilon$, then there exists an $|h(q)|<H$ such that $\rho(\Phi(p, t+h(q)),$ $\Phi(q, t))<\alpha(t)$ for $t\geqslant 0$. Choose such a fixed ε smaller than the radius of the neighborhood U chosen above for the point p.

Now choose an arbitrary point $r\in\bar{S}$ such that $\rho(r, p)\leqslant\varepsilon/2$. Since the $(n-1)$-dimensional sphere $\bar{S}$ does not meet the direction field, there exists a $\delta>0$ that is independent of r and has the following properties. Let $\Phi(r, -H, H)$ be the part of the trajectory $\Phi(r, t)$ corresponding to the time interval $-H\leqslant t\leqslant H$, and let V be the δ-neighborhood of this part of the trajectory. Then, if a point l belongs to V and $-2H\leqslant t\leqslant 2H$, the trajectory $\Phi(l, t)$ intersects $\bar{S}$ exactly once; the point of intersection $\Phi(l, \tau)$ is at a distance of less than $\varepsilon/2$ from r and is a continuous function of l.

Since, by hypothesis, $\alpha(t)\to 0$ for $t\to\infty$, there exists a T such that $\alpha(t)\leqslant\delta$ for $t\geqslant T$. By hypothesis, the motion $\Phi(p, t)$ is positive Poisson-stable; as a result, there exists a $t_1>T+2H$ such that the point $\Phi(p, t_1)$ belongs to $\bar{S}$ and $\rho(\Phi(p, t_1), p) < \varepsilon/2$ choose an arbitrary point $q \in S$ such that $\rho(q, p) \leqslant \varepsilon$. By hypothesis, for $t > 0$ we have the inequality $\rho(\Phi(p, t+h(q)), \Phi(q, t)) < \alpha(t)$; consequently, $\rho(\Phi(p, t_1+h(q)), \Phi(q, t_1)) < \delta$. Since $|h(q)| < H$ by virtue of the choice of ε, then for the chosen δ there exists a $\tau \in [t_1-2H, t_1+2H]$ such that the point $\Phi(q, \tau)$ belongs to $\bar{S}$, $\rho(\Phi(q, \tau), \Phi(p, t_1)) < \varepsilon/2$, and $\Phi(q, \tau)$ is a continuous function of $\Phi(q, t_1)$ as well as (by virtue of the theorem on integral continuity) of q.

It follows from the triangle inequality that $\rho(\Phi(q, \tau), p) < \varepsilon$. Let S_ε denote the intersection of S and $U(p, \varepsilon)$. We associate the point $\Phi(q, \tau)$ with the point $q \in S_\varepsilon$. Since $\rho(p, \Phi(q, \tau)) < \varepsilon$, we obtain a mapping P of the closed (n-1)-dimensional sphere $\bar{S}_\varepsilon$ into itself. As we have already noted, the point $\Phi(q, \tau)$ is a continuous function of q, so the transformation P is continuous. Thus, by virtue of Brouwer's theorem, it follows that the transformation P has a stationary point $q_0 \in S_\varepsilon$. This means that $\Phi(q_0, \tau) = q_0$, i.e., the trajectory $\Phi(q_0, t)$ is closed.

We will now show that the trajectories $\Phi(q_0, I_0)$ and $\Phi(p, I_0)$ coincide. Assume that this is not so, i.e., assume that $\rho(p, \Phi(q_0, I_0)) = d > 0$. Since $q_0 \in \bar{S}_\varepsilon$, there exists, by hypothesis, an $h(q_0)$ such that $\rho(\Phi(p, t+h(q_0)) \Phi(q_0, t)) < \alpha(t)$ for $t \geqslant 0$. Again by hypothesis, $\alpha(t) \to 0$ as $t \to +\infty$, so that there exists a T_0 such that $\alpha(t) < (d/2)$ for $t \geqslant T_0$. As a result, $\rho(\Phi(p, t+h(q_0)), \Phi(q_0, t)) < d/2$ for $t \geqslant T_0$. The triangle inequality now implies that $\rho(p, \Phi(p, t+h(q_0))) > d/2$ for all $t \geqslant T_0$. This last inequality contradicts the fact that the motion $\Phi(p, t)$ is positive Poisson-stable, which proves that the trajectories $\Phi(p, I_0)$ and $\Phi(q_0, I_0)$ coincide. The trajectory $\Phi(q_0, I_0)$ is closed, and, therefore, so is $\Phi(p, I_0)$.

The theorem is proved.

4. Let us now consider system (1.1) under the assumptions made above. One might suppose that the period of any periodic solution is commensurable with the period ω of the right sides of the system. It has been noted [5, 6], however, that this is not always true. As an example [7], consider the system

$$\frac{dx}{dt} = y + (x^2 + y^2 - 1)\sin\lambda t, \quad \frac{dy}{dt} = -x. \tag{1.22}$$

Although the period of the right sides of this system relative to t is $2\pi/\lambda$, the system admits the periodic solution $x = -\cos t$, $y = \sin t$ with period 2π, which, generally speaking, is not commensurable with $2\pi/\lambda$. System (1.22) is such that the right sides are independent of time at the points through which the periodic solution passes in the (x, y) plane, i.e., it is independent of time at points on the circle $x^2 + y^2 = 1$. It turns out that this is true not only for system (1.22), but for any system with a periodic solution whose period is not commensurable with the period of the right sides. We will prove the following theorem [8].

Theorem 1.7. Let $X(t)$ be a periodic solution of system (1.1) with period Ω, not commensurable with ω; then the vector function $F(X(t_0), t)$ is constant for all t_0.

Before proving this theorem, we will prove the following arithmetic lemma.

Lemma 1.1. Let a and μ be incommensurable numbers. Then, for any b and $\varepsilon > 0$ it is possible to find two integers M and N such that

$$|b + M\mu - Na| < \varepsilon.$$

Proof. Select a natural number p so large that $a/p < \varepsilon$ and partition the segment [0, 1] into segments of the form $[(h-1)/p, (h/p)]$. Denote the integral part of a number β by $[\beta]$, and the fractional part by (β). Consider the $p+1$ numbers $(k\mu/a)$, $k = 1, 2, \ldots, p+1$. Since there are p segments in our partition of [0, 1], there are two different numbers k_1 and k_2 such that $(k_1\mu/a)$ and $(k_2\mu/a)$ lie in the same segment of the partition. Let

$$\frac{h-1}{p} \leqslant \left(k_1 \frac{\mu}{a}\right) \leqslant \frac{h}{p} \tag{1.23}$$

and

$$\frac{h-1}{p} \leqslant \left(k_2 \frac{\mu}{a}\right) \leqslant \frac{h}{p}. \tag{1.24}$$

Here, for definiteness, we assume that $k_1 < k_2$. Subtracting inequality (1.23) from inequality (1.24), we obtain the inequality

$$-\frac{1}{p} \leqslant \left(k_2 \frac{\mu}{a}\right) - \left(k_1 \frac{\mu}{a}\right) \leqslant \frac{1}{p}$$

or, by the definition of $(k\mu/a)$,

$$-\frac{1}{p} \leqslant (k_2 - k_1)\frac{\mu}{a} - \left\{\left[k_2 \frac{\mu}{a}\right] - \left[k_1 \frac{\mu}{a}\right]\right\} \leqslant \frac{1}{p}. \tag{1.25}$$

Set $k_2 - k_1 = m$, $(k_2\mu/a) - (k_1\mu/a) = n$; because $k_2 > k_1$, it is clear that $m > 0$, and $n \geqslant 0$. Multiplying (1.25) by a, we obtain the inequalities

$$-\varepsilon \leqslant m\mu - na \leqslant \varepsilon.$$

Since the number μ/a is, by hypothesis, irrational, one of the following two cases must occur: either

$$m\mu - na = \gamma > 0, \tag{1.26}$$

or

$$m\mu - na = -\gamma < 0. \tag{1.27}$$

In either case, $0 < \gamma \leqslant \varepsilon$. We first assume that inequality (1.27) holds. Multiplying (1.27) by $[b/\gamma]$ and adding b to both sides, we find that

$$b + m\left[\frac{b}{\gamma}\right]\mu - n\left[\frac{b}{\gamma}\right]a = b - \left[\frac{b}{\gamma}\right]\gamma. \tag{1.28}$$

But, by the definition of $[b/\gamma]$, we have

$$\gamma\left[\frac{b}{\gamma}\right] \leqslant b < \gamma\left[\frac{b}{\gamma}\right] + \gamma;$$

thus,

$$0 \leqslant b - \gamma\left[\frac{b}{\gamma}\right] < \gamma \leqslant \varepsilon.$$

Setting $m[b/\gamma] = M$ and $n[b/\gamma] = N$, we obtain the lemma.

Now assume that (1.26) holds. Choose a number $l \geqslant 1$ such that

$$(l-1)a \leqslant b < la.$$

Multiplying (1.26) by $[(la-b)/\gamma]$ and subtracting $la-b$ from it, we find that

$$b - la + m\left[\frac{la-b}{\gamma}\right]\mu - n\left[\frac{la-b}{\gamma}\right]a = b - la + \gamma\left[\frac{la-b}{\gamma}\right]. \tag{1.29}$$

Moreover, by definition of $[(la-b)/\gamma]$, we have

$$\left[\frac{la-b}{\gamma}\right] \leqslant \frac{la-b}{\gamma} < \left[\frac{la-b}{\gamma}\right] + 1$$

or

$$0 \leqslant la - b - \gamma\left[\frac{la-b}{\gamma}\right] < \gamma \leqslant \varepsilon.$$

Setting $m[(la-b)/\gamma] = M$ and $n[(la-b)/\gamma] + 1 = N$, we obtain the lemma.

The lemma is proved.

We now return to the proof of Theorem 1.7. Choose a fixed number t_0 and let M and N be arbitrary integers (positive, negative, or zero). We have

$$F(X(t_0),\ t_0+M\omega+N\Omega)=F(X(t_0),\ t_0+N\Omega) \tag{1.30}$$

because, by hypothesis, the period of the function F relative to t is ω. Further, by hypothesis, $X(t_0+N\Omega)=X(t_0)$, so we can write

$$F(X(t_0),\ t_0+N\Omega)=F(X(t_0+N\Omega),\ t_0+N\Omega). \tag{1.31}$$

But

$$\left.\frac{dX}{dt}\right|_{t=t_0+N\Omega}=F(X(t_0+N\Omega),\ t_0+N\Omega), \tag{1.32}$$

and, because $X(t)$ is periodic, we have

$$\left.\frac{dX}{dt}\right|_{t=t_0+N\Omega}=\left.\frac{dX}{dt}\right|_{t=t_0}=F(X_0(t_0),\ t_0).$$

Hence, it follows from (1.30), (1.31) and (1.32) that

$$F(X(t_0),\ t_0+M\omega+N\Omega)=F(X(t_0),\ t_0). \tag{1.33}$$

By hypothesis, the number Ω/ω is irrational, so that, by virture of Lemma (1.1), the set of numbers $M\omega+N\Omega$ is everywhere dense on the real axis t, and because, by hypothesis, the function $F(X,\ t)$ is continuous, it follows from (1.33) that the equation

$$F(X(t_0),\ t)=F(X(t_0),\ t_0) \tag{1.34}$$

is satisfied for all t. This proves the theorem.

Assume that system (1.1) has a periodic solution $X(t)$ with period Ω not commensurable with ω. Then it follows from Theorem (1.7) that the vector function $X(t+h)$, where $h=\text{const}$, is also a solution of system (1.1). Indeed,

$$\frac{d}{dt}X(t+h)=F(X(t+h),\ t+h)$$

because $X(t)$ is a solution of system (1.1). From Theorem 1.7, $F(X(t+h),\ t+h)=F(X(t+h),\ t)$. Hence it follows that

$$\frac{d}{dt}X(t+h)=F(X(t+h),\ t)$$

and this proves the theorem.

Thus, if the period Ω of the solution $X(t)$ of system (1.1) is not commensurable with the period ω of the right sides, $X(t)$ behaves like the solution to dynamical system (1.2): Along it the right sides are independent of time, and it is a member of the family $X(t+h)$.

Erugin [7] developed methods for finding this type of periodic solution. He proved in [9] that a second-order linear system, whose coefficients do not degenerate into constants, may not have periodic solutions whose period is not commensurable with the period of the coefficients.

5. As the considerations of the preceding paragraph show, periodic solutions of system (1.1) with period not commensurable with the period of the right sides are, in some sense, an exceptional occurrence.

Of primary interest are natural solutions with periods commensurable with ω. We will now study these solutions.

We introduce the following definitions [10].

Definition 1.5. A solution of system (1.1) with period ω is said to be a harmonic oscillation or, simply, a harmonic.

Definition 1.6. The solution of system (1.1) with smallest period $k\omega (k \geqslant 2$ is a natural number) is called the kth order subharmonic oscillation or, simply, the kth subharmonic.

Let $X(t)$ be a kth subhamonic. It is then clear that for any integers $l, X = X(t + l\omega)$ is also a kth subharmonic. In this case, the set of functions $X(t+l\omega)$ has exactly k different subharmonics (here we refer to the Eucliden (X, t) space; the subharmonics of the toroidal space defined above are identical to each other). The set of all such functions for a given dynamical system is called its system of subharmonics.

The study of harmonic and subharmonic oscillations of system (1.1) is facilitated by the following transformation. Let $X = X(t, X_0$ $t_0)$ be the solution of system (1.1) with the initial data $t = t_0$, $X = X_0$. Assume that the point X_0 of the hyperplane $t = 0$ is such that the solution $X(t, X_0, 0)$ can be extended to all times $0 \leqslant t \leqslant \omega$. By associating the point $X(\omega, X_0, 0)$ with the point X_0, we obtain a transformation T of the section of the hyperplane $t = 0$ through which solutions extended by integral multiples of the period pass into the hyperplane $t = 0$.

It follows from uniqueness and the theorem on integral continuity that the set of all points (of the hyperplane $t = 0$) at which the transformation T is defined is open, and that on this set the transformation T is one-to-one and continuous in both directions.

It follows from the ω-periodicity of the function $F(X, t)$ that if $TX_0 = X_0$, then the solution $X(t, X_0, 0)$ is ω-periodic and, conversely, if $X(t+\omega, X_0, 0) = X(t, X_0, 0)$, then $TX_0 = X_0$. Thus, in order for a solution $X(t, X_0, 0)$ to be a harmonic oscillation, it is necessary and sufficient that the point X_0 be stationary under the transformation T.

Moreover, it is clear that if a solution $X(t, X_0, 0)$ has the period $k\omega$, then $T^k X_0 = X_0$. The converse is implied by the ω-periodicity of the right sides of system (1.1): If $T^k X_0 = X_0$, then the solution $X(t, X_0, 0)$ has the period $k\omega$.

6. Consider system (1.1) under the assumption that its right sides are continuously differentiable with respect to all of their arguments. We will prove the following.

Theorem 1.8. If the right sides of system (1.1) are continuously differentiable with respect to all of their arguments and

$$\frac{\partial f_1}{\partial x_1} + \frac{\partial f_2}{\partial x_2} + \ldots + \frac{\partial f_n}{\partial x_n} < 0 \tag{1.35}$$

for all X *and* t, *and if all the solutions* $X(t, X_0, 0)$ *exist for* $0 \leqslant t \leqslant \omega$, *then any set of points in the hyperplane* $t = 0$ *that is bounded and invariant with respect to the transformation T has Lebesgue measure zero.*

Proof. Under the transformation T, the point X_0 with coordinates $\{x_{10}, \ldots, x_{n0}\}$ is mapped into the point $X(\omega, X_0, 0)$ with the coordinates $\tilde{x}_1 = x_1(\omega, x_{10}, \ldots, x_{n0}, 0), \ldots, \tilde{x}_n = x_n(\omega, x_{10}, \ldots, x_{n0}, 0)$. Consider the Jacobian of this transformation:

$$J = \begin{vmatrix} \dfrac{\partial \tilde{x}_1}{\partial x_{10}}, & \ldots, & \dfrac{\partial \tilde{x}_1}{\partial x_{n0}} \\ \cdot\ \cdot\ \cdot & \cdot\ \cdot\ \cdot & \cdot\ \cdot\ \cdot \\ \dfrac{\partial \tilde{x}_n}{\partial x_{10}}, & \ldots, & \dfrac{\partial \tilde{x}_n}{\partial x_{n0}} \end{vmatrix}. \tag{1.36}$$

By substituting the solution $X = X(t, X_0, 0)$ of system (1.1) into this system and differentiating the identities thus obtained with respect to each of the variables $x_{10}, \ldots, x_{n0}$ in turn we obtain n sets of identities:

$$\begin{aligned} \frac{d}{dt}\frac{\partial x_1}{\partial u} &= \frac{\partial f_1}{\partial x_1}\frac{\partial x_1}{\partial u} + \ldots + \frac{\partial f_1}{\partial x_n}\frac{\partial x_n}{\partial u}, \\ &\cdots\cdots\cdots\cdots\cdots \\ \frac{d}{dt}\frac{\partial x_n}{\partial u} &= \frac{\partial f_n}{\partial x_1}\frac{\partial x_1}{\partial u} + \ldots + \frac{\partial f_n}{\partial x_n}\frac{\partial x_n}{\partial u} \end{aligned} \tag{1.37}$$

where $u = x_{i0}$ $(i = 1, 2, \ldots, n)$ and $f_i = f_i(X(t, X_0, 0))$, $i = 1, 2, \ldots, n$. System (1.37) can be treated as a system of linear differential equations in $\partial x_i / \partial u$ $(i = 1, 2, \ldots, n)$. By definition we have $X(0, X_0, 0) = X_0$, so that $(\partial x_i / \partial x_{k0}) = \delta_{ik}$ for $t = 0$, where δ_{ik} is the Kronecker delta. It thus follows that the system of functions

$$\begin{matrix} \frac{\partial x_1}{\partial x_{10}}, \dots, \frac{\partial x_1}{\partial x_{n0}} \\ \dots\dots\dots \\ \frac{\partial x_n}{\partial x_{10}}, \dots, \frac{\partial x_n}{\partial x_{n0}} \end{matrix} \tag{1.38}$$

is the fundamental solution matrix (normalized to yield the identity matrix when $t=0$) of the system of linear differential equations

$$\begin{aligned} \frac{d\zeta_1}{dt} &= \frac{\partial f_1}{\partial x_1}\zeta_1 + \dots + \frac{\partial f_1}{\partial x_n}\zeta_n, \\ &\dots\dots\dots\dots\dots \\ \frac{d\zeta_n}{dt} &= \frac{\partial f_n}{\partial x_1}\zeta_1 + \dots + \frac{\partial f_n}{\partial x_1}\zeta_n. \end{aligned} \tag{1.39}$$

By Liouville's theorem, the determinant of this system is given by

$$\begin{vmatrix} \frac{\partial x_1}{\partial x_{10}}, \dots, \frac{\partial x_1}{\partial x_{n0}} \\ \dots\dots\dots \\ \frac{\partial x_n}{\partial x_{10}}, \dots, \frac{\partial x_n}{\partial x_{n0}} \end{vmatrix} = e^{\int\limits_0^t \sum\limits_{i=1}^n \frac{\partial f_i}{\partial x_i} dt}. \tag{1.40}$$

Now contrary to the assertion of the theorem, assume that the transformation T has an invariant bounded set M of nonzero measure. It is not difficult to see that the closure $\overline{M}$ of M is also bounded and invariant under the transformation T.

The set $\overline{M}$ clearly has a positive Lebesgue measure μ. Consider the set S in the (X, t) space consisting of those solution curves of system (1.1) that pass through $\overline{M}$. This set is bounded for $0 \leqslant t \leqslant \omega$, so, in the hyperplane $t=0$, there exists a sphere K such that the set S is contained in the cylinder

$$L\{X \in K,\ t \in [0,\ \omega]\} \text{ for } 0 \leqslant t \leqslant \omega.$$

It follows from inequality (1.35) and the fact that the derivatives in (1.35) are continuous that there exists an $\alpha > 0$ such that for $X \in \overline{K},\ 0 \leqslant t \leqslant \omega$, the inequality

$$\frac{\partial f_1}{\partial x_1} + \dots + \frac{\partial f_n}{\partial x_n} < -\alpha \tag{1.41}$$

is satisfied.

Now partition the hyperplane $t=0$ into cubes with faces parallel to the coordinate planes and consider the set G composed of the cubes that have at least one point in common with $\overline{M}$. This partition can be made so fine that: 1) any solution passing through the set $\overline{G}$ when $t=0$ lies in the cylinder L when $0 \leqslant t \leqslant \omega$, and 2) the volume a of the set G satisfies the inequalities $\mu < a < \mu e^{\alpha\omega}$.

Now consider the set TG: since $\overline{M} \subset G$, we have $T\overline{M} \subset TG$, and the invariance of $\overline{M}$ implies that $\overline{M} \subset TG$. We now estimate the volume a_1 of the set TG. We have

$$a_1 = \int_G J dx_1 \ldots dx_n. \tag{1.42}$$

It follows from the definition of J [Eq. (1.36)], Eq. (1.40) and inequality (1.41) that

$$J < e^{-\alpha\omega}, \tag{1.43}$$

and this, together with (1.42), implies that

$$a_1 < e^{-\alpha\omega} \int_G dx_1 \ldots dx_n = e^{-\alpha\omega} a. \tag{1.44}$$

By the choice of the set G, we have $a < \mu e^{\alpha\omega}$, while this and (1.44) give us the inequality

$$a_1 < \mu. \tag{1.45}$$

On the other hand, $\overline{M} \subset TG$; consequently, by the definition of Lebesgue measure, $\mu \leqslant a_1$. This inequality contradicts (1.45).

The contradiction we have obtained proves the theorem.

2. GENERAL THEOREMS ON DISSIPATIVE SYSTEMS

Consider the following system of differential equations describing forced oscillations:

$$\frac{dX}{dt} = F(X, t) \tag{2.1}$$

where $X = \{x_1, \ldots, x_n\}$ is an n-dimensional vector and the vector $F = \{f_1, \ldots, f_n\}$ is defined, continuous, and satisfies the uniqueness condition for solutions of system (2.1) for all X, t; moreover, it has period ω with respect to t: $F(X, t+\omega) \equiv F(X, t)$.

We denote the solution of system (2.1) with initial data $X=X_0$ for $t=t_0$ by $X(t, X_0, t_0)$, i.e., $X(t_0, X_0, t_0)=X_0$.

In practice we frequently encounter systems for which natural dissipation causes every solution to reach a fixed region and remain there after a sufficiently long time. Such systems are said to be [10, 11] dissipative. The following definition refines this concept.

Definition 2.1. We will say that system (2.1) is dissipative, or a D-system, if there exists an $R > 0$ such that

$$\overline{\lim_{t \to +\infty}} \|X(t, X_0, t_0)\| < R \tag{2.2}$$

for all X_0 and t_0. As usual, we assume that

$$\|X\| = \sqrt{x_1^2 + \ldots + x_n^2}.$$

It follows from the definition that all solutions $X(t, X_0, t_0)$ of a D-system can be extended to all times $t \geqslant t_0$.

Here and in the following sections we will study the class of D-systems.

1. First, let us state one characteristic property of D-systems.

Theorem 2.1. System (2.1) will be dissipative if and only if there exists an $r > 0$ such that for any X_0 and t_0 there exists a $\tau(X_0, t_0) > t_0$ such that

$$\|X(\tau, X_0, t_0)\| < r. \tag{2.3}$$

Proof. Necessity is obvious, so we will proceed directly to sufficiency.

Assume, contrary to the assertion of the theorem, that condition (2.3) does not imply relation (2.2), i.e., assume that there exist sequences $\overline{X}_0^{(1)}$ $\overline{X}_0^{(2)}, \ldots, t_0^{(1)}, t_0^{(2)}, \ldots$ and $R_1, R_2, \ldots \to +\infty$ such that

$$\overline{\lim_{t \to +\infty}} \left\|X\left(t, \overline{X}_0^{(k)}, t_0^{(k)}\right)\right\| > R_k. \tag{2.4}$$

Here we can and will assume that $R_k > r$. But, from condition (2.3), there exist $\tau_k > t_0^{(k)}$ such that the inequalities

$$\left\|X\left(\tau_k, \overline{X}_0^{(k)}, t_0^{(k)}\right)\right\| < r \tag{2.5}$$

are satisfied.

It follows from (2.4) that there exists a sequence $\bar{t}_k > \tau_k$ with the property

$$\left\|X\left(\bar{t}_k, X_0^{(k)}, t_0^{(k)}\right)\right\| > R_k.$$

But then, because the solutions are continuous, we can find $\overline{\theta}_k \in [\tau_k, \bar{t}_k]$ such that

$$\left\|X\left(\overline{\theta}_k, \overline{X}_0^{(k)}, t_0^{(k)}\right)\right\| = r \tag{2.6}$$

and, for $\overline{\theta}_k < t \leqslant \overline{t}_k$,

$$\|X(t, \overline{X}_0^{(k)}, t_0^{(k)})\| > r. \tag{2.7}$$

It follows from (2.6), (2.7), and the ω-periodicity of the vector function $F(X, t)$ that there exist sequences θ_k, $X_0^{(k)}$ and $t_k > \theta_k$ such that $0 \leqslant \theta_k \leqslant \omega$, $\|X_0^{(k)}\| = r$,

$$\|X(t_k, X_0^{(k)}, \theta_k)\| > R_k \tag{2.8}$$

and, for $\theta_k < t \leqslant t_k$, the inequalities

$$\|X(t, X_0^{(k)}, \theta_k)\| > r \tag{2.9}$$

are satisfied.

Because the sequences θ_k and $X_0^{(k)}$ are bounded, we can assume that they converge (otherwise we would choose convergent subsequences). Let

$$\lim_{k\to\infty} \theta_k = \theta_0, \quad \lim_{k\to\infty} X_0^{(k)} = X_0' . \tag{2.10}$$

Consider the solution $X(t, X_0', \theta_0)$ of system (2.1). It follows from condition (2.3) that there exists a $\tau_0 > \theta_0$ satisfying the inequality

$$\|X(\tau_0, X_0', \theta_0)\| < r. \tag{2.11}$$

Let $M > r$ be such that the inequality

$$\|X(t, X_0', \theta_0)\| < M \tag{2.12}$$

is satisfied in the interval $\theta_0 \leqslant t \leqslant \tau_0$. Then, since $\lim_{k\to\infty} R_k = \infty$, it follows from Eqs. (2.10) that for $k > k_0$, where k_0 is a sufficiently large natural number, $\theta_k < \tau_0$, $\|X(\tau_0, X_0^{(k)}, \theta_k)\| < r$, $\|X(t, X_0^{(k)}, \theta_k)\| < M$ for $\theta_k \leqslant t \leqslant \tau_0$, $R_k > M$. This contradicts inequalities (2.8) and (2.9). The contradiction we have obtained proves that condition (2.3) implies relation (2.2).

The theorem is proved.

2. Consider the transformation T introduced at the end of the last section. In the case of a dissipative system, this transformation has the property that any sphere with its center at the origin and a sufficiently large radius is mapped into itself upon application of a sufficiently large power of the transformation T. We will now prove this statement.

Theorem 2.2. Let system (2.1) be dissipative. Then there exists a sphere $H\{\|X\| < h\}$ *such that for any sphere* $A\{\|X\| < a\}$ *there is a natural number* $k(a)$ *such that for* $k \geqslant k(a)$

$$T^k A \subset H. \tag{2.13}$$

Proof. We will prove that there exists an h such that if $\|X\| \leqslant R$, where R is the quantity contained in Definition (2.1) of dissipative systems, then

$$\|T^k X\| < h \tag{2.14}$$

for all integral nonnegative k. Assume that this is not the case. Then we must assume that there exist sequences X_i, h_i, and k_i such that

$$\|X_i\| \leqslant R, \; h_i > R, \; \lim_{i \to \infty} h_i = \infty$$
$$\|T^{k_i} X_i\| > h_i \tag{2.15}$$

and

$$\|T^k X_i\| > R \; \text{for} \; 0 < k \leqslant k_i. \tag{2.16}$$

Since the sequence X_i is bounded, we can assume that it converges (otherwise we would consider a convergent subsequence). Let

$$\lim_{i \to \infty} X_i = X_0.$$

It follows from inequality (2.2) and the definition of the transformation T that there exist a natural number l and a positive quantity M such that

$$\|T^l X_0\| < R,$$
$$\|T^k X_0\| < M \; \text{for} \; 0 \leqslant k \leqslant l.$$

Then there exists an i_0 such that for $i \geqslant i_0$ $h_i > M$,

$$\|T^l X_i\| < R, \tag{2.17}$$

$$\|T^k X_i\| < M < h_i \; \text{for} \; 0 \leqslant k \leqslant l. \tag{2.18}$$

This contradicts inequalities (2.15) and (2.16), which proves the existence of an h with property (2.14).

We will now show that this h is the one required by the theorem. Take an arbitrary point $X' \in A$. It follows from (2.2) that there exists a natural k such that $\|T^k X'\| < R$. But then, for all X for which $\|X - X'\|$ is sufficiently small, we have $\|T^k X\| < R$.

Then, by the Heine–Borel theorem, there exists a $k(a)$ such that for any $X \in A$ there is an $m \leqslant k(a)$ with the property $\|T^m X\| < R$. But then inequality (2.14) implies that the inequality $\|T^k X\| < h$ is satisfied for all $k \geqslant m$. Since $k(a) \geqslant m$, it means that $X \in A$, and $k > k(a)$ implies that $\|T^k X\| < h$. This proves inclusion (2.13).

Corollary 2.1. If system (2.1) is dissipative, then it admits at least one periodic solution.

Indeed, take H for the sphere A in Theorem 2.2. It follows from inclusion (2.13) that $T^{k(h)}\bar{H}\subset\bar{H}$ where $\bar{H}$ denotes the closure of the sphere H. By the Brouwer fixed-point theorem, it then follows that the sphere H has a point X_0 that is stationary under the transformation $T^{k(h)}$. It is then clear that the solution $X(t, X_0, 0)$ has a period equal to $\omega k(h)$.

3. Here we will present several more properties of D-systems. Consider an arbitrary sphere $A\{\|X\|<a\}$ containing the closed sphere $\bar{H}$ (see Theorem 2.2). From Theorem 2.2, we have

$$T^{k(a)}\bar{A}\subset\bar{H}\subset A. \tag{2.19}$$

Apply the transformation $T^{lk(a)}$ to the sets in relation (2.19), where l is an arbitrary nonnegative integer; we than obtain

$$T^{(l+1)k(a)}\bar{A}\subset T^{lk(a)}A \tag{2.20}$$

for any nonnegative integer l.

Consider the nonempty set $I=\prod_{l=0}^{\infty} T^{lk(a)}A$.

It is not difficult to see that this set is closed and bounded. We will show that it is invariant under the transformation T. It follows from (2.20) that

$$T^{(l+1)(k(a)+1)k(a)}A\subset T^{l(k(a)+1)k(a)+k(a)k(a)}A\subset$$
$$\subset T^{l(k(a)+1)k(a)+(k(a)-1)k(a)}A\subset\ldots\subset T^{l(k(a)+1)k(a)}A. \tag{2.21}$$

This and the definition of set I imply that

$$I=\prod_{l=0}^{\infty} T^{l(k(a)+1)k(a)}A. \tag{2.22}$$

But, from Theorem 2.2, we have

$$T^{k(a)+1}\bar{A}\subset A$$

and, therefore,

$$T^{(l+1)(k(a)+1)}\bar{A}\subset T^{l(k(a)+1)}A$$

for any nonnegative integer l. Therefore,

$$T^{(l+1)(k(a)+1)k(a)}A\subset T^{l(k(a)+1)k(a)+(k(a)-1)(k(a)+1)}A\subset\ldots$$
$$\ldots\subset T^{l(k(a)+1)k(a)}A. \tag{2.23}$$

Relations (2.22) and (2.23) imply that

$$\prod_{l=0}^{\infty} T^{l(k(a)+1)} A = \prod_{l=0}^{\infty} T^{l(k(a)+1)k(a)} A = I. \tag{2.24}$$

It is easily seen that

$$T^{k(a)} \prod_{l=0}^{\infty} T^{lk(a)} A = \prod_{l=1}^{\infty} T^{lk(a)} A$$

which means that

$$T^{k(a)} I = I.$$

Similarly, Eq. (2.24) yields $T^{k(a)+1} I = I$; consequently,

$$T^{k(a)+1} I = T^{k(a)} I.$$

Applying the transformation $T^{-k(a)}$ to the sets in this last equation, we find that

$$TI = I. \tag{2.25}$$

Thus, the set I is invariant under the transformation T.

We will now show that the set I is independent of the choice of the sphere A. Let $k(h)$ be such that for $k \geqslant k(h)$ we have $T^k H \subset H$. Then we will show that

$$I = \prod_{m=0}^{\infty} T^{mk(h)} H. \tag{2.26}$$

Since $H \subset A$, for any natural j we will have

$$T^{jk(a)k(h)} H \subset T^{jk(a)k(h)} A.$$

This and the definition of I imply that

$$\prod_{m=0}^{\infty} T^{mk(h)} H \subset I. \tag{2.27}$$

On the other hand, it follows from the definition of the number $k(a)$ that $T^{k(a)} A \subset H$ and, therefore, for any natural j

$$T^{jk(a)k(h)+k(a)} A \subset T^{jk(a)k(h)} H.$$

This relationship implies that

$$I \subset \prod_{m=0}^{\infty} T^{mk(h)} A. \tag{2.28}$$

Equation (2.26) follows from (2.27) and (2.28). Thus, Eq. (2.26) holds for any sphere A. This also means that the set I is independent of the choice of the sphere A.

In an absolutely analogous manner we can show that for any bounded domain B containing the sphere H we have the relationship

$$\prod_{l=0}^{\infty} T^{lk} B = I \tag{2.29}$$

where k is some natural number.

Let M and N be two point sets, and let $\rho(M, N)$ denote the distance between them.

We will show that for any point X_0 in the hyperplane $t=0$ we always have

$$T^m X_0 \to I \text{ for } m \to \infty \tag{2.30}$$

Consider a sphere $A\{\|X\| < a\}$, such that $a > h$ and $X_0 \in A$. Then, by definition of I,

$$\prod_{l=0}^{\infty} T^{lk(a)} A = I.$$

Now, choose an arbitrary $\varepsilon > 0$. Since the transformation T is continuous, there exists for this ε a $\delta > 0$ such that if $\rho(X, I) < \delta$, then for any integer $k \in [0, k(a)]$ we have $\rho(T^k X, I) < \varepsilon$. Let M be a point set, and let $U(M, \delta)$ be the δ-neighborhood of the set M, i.e., the set of points for which $\rho(M, X) < \delta$. By the definition of I, there exists an l_0 such that for $l \geqslant l_0$, $T^{lk(a)} A \subset U(I, \delta)$. But then it is clear that for $l \geqslant l_0$ we will also have $T^{lk(a)} X_0 \in U(I, \delta)$. By the choice of δ, therefore, it turns out that for $lk(a) \leqslant j \leqslant (l+1)k(a)$ we have $T^j X_0 \in U(I, \varepsilon)$. Since, for any $j > l_0 k(a)$, there exists an $l \geqslant l_0$ such that $lk(a) \leqslant j \leqslant (l+1)k(a)$. Then for all $j > l_0 k(a)$ we have the following inequality:

$$\rho(T^j X_0, I) < \varepsilon.$$

This proves relation (2.30).

Now, let $X_0 \in I$, consider the solution $X(t, X_0, 0)$ of system (2.1) that passes through the point $X = X_0 \in I$ when $t=0$. Since the set I is invariant under the transformation T, it is clear that this solution can be extended to all times between $-\infty$ and $+\infty$.

Now consider the set of all solutions $X(t, X_0, 0)$ for $X_0 \in I$. Let S denote the set of such solution in the space (X, t).

It is clear that the set S is bounded and closed. This set has a number of additional remarkable properties. In order to formulate them, we will need the following definitions.

Definition 2.2. We will say that a nonempty set M in an $(n+1)$-dimensional space (X, t) is Ω-periodic if the relationship $(X, t) \in M$ implies that $(X, t+l\Omega) \in M$ for any integer l.

Definition 2.3. We will say that a nonempty set M in an $(n+1)$-dimensional space (X, t) is invariant if it consists of entire solution curves of system (2.1), i.e., the inclusion $(X_0, t_0) \in M$ implies that $(X(t, X_0, t_0), t) \in M$ for all t for which the solution $X(t, X_0, t_0)$ exists.

Let M_t denote the intersection of the set M and the corresponding hyperplane in the space (X, t).

Definition 2.4. An invariant set M is said to be stable if for any $\varepsilon > 0$ there exists a $\delta > 0$ such that if $\rho(X_0, M_{t_0}) < \delta$, then $\rho(X(t, X_0, t_0), M_t) < \varepsilon$ for all $t \geqslant t_0$.

Definition 2.5. An invariant set M is said to be asymptotically stable if it is stable and there exists a δ such that the inequality $\rho(X_0, M_{t_0}) < \delta$ implies

$$\lim_{t\to\infty} \rho(X(t, X_0, t_0), M_t) = 0. \tag{2.31}$$

Definition 2.6. An invariant set M is said to be stable in the large if it is stable and the relation (2.31) is satisfied for all solutions of system (2.1).

Note that the definition of stability for invariant sets of dynamical systems is due to Barbashin [12].

It is not difficult to see that the set S is ω-periodic and invariant. We will now show that it is stable in the large.

Theorem 2.3. The set S is stable in the large.

Proof. We will first show that the set S is stable. Choose an arbitrary $\varepsilon > 0$ and, for it, attempt to find a $\delta_1 > 0$ such that if $\rho(X_0, S_{t_0}) < \delta_1$, then $\rho(X(t, X_0, t_0), S_t) < \varepsilon$ for $t_0 \leqslant t \leqslant t_0 + k(h)\omega$, where $k(h)$ is the number in Theorem 2.2. The existence of such a δ_1 follows from the theorem on integral continuity and the ω-periodicity of the function $F(X, t)$ and of the set S. By the definition of set S, we can find for this δ_1 an l_1 such that for $l \geqslant l_1$ we have $T^{lk(h)}\overline{H} \subset U(S_0, \delta_1)$ where, by definition, $S_0 = I$. Now, let Γ denote the boundary of the domain $T^{l_1 k(h)}H$. Since $I \subset H$, it is clear that the sets Γ and I are disjoint. Let d be the distance between them. For this d we can find a δ such that if $\rho(X_0, S_{t_0}) < \delta$, then $\rho(X(t, X_0, t_0), S_t) < d$ for $t_0 \leqslant t \leqslant t_0 + \omega$. This will be the δ desired. Indeed, consider an arbitrary point (X_0, t_0) such that $\rho(X_0, S_{t_0}) < \delta$. Then, by the choice of δ, the solution $X(t, X_0, t_0)$ will intersect the hyperplane of the form $t = t_0$ nearest $t = m$ (m is an integer such that $m - 1 \leqslant t_0 \leqslant m$) at a point in the domain $T^{l_1 k(h)}H$. Thus, for $t = m + jk(h)$ $(j = 1, 2, \ldots)$ we will have $X(t, X_0, t_0) \in T^{l_1 k(h)}H \subset U(S_t, \delta_1)$, and then, again by the choice of δ_1, we will have $\rho(X(t, X_0, t_0), S_t) < \varepsilon$ for all $t \geqslant t_0$. This proves that the set S is stable. Now (2.31) itself can easily be derived from (2.30) with the aid of the theorem on integral continuity.

The theorem is proved.

4. Here we will note another property of D-system that is important in what follows. Assume that system (2.1) is dissipative. Choose an arbitrary $g \geqslant h$ (the h in the statement of Theorem 2.2) and consider the cylinder $G\{\|X\| \leqslant g,\ 0 \leqslant t \leqslant \omega\}$. We will study all the solutions $X(t, X_0, t_0)$ passing through G. These solutions are uniformly bounded in the interval $t_0 \leqslant t \leqslant \omega$, for if we assume the opposite to be true, i.e., if we assume that there exist sequences $X_0^{(i)}$, $t_0^{(i)}$, and t_i such that $\|X_0^{(i)}\| \leqslant g$ $0 \leqslant t_0^{(i)} \leqslant \omega$, $t_0^{(i)} \leqslant t_i \leqslant \omega$,

$$\|X(t_i, X_0^{(i)}, t_0^{(i)})\| \geqslant g_i > g,\ \underset{i \to \infty}{g_i \to \infty}$$

then it turns out that a solution that does not extend to $\bar{t}_0 \leqslant t \leqslant \omega$ passes through the limit point $(\bar{X}_0, \bar{t}_0)$ of the sequence $(X_0^{(i)}, t_0^{(i)})$. But, by the definition of D-systems, this is impossible. Thus, there exists a $c > g$ such that $\|X(t, X_0, t_0)\| < c$ for $t_0 \leqslant t \leqslant \omega$ provided $\|X_0\| \leqslant g$ and $0 \leqslant t_0 \leqslant \omega$.

Now choose an arbitrary number $a > c$ and let $\Omega(t)$ denote the set $\{X(t, X_0, t_0), t\}$ for $\|X_0\| \leqslant a$ $t \geqslant t_0$, $0 \leqslant t_0 \leqslant \omega$.

Consider the function $\alpha_1(t)$ defined for $t \geqslant \omega$ in the following manner: Let $\alpha_1(t)$ be such that

$$\Omega(t) \subset U(S_t, \alpha_1(t)),\ \Omega(t) \not\subset U(S_t, \alpha_1(t) - \varepsilon)$$

for any $\varepsilon > 0$. Since $I \subset H$ by the definition of I, it follows from the choice of c that S_t lies entirely within the cylinder $\|X\| < c$. It is therefore clear that the set $\Omega(t)$ contains points not belonging to the set S_t, and this proves that $\alpha_1(t) > 0$ for $t \geqslant \omega$.

We will now show that

$$\lim_{t \to \infty} \alpha_1(t) = 0. \tag{2.32}$$

Choose an arbitrary $\varepsilon > 0$. In virtue of the theorem on integral continuity, there exists for this a $\delta > 0$ such that if $\rho(X_0, S_{t_0}) < \delta$, then $\rho(X(t, X_0, t_0), S_t) < \varepsilon$ for $t_0 \leqslant t \leqslant t_0 + k(a)\omega$, where $k(a)$ is the number given in Theorem 2.2. By definition of I, there exists an l_1 such that $T^{lk(a)}\bar{A} \subset U(I, \delta)$ for $l \geqslant l_1$, where A denotes the sphere $\|X\| < a$. This means that $\Omega(t) \subset U(S_t, \delta)$ for $t = lk(a)\omega$, where $l \geqslant l_1$. Therefore, it follows from the choice of δ that $\Omega(t) \subset U(S_t, \delta)$ for all $t \geqslant l_1 k(a)$, which proves (2.32).

It follows from the definitions of the function $\alpha_1(t)$ and the set $\Omega(t)$ that if $\|X_0\| \leqslant a$ and $0 \leqslant t_0 \leqslant \omega$, then

$$\rho(X(t, X_0, t_0), S_t) < \alpha_1(t) \tag{2.33}$$

for $t \geqslant \omega$.

Note that the argument which was used to prove the existence of c implies also that set $\Omega(t)$ is bounded. We now introduce a function $\alpha(t)$ with the following properties: $\alpha(t)$ is defined and continuously differentiable for $t>0$, $\alpha'(t)<0$ for $t>0$, $|\alpha'(t)|<1/2$ for sufficiently large t, $\alpha(t)>\alpha_1(t)$ for $t\geqslant\omega$, $\alpha(t)\to 0$ for $t\to\infty$, $\alpha(t)\to\infty$ for $t\to 0$, and, for $0\leqslant t_0<\omega$ and $t_0<t$,

$$\rho(X(t, X_0, t_0), S_t)<\alpha(t) \tag{2.34}$$

if $\|X_0\|\leqslant a$.

Then it follows from (2.33) that (2.34) is satisfied for all $t_0\leqslant t<+\infty$ if $0\leqslant t_0\leqslant\omega$ and $\|X_0\|\leqslant a$.

Now consider a region of the form $c<\|X\|<a$, $0<t<\omega$, which we will denote by L. We will show that a function $\beta(t)$ with the following properties exists: $\beta(t)$ is defined and continuously differentiable for $t\geqslant 0$, $\beta'(t)<0$ for $t\geqslant 0$ and

$$\rho(X(t, X_0, t_0), S_t)>\beta(t) \text{ for } t\geqslant t_0 \tag{2.35}$$

if $(X_0, t_0)\in\bar{L}$.

As proved above, S_t lies inside the sphere $\|X\|<c$ for all t. As a result, the closed region $\bar{L}$ and the set S are disjoint.

Let $\Phi(t)$ be the set of points of the form $X(t, X_0, t_0)$ for $(X_0, t_0)\in\bar{L}$ and $t\geqslant t_0$. Since the set S is invariant and does not intersect $\bar{L}$, it is clear that S_t does not intersect $\Phi(t)$. But the sets S_t and $\Phi(t)$ are closed, so that $\rho(\Phi(t), S_t)>0$. It is not difficult to find a function $\beta(t)$ that is defined, continuously differentiable for $t\geqslant 0$ and satisfies the inequalities $\beta'(t)<0$ and $0<\beta(t)<\rho(\Phi(t), S_t)$. It is then clear that the function $\beta(t)$ is also the one desired.

Thus, we have proved the existence of smooth functions $\alpha(t)$ and $\beta(t)$ such that inequalities (2.34) and (2.35) are satisfied.

5. We will now state a proposition which, in certain cases, permits us to determine whether or not a given system is dissipative.

Theorem 2.4. In order for system (2.1) to be dissipative, it is necessary and sufficient that the following conditions be satisfied.

I. All solutions $X(t, X_0, t_0)$ of system (2.1) can be extended to $t\geqslant t_0$.

II. There exists a continuous function $v(X)$ with the following properties:

1. *$v(X)$ is defined and continuous for $\|X\|\geqslant a$, where a is some positive number;*

2) $v(X)>0$ for $\|X\|\geqslant a$;

3) $v(X)\to\infty$ for $\|X\|\to\infty$;

4) If X is such that $\|X\|>a$, and $\|TX\|>a$, then $v(TX)<v(X)$.

Proof. Sufficiency. As before, we denote the sphere $\|X\|<a$ by A, and its closure by $\bar{A}$. Consider the set $T\bar{A}+\bar{A}-A$, which is closed. Let $l=\max_{X\in T\bar{A}+\bar{A}-A} v(X)$. Since, by hypothesis, $v(X)\to\infty$ for

$\|X\| \to \infty$ there exists a $b > a$ such that $v(X) \geqslant 2l$ for $\|X\| \geqslant b$. We now choose an arbitrary point X_0, and show that there exists a k_0 such that $\|T^k X_0\| < b$ for $k > k_0$.

Initially assume that X_0 is such that either $\|X_0\| < a$ or $v(X_0) < l$. Then one of two cases must occur: either $\|TX_0\| < a$ or $TX_0 \in T\bar{A}$ and, consequently, $v(TX_0) \leqslant l$. Again considering TX_0 as an arbitrary point, we can see that for all $k \geqslant 0$, one of two cases must occur: either $\|T^k X_0\| < a$ or $v(T^k X_0) \leqslant l$. The inequality $\|T^k X_0\| < b$ will be satisfied in both of these cases.

Now assume that X_0 is such that $v(X_0) = v_0 > l$. Let G_1 be the set of all those points of the hyperplane $t = 0$ at which the inequality $v(X) < v_0$ is satisfied, and let $G = G_1 + A$. We will show that there exists a k_0 such that $\|T^k X_0\| < b$ for $k \geqslant k_0$ Assume that this is not true, and consider the sequence of points $T^k X_0$. It follows from the above considerations that $\|T^k X_0\| > a$ and $v(T^k X_0) > l$, because otherwise, according to the last paragraph, we would have $\|T^k X_0\| < b$ for all sufficiently large k. By hypothesis, the sequence $v(T^k X_0)$ is a decreasing sequence which implies $\bar{v} = \lim_{k\to\infty} v(T^k X_0)$. Moreover, because $v(X) \to \infty$ for $\|X\| \to \infty$, the set $\bar{G}$ is bounded and $T^k X_0 \in \bar{G}$ for all $k \geqslant 0$. As a result, $T^k X_0$ has a nonempty limit set P. It is clear that if $\bar{X} \in P$, then $v(\bar{X}) = \bar{v}$. But then $\bar{v} \geqslant 2l$, because otherwise the set P would be contained in the sphere $\|X\| < b$, which would imply that $\|T^k X_0\| < b$ for sufficiently large k. Choose some point $\bar{X} \in P$. By hypothesis, $v(T\bar{X}) < v(\bar{X}) = \bar{v}$, from which it is clear that there exists a k such that $v(T^k X_0) < \bar{v}$, which, by definition of $\bar{v}$, is impossible. The contradiction obtained proves that $\|T^k X_0\| < b$ for sufficiently large k.

Sufficiency now follows from Theorem 2.1.

Necessity. Assume that system (2.1) is dissipative. Then, as we have already noted, all of its solutions $X(t, X_0, t_0)$ can be extended to $t \geqslant t_0$.

Consider the sphere H discussed in Theorem 2.2, the set $I = \prod_{l=0}^{\infty} T^{lk(h)} H$, and the function $\alpha(t)$ defined in Paragraph 4. It follows from inequality (2.34) that

$$\rho(T^k X, I) < \alpha(k) \tag{2.36}$$

for $X \in H$ and $k > 0$.

By inverting the function $\alpha = \alpha(t)$ we obtain the function $t = t(\alpha)$, which is defined and continuously differentiable for $0 < \alpha < +\infty$; for such α, $t'(\alpha) < 0$, $t(\alpha) \to 0$ for $\alpha \to \infty$, and $t(\alpha) \to \infty$ for $\alpha \to 0$.

We define the function

$$v(X) = \sum_{k=0}^{\infty} \frac{1}{t^2(\rho(T^k X, I))} \tag{2.37}$$

for $X \notin I$. We will now show that the series in the right side of (2.37) converges uniformly in any sphere A of the form $\|X\| < a$. Let $k(a)$ be a natural number such that $T A \subset H$ for all $k \geqslant k(a)$; from Theorem 2.2, such a number exists. It then follows from inequality (2.36) that

$$\rho(T^k X, I) < \alpha(k - k(a))$$

for all $k > k(a)$.

Since the function $t(\alpha)$ is monotonic, it follows that

$$t(\rho(T^k X, I)) > t(\alpha(k - k(a)) = k - k(a)$$

and, consequently,

$$\frac{1}{t^2(\rho(T^k X, I))} < \frac{1}{[k - k(a)]^2} \tag{2.38}$$

for $X \in A$ and $k > k(a)$.

This shows that the series defining the function $v(X)$ converges uniformly in A. It then follows that the function $v(X)$ is continuous for $\|X\| > h$, and it is clear that $\|X\| > h$ for $v(X) > 0$.

Since $\rho(X, I) \to \infty$ for $\|X\| \to \infty$, we have $t(\rho(X, I)) \to 0$ for $\|X\| \to \infty$ and, consequently, $v(X) \to \infty$ for $\|X\| \to \infty$.

In order that the theorem be proved valid, it remains necessary merely to prove the inequality $v(TX) < v(X)$. We now have

$$v(TX) = \sum_{k=0}^{\infty} \frac{1}{t^2(\rho(T^{k+1}X, I))} = \sum_{k=1}^{\infty} \frac{1}{t^2(\rho(t^k X, I))} = v(X) - \frac{1}{t^2(\rho(X, I))}.$$

Since $1/t^2(\rho(X, I))$ is positive for $X \notin I$, this proves the inequality $v(TX) < v(X)$.

The theorem is proved.

6. It is frequently possible to construct a smooth function v that depends not only on X but also on t and decreases along all solutions located near ∞. In such cases it proves desirable to use the following theorem.

Theorem 2.5. Assume that the right sides of system (2.1) are such that there exists a function $v(X, t)$ that is continuously differentiable for $\|X\| > a$ (a is some number) with respect to all of its arguments and has the following properties:

1) $v(X, t + \omega) = v(X, t)$;

2) $v(X, t) > 0$ *for* $\|X\| > a$;

3) $v(X, t) \to \infty$ *for* $\|X\| \to \infty$ *uniformly with respect to* $t \in [0, \omega]$;

4) $\frac{\partial v}{\partial t} + \sum_{i=1}^{n} \frac{\partial v}{\partial x_i} f_i < 0$ *for* $\|X\| > a$.

Then system (2.1) is dissipative.

Proof. Consider the solution $X(t, X_0, t_0)$ for sufficiently large $\|X_0\|$. By virtue of Condition 4 of the theorem, this solution is contained in the set $v \leqslant v(X_0)$ for all $t \geqslant t_0$, and, from Condition 3, this set is bounded. Consequently, all solutions of system (2.1) can be extended to $t \geqslant t_0$. Since, from Condition 4, the function v decreases along all solutions of system (2.1), it is not difficult to see that the function $v(X, 0)$ satisfies Condition II of Theorem 2.4, to which we appeal for the conclusion of the proof.

It is also possible to give other conditions for a system to be dissipative based on consideration of functions similar to the function $v(X, t)$ of Theorem 2.5 (see, for example, [13]), but we will not dwell on this point, since the conditions of Theorems 2.4 and 2.5 are sufficient for our purposes.

Considerations due to Kurtsveyl' [14] can be used to reverse Theorem 2.5. Here we will do this under the assumption that the right sides of the system under study are smooth. Our considerations are, to a great extent, analogous to the considerations used by Massera to reverse Lyapunov's theorem on asymptotic stability (see Malkin [15] and Massera [16]).

Theorem 2.6. If the right sides of system (2.1) are continuously differentiable with respect to all of their arguments, then the conditions of Theorem 2.5 are necessary for the system to be dissipative.

Proof. We define a function $w(X, t)$ with the following properties: 1) $w(X, t) = w(X, t+\omega)$ for all X and t; 2) if $(X, t) \in S$, then $w(X, t) = 0$; 3) if $(X, t) \notin S$, then we have the inequality

$$\frac{1}{2} < \frac{w(X, t)}{\rho(X, t)} < \frac{3}{2};$$

4) the function $w(X, t)$ is continuously differentiable at any point $(X, t) \notin S$. It is not difficult to use Whithey's theorem [17] to prove the existence of such a function.

We again consider the quantities a and c and the set L introduced in Paragraph 4 of the present section, and use the notation $\gamma(t) = 3/2\, \alpha(t)$, $\delta(t) = 1/2\, \beta(t)$. By definition of $w(X, t)$, inequalities (2.34) and (2.35) give us the inequality

$$\delta(t) < w(X(t, X_0, t_0), t) < \gamma(t) \tag{2.39}$$

for $(X_0, t_0) \in L$.

Let $X = X(\tau, \Xi, t)$, where $\Xi = \{\xi_1, \ldots, \xi_n\}$ is the solution of the system $dX/d\tau = F(X, \tau)$ with the initial data $X = \Xi$ for $\tau = t$. Consider the function

$$v(\Xi, t) = \int_t^\infty G(w(X(\tau, \Xi, t), \tau))\, d\tau \tag{2.40}$$

where $G(\eta)$ is some function that is continuously differentiable when $\eta \geqslant 0$, has positive values when $\eta > 0$; and vanishes with its derivative when $\eta = 0$. In what follows, the function G is defined so that the integral in the right side of (2.40) is defined, continuous, continuously differentiable with respect to all of its arguments, and satisfies all of the conditions of Theorem 2.5.

We will now show that the function v is periodic with respect to t and has period ω. We have

$$v(\Xi, t+\omega) = \int_{t+\omega}^{\infty} G(w(X(\tau, \Xi, t), \tau))\, d\tau.$$

We make the substitution $\tau = \theta + \omega$ in the right side of the integral above, obtaining

$$v(\Xi, t+\omega) = \int_{t}^{\infty} G(w(X(\theta+\omega, \Xi, t+\omega), \theta+\omega))\, d\theta.$$

The periodicity of the right side of system (2.1) implies that

$$X(\theta+\omega, \Xi, t+\omega) = X(\theta, \Xi, t)$$

so that we can write

$$v(\Xi, t+\omega) = \int_{t}^{\infty} G(w(X(\theta, \Xi, t), \theta+\omega))\, d\theta$$

from which, by virtue of the periodicity of w, we obtain

$$v(\Xi, t+\omega) = \int_{t}^{\infty} G(w(X(\theta, \Xi, t), \theta))\, d\theta = v(\Xi, t).$$

This proves that the function v is periodic.

The function G will not be determinant for large η. It follows from the considerations used when the function $\alpha(t)$ was introduced (see Paragraph 4) and the periodicity of the right sides of system (2.1) that there exists a b_1 such that if $\|\Xi\| < a$, then, for $\tau \geqslant t$, we have $\|X(\tau, \Xi, t)\| < b_1$, $w(X(\tau, \Xi, t), \tau) < b_1$. Now choose a $b > 2b_1$ such that the inequality $1/3\, \|X\| < w(X, t) < 5/3\, \|X\|$ will be satisfied for $\|X\| > b$. We will now determine the function $G(\eta)$ for $\eta \geqslant b$.

Consider the function $N_1(\varphi) = n \max\limits_{\|X\| = \varphi,\ i = 1, 2, \ldots, n} |f_i(X, t)|$ and define a function $N(\varphi)$ with the following properties: 1) $N(\varphi)$ is defined and continuously differentiable for $\varphi \geqslant b$; 2) $N'(\varphi) > 0$ for $\varphi \geqslant b$; and 3) $N(\varphi) > N_1(\varphi)$. Now consider the differential equation

$$\frac{d\varphi}{d\tau} = -N(\varphi) \text{ for } \varphi \geqslant b. \tag{2.41}$$

Without loss of generality, we can assume that all of its solutions cannot be extended to $t\to-\infty$, (otherwise, it would be sufficient to add $-\varphi^2$ to the right side of the equation). Note that if $\varphi(\tau)$ is a solution of Eq. (2.41), then so is $\varphi(\tau+c)$, where c is an arbitrary constant.

Henceforth, $\varphi(\tau)$ will denote a solution of Eq. (2.41) such that $\varphi(\tau_0)=b$, $\varphi(\tau)$ is defined for $0<\tau\leqslant\tau_0$, and $\varphi(\tau)\to\infty$ for $\tau\to+0$. Assume that $\varphi(\tau)$ admits an inverse, $\tau=\tau(\varphi)$ which is a decreasing function, defined for $b\leqslant\varphi<\infty$; $\tau(\varphi)\to 0$ for $\varphi\to\infty$, and $\tau(\varphi)\to\tau_0$ for $\varphi\to b$.

Set

$$G(\eta)=\frac{1}{\tau(\eta)} \text{ for } \eta\geqslant b. \tag{2.42}$$

Then we will show that

$$\int_t^\infty G(w(X(\tau, \Xi, t), \tau))\,d\tau\to\infty \text{ for } \|\Xi\|\to\infty \tag{2.43}$$

uniformly with respect to t. Choose an arbitrary $D>0$, set $\bar{t}=e^{-D+\ln\tau_0}$, and assume that Ξ satisfies the condition $\|\Xi\|>3\varphi(\bar{t})$. Then we will show that

$$\|X(\tau, \Xi, t)\|>3\varphi(\tau+\bar{t}-t) \tag{2.44}$$

for $t\leqslant\tau\leqslant\tau_0+t-\bar{t}$.

Indeed, we have

$$\frac{d}{d\tau}\|X(\tau, \Xi, t)\|=\sum_{k=1}^{n}\frac{x_k}{\|X\|}f_k(X(\tau, \Xi, t), \tau). \tag{2.45}$$

It follows from the conditions $\|\Xi\|>3\varphi(\bar{t})$ that inequality (2.44) is satisfied for all τ sufficiently close to t. Now assume that inequality (2.44) is not satisfied for all $\tau\in[t, \tau_0+t-\bar{t}]$. This means that there exists a $\tau^*\in[t, \tau_0+t-\bar{t}]$ such that

$$\|X(\tau^*, \Xi, t)\|=3\varphi(\tau^*+\bar{t}-t) \tag{2.46}$$

and inequality (2.44) is satisfied for $t\leqslant\tau<\tau^*$. Then (2.45) and the definition of $N(\varphi)$ give us

$$\frac{d}{d\tau}\|X(\tau^*, \Xi, t)\|\geqslant -n\max_{i=1, 2, \dots, n}|f_i(X(\tau^*, \Xi, t), \tau^*)|>$$
$$>-3N(\varphi(\tau^*+\bar{t}-t))=3\frac{d}{d\tau}\varphi(\tau^*+\bar{t}-t).$$

But this is impossible, because inequality (2.44) is satisfied for $t\leqslant\tau<\tau^*$. The contradiction we have obtained proves that inequality (2.44) holds for $t\leqslant\tau\leqslant\tau_0+t>\bar{t}$.

Since the function $G(\eta)$ is nonnegative for $\eta \geqslant 0$, we have

$$\int_t^\infty G(w(X(\tau, \Xi, t), \tau))\,d\tau > \int_t^{\tau_0+t-\bar{t}} G(w(X(\tau, \Xi, t), \tau))\,d\tau. \qquad (2.47)$$

It follows from (2.43) and the choice of b that

$$w(X(\tau, \Xi, t), \tau) > \varphi(\tau + \bar{t} - t) \qquad (2.48)$$

for $t \leqslant \tau \leqslant \tau_0 + t - \bar{t}$.

Since the function $G(\eta)$ increases monotonically for $\eta \geqslant b$, inequalities (2.47) and (2.48) give us

$$\int_t^\infty G(w(X(\tau, \Xi, t), \tau))\,d\tau > \int_t^{\tau_0+t-\bar{t}} G(\varphi(\tau + \bar{t} - t))\,d\tau = \int_t^{\tau_0+t-\bar{t}} \frac{d\tau}{\tau(\varphi(\tau + \bar{t} - t))}$$

and then the definitions of $\tau(\varphi)$ and $\bar{t}$ yield

$$\int_t^\infty G(w(X(\tau, \Xi, t), \tau))\,d\tau > \int_t^{\tau_0+t-\bar{t}} \frac{d\tau}{\tau + \bar{t} - t} = \ln \tau_0 - \ln \bar{t} = D,$$

which proves relation (2.43).

We will now determine the function $G(\eta)$ for $0 \leqslant \eta \leqslant b_1$. Take the derivatives of v with respect to t and ξ_s differentiating under the integral sign:

$$\frac{\partial v}{\partial \xi_s} = \int_t^\infty G'(w(X(\tau, \Xi, t), \tau)) \sum_{k=1}^n \frac{\partial w}{\partial x_k} \frac{\partial x_k}{\partial \xi_s}\,d\tau \qquad (2.49)$$

$$\frac{\partial v}{\partial t} = -G(w(\Xi, t)) + \int_t^\infty G'(w(X(\tau, \Xi, t), \tau)) \sum_{k=1}^n \frac{\partial \omega}{\partial x_k} \frac{\partial x_k}{\partial t}\,d\tau. \qquad (2.50)$$

Assume that the point (Ξ, t) belongs to the closed set $\bar{L}$ ($\bar{L}$ is the set $0 \leqslant t \leqslant \omega$, $c \leqslant \|\Xi\| \leqslant a$).

It follows from inequality (2.39) and the continuity of the derivatives $\partial w/\partial x_k$, $\partial x_k/\partial \xi_s$, and $\partial x_k/\partial t$ that if $(\Xi, t) \in \bar{L}$, then it is possible to find a function $M(\tau)$ that is defined for $\tau \geqslant 0$ such that

$$\left| \sum_{k=1}^n \frac{\partial w}{\partial x_k} \frac{\partial x_k}{\partial \xi_s} \right| < M(\tau) \quad (s = 1, \ldots, n),$$

$$\left| \sum_{k=1}^n \frac{\partial w}{\partial x_k} \frac{\partial x_k}{\partial t} \right| < M(\tau) \qquad (2.51)$$

for $\tau \geqslant t$. Here we can and will assume that the function $M(\tau)$ is continuous and increasing.

Since the function $\gamma(t)$ is a decreasing function, it has an inverse $t = t(\gamma)$. It is clear that the function $t(\gamma)$ is positive, has a negative derivative, $t(\gamma) \to \infty$ for $\gamma \to 0$, and $t(\gamma) \to 0$ for $\gamma \to \infty$.

Set

$$G(\eta) = \int_0^\eta \frac{e^{-t(\eta)}}{M(t(\eta))} d\eta \tag{2.52}$$

for $0 \leqslant \eta \leqslant b_1$. Thus the function $G(\eta)$ is determined for $0 \leqslant \eta \leqslant b_1$ and $\eta \geqslant b$. We will now determine this function for $b_1 \leqslant \eta \leqslant b$ so that $G(\eta)$ is positive and continuously differentiable for $b_1 \leqslant \eta \leqslant b$. We will show that for such a choice of G, the integrals in the right sides of (2.49) and (2.50) converge uniformly when $(\Xi, t) \in \bar{L}$. We have

$$\left| \int_t^\infty G'(w) \sum_{k=1}^n \frac{\partial w}{\partial x_k} \frac{\partial x_k}{\partial \xi_s} d\tau \right| =$$
$$= \left| \int_t^\infty \frac{e^{-t(w)}}{M(t(w))} \sum_{k=1}^n \frac{\partial w}{\partial x_k} \frac{\partial x_k}{\partial \xi_s} d\tau \right| < \int_t^\infty \frac{e^{-t(w)}}{M(t(w))} M(\tau)\, d\tau.$$

Since $M(\tau)$ is an increasing function and $t(\gamma)$ is a decreasing function, inequality (2.39) yields

$$t(w(X(\tau, \Xi, t), \tau)) > \tau, \quad M(t(w(X(\tau, \Xi, t), \tau))) > M(\tau),$$

and, consequently,

$$\left| \int_t^\infty G'(w) \sum_{k=1}^n \frac{\partial w}{\partial x_k} \frac{\partial x_k}{\partial \xi_k} d\tau \right| < \int_t^\infty e^{-\tau} d\tau \leqslant \int_0^\infty e^{-\tau} d\tau = 1. \tag{2.53}$$

This proves uniform convergence of the integral in the right side of (2.49); a similar argument can be used to show that the integral in Eq. (2.50) converges uniformly for $(\Xi, t) \in \bar{L}$. Since the function $v(\Xi, t)$ is periodic, it is clear that the integrals in the right sides of (2.49) and (2.50) converge uniformly for $c \leqslant \|\Xi\| \leqslant a$ and all t.

Now choose an arbitrary point (Ξ, t), assuming that $\|\Xi\| \geqslant a$. We will show that the integrals in the right sides of Eqs. (2.49) and (2.50) converge uniformly in some neighborhood of the point (Ξ, t).

Since the function $v(\Xi, t)$ is periodic, we can, without loss of generality, assume that $0 \leqslant t < \omega$. Consider the solution $X(\tau, \Xi, t)$.

Since any solution of a dissipative system approaches the set S as $t \to +\infty$ and S lies in the cylinder $\|X\| \leqslant c$ for all t, it is clear that there exists a $\bar{t} > t$ such that $c < \|X(\bar{t}, \Xi, t)\| < a$.

It follows from the theorem on integral continuity that this same relationship is also valid for solutions of system (2.1) originating sufficiently close to the point (Ξ, t). If we set

$$X(\bar{t}, \Xi, t) = \bar{X} = \{\bar{x}_1, \ldots, \bar{x}_n\}$$

we will obtain

$$X(\tau, \Xi, t) = X(\tau, \bar{X}, \bar{t}). \tag{2.54}$$

Using the relationship, we can write

$$\int_t^\infty G'(w) \sum_{k=1}^n \frac{\partial w}{\partial x_k} \frac{\partial x_k}{\partial \xi_s} d\tau = \\ = \int_t^\infty G'(w) \sum_{k,\, l=1}^n \frac{\partial w}{\partial x_k} \frac{\partial x_k}{\partial \bar{x}_l} \frac{\partial \bar{x}_l}{\partial \xi_s} d\tau. \tag{2.55}$$

From the fact that the derivatives of the solutions are continuous with respect to the initial data it follows that there exists a constant P such that

$$\left| \frac{\partial \bar{x}_k}{\partial \xi_s} \right| < P \quad (k,\ s = 1, 2, \ldots, n) \tag{2.56}$$

for all solutions sufficiently close to $X(\tau, \Xi, t)$.

Since $c < \|X(\bar{t}, \Xi, t)\| < a$, inequality (2.39) implies

$$\delta(\tau - \bar{t}) < w(X(\tau, \Xi, t), \tau) < \gamma(\tau - \bar{t}) \tag{2.57}$$

for $\tau > \bar{t}$. It then follows from (2.51) that

$$\left| \sum_{k=1}^n \frac{\partial w}{\partial x_k} \frac{\partial x_k}{\partial \bar{x}_l} \right| < M(\tau - \bar{t}) \quad (l = 1, 2, \ldots, n). \tag{2.58}$$

Using relationships (2.55), (2.56) and (2.58), we find that

$$\left| \int_{\bar{t}}^\infty G'(w) \sum_{k=1}^n \frac{\partial w}{\partial x_k} \frac{\partial x_k}{\partial \xi_s} d\tau \right| < \int_{\bar{t}}^\infty G'(w) \cdot nP \cdot M(\tau - \bar{t})\, d\tau = \\ = \int_t^\infty \frac{e^{-t(w)}}{M(t(w))} nPM(\tau - \bar{t})\, d\tau,$$

which in conjunction with (2.57) yields, as before,

$$\left| \int_{\bar{t}}^{\infty} G'(w) \sum_{k=1}^{n} \frac{\partial w}{\partial x_k} \frac{\partial x_k}{\partial \xi_k} d\tau \right| < nP \int_{\bar{t}}^{\infty} \frac{e^{-(\tau-\bar{t})}}{M(\tau-\bar{t})} M(\tau-\bar{t})\, d\tau$$

whence follows uniform convergence of the integral in the right side of (2.49). A similar argument holds for the integral in (2.50).

We will now show that the integral in the right side of Eq. (2.40) converges uniformly in the region $\|\Xi\| \leqslant a$ $0 \leqslant t \leqslant \omega$. By definition of G, we have

$$\int_{t}^{\infty} G(w)\, d\tau = \int_{t}^{\infty} d\tau \int_{0}^{w} \frac{e^{-t(\eta)}}{M(t(\eta))} d\eta.$$

Since $w(X(\tau, \Xi, t), \tau) < \gamma(\tau)$ for $\tau > t$, we can write

$$\int_{t}^{\infty} G(w)\, d\tau < \int_{t}^{\infty} d\tau \int_{0}^{\gamma(\tau)} \frac{e^{-t(\eta)}}{M(0)} d\eta.$$

Substituting $t(\eta)$ for the variable of integration η in the inner integral, we obtain the expression

$$\int_{t}^{\infty} G(w)\, d\tau < \int_{t}^{\infty} d\tau \int_{\infty}^{\tau} \gamma'(t) \frac{e^{-t}}{M(0)} dt.$$

But, by the choice of $\alpha(t)$, we will have $|\gamma'(t)| < 1$ for sufficiently large t: this implies uniform convergence of the integral under discussion.

Since v is periodic, it is clear that this integral converges uniformly for all t when $\|\Xi\| \leqslant a$.

Now assume that the point (Ξ, t) is such that $\|\Xi\| \geqslant a$. As already noted, there exists a $\bar{t} > t$ such that $\|X(\bar{t}, \Xi, t)\| < a$ and this relationship is satisfied for all solutions beginning sufficiently close to the point (Ξ, t). If we set $X(\bar{t}, \Xi, t) = \bar{X}$, then

$$\int_{t}^{\infty} G(w(X(\tau, \Xi, t))\, d\tau = \int_{t}^{\bar{t}} G(w(X(\tau, \Xi, t), \tau))\, d\tau + \\ + \int_{\bar{t}}^{\infty} G(w(X(\tau, \bar{X}, \bar{t}))\, d\tau.$$

But we have just proved that $\int_{\bar{t}}^{\infty} G(w(X(\tau, \bar{X}, \bar{t}), \tau))\, d\tau$ converges uniformly for $\|\bar{X}\| \leqslant a$.

Thus, the integral in the right side of Eq. (2.40) converges uniformly in the neighborhood of each point (Ξ, t).

It follows from what we have proved that the function $v(\Xi, t)$ is continuous and continuously differentiable with respect to all of its arguments when $\|\Xi\| > c$. Moreover, it satisfies Conditions 1, 2, and 3 of Theorem 2.5. We will now show that it also satisfies Condition 4 of this theorem. We have

$$\frac{\partial v}{\partial t} + \sum_{i=1}^{n} \frac{\partial v}{\partial \xi_i} f_i = \frac{d}{dt} v(\Xi(t), t)$$

where $\Xi(t)$ denotes the solution of system (2.1) with initial data $t = t_0$, $\Xi = \Xi_0$. But it is not difficult to see that

$$X(\tau, \Xi(t, \Xi_0, t_0), t) = X(\tau, \Xi_0, t_0)$$

and, therefore,

$$\frac{d}{dt} v(\Xi(t), t) = \frac{d}{dt} \int_{t}^{\infty} G(w(X(\tau, \Xi_0, t_0), \tau))\, d\tau = \\ = -G(w(X(t, \Xi_0, t_0), t)) < 0.$$

This proves that Condition 4 is satisfied. Q.E.D.

3. SUFFICIENT CONDITIONS FOR MULTIDIMENSIONAL SYSTEMS TO BE DISSIPATIVE

In this section we will study certain nonlinear systems with regard to their membership in the class of D-systems.

1. Consider the system

$$\frac{dX}{dt} = AX + G(X, t) + F(X, t), \tag{3.1}$$

where A is a constant square matrix with elements a_{ij} $(i, j = 1, 2, \ldots, n)$, while X, G, and F are n-dimensional vectors with components x_i, g_i, and f_i, respectively. We will assume that the functions G and F are continuous, satisfy requirements for the uniqueness of solutions of system (3.1), are periodic with respect to t, and have period ω. Moreover, we will assume that the inequalities

$$|f_i(X, t)| < d_0, \quad |g_i(X, t)| < \varkappa_0 \|X\| \quad (i = 1, 2, \ldots, n) \tag{3.2}$$

are satisified for all X and t.

A system of the form (3.1) that satisfies conditions (3.2) is said to be quasi-linear [1]. With regard to their dissipative property, such systems have been studied by Nemtskiy [18] and Atrashenok [19]. In the following discussion we will use an approach suggested by Atrashenok.

2. Consider a quadratic form in the variables $y_1, \ldots, y_n$:

$$Y = \sum_{i, k=1}^{n} b_{ik} y_i y_k, \quad b_{ik} = b_{ki}.$$

Introduce the notation:

$$\Delta_k = \begin{vmatrix} b_{11}, & \ldots, & b_{1k} \\ \cdot & \cdot & \cdot \\ b_{k1}, & \ldots, & b_{kk} \end{vmatrix} \quad (k = 1, 2, \ldots, n).$$

It is well known that a quadratic form Y is positive definite if and only if the inequalities $\Delta_i > 0$ $(i = 1, 2, \ldots, n)$ are satisfied (Silvester's criterion).

Consider the quadratic form

$$\Phi = 2\lambda^2 y_1^2 + \sum_{\alpha=2}^{n} 2\lambda^{2\alpha-1} y_\alpha (-y_{\alpha-1} + \lambda y_\alpha), \tag{3.3}$$

where λ is an arbitrary nonzero real number; we will show that this form is positive definite. Silvester's determinants Δ_k are:

$$\Delta_1 = 2\lambda^2, \quad \Delta_2 = \begin{vmatrix} 2\lambda^2, & -\lambda^3 \\ -\lambda^3, & 2\lambda^4 \end{vmatrix} = 3\lambda^6,$$

$$\Delta_k = \begin{vmatrix} 2\lambda^2, & -\lambda^3, & 0, \ldots, & 0 \\ -\lambda^3, & 2\lambda^4, & -\lambda^5, \ldots, & 0 \\ \cdot & \cdot & \cdot & \cdot \\ 0, & 0, & 0, \ldots, & 2\lambda^{2k} \end{vmatrix}.$$

Expanding the last determinant by the elements of the last column, we obtain the recurrence relation

$$\Delta_k = 2\lambda^{2k}\Delta_{k-1} - \lambda^{4k-2}\Delta_{k-2}. \tag{3.4}$$

We will show that

$$\Delta_k = (k+1)\lambda^{(k+1)k}. \tag{3.5}$$

When $k = 1$ Eq. (3.5) obviously holds. Assume that it is true for $k-1$ and $k-2$, i.e., assume that the equations

$$\Delta_{k-2}=(k-1)\lambda^{(k-1)(k-2)}, \qquad \Delta_{k-1}=k\lambda^{k(k-1)},$$

are satisfied.

Substituting these equations into (3.4), we find that

$$\Delta_k=2\lambda^{2k}\cdot k\lambda^{k(k-1)}-\lambda^{4k-2}(k-1)\lambda^{(k-1)(k-2)}=(k+1)\lambda^{(k+1)k}$$

This and the principle of mathematical induction give us Eq. (3.5) for $k=1, 2, \ldots, n$. It follows from (3.5) that $\Delta_k>0$ for $k=1, 2, \ldots, n$. Thus, quadratic form (3.3) is positive definite, and for sufficiently small μ the quadratic form

$$\Phi_1=\Phi-\mu\sum_{i=1}^{n} y_i^2 \tag{3.6}$$

is also clearly positive definite.

Remark 3.1. If $\alpha>0$ is sufficiently small, then, in the interval $0\leqslant\mu\leqslant\alpha$, the determinants

$$\Delta_k(\mu)=\begin{vmatrix} 2\lambda^2-\mu, & -\lambda^3, & 0, \ldots, 0 \\ -\lambda^3, & 2\lambda^4-\mu, & -\lambda^5, \ldots, 0 \\ \cdots & \cdots & \cdots \\ 0, & 0, & 0, \ldots, 2\lambda^{2k}-\mu \end{vmatrix} \tag{3.7}$$

have their largest values at $\mu=0$.

Indeed, let σ_l be the sum of all lth-order principal minors of the determinant Δ_k. All of the σ_l are greater than zero, because they are the sums of products of determinants of the form Δ_k and even powers of λ. We have

$$\Delta_k(\mu)=\Delta_k-\mu\sigma_{k-1}+\mu^2\sigma_{k-2}-\ldots+(-1)^k\mu^k. \tag{3.8}$$

This implies that $\Delta_k(\mu)<\Delta_k$ for sufficiently small positive μ.

We will now find the upper limit for the values of μ for which quadratic form (3.6) is positive definite. Contruct the determinants $\Delta_1(\mu), \ldots, \Delta_n(\mu)$ and find the slower bound l_k of the real roots of the equations

$$\Delta_k(\mu)=0 \quad (k=1, 2, \ldots, n). \tag{3.9}$$

It follows from formula (3.8) that $l_k>0$.

If we set

$$m_n=\min\{l_1, \ldots, l_n\} \tag{3.10}$$

then, when $\mu<m_n$, the inequalities $\Delta_k(\mu)>0$ are satisfied and, consequently, quadratic form (3.6) will be positive definite.

Remark 3.2. The number m_n can also be defined as the smallest value of the form (3.3) on the surface of the sphere $y_1^2+y_2^2+\ldots+y_n^2=1$.

Indeed, if m_n is the smallest value of quadratic form (3.3) on the surface $y_1^2+y_2^2+\ldots+y_n^2=1$, then

$$\Phi \geqslant m_n \sum_{i=1}^{n} y_i^2,$$

consequently,

$$\Phi_1 = \Phi - m_n \sum_{i=1}^{n} y_i^2 \geqslant 0$$

and it is clear that the form Φ_1 will be positive definite when $\mu < m_n$.

3. Let λ_l denote the real and p_j+iq_j the complex characteristic roots of matrix A, and let k_l and k_j denote the multiplicities of the respective characteristic roots. If r and r_1 are the numbers of elementary divisors of A corresponding to the real and complex roots, then

$$\sum_{l=1}^{r} k_l + \sum_{j=1}^{r_1} k_j = n.$$

System (3.1) can be reduced to the following canonical form:

$$\left.\begin{aligned}
&\frac{dz_{1,l}}{dt} = \lambda_l z_{1,l} + \xi_{1,l} + \eta_{1,l},\\
&\cdots\cdots\cdots\cdots\cdots\cdots\cdots\cdots\\
&\frac{dz_{k_l,l}}{dt} = -z_{k_l-1,l} + \lambda_l z_{k_l,l} + \xi_{k_l,l} + \eta_{k_l,l},\\
&\frac{du_{1,j}}{dt} = p_j u_{1,j} - q_j v_{1,j} + \xi_{\nu_j+1,j} + \eta_{\nu_j+1,j},\\
&\frac{dv_{1,j}}{dt} = p_j v_{1,j} + q_j u_{1,j} + \xi_{\rho_j+1,j} + \eta_{\rho_j+1,j},\\
&\cdots\cdots\cdots\cdots\cdots\cdots\cdots\cdots\\
&\frac{du_{k_j,j}}{dt} = p_j v_{k_j,j} - q_j v_{k_j,j} - u_{k_j-1,j} + \xi_{\nu_j+k_j,j} + \eta_{\nu_j+k_j,j},\\
&\frac{dv_{k_j,j}}{dt} = p_j v_{k_j,j} + q_j u_{k_j,j} - v_{k_j-1,j} + \xi_{\rho_j+k_j,j} + \eta_{\rho_j+k_j,j}.
\end{aligned}\right\} \quad (3.11)$$

The functions $\xi_{\alpha,\beta}$ and $\eta_{\alpha,\beta}$ are linear combinations of the functions f_i and g_i, respectively, with constant coefficients. It is clear that $\xi_{\alpha,\beta}$ and $\eta_{\alpha,\beta}$ satisfy conditions of the same form as the functions f_i and g_i, respectively. Thus, for all z, u, v, and t we will have

$$|\xi_{\alpha,\beta}| < d, \quad |\eta_{\alpha,\beta}| < \varkappa \sqrt{\sum z_\alpha^2 + \sum (u_\beta^2 + v_\beta^2)}. \tag{3.12}$$

In addition, we will hereafter assume that the real parts of all characteristic roots of the matrix A are negative.

Following Bol' [20], we define functions

$$Z_i = \sum_{\alpha=1}^{k_i} \lambda_i^{2\alpha-1} z_{\alpha,i}^2, \quad U_j = \sum_{\beta=1}^{k_j} p_j^{2\beta-1} (u_{\beta,j}^2 + v_{\beta,j}^2) \tag{3.13}$$

and set

$$S = \sum_{i=1}^{r} Z_i + \sum_{j=1}^{r_1} U_j. \tag{3.14}$$

The function S is a quadratic form with coefficients that are odd powers of the real parts of the characteristic roots of matrix A. We now obtain the total derivative of S with respect to t, which, by virtue of the differential equations of system (3.11) is

$$\frac{dS}{dt} = \sum_{i=1}^{r} \sum_{\alpha=1}^{k_i} 2\lambda_i^{2\alpha-1} z_{\alpha,i} \frac{dz_{\alpha,i}}{dt} +$$

$$+ \sum_{j=1}^{r_1} \sum_{\beta=1}^{k_j} 2p_j^{2\beta-1} \left(u_{\beta,j} \frac{du_{\beta,j}}{dt} + v_{\beta,j} \frac{dv_{\beta,j}}{dt} \right) =$$

$$= \sum_{i=1}^{r} \Big\{ 2\lambda_i z_{1,i} (\lambda_i z_{1,i} + \xi_{1,i} + \eta_{1,i}) +$$

$$+ \sum_{\alpha=2}^{k_i} 2\lambda^{2\alpha-1} z_{\alpha,i} (-z_{\alpha-1,i} + \lambda_i z_{\alpha,i} + \xi_{\alpha,i} + \eta_{\alpha,i}) \Big\} +$$

$$+ \sum_{j=1}^{r_1} \Big\{ 2p_j u_{1,j} (p_j u_{1,j} - q_j v_{1,j} + \xi_{\nu_j+1,j} + \eta_{\nu_j+1,j}) +$$

$$+ \sum_{\beta=2}^{k_j} 2p_j^{2\beta-1} u_{\beta,j} (-u_{\beta-1,j} + p_j u_{\beta_j} -$$

$$- q_j v_{\beta,j} + \xi_{\nu_j+\beta,j} + \eta_{\nu_j+\beta,j}) \Big\} +$$

$$+ \sum_{j=1}^{r_1} \Big\{ 2p_j v_{1,j} (p_j v_{1,j} + q_j u_{1,j} + \xi_{\rho_j+1,j} + \eta_{\rho_j+1,j}) +$$

$$+ \sum_{\beta=2}^{k_j} 2p_j^{2\beta-1} v_{\beta,j} (p_j v_{\beta,j} + q_j u_{\beta,j} - v_{\beta-1,j} + \xi_{\rho_j+\beta,j} + \eta_{\rho_j+\beta,j}) \Big\} =$$

$$= \sum_{i=1}^{r}\left[2\lambda_i^2 z_{1,i}^2 + \sum_{\alpha=2}^{k_i} 2\lambda_i^{2\alpha-1} z_{\alpha,i}(-z_{\alpha-1,i}+\lambda_i z_{\alpha,i})\right]+$$

$$+\sum_{j=1}^{r_1}\left[2p_j^2 u_{1,j}^2 + \sum_{\beta=2}^{k_j} 2p_j^{2\beta-1} u_{\beta,j}(-u_{\beta-1,j}+p_j u_{\beta,j})\right]+$$

$$+\sum_{j=1}^{r_1}\left[2p_j^2 v_{1,j}^2 + \sum_{\beta=1}^{k_j} 2p_j^{2\beta-1} v_{\beta,j}(-v_{\beta-1,j}+p_j v_{\beta,j})\right]+$$

$$+\sum_{i=1}^{r}\sum_{\alpha=1}^{k_i} 2\lambda_i^{2\alpha-1} z_{\alpha,i}\xi_{\alpha,i}+$$

$$+\sum_{j=1}^{r_1}\sum_{\beta=1}^{k_j} 2p_j^{2\beta-1}(u_{\beta,j}\xi_{\nu_j+\beta,j}+v_{\beta,j}\xi_{\rho_j+\beta,j})+$$

$$+\sum_{i=1}^{r}\sum_{\alpha=1}^{k_i} 2\lambda_i^{2\alpha-1} z_{\alpha,i}\eta_{\alpha,i}+$$

$$+\sum_{j=1}^{r_1}\sum_{\beta=1}^{k_j} 2p_j^{2\beta-1}(u_{\beta,j}\eta_{\nu_j+\beta,j}+v_{\beta,j}\eta_{\rho_j+\beta,j}).$$

The expressions in each of the square brackets are quadratic forms of the same form as (3.3). Let m_{k_i} be numbers satisfying conditions (3.10) and set

$$m_0 = \min_i \{m_{k_i}\}. \tag{3.15}$$

Now consider the linear form

$$L = \sum_{i=1}^{r}\sum_{\alpha=1}^{k_i} \lambda_i^{2\alpha-1} z_{\alpha,i} + \sum_{j=1}^{r_1}\sum_{\beta=1}^{k_j} p_j^{2\beta-1}(u_{\beta,j}+v_{\beta,j}), \tag{3.16}$$

denote its largest value on the surface

$$\sum_{\alpha=1}^{k} z_\alpha^2 + \sum_{\beta=1}^{l}(u_\beta^2+v_\beta^2) = 1$$

by M_0 and set $\lambda_0 = 2M_0$. In virtue of the Cauchy inequality we have

$$M = \sqrt{\sum_{i=1}^{r}\sum_{\alpha=1}^{k_i} \lambda_i^{4\alpha-2} + 2\sum_{j=1}^{r_1}\sum_{\beta=1}^{k_j} p_j^{4\beta-2}}. \tag{3.17}$$

Using (3.12), we obtain the following estimate for dS/dt:

$$\frac{dS}{dt} \geqslant m_0\left(\sum_{i=1}^{r}\sum_{\alpha=1}^{k_i} z_{\alpha,i}^2 + \sum_{j=1}^{r_1}\sum_{\beta=1}^{k_j}(u_{\beta,j}^2 + v_{\beta,j}^2)\right) -$$

$$-\lambda_0 d \sqrt{\sum_{i=1}^{r}\sum_{\alpha=1}^{k_i} z_{\alpha,i}^2 + \sum_{j=1}^{r_1}\sum_{\beta=1}^{k_j}(u_{\beta,j}^2 + v_{\beta,j}^2)} -$$

$$-\lambda_0 \varkappa\left(\sum_{i=1}^{r}\sum_{\alpha=1}^{k_i} z_{\alpha,i}^2 + \sum_{j=1}^{r_1}\sum_{\beta=1}^{k_j}(u_{\beta,j}^2 + v_{\beta,j}^2)\right),$$

or, letting

$$\sigma^2 = \sum_{i=1}^{r}\sum_{\alpha=1}^{k_i} z_{\alpha,j}^2 + \sum_{j=1}^{r_1}\sum_{\beta=1}^{k_j}(u_{\beta,j}^2 + v_{\beta,j}^2), \tag{3.18}$$

we obtain

$$\frac{dS}{dt} \geqslant (m_0 - \lambda_0\varkappa)\,\sigma^2 - \lambda_0\, d\sigma. \tag{3.19}$$

4. The inequality which we have just established makes it possible to prove the following proposition.

Theorem 3.1. If the real parts of the characteristic roots of matrix A are negative and $\varkappa < m_0/\lambda_0$, where m_0 is defined by Eq. (3.15) and $\lambda_0 = 2M_0$ is defined by Eq. (3.17), then system (3.1) is dissipative.

Proof. Consider the function $V = -S$. It follows from the form of this function and inequality (3.19) that this function satisfies all conditions of Theorem 2.5, and the theorem follows.

Theorem 3.2. When the conditions of the above theorem are satisfied, system (3.1) has at least one periodic solution (harmonic oscillation) with period equal to ω.

Proof. As before, let $V = -S$. Then it follows from inequality (3.19) and the proofs of Theorems 2.4 and 2.5 that the set $V \leqslant h$ is mapped into itself by the transformation T when h is sufficiently large. But the function V is a positive definite quadratic form, so that the set $V \leqslant h$ is homeomorphic to a closed sphere. It then follows from the Brouwer theorem that the transformation T has a stationary point in the set $V \leqslant h$. Consequently, system (3.1) has a harmonic.

The theorem is proved.

5. Again considering system (2.1), we will prove the following theorem with regard to the system being dissipative.

Theorem 3.3. Let the functions f_i be continuously differentiable with $\partial f_i/\partial x_i \leqslant -m < 0$ $(i=1, 2, \ldots, n)$ and, in addition, assume that the functions $f_i(x_1, \ldots, x_{i-1}, 0, x_{i+1}, x_n, t)$ are bounded; then system (2.1) is dissipative.

Proof. We have

$$f_i(x_1, \ldots, x_n, t) = \int_0^{x_i} \frac{\partial f_i}{\partial x_i} dx_i + f_i(x_1, \ldots, x_{i-1}, 0, x_{i+1}, \ldots, x_n, t). \quad (3.20)$$

By hypothesis, there exists an $M > 0$ such that

$$|f_i(x_1, \ldots, x_{i-1}, 0, x_{i+1}, \ldots, x_n, t)| < M. \quad (3.21)$$

By hypothesis, therefore, it follows that there exists an $a > 0$ such that for $|x_i| \geqslant a$ the inequality

$$f_i x_i < -\frac{m}{2} x_i^2 \quad (3.22)$$

is satisfied. Moreover, it follows from (3.20) and (3.21) that when $|x_i| \leqslant a$

$$f_i(x_1, \ldots, x_n, t)\, x_i < Na \quad (3.23)$$

where $N > 0$ is some constant.

Consider the function

$$v = x_1^2 + \ldots + x_n^2. \quad (3.24)$$

By virtue of the differential equations of system (2.1), the derivative of this function with respect to time is clearly

$$\frac{dv}{dt} = \sum_{i=1}^{n} 2x_i f_i(x_1, \ldots, x_n, t). \quad (3.25)$$

We select a number A sufficiently large to satisfy the inequality

$$mA^2 > 2nNa. \quad (3.26)$$

Now consider the domain $\|X\| \geqslant nA$. Because $\sum_{k=1}^{n} |x_k| \geqslant \|X\|$ it is clear that in this region the inequality $\max_{i=1,\ldots,n} |x_i| \geqslant A$ will be satisfied. With the aid of inequalities (3.22) and (3.23), the following estimate is easily obtained:

$$\frac{dv}{dt} < -mA^2 + 2nNa.$$

It follows from this inequality and (3.26) that when $\|X\| \geqslant nA$

$$\frac{dv}{dt} < 0. \tag{3.27}$$

The theorem then follows from this and Theorem 2.5.

The following theorem is a consequence of inequality (3.27) and the Brouwer theorem.

Theorem 3.4. If system (2.1) satisfies the conditions of the preceding theorem, then it has at least one harmonic.

The results of Theorems 3.3 and 3.4 and other similar ones, were obtained by Corduneanu [21–24]. Manfredi [25], Graffi [26], Castro [27], and others have obtained a number of interesting results pertaining to dissipative systems of second-order differential equations. We will not dwell on these results; instead, we refer the interested reader to the original papers.

In the next two sections we will consider the dissipative properties of several concrete second- and third-order systems encountered in applications.

4. DISSIPATIVE PROPERTIES OF CERTAIN SECOND-ORDER SYSTEMS ENCOUNTERED IN APPLICATIONS

Consider the second-order differential equation

$$\frac{d^2x}{dt^2} + f(x)\frac{dx}{dt} + g(x) = p(t). \tag{4.1}$$

The dissipative property of such an equation and various generalizations of it have been considered by many authors. In this section we will merely consider some conditions, together with their generalizations, which are sufficient for Eq. (4.1) to be dissipative [28].

1. Using the following notation: $q(t) = \int\limits_0^t p(t)\,dt,\ F(x) = \int\limits_0^x f(x)\,dx,$

and $y = \frac{dx}{dt} + F(x) - q(t)$ results in the system

$$\frac{dx}{dt} = y - F(x) + q(t), \quad \frac{dy}{dt} = -q(x).$$

Instead of this system, let us consider the more general system

$$\frac{dx}{dt}=y-F(x)+Q(x,\ y,\ t),\quad \frac{dy}{dt}=-q(x). \tag{4.2}$$

Theorem 4.1. Assume that the functions $F(x)$, $g(x)$, *and* $Q(x, y, t)$ *are continuous and satisfy the condition required for uniqueness of solutions of system (4.2) for all initial data, that* $xg(x)>0$ *for* $|x|\geqslant 1$, *and that u* $\int_0^{+\infty} g(x)\,dx=\int_0^{-\infty} g(x)\,dx=+\infty$. *Moreover, assume that there exists constants* $L>H>0$ *such that* $|Q(x,\ y,\ t)|<H$ *for all* $x,\ y,\ t$ *and that* $F(x)$ *sign* $x>L$ *for* $|x|\geqslant 1$. *Finally, assume that* $Q(x,\ y,\ t+1)=Q(x,\ y,\ t)$ *for all* x, y, *and* t. *Then system (4.2) is dissipative.*

Proof. Set

$$F_m=\max_{|x|\leqslant 1}|F(x)|.$$

Since, by hypothesis, the integrals $\int_0^{+\infty} g(x)\,dx$ and $\int_0^{-\infty} g(x)\,dx$ diverge, there exists a $\xi>1$ such that

$$(L-H)\int_1^{\xi} g(x)\,dx>4(F_m+H)\int_{-1}^{+1}|g(x)|\,dx$$

and

$$(L-H)\int_{-1}^{-\xi} g(x)\,dx>4(F_m+H)\int_{-1}^{+1}|g(x)|\,dx.$$

Introduce the following notation:

$$a=\max_{|x|\leqslant\xi}|g(x)|,\quad b=\max_{|x|\leqslant\xi}|F(x)|+H$$

$$\eta_1=\frac{4b+\sqrt{4b^2+24(1+\xi)a}}{3}.$$

Consider the solution $x=\varphi(t)$, $y=\psi(t)$ of system (4.2) with the initial data $\varphi(t_0)=x_0$, $\psi(t_0)=y_0$, and assume that $|x_0|\leqslant 1$, $y_0\geqslant\eta_1$.

It follows from the first equation in system (4.2) that x increases along any solution in the region $|x|\leqslant\xi$, $y>b$. In this region, the relationship between y and x along our solution is given by

$$\frac{dy}{dx} = -\frac{g(x)}{y - F(x) + Q(x, y, t)}. \tag{4.3}$$

From Eq. (4.3), we have the following estimate in the region $|x| \leqslant \xi$ $y > b$:

$$\frac{dy}{dx} > -\frac{a}{y - b}. \tag{4.4}$$

Let $Y(x)$ be the solution of the equation

$$\frac{dY}{dx} = -\frac{a}{Y - b} \tag{4.5}$$

with the initial data $x = x_0$, $Y = y_0$. It follows from inequality (4.4) that the inequality $x \in (x_0, \xi]$ will be satisfied for those $Y(x) > b$ for which $y > Y(x)$.

Let us find the function $Y(x)$; integrating (4.5), we obtain

$$\frac{1}{2} Y^2 - bY - \frac{1}{2} y_0^2 + by_0 + a(x - x_0) = 0$$

and, consequently,

$$Y = b + \sqrt{(y_0 - b)^2 - 2a(x - x_0)}.$$

Since $|x_0| \leqslant 1$ and $x \leqslant \xi$, we can write

$$y \geqslant b + \sqrt{(y_0 - b)^2 - 2a(1 + \xi)} \text{ for } x_0 \leqslant x \leqslant \xi. \tag{4.6}$$

Since η_1 is a root of the equation

$$\sqrt{(y_0 - b)^2 - 2a(1 + \xi)} = \frac{1}{2} y_0,$$

the inequality (4.6) leads to

$$y - b > \frac{1}{2} y_0 \text{ for } x_0 \leqslant x \leqslant \xi. \tag{4.7}$$

Now consider our solution as x varies from x_0 to +1. It follows from Eq. (4.3) that

$$\frac{dy}{dx} < \frac{a}{y - b}. \tag{4.8}$$

This shows that if $y_1(x)$ is the solution of the equation

$$\frac{dy_1}{dx}=\frac{a}{y_1-b}, \tag{4.9}$$

with initial data $x=x_0$, $y_1=y_0$, the inequality $y(x)<y_1(x)$ when $x_0\leqslant x\leqslant 1$ is satisfied along our solution. But integration of (4.9) gives us

$$\frac{1}{2}y_1^2-by_1-\frac{1}{2}y_0+by_0-a(x-x_0)=0$$

consequently,

$$y_1=b+\sqrt{(y_0-b)^2+2a(x-x_0)}.$$

Since $|x_0|\leqslant 1$ and $x\leqslant 1$, for $x_0\leqslant x\leqslant 1$ we have the inequality

$$y<b+\sqrt{(y_0-b)^2+4a}<y_0+2\sqrt{a}.$$

Since, along our solution, when $1\leqslant x\leqslant \xi$ y, y decreases as time increases, we have the inequality

$$y<y_0+2\sqrt{a}$$

when $x_0\leqslant x\leqslant \xi$. The inequality $y_0+2\sqrt{a}+b>2y_0$ is easily derived from the condition $y_0>\eta_1$; as a result,

$$y+b<2y_0 \text{ for } x_0\leqslant x\leqslant \xi. \tag{4.10}$$

Consider the function

$$v(x, y)=\frac{1}{2}y^2+\int_0^x g(x)\,dx. \tag{4.11}$$

By virtue of the differential equations of system (4.2), the derivative of this function is, as we can easily verify,

$$\dot{v}=-g(x)[F(x)-Q(x, y, t)]. \tag{4.12}$$

Let t_1 be the first instant after t_0 at which $x=\xi$ on the solution under discussion, i.e., $\varphi(t_1)=\xi$ and $x_0\leqslant\varphi(t)<\xi$ for $t_0\leqslant t<t_1$. We will show that

$$v(\varphi(t_1), \psi(t_1))<v(x_0, y_0). \tag{4.13}$$

Dividing Eq. (4.12) by the first equation of (4.2) we obtain

$$\frac{dv}{dx} = -\frac{g(x)[F(x) - Q(x, y, t)]}{y - F(x) + Q(x, y, t)}. \tag{4.14}$$

Integrating this equation, we find

$$v(\varphi(t_1), \psi(t_1)) = v(x_0, y_0) - \int_{x_0}^{1} \frac{g(x)[F(x) - Q(x, y, t)]}{y - F(x) + Q(x, y, t)} dx - \\ - \int_{1}^{\xi} \frac{g(x)[F(x) - Q(x, y, t)]}{y - F(x) + Q(x, y, t)} dx. \tag{4.15}$$

We now estimate the integrals in the right side of this equation. By virtue of (4.7),

$$-\int_{x_0}^{1} \frac{g(x)[F(x) - Q(x, y, t)]}{y - F(x) + Q(x, y, t)} dx < \frac{2(F_m + H)}{y_0} \int_{-1}^{+1} |g(x)| dx.$$

The following estimate is easily derived from (4.10):

$$\int_{1}^{\xi} \frac{g(x)[F(x) - Q(x, y, t)]}{y - F(x) + Q(x, y, t)} dx > \frac{L - H}{2y_0} \int_{1}^{\xi} g(x) dx.$$

This and (4.15) give us the inequality

$$v(\varphi(t_1), \psi(t_1)) < v(x_0, y_0) + \frac{2(F_m + H)}{y_0} \int_{-1}^{+1} |g(x)| dx - \\ - \frac{L - H}{2y_0} \int_{1}^{\xi} g(x) dx.$$

Inequality (4.13) follows from this last inequality and the choice of ξ.

Similarly, we can prove that, along the solution $x = \varphi(t)$, $y = \psi(t)$, x decreases as t decreases from t_0 until $x = -\xi$ at $t = t_2$. Here $t = t_2$ denotes the first such instant, i.e., $\varphi(t_2) = -\xi$ and $-\xi < \varphi(t) \leqslant x_0$ when $t_2 < t \leqslant t_0$. Moreover, it is clear that inequalities (4.7) and (4.10) will be satisfied in the time interval $t_2 \leqslant t \leqslant t_0$. Now, using the same argument, we show that

$$v(\varphi(t_2), \psi(t_2)) > v(x_0, y_0). \tag{4.16}$$

Let $x=\varphi_1(t)$, $y=\psi_1(t)$ be the solution with the initial data $t=t_0$, $x=x_0$, $y=y_0$, and $|x_0|\leqslant 1$, $y_0<-\eta_1$. Then, as above, we will show that there exist times $t_2'<t_0'<t_1'$ such that $\varphi_1(t_1')=-\xi$, $\varphi_1(t_2')=\xi$, $-\xi<\varphi(t)<\xi$ for $t_2'<t<t_1'$ and the inequalities

$$y+b<\frac{1}{2}y_0,\quad y-b>2y_0 \tag{4.17}$$

are satisfied in the time interval $t_2'\leqslant t\leqslant t_1'$. As above, these relationships make it possible to prove that the following inequality holds:

$$v\left(\varphi_1(t_1'),\ \psi_1(t_1')\right)<v(x_0,\ y_0)<v\left(\varphi_1(t_2'),\ \psi_1(t_2')\right). \tag{4.18}$$

Now we estimate the length of the interval $[t_0,\ t_1]$. The inequality

$$\frac{dt}{dx}<\frac{1}{y-b}\ \text{for}\ x_0\leqslant x\leqslant\xi$$

which is a consequence of the first equation of (4.2), and, together with (4.7) gives us

$$\frac{dt}{dx}<\frac{2}{y_0}.$$

Integrating this inequality between $x=x_0$ and $x=\xi$, we find that

$$t_1-t_0<\frac{2}{y_0}(\xi-x_0)\leqslant\frac{2}{y_0}(\xi+1). \tag{4.19}$$

Set

$$\eta=\max\{\eta_1,\ 4(\xi+1)\}. \tag{4.20}$$

Then, for $y_0>\eta$, we will have the inequality $t_1-t_0<1/2$. Similarly, we can also prove the inequalities $t_0-t_2<1/2$, $t_1'-t_0<1/2$ and $t_0-t_2'<1/2$.

Let

$$\bar{v}=\frac{1}{2}\eta^2+\int_{-1}^{+1}|g(x)|\,dx. \tag{4.21}$$

Since, by hypothesis, the integrals $\int_0^{+\infty}g(x)\,dx$ and $\int_0^{-\infty}g(x)\,dx$ diverge, there exists an $A>0$ such that $x^2+y^2\geqslant A^2$ when $v(x,\ y)>\bar{v}$.

Consider the solution $x=\varphi(t)$, $y=\psi(t)$ of system (4.2) with the initial data $t=0$, $x=x_0$, $y=y_0$ and $x_0^2+y_0^2 \geqslant A^2$. We will now prove the inequality

$$v(\varphi(1), \psi(1)) < v(x_0, y_0). \tag{4.22}$$

The proof is indirect. Assume that this inequality is not satisfied, and, initially, that $|x_0| \geqslant 1$. It then follows from Eq. (4.12) and the conditions of the theorem that $\dot{v}(x_0, y_0) < 0$. As a result, $v(\varphi(t), \psi(t))$ decreases in the neighborhood of the point $t=0$. Since, by hypothesis, inequality (4.22) is not satisfied, it is clear that there exists a $\tau_0 \in (0, 1]$ such that $v(\varphi(\tau_0), \psi(\tau_0)) = v(x_0, y_0)$ and that, when $0 < t < \tau_0$, the inequality $v(\varphi(t) \ \psi(t)) < v(x_0, y_0)$ is satisfied. It follows from Eq. (4.12) that $\dot{v}(x, y) < 0$ when $|x| \geqslant 1$; it is thus clear that $|\varphi(\tau_0)| < 1$. If $|x_0| < 1$, we simply set $\tau_0 = 0$.

We will now show that $\tau_0 < 1/2$. Since $x_0^2+y_0^2 \geqslant A^2$, we have $v(x_0, y_0) > \bar{v}$ and, by definition of τ_0,

$$v(\varphi(\tau_0), \psi(\tau_0)) = v(x_0, y_0) > \bar{v}. \tag{4.23}$$

But $|\varphi(\tau_0)| < 1$, so that from Eq. (4.21), we have

$$|\psi(\tau_0)| > \eta. \tag{4.24}$$

This and the preceding considerations imply that there exists a τ^* (this τ^* corresponds to the time t_2 when $\psi(\tau_0) > \eta$ or the time t_2' when $\psi(\tau_0) < -\eta$) such that $\tau^* < \tau_0$ and

$$v(\varphi(\tau^*), \psi(\tau^*)) > v(\varphi(\tau_0), \psi(\tau_0)). \tag{4.25}$$

Here, as proved above, $\tau_0 - \tau^* < 1/2$. This shows that $\tau_0 < 1/2$, because if we had $\tau_0 \geqslant 1/2$, we would have $0 < \tau^* < \tau_0$, which, together with (4.25), would contradict the definition of τ_0 as the first instant after $t=0$ which the inequality $v(\varphi(t), \psi(t)) < v(x_0, y_0)$ is violated.

As shown above, there exists a $\tau_1 > \tau_0$ (this τ_1 corresponds to the time t_1 if $\psi(\tau_0) > \eta$ or the time t_1' if $\psi(\tau_0) < -\eta$) such that $\varphi(\tau_1) = \xi$ $\varphi(\tau_0) < \varphi(t) < \xi$ when $\tau_0 < t < \tau_1$ (for $\psi(\tau_0) > \eta$) or $\varphi(\tau_1) = -\xi$, $-\xi < \varphi(t) < \varphi(\tau_0)$ when $\tau_0 < t < \tau_1$ (for $\psi(\tau_0) < -\eta$) and

$$v(\varphi(\tau_1), \psi(\tau_1)) < v(\varphi(\tau_0), \psi(\tau_0)) = v(x_0, y_0). \tag{4.26}$$

Moreover, we have shown that $\tau_1 - \tau_0 < 1/2$ and, consequently, $\tau_1 < 1$.

By hypothesis, inequality (4.22) is not satisfied, so there exists a $\bar{\tau} \in (\tau_1, 1]$ such that

$$v(\varphi(\bar{\tau}), \psi(\bar{\tau})) = v(x_0, y_0)$$

and $v(\varphi(t), \psi(t)) < v(x_0, y_0)$ for $\tau_1 \leqslant t < \bar{\tau}$; it is clear that $|\varphi(\bar{\tau})| < 1$.

From the statements proved above it follows that there exists a $\tau' < \bar{\tau}$ such that $\varphi(\tau') = -\xi$, $\xi < \varphi(t) < \varphi(\bar{\tau})$ for $\tau' < t < \bar{\tau}$ (if $\psi(\bar{\tau}) > \eta$) or $\varphi(\tau') = \xi$, $\varphi(\bar{\tau}) < \varphi(t) < \xi$ for $\tau' < t < \bar{\tau}$ (if $\psi(\bar{\tau}) < -\eta$) and

$$v(\varphi(\tau'), \psi(\tau')) > v(\varphi(\bar{\tau}), \psi(\bar{\tau})) = v(x_0, y_0). \tag{4.27}$$

It follows from the definition of τ_1 that the inequality $\tau_1 < \tau' < \bar{\tau} \leqslant 1$ is satisfied. This contradicts the fact that $v(\varphi(t), \psi(t)) < v(x_0, y_0)$ when $\tau_1 \leqslant t < \bar{\tau}$. The contradiction we have obtained proves inequality (4.22).

Our argument also shows that $v(\varphi(t), \psi(t)) < v(x_0, y_0)$ when $\tau_1 \leqslant t \leqslant 1$. Thus, it follows from the definition of v that the solution $x = \varphi(t)$, $y = \psi(t)$ is bounded when $0 \leqslant t \leqslant 1$ and, therefore, extends to the entire interval between $t = 0$ and $t = 1$.

Having satisfied the conditions of Theorem 2.4, the theorem follows.

Remark 4.1. It follows from our argument that when system (4.2) satisfies the conditions of the preceding theorem it has at least one periodic solution with unit period. Indeed, it is easily seen that for sufficiently large c the set $v(x, y) \leqslant c$ is a closed topological disk. Since the disk is mapped into itself under the transformation T, the proposition follows from the Brouwer theorem.

2. We will now consider an equation somewhat more complex than Eq. (4.1):

$$\frac{d^2x}{dt^2} + f(x)\frac{dx}{dt} + g(x) = R(x, \dot{x}, t). \tag{4.28}$$

We set $y = \dot{x} + F(x)$, where, as before $F(x) = \int_0^x f(x)\,dx$; then we obtain the system

$$\frac{dx}{dt} = y - F(x), \quad \frac{dy}{dt} = -g(x) + R(x, y, t). \tag{4.29}$$

Theorem 4.2. Let the functions $f(x)$, $g(x)$, *and* $R(x, y, t)$ *be continuous and satisfy the condition required for uniqueness of solutions of system (4.29) with arbitrary initial data,* $R(x, y, t+1) = R(x, y, t)$ *for all* x, y, t. *Moreover, assume that there exist constants* $L > H > 0$ *and* $K > 0$ *such that*

1) $|R(x, y, t)| < H$ *for all* x, y, t;
2) $g(x)\,\mathrm{sign}\,x \geqslant L$ *for* $|x| \geqslant 1$;
3) $f(x) \geqslant K$ *for* $|x| \geqslant 1$.

Then system (4.29) is dissipative.

Proof. Consider the function

$$v(x, y) = y^2 - yF(x) + \frac{1}{2} F^2(x) + 2 \int_0^x g(x)\, dx. \qquad (4.30)$$

By virtue of the differential equations of system (4.29), the derivative of this function is, as we can easily verify,

$$\dot{v} = -[y - F(x)]^2 f(x) - g(x) F(x) + [2y - F(x)] R(x, y, t). \qquad (4.31)$$

We now show that there exists an $h_1 > 0$ such that for $|x| \geqslant h_1$

$$\dot{v}(x, y, t) < 0. \qquad (4.32)$$

For definiteness, assume that $x > 0$ (the proof for $x < 0$ is similar). By hypothesis, we have

$$\dot{v} < -[y - F(x)]^2 K - LF(x) + [2y - F(x)] H$$

when $x \geqslant 1$ and $y \geqslant (1/2) F(x)$. We will show that, for sufficiently large x, the equation

$$[y - F(x)]^2 K + LF(x) - [2y - F(x)] H = 0$$

has no real solutions. The discriminant D of this equation is

$$\frac{1}{4} D = K^2F^2 + 2KHF + H^2 - K^2F^2 - KLF - KHF =$$
$$= KHF + H^2 - KLF = -K(L - H) F(x) + H^2.$$

Since by hypothesis $f(x) \geqslant K$ for $|x| \geqslant 1$, it is clear that $\lim F(x) = \infty$ as $x \to \infty$, so that we will have $L > H$ for sufficiently large x because $D < 0$. This shows that $\dot{v} < 0$ for sufficiently large x and $y \geqslant (1/2) F(x)$.

When $x \geqslant 1$ and $y \leqslant (1/2) F(x)$, we will have $\dot{v} < -[y - F(x)]^2 K - LF(x) - [2y - F(x)] H$. As before, we now show that the equation

$$[y - F(x)]^2 K + LF(x) + [2y - F(x)] H = 0$$

has no real solutions when x is sufficiently large. It follows from what we have said that there exists an $h_1 > 0$ such that inequality (4.32) is satisfied when $|x| \geqslant h_1$.

It follows from the very form of the function $\dot{v}$ that there exists an h_2 such that

$$\dot{v}(x, y, t) < 0$$

when $|x| \leqslant h_1$ and $|y| \geqslant h_2$. As a result, there exists an $a > 0$ such that $\dot{v} < 0$ when $x^2 + y^2 \geqslant a$.

Thus, we have satisfied the hypothesis of Theorem 2.5, from which our proposition follows.

Remark 4.2. It is not difficult to show that system (4.29) has at least one harmonic oscillation when the hypothesis of the preceding theorem is satisfied.

5. AN INVESTIGATION OF ONE THIRD-ORDER NONLINEAR EQUATION

Consider the differential equation [29, 30]

$$\frac{d^3x}{dt^3} + a\frac{d^2x}{dt^2} + b\frac{dx}{dt} + f(x) = p_1\left(x, \frac{dx}{dt}, \frac{d^2x}{dt^2}, t\right). \tag{5.1}$$

If we set $y = ax + \dot{x}$, $z = bx + a\dot{x} + \ddot{x}$ then Eq. (5.1) may be replaced by the system

$$\frac{dx}{dt} = y - ax, \quad \frac{dy}{dt} = z - bx, \quad \frac{dz}{dt} = -f(x) + p(x, y, z, t). \tag{5.2}$$

We will prove the following sufficient conditions for system (5.2) to be dissipative.

Theorem 5.1. Let the functions $f(x)$ and $p(x, y, z, t)$ be continuous and satisfy the required conditions for uniqueness of solutions of system (5.2) for all x, y, z, and t and assume that the following conditions hold;

1) $a > 0$, $b > 0$;
2) $0 < f(x)/x < ab$ *for* $|x| \geqslant 1$;
3) $\lim_{|x| \to \infty} |f(x)| = \infty$;
4) $\lim_{|x| \to \infty} |f(x) - abx| = \infty$;
5) $p(x, y, z, t + \omega) = p(x, y, z, t)$ *for all x, y, z, and t;*
6) *there exists a constant $A > 0$ such that $|p(x, y, z, t)| < A$ for all x, y, z, and t. Then system (5.2) is dissipative.*

In order to prove this theorem, consider the function

$$v = \frac{1}{2}(a^2x - ay + z)^2 + \frac{1}{2}(z - bx)^2 + \frac{b}{2}y^2 + a\int_0^x [f(x) - abx]\,dx. \tag{5.3}$$

By virtue of the differential equations of system (5.2), it is not difficult to show that the time derivative of this function is

$$\dot{v} = -a(a^2x - ay + z)^2 + [abx - f(x)] \times \times [2(a^2x - ay + z) - bx] + [(a^2 - b)x - ay + + 2z]\, p(x, y, z, t). \quad (5.4)$$

Let us examine the behavior of $\dot{v}$ for sufficiently large x, y, and z. Set

$$w = -a(a^2x - ay + z)^2 + + [abx - f(x)][2(a^2x - ay + z) - bx]. \quad (5.5)$$

We will now prove the following lemmas.

Lemma 5.1. When the hypothesis of Theorem 5.1 is satisfied, the following relationship holds uniformly for all y and z:

$$\lim \left| \frac{w}{x} \right| = +\infty \text{ for } |x| \to \infty. \quad (5.6)$$

Proof. Let us set $u = a^2x - ay + z$ and find the maximum of the function w for fixed x. Since

$$\frac{\partial w}{\partial u} = -2au + 2[abx - f(x)].$$

It follows that for fixed x, the maximum of w is realized at $u = (1/a)[abx - f(x)]$. Denoting this maximum by $w_1(x)$, we have

$$w_1(x) = -\frac{1}{a}[abx - f(x)]^2 + \frac{2}{a}[abx - f(x)]^2 - - bx[abx - f(x)] = -\frac{1}{a} f(x)[abx - f(x)],$$

which in turn yields

$$\left| \frac{w(x, y, z)}{x} \right| \geqslant \left| \frac{w_1(x)}{x} \right| = \frac{f(x)}{a|x|}[abx - f(x)]. \quad (5.7)$$

Choose an arbitrary $L > 0$. By virtue of Conditions 3 and 4 of the theorem, there exists for this L an $x_0 > 1$ such that $|f(x)| > 2L/b$ and $|abx - f(x)| > 2L/b$ when $|x| \geqslant x_0$. Now consider an arbitrary $x > x_0$. Two possibilities exist: Either

$$0 < \frac{f(x)}{x} \leqslant \frac{1}{2} ab, \quad (5.8)$$

or

$$\frac{1}{2} ab < \frac{f(x)}{x} < ab. \quad (5.9)$$

Assume initially that (5.9) is satisfied; it then follows from (5.7) that

$$\left|\frac{w(x, y, z)}{x}\right| \geqslant \frac{b}{2}\,|abx - f(x)| > L. \tag{5.10}$$

If, on the other hand, (5.8) is satisfied, we obtain the inequality

$$\left|\frac{w(x, y, z)}{x}\right| \geqslant \frac{b}{2}\,|f(x)| > L. \tag{5.11}$$

Inequalities (5.10) and (5.11) prove that relation (5.6) is satisfied uniformly for all y and z.

Let α be an arbitrary, sufficiently small, positive constant, and let $D(\alpha)$ denote the set of points defined by the inequalities $\{-\alpha^2 z < x < \alpha^2 z,\ (1-\alpha/a)z < y < (1+\alpha/a)z$ for $z > 0$ and $\alpha^2 z < x < -\alpha^2 z\ (1+\alpha/a)z < y < (1-\alpha/a)z$ for $z < 0\}$.

Lemma 5.2. There exists a number $r(\alpha)$ *such that outside the set* $D(\alpha)$ *and the sphere* $R(\alpha)$ *defined by the inequality* $\{x^2 + y^2 + z^2 < r^2(\alpha)\}$ *the function* $\dot{v}(x, y, z, t)$ *is negative.*

We will prove this proposition for the region $x \geqslant 0$, $y \geqslant 0$, and $z \geqslant 0$; the proof is analogous for the remaining quadrants.

First, consider the region $E_1\{x \geqslant 0,\ y \geqslant 0,\ z \geqslant 0\ x \geqslant \alpha^2 z,\ x \geqslant (a\alpha^2/1+\alpha)\,y\}$. It follows from the form of the function $\dot{v}$ and from (5.6) that there exists a number r_1, such that $\dot{v} < 0$ in the region E outside the sphere $\{x^2 + y^2 + z^2 < r_1^2\}$.

Let E_2 denote the region defined by the inequalities $\{x \geqslant 0,\ y \geqslant 0$. $z \geqslant 0,\ y \geqslant (1+\alpha/a)z,\ x \leqslant (a\alpha^2/1+\alpha)y\}$. Then we have

$$\frac{\dot{v}}{(a^2x - ay + z)^2} = -a + 2\,\frac{abx - f(x)}{a^2x - ay + z} - \frac{bx\,[abx - f(x)]}{(a^2x - ay + z)^2} + \\ + \frac{(a^2 - b)\,x - ay + 2z}{(a^2x - ay + z)^2}\,p(x, y, z, t). \tag{5.12}$$

It is easily seen that there exists a number A_1 such that in the region E_2 the following inequalities will be satisfied for sufficiently small α:

$$\left|\frac{abx - f(x)}{a^2x - ay + z}\right| < A_1\alpha, \quad \left|\frac{bx\,[abx - f(x)]}{(a^2x - ay + z)^2}\right| < A_1\alpha^2. \tag{5.13}$$

It follows from the definition of E_2 that, in this region, the quantity

$$\frac{(a^2 - b)\,x - ay + 2z}{(a^2x - ay + z)^2}$$

will be arbitrarily small when $x^2+y^2+z^2$ is sufficiently large. It then follows from expression (5.12), inequality (5.13), and Condition 6 of the theorem that there exists an r_2 such that $\dot{v}<0$ when $x^2+y^2+z^2\geqslant r_2^2$ in the region E_2.

Similarly, we can prove the existence of an r_3 such that $\dot{v}<0$ in the region $E_3\left\{x\geqslant 0,\ y\geqslant 0,\ z\geqslant 0,\ x\leqslant \alpha^2 z,\ y\leqslant (1-\alpha/a)z\right\}$ when $x^2+y^2+z^2\geqslant r_3^2$.

We have thus proved that $\dot{v}(x, y, z, t)<0$ outside the set $\Sigma(\alpha)=R(\alpha)+D(\alpha)$.

Now we will prove the following lemma.

Lemma 5.3. There exists an $\alpha_1>0$ *and a function* $q_1(\alpha)$ *with the following properties: Let the point* (x_0, y_0, z_0) *be in* $D(\alpha)$, *where* $0<\alpha\leqslant\alpha_1$, *and* $z_0\geqslant q_1(\alpha)>0$, *and let* $x=x(t),\ y=y(t),\ z=z(t)$ *be the solution of system (5.2) with initial data* $t=t_0,\ x=x_0,\ y=y_0$ *and* $z=z_0$. *Then there exists a* $\theta_1>t_0$ *such that*

1) $x(\theta_1)=2\alpha^2 z(\theta_1)$ *and for* $t_0\leqslant t<\theta_1$, $|x(t)|<2\alpha^2 z(t)$;

2) *for* $t_0\leqslant t\leqslant\theta_1$, $|z-z_0|<\alpha^2 z_0$;

3) *for* $t_0\leqslant t\leqslant\theta_1$, $0\leqslant y-y_0<\alpha z_0$;

4) $\theta_1-t_0<\omega/2$.

Proof. Choose an $\alpha_1^2<1/2b$; then the solution under discussion first intersects the plane $x=2\alpha^2 z$, and only then intersects the plane $x=(1/b)z$. In the time interval $t_0\leqslant t\leqslant\theta_1$, therefore, y increases along our solution. We will show that for sufficiently small α_1 and sufficiently large $q_1(\alpha)$, statements 2 and 3 of the lemma are satisfied. By virtue of continuity, both of the inequalities

$$|z(t)-z_0|<\alpha^2 z_0,\quad 0\leqslant y-y_0<\alpha z_0 \tag{5.14}$$

are satisfied when $t>t_0$ and $(t-t_0)$ is sufficiently small. Assume that one of these inequalities does not hold when $t=t^*\in(0,\theta_1]$; here we assume that t^* is the first point at which one of inequalities (5.14) is violated. Assume initially that the second inequality (5.14) is the first to be violated, i.e., we assume that

$$y(t^*)-y_0=\alpha z_0 \tag{5.15}$$

and that both inequalities in (5.14) are satisfied when $t_0\leqslant t<t^*$. Dividing the second equation of system (5.2) by the first, we find that

$$\frac{dy}{dx}=\frac{z-bx}{y-ax}. \tag{5.16}$$

It then follows that the inequality

$$\frac{dy}{dx}<2a \tag{5.17}$$

is satisfied when $t_0 \leqslant t \leqslant t^*$ if α_1 is sufficiently small and $q_1(\alpha)$ is sufficiently large. Integrating inequality (5.17) along the solution $x = x(t)$, $y = y(t)$, $z = z(t)$, we find that

$$y - y_0 < 2a(x - x_0).$$

Since $x_0 > -\alpha^2 z$, $x < 3\alpha^2 z_0$ for sufficiently small α, the last inequality implies the relationship

$$y(t^*) - y_0 < \alpha z_0.$$

which contradicts Eq. (5.15). This contradiction proves that the second inequality of (5.14) can only be violated after the first one. We now assume that

$$|z(t^*) - z_0| = \alpha^2 z_0 \tag{5.18}$$

and both inequalities are satisfied when $t_0 \leqslant t < t^*$.

Dividing the third equation of system (5.2) by the first, we obtain the expression

$$\frac{dz}{dx} = \frac{-f(x) + p(x, y, z, t)}{y - ax}. \tag{5.19}$$

It follows from inequalities (5.14) and the hypothesis of the theorem that the inequality

$$\left|\frac{dz}{dx}\right| < \alpha \tag{5.20}$$

will be satisfied when $t_0 \leqslant t \leqslant t^*$ if α_1 is sufficiently small and $q_1(\alpha)$ is sufficiently large. Integrating this last inequality, we find that

$$|z - z_0| < \alpha |x - x_0|.$$

Since $|x(t)| \leqslant 2\alpha^2 z(t)$ when $t_0 \leqslant t \leqslant t^*$, it follows from the last inequality that

$$|z - z_0| < \alpha^2 z_0$$

which contradicts Eq. (5.18). The contradiction which we have obtained proves that inequalities (5.14) are satisfied for all $t_0 \leqslant t \leqslant \theta_1$.

We will now show that the last statement of the lemma holds. From the first equation of system (5.2) we find

$$\frac{dt}{dx} = \frac{1}{y - ax}. \tag{5.21}$$

For sufficiently small α, inequalities (5.14) yield the inequality

$$\frac{dt}{dx} < \frac{2a}{z_0}$$

which holds for $t_0 \leqslant t \leqslant \theta_1$. Integrating this inequality, we obtain

$$\theta_1 - t_0 < \frac{2a}{z_0}(x - x_0) < \alpha.$$

If $\alpha_1 < \omega/2$, we obtain the inequality $\theta_1 - t_0 < \omega/2$.

The lemma is proved.

Similar proofs hold for the following three lemmas.

Lemma 5.4. There exists an $\alpha_1 > 0$ *and a function* $q_1(\alpha)$ *with the following properties: Let the point* (x_0, y_0, z_0) *be in* $D(\alpha)$*, where* $0 < \alpha \leqslant \alpha_1$ *and* $z_0 \geqslant q_1(\alpha) > 0$*, and let* $x = x(t)$, $y = y(t)$, $z = z(t)$ *be the solution of system (5.2) with initial data* $t = t_0$, $x = x_0$, $y = y_0$, $z = z_0$. *Then there exists a* $\theta_2 < t_0$ *such that*

1) $x(\theta_2) = -2\alpha^2 z(\theta_2)$ *and for* $\theta_2 < t \leqslant t_0$, $x(t) > -2\alpha^2 z(t)$;
2) *for* $\theta_2 \leqslant t \leqslant t_0$, $|z - z_0| < \alpha^2 z_0$;
3) *for* $\theta_2 \leqslant t \leqslant t_0$, $0 \leqslant y_0 - y < \alpha z$;
4) $t_0 - \theta_2 < \omega/2$.

Lemma 5.5. There exists an $\alpha_1 > 0$ *and a function* $q_1(\alpha)$ *with the following properties: Let the point* (x_0, y_0, z_0) *be in* $D(\alpha)$, *where* $0 < \alpha \leqslant \alpha_1$ *and* $z_0 \leqslant -q_1(\alpha) < 0$, *and let* $x = x(t)$, $y = y(t)$, $z = z(t)$ *be the solution with initial data* $t = t_0$, $x = x_0$, $y = y_0$, $z = z_0$. *Then there exists* $\theta_3 > t_0$ *such that*

1) $x(\theta_3) = 2\alpha^2 z(\theta_3)$ *and for* $t_0 \leqslant t < \theta_3$, $x(t) > 2\alpha^2 z(t)$;
2) *for* $t_0 \leqslant t \leqslant \theta_3$, $|z(t) - z_0| < -\alpha^2 z_0$;
3) *for* $t_0 \leqslant t \leqslant \theta_3$, $0 \leqslant y_0 - y < -\alpha z_0$;
4) $\theta_3 - t_0 < \omega/2$.

Lemma 5.6. There exists an $\alpha_1 > 0$ *and a function* $q_1(\alpha)$ *with the following properties: Let the point* (x_0, y_0, z_0) *be* $D(\alpha)$, *where* $0 < \alpha \leqslant \alpha_1$ *and* $z_0 \leqslant -q_1(\alpha)$, *and let* $x = x(t)$, $y = y(t)$, $z = z(t)$, *be the solution with initial data* $t = t_0$, $x = x_0$, $y = y_0$, $z = z_0$. *Then there exists a* $\theta_4 < t_0$ *such that*

1) $x(\theta_4) = -2\alpha^2 z(\theta_4)$ *and for* $\theta_4 < t \leqslant t_0$, $x(t) < -2\alpha^2 z(t)$;
2) *for* $\theta_4 \leqslant t \leqslant t_0$, $|z(t) - z_0| < -\alpha^2 z_0$;
3) *for* $\theta_4 \leqslant t \leqslant t_0$, $0 \leqslant y - y_0 < -\alpha z_0$;
4) $t_0 - \theta_4 < \omega/2$.

We will now prove the following four lemmas about the behavior of the function $v(x, y, z)$ along the solutions of system (5.2).

Lemma 5.7. Let $\alpha > 0$ *be sufficiently small, and let* $q_2(\alpha) > 0$ *be sufficiently large, and suppose that* $x = x(t)$, $y = y(t)$, $z = z(t)$ *is the solution of system (5.2) with initial data* $t = t_0$, $x = x_0$, $y = y_0$, $z = z_0$, *with the point* (x_0, y_0, z_0) *lying inside* $D(\alpha)$, *while* $z_0 \geqslant q_2(\alpha)$. *Then*

$$v(x_0, y_0, z_0) > v(x(\theta_1), y(\theta_1), z(\theta_1)) \tag{5.22}$$

where θ_1 *is the time determined by Lemma 5.3.*

Proof. Dividing Eq. (5.4) by the first equation of system (5.2), yields

$$\frac{dv}{dx} = -\frac{a(a^2x - ay + z)^2}{y - ax} + \\ + \frac{abx - f(x)}{y - ax}[2(a^2x - ay + z) - bx) + \\ + \frac{(a^2 - b)x - ay + 2z}{y - ax} p(x, y, z, t). \tag{5.23}$$

For definiteness, assume that $x_0 < -1$. It then follows from Lemma 5.3 that there exist times t_1, t_2, and t_3 such that $t_0 < t_1 < t_2 < t_3 < \theta_1$ and chosen so that $x(t_1) = -1$ $x(t_2) = 1$, $x(t_3) = \alpha^2 z(t_3)$ $x_0 \leqslant x(t) \leqslant -1$, for $t_0 \leqslant t \leqslant t_1$, $-1 \leqslant x(t) \leqslant 1$ for $t_1 \leqslant t \leqslant t_2$ $1 \leqslant x(t) \leqslant \alpha^2 z(t)$, for $t_2 \leqslant t \leqslant t_3$, $\alpha^2 z(t) \leqslant x(t) \leqslant 2\alpha^2 z(t)$, for $t_3 \leqslant t \leqslant \theta_1$. Thus,

$$v(x(\theta_1), y(\theta_1), z(\theta_1)) - v(x_0, y_0, z_0) = \\ = \int_{x_0}^{-1} \frac{dv}{dx} dx + \int_{-1}^{+1} \frac{dv}{dx} dx + \int_{1}^{x(t_3)} \frac{dv}{dx} dx + \int_{x(t_3)}^{x(\theta_1)} \frac{dv}{dx} dx. \tag{5.24}$$

We will now estimate the integrals in the right side of Eq. (5.24). It follows from the proof of Lemma 5.1 that

$$w(x, y, z) \leqslant -\frac{1}{a} f(x)[abx - f(x)] = w_1(x).$$

It then follows from (5.23) that

$$\int_{x_0}^{-1} \frac{dv}{dx} dx \leqslant \int_{x_0}^{-1} \frac{(a^2 - b)x - ay + 2z}{y - ax} p(x, y, z, t)\, dx.$$

From Lemma 5.3 it follows that, when α is fixed, the quantity $[(a^2 - b)x - ay + 2z]/(y - ax)$ is uniformly bounded with respect to z_0 on the solution $x = x(t)$, $y = y(t)$, $z = z(t)$ when $t_0 \leqslant t \leqslant \theta_1$. The hypothesis of the theorem then yields

$$\left| \frac{(a^2 - b)x - ay + 2z}{y - ax} p(x, y, z, t) \right| < B_1 \tag{5.25}$$

where B_1 is a sufficiently large constant. As a result, we have

$$\int_{x_0}^{-1} \frac{dv}{dx} dx \leqslant - B_1 (1 + x_0) < B_1 \alpha z_0. \tag{5.26}$$

From Eq. (5.23) we obtain

$$\int_{-1}^{+1} \frac{dv}{dx} dx \leqslant \int_{-1}^{+1} \frac{abx - f(x)}{y - ax} [2(a^2 x - ay + z) - bx]\, dx + \\ + \int_{-1}^{+1} \frac{(a^2 - b)x - ay + 2z}{y - ax} p\, dx.$$

But the function $f(x)$ is continuous and therefore bounded when $-1 \leqslant x \leqslant 1$. Therefore,

$$\left| \frac{abx - f(x)}{y - ax} [2(a^2 x - ay + z) - bx] \right| < B_2$$

on the solution under discussion when $t_1 \leqslant t \leqslant t_2$. The constant B_2 is independent of the choice of initial data x_0, y_0, z_0. Thus, we find that

$$\int_{-1}^{+1} \frac{dv}{dx} dx \leqslant 2B_2. \tag{5.27}$$

The estimate

$$\int_{1}^{x(t_3)} \frac{dv}{dx} dx \leqslant B_1 (x(t_3) - 1) \leqslant 2B_1 \alpha^2 z_0 \tag{5.28}$$

follows from inequality (5.25). Combining inequalities (5.26), (5.27), and (5.28), we find that

$$\int_{x_0}^{x(t_3)} \frac{dv}{dx} dx \leqslant 3B_1 \alpha^2 z_0 + 2B_2. \tag{5.29}$$

We will now estimate the last term in the right side of Eq. (5.24):

$$\int_{x(t_3)}^{x(\theta_1)} \frac{dv}{dx} dx = \int_{x(t_3)}^{x(\theta_1)} \frac{w(x, y, z)}{y - ax} dx + \\ + \int_{x(t_3)}^{x(\theta_1)} \frac{(a^2 - b)x - ay + 2z}{y - ax} p\, dx. \tag{5.30}$$

Lemmas 5.1 and 5.3 imply that

$$\frac{w(x,\ y,\ z)}{y-ax} \to -\infty \text{ for } z_0 \to +\infty$$

along the solution under discussion, and that the limit is approached uniformly with respect to $t \in [t_3,\ \theta_1]$ and the choice of initial data $x_0,\ y_0,\ z_0$. Thus,

$$\frac{w(x,\ y,\ z)}{y-ax} < -B \tag{5.32}$$

where B can be made arbitrarily large by choosing a sufficiently large z_0. Then it follows from (5.25), (5.30), (5.32), and Lemma 5.3 that

$$\int_{x(t_3)}^{x(\theta_1)} \frac{dv}{dx}\,dx < -\frac{1}{2}\alpha^2 z_0 B + 2B_1\alpha^2 z_0.$$

Combining this inequality with inequality (5.29), we find that

$$v(x(\theta_1),\ y(\theta_1),\ z(\theta_1)) - v(x_0,\ y_0,\ z_0) < -\frac{1}{2}\alpha^2 z_0 B + 5B_1\alpha^2 z_0 + 2B_2.$$

By definition of B, therefore,

$$v(x(\theta_1),\ y(\theta_1),\ z(\theta_1)) - v(x_0,\ y_0,\ z_0) < 0. \tag{5.33}$$

This relationship proves the lemma.

The following three lemmas may be proved in a similar manner.

Lemma 5.8. Let $\alpha > 0$ *be sufficiently small and let* $q_2(\alpha) > 0$ *be sufficiently large. Moreover, assume that* $x = x(t),\ y = y(t),\ z = z(t)$ *is the solution of system (5.2) with initial data* $t = t_0\ x = x_0\ y = y_0\ z = z_0$ *that the point* $(x_0,\ y_0,\ z_0)$ *is in* $D(\alpha)$*, and that* $z_0 \geqslant q_2(\alpha)$*. Then*

$$v(x(\theta_2),\ y(\theta_2),\ z(\theta_2)) > v(x_0,\ y_0\ z_0). \tag{5.34}$$

where θ_2 *is the time determined by Lemma 5.4.*

Lemma 5.9. Let $\alpha > 0$ *be sufficiently small and let* $q_2(\alpha) > 0$ *be sufficiently large. Assume that* $x = x(t),\ y = y(t),\ z = z_0(t)$ *is the solution of system (5.2) with initial data* $t = t_0\ x = x_0,\ y = y_0,\ z = z_0,$ *that the point* $(x_0,\ y_0,\ z_0)$ *is in* $D(\alpha)$*, and that* $z_0 \leqslant -q_2(\alpha)$*. Then*

$$v(x(\theta_3),\ y(\theta_3),\ z(\theta_3)) < v(x_0,\ y_0,\ z_0) \tag{5.35}$$

where θ_3 *is the time determined by Lemma 5.5.*

Lemma 5.10. Let $\alpha > 0$ be sufficiently small, and let $q_2(\alpha) > 0$ be sufficiently large. Moreover, assume that $x = x(t)$, $y = y(t)$, $z = z(t)$ is the solution of system (5.2) with initial data $t = t_0$, $x = x_0$, $y = y_0$, $z = z_0$ that the point (x_0, y_0, z_0) is in $D(\alpha)$, and that $z_0 \leqslant -q_2(\alpha)$. Then

$$v(x(\theta_4), y(\theta_4), z(\theta_4)) > v(x_0, y_0, z_0), \tag{5.36}$$

where θ_4 is the time determined by Lemma 5.6.

We will now examine the behavior of the function $v(x, y, z)$ for sufficiently large $x^2 + y^2 + z^2$.

Lemma 5.11. The following relationship holds:

$$v(x, y, z) \to \infty \text{ for } x^2 + y^2 + z^2 \to \infty. \tag{5.37}$$

Proof. From the hypothesis of the theorem it follows that there exists an $x_0 > 0$ such that

$$\int_0^x f(x)\,dx > 0 \tag{5.38}$$

for $|x| \leqslant x_0$. For $|x| \geqslant x_0$ relationship (5.37) is satisfied. Now consider the function v for $|x| \geqslant x_0$. Set

$$V(x, y, z) = (a^2x - ay + z)^2 + (z - bx)^2 + by^2 - a^2bx^2. \tag{5.39}$$

Then for $|x| \geqslant x_0$

$$v(x, y, z) = \frac{1}{2} V(x, y, z) + a \int_0^x f(x)\,dx > \frac{1}{2} V(x, y, z) \tag{5.40}$$

We will now show that the form V is positive definite.

By making the substitutions

$$x_1 = a^2x - ay + z, \quad y_1 = z - bx, \quad z_1 = y,$$

so that

$$x = \frac{x_1 - y_1 + az_1}{a^2 + b}$$

we find that V takes the form

$$V = x_1^2 + y_1^2 + bz_1^2 - \frac{a^2b}{(a^2 + b)^2}(x_1 - y_1 + az_1)^2. \tag{5.41}$$

Consider the form

$$V_h = x_1^2 + y_1^2 + bz_1^2 - h(x_1 - y_1 + az_1)^2. \tag{5.42}$$

Necessary and sufficient conditions for positive definiteness of this form will clearly be provided by the inequalities $1 - h > 0$, $1 - 2h > 0$, and

$$\begin{vmatrix} 1-h, & h, & -ah \\ h, & 1-h, & ah \\ -ah, & ah, & b-a^2h \end{vmatrix} > 0.$$

The last inequality can be written in the form

$$b - (2b + a^2)h > 0 \text{ or } h < \frac{b}{2b + a^2}.$$

But it is easily verified that $(a^2b)/(a^2 + b^2) < 1/2$ and $(a^2b)/(a^2 + b)^2 < (b)/(2b + a^2)$. It then follows that the form V is positive definite, and the lemma follows from (5.40).

We will now proceed directly to the proof of Theorem 5.1 by showing that there exists a $q > 0$ such that if $x_0^2 + y_0^2 + z_0^2 \geqslant q^2$, then

$$v(x_0, y_0, z_0) > v(x(\omega), y(\omega), z(\omega)), \tag{5.43}$$

where $x = x(t)$, $y = y(t)$, $z = z(t)$ is the solution of system (5.2) with initial data $t = 0$, $x = x_0$, $y = y_0$, $z = z_0$. Choose $\bar{q}$ so that, for a sufficiently small fixed α and $x_0^2 + y_0^2 + z_0^2 \geqslant \bar{q}^2$, Lemmas 5.1-5.10 hold, and let

$$\bar{v} = \max_{x^2+y^2+z^2 \leqslant \bar{q}^2} v(x, y, z). \tag{5.44}$$

By virtue of Lemma 5.11, there exists a $q > \bar{q}$ such that $v \geqslant 2\bar{v}$ when $x^2 + y^2 + z^2 \geqslant q^2$. We will show that this q is the one desired.

Inequality (5.43) will be proved indirectly: Assume that it does not hold and that, initially, the point (x_0, y_0, z_0) does not belong to $D(\alpha)$; then, by virtue of Lemma 5.2, we have $\dot{v}(x_0, y_0, z_0) < 0$. As a result, $v(x(t), y(t), z(t))$ decreases in the neighborhood of the point $t = 0$. Since, by hypothesis, inequality (5.43) does not hold, it is clear that there exists a $\tau_0 \in (0, \omega]$ such that

$$v(x(\tau_0), y(\tau_0), z(\tau_0)) = v(x_0, y_0, z_0) \tag{5.45}$$

and the inequality

$$v(x(t),\ y(t),\ z(t)) < v(x_0,\ y_0,\ z_0) \tag{5.46}$$

is satisfied when $0 < t < \tau_0$.

It follows from Lemma 5.2 that the point $x(\tau_0),\ y(\tau_0),\ z(\tau_0)$ is in $D(\alpha)$. If the point $(x_0,\ y_0,\ z_0)$ is contained in $D(\alpha)$, then we simply set $\tau_0 = 0$.

We will now show that $\tau_0 < \omega/2$. By the choice of q, we have $v(x(\tau_0),\ y(\tau_0),\ z(\tau_0)) = v(x_0,\ y_0,\ z_0) > 2\bar{v}$; consequently, by definition of $\bar{v}$, we have $x^2(\tau_0) + y^2(\tau_0) + z^2(\tau_0) > \bar{q}$ and, therefore, there exists a $\tau^* < \tau_0$, this τ^* corresponds to the time θ_2 in Lemma 5.4 if $z(\tau_0) > 0$ and the time θ_4 of Lemma 5.6 if $z(\tau_0) < 0$), such that

$$v(x(\tau^*),\ y(\tau^*),\ z(\tau^*)) > v(x(\tau_0),\ y(\tau_0),\ z(\tau_0)) = v(x_0,\ y_0,\ z_0). \tag{5.47}$$

Here, as Lemmas 5.4 and 5.6 imply, $\tau_0 - \tau^* < \omega/2$, since $\tau_0 < \omega/2$ would imply $0 < \tau^* < \tau_0$, which would contradict the fact that inequality (5.46) holds for $0 < t < \tau_0$.

From Lemmas 5.7 and 5.9 it follows that there exists a $\tau_1 > \tau_0$ (this τ_1 corresponds to the time θ_1 of Lemma 5.3 if $z(\tau_0) > 0$ and to the time θ_3 of Lemma 5.5 if $z(\tau_0) < 0$) such that

$$v(x(\tau_1),\ y(\tau_1),\ z(\tau_1)) < v(x(\tau_0),\ y(\tau_0),\ z(\tau_0)) \tag{5.48}$$

and $\tau_1 - \tau_0 < \omega/2$; therefore, $\tau_1 < \omega$.

By hypothesis, inequality (5.43) does not hold; consequently, there exists a $\bar{\tau} \in (\tau_1,\ \omega]$ such that

$$v(x(\bar{\tau}),\ y(\bar{\tau}),\ z(\bar{\tau})) = v(x_0,\ y_0,\ z_0)$$

and, when $\tau_1 \leqslant t < \bar{\tau}$, inequality (5.46) holds. It is not difficult to see that, under these conditions, the point $(x(\bar{\tau}),\ y(\bar{\tau}),\ z(\bar{\tau}))$ is contained in $D(\alpha)$ and $x^2(\bar{\tau}) + y^2(\bar{\tau}) + z^2(\bar{\tau}) > \bar{q}$. It then follows from Lemmas 5.8 and 5.10 that there exists a τ' such that

$$v(x(\tau'),\ y(\tau'),\ z(\tau')) > v(x(\bar{\tau}),\ y(\bar{\tau}),\ z(\bar{\tau})) = v(x_0,\ y_0,\ z_0).$$

In that case, it follows from Lemmas 5.4–5.10 that $\tau_1 < \tau' < \bar{\tau} \leqslant \omega$. This contradicts the fact that inequality (5.46) holds when $\tau_1 \leqslant t < \bar{\tau}$. The contradiction obtained proves inequality (5.43).

Moreover, from the previous considerations it follows that any solution of system (5.2) can be extended in the direction of increasing time. But then we have satisfied the conditions of Theorem 2.4, from which the proof follows.

Theorem 5.2. When the hypothesis of Theorem 5.1 is satisfied, system (5.2) has at least one ω-periodic solution.

Proof. We will show that, for sufficiently large c, the domain $v(x,\ y,\ z) < c$ is star-shaped. Let $x = \alpha l,\ y = \beta l,\ z = \gamma l\ (\alpha^2 + \beta^2 + \gamma^2 = 1)$.

We will show that when $l > 0$, this line intersects the surface $v(x, y, z) = c$, c being taken sufficiently large, exactly once. Consider the equation

$$v(\alpha l, \beta l, \gamma l) = c. \tag{5.49}$$

It is easily seen that if c is made sufficiently large, the roots of Eq. (5.49) will be arbitrarily large. We will now show that, for sufficiently large l, $d/dl\, v(\alpha l, \beta l, \gamma l) > 0$. Thus,

$$\frac{d}{dl} v(\alpha l, \beta l, \gamma l) = l(a^2\alpha - a\beta + \gamma)^2 + l(\gamma - b\alpha)^2 + bl\beta^2 + \\ + a\alpha[f(\alpha l) - ab\alpha l] = lV(\alpha, \beta, \gamma) + a\alpha f(\alpha l).$$

In the proof of Lemma 5.11 it was established that the form $V(\alpha, \beta, \gamma)$ is positive definite. It then follows from the hypothesis of Theorem 5.1 and the last equation that

$$\frac{d}{dl} v(\alpha l, \beta l, \gamma l) > 0$$

for sufficiently large $\bar{l}$. This shows that, when c is sufficiently large, the domain $v(x, y, z) < c$ is star-shaped. It is now easily shown that the closed domain $v(x, y, z) \leqslant c$ is homeomorphic to a sphere. It follows from inequality (5.43) that the transformation T maps the topological sphere $v(x, y, z) \leqslant c$ into itself, and, by Brouwer's theorem, the transformation T has a stationary point. This proves the theorem.

6. THE EXISTENCE OF HARMONIC OSCILLATIONS FOR HIGHER-ORDER SYSTEMS THAT ARE NOT D-SYSTEMS

As already noted, any stationary point of the transformation T represents the initial value of an ω-periodic solution of the system

$$\frac{dX}{dt} = F(X, t). \tag{6.1}$$

Therefore, in order to prove existence theorems for harmonic oscillations, we can use different tests for the existence of stationary points of topological mappings of Euclidean space into itself.

1. The following test for the existence of a stationary point for the transformation T [31] is frequently found to be very convenient in applications.

Theorem 6.1. Assume that the net rotation of the vector $F(X, 0)$ *on some* $(n-1)$*-dimensional sphere S of the space* $x_1, \ldots, x_n$ *is* *nonzero. Moreover, assume that all of the solutions that pass through the closed sphere* $\bar{K}$ *when* $t=0$ *are bounded by the sphere* S, *and may be extended to* $0 \leqslant t \leqslant \omega$, *and that for* $X_0 \in S$ *and* $0 < t \leqslant \omega$, *the inequality*

$$X(t, X_0, 0) \neq X_0 \tag{6.2}$$

is satisfied. Then the sphere K contains at least one point that is stationary under the transformation T.

Proof. Consider the vector

$$V(X_0, t) = X(t, X_0, 0) - X_0. \tag{6.3}$$

For sufficiently small $t > 0$ we will have

$$V(X_0, t) = F(X_0, 0)t + \varepsilon(X_0, t) \cdot t \tag{6.4}$$

where $\varepsilon(X_0, t) \to 0$ when $t \to 0$ uniformly with respect to $X_0 \in S$. For sufficiently small $t > 0$, therefore, the vector V will neither vanish nor will it be directed opposite to the vector $F(X_0, 0)$ at any point of the sphere S. Consequently, the net rotations of the vectors $V(X_0, t)$ and $F(X_0, 0)$ coincide when $t > 0$ is sufficiently small. Since, by hypothesis, the net rotation of the vector $F(X_0, 0)$ is nonzero on the sphere S, the net rotation of the vector $V(X_0, t)$ is also nonzero for sufficiently small $t > 0$. But, from condition (6.2), the vector $V(X_0, t)$ has no singular points on the sphere S for any $t \in (0, \omega]$. Moreover, $V(X_0, t)$ is a continuous function of t and, therefore, the net rotation of $V(X_0, t)$ is constant on the half-open interval $0 < t \leqslant \omega$. Thus, it follows that the net rotation of the vector $V(X_0, \omega)$ is nonzero. The vector $V(X_0, \omega)$ is the displacement vector of the mapping T at the point X_0. Hence, the degree of the mapping T is nonzero, which proves the theorem.

2. The theorem which we have just proved makes it possible to establish the following test for the existence of harmonic oscillations for system (6.1) (see [22, 23, 24]).

Theorem 6.2. Let the function $F(X, t) = \{f_1(x_1, \ldots, x_n, t), \ldots, f_n(x_1, \ldots, x_n, t)\}$ *be continuous,* ω*-periodic in* t, *and have continuous partial derivatives* $\partial f_i / \partial x_j$, $i, j = 1, 2, \ldots, n$ *satisfying the conditions*

$$\frac{\partial f_i}{\partial x_i} \geqslant m > 0$$

or

$$\frac{\partial f_i}{\partial x_i} \leqslant -m < 0.$$

Moreover, assume that the functions $f_i(x_1, \ldots, x_{i-1}, 0, x_{i+1}, \ldots x_n, t)$ *are bounded. Then harmonic oscillations exist for system (6.1).*

Proof. It follows from the hypothesis of the theorem that there exists an r such that

$$\frac{\partial f_i}{\partial x_i} \geqslant m > 0 \text{ for } i = 1, 2, \ldots, r \tag{6.5}$$

and

$$\frac{\partial f_i}{\partial x_i} \leqslant -m < 0 \text{ for } i = r+1, \ldots, n. \tag{6.6}$$

Here we can assume that r is equal to neither zero nor n, because otherwise the situation would reduce to that of Theorem 3.4. Thus,

$$f_i = \int_0^{x_i} \frac{\partial f_i}{\partial x_i} dx_i + f_i(x_1, \ldots, x_{i-1}, 0, x_{i+1}, \ldots, x_n, t). \tag{6.7}$$

By the hypothesis of the theorem, there exists an $M > 0$ such that

$$|f_i(x_1, \ldots, x_{i-1}, 0, x_{i+1}, \ldots, x_n, t)| < M. \tag{6.8}$$

It thus follows from conditions (6.5) and (6.6) that there exists an $a > 0$ such that the inequalities

$$f_i(x_1, \ldots, x_n, t)\, x_i > \frac{m}{2} x_i^2 \text{ for } i = 1, 2, \ldots, r, \tag{6.9}$$

$$f_i(x_1, \ldots, x_n, t)\, x_i < -\frac{m}{2} x_i^2 \text{ for } i = r+1, \ldots, n, \tag{6.10}$$

are satisfied when $|x_i| \geqslant a$. In conjunction with system (6.1), consider the system

$$\frac{dx_i}{dt} = \varphi_i(x_1, \ldots, x_n, t) \quad (i = 1, \ldots, n), \tag{6.11}$$

where the functions $\varphi_i(x_1, \ldots, x_n, t)$ are defined by the equations

$$\varphi_i(x_1, \ldots, x_n, t) = \begin{cases} f_i(x_1, \ldots, x_n, t) & \text{for } |x_i| \leqslant a, \\ a\dfrac{f_i(x_1, \ldots, x_n, t)\, x_i}{(2a - |x_i|)\, x_i + (|x_i| - a)\, f_i} & \text{for } a \leqslant |x_i| \leqslant 2a \\ x_i & \text{for } |x_i| \geqslant 2a \end{cases}$$

for $i = 1, 2, \ldots, r$.

$$\varphi_i(x_1, \ldots, x_n, t) = \begin{cases} f_i(x_1, \ldots, x_n, t) & \text{for } |x_i| \leqslant a, \\ a \dfrac{f_i(x_1, \ldots, x_n, t)}{(2a - |x_i|) x_i - (|x_i| - a) f_i} x_i & \text{for } a \leqslant |x_i| \leqslant 2a, \\ -x_i & \text{for } |x_i| \geqslant 2a \end{cases}$$

for $i = r+1, \ldots, n$.

It is not difficult to see that the functions φ_i are continuous, satisfy a Lipschitz condition with respect to the variables x_k in the neighborhood of each point (X, t) and are ω-periodic. In addition, $\operatorname{sign} \varphi_i = \operatorname{sign} x_i$ for $|x_i| \geqslant a$, $i = 1, 2, \ldots, r$ and $\operatorname{sign} \varphi_i = -\operatorname{sign} x_i$ for $|x_i| \geqslant a$ $i = r+1, \ldots, n$.

Choose a positive constant A large enough so that

$$A^2 > nMa, \quad A > 2a. \tag{6.12}$$

Now let S be the sphere defined by the equation $\|X\| = nA$ with its center at the coordinate origin, and consider the vector field $Z(X)$ with components

$$\left.\begin{aligned} z_i(X) &= x_i \quad \text{for } i = 1, 2, \ldots, r, \\ z_i(X) &= -x_i \quad \text{for } i = r+1, \ldots, n. \end{aligned}\right\} \tag{6.13}$$

Let Φ be the vector with components $\varphi_1(x_1, \ldots, x_n, 0) \ldots, \varphi_n(x_1, \ldots, x_n, 0)$, and consider the scalar product $Z \cdot \Phi = \sum_{i=1}^{n} z_i \varphi_i$. We will show that this scalar product is positive on the sphere S. We have

$$Z \cdot \Phi = \sum_{i=1}^{r} \varphi_i x_i - \sum_{i=r+1}^{n} \varphi_i x_i \tag{6.14}$$

and, clearly, $\max_{i=1,\ldots,n} |x_i| \geqslant A$ on the sphere S. Moreover, it follows from conditions (6.5) and (6.6), Eq. (6.7), and condition (6.8) that

$$f_i(x_1, \ldots, x_n, t) x_i > -Ma, \quad i = 1, 2, \ldots, r, \tag{6.15}$$

$$f_i(x_1, \ldots, x_n, t) x_i < Ma, \quad i = r+1, \ldots, n. \tag{6.16}$$

These inequalities give us the estimate

$$Z \cdot \Phi > A^2 - nMa,$$

and then, by virtue of the choice of A, the inequality $Z \cdot \Phi > 0$, valid on the sphere S, follows. This means that, on the sphere S, the vectors Z and Φ never have opposite directions; consequently, their net rotations coincide. But it is well known [32], that the net rotation of the vector Z is nonzero, and, therefore, so is the net rotation of the vector Φ,

Let the vector $\Psi(t, X_0, t_0)$ with components $\psi_1, \ldots, \psi_n$ be the solution of system (6.11) with initial data $t=t_0$, $X=X_0$. We will show that if $X_0 \in S$, then the inequality

$$\Psi(t, X_0, t_0) \neq X_0 \tag{6.17}$$

is satisfied when $0 < t \leqslant \omega$. Let $X_0 = \{x_1^{(0)}, \ldots, x_n^{(0)}\} \in S$. Initially, assume that the inequality $|x_k^{(0)}| \geqslant a$ is satisfied for some k, $1 \leqslant k \leqslant r$. But then the fact that $\varphi_k x_k > 0$ when $|x_k| \geqslant a$ implies that the inequality $|x_k| > |x_k^{(0)}|$ will be satisfied along our solution for all $t > 0$, which proves inequality (6.17). Now assume that $|x_i^{(0)}| \leqslant a$ for $i=1$ $2, \ldots, r$; then $|x_k^{(0)}| \geqslant a$ for some k, $r+1 \leqslant k \leqslant n$. Because $\varphi_k x_k < 0$ for $|x_k| \geqslant a$, it is easily shown that the inequality $|x_k| < |x_k^{(0)}|$ holds for all $t > 0$, which proves (6.17).

It follows from the choice of the functions φ_i that all solutions (6.11) can be extended to all times t between $t=-\infty$ and $t=+\infty$.

Thus, all conditions of Theorem 6.1 are satisfied by system (6.11), so that system (6.11) has an ω-periodic solution, which we will denote by $x_i = \psi_i(t)$. $(i=1, 2, \ldots, n)$. We will now show that the inequalities $|\psi_i(t)| < a$ $(i=1, \ldots, n)$ are satisfied for all t. Assume that this is not true, i.e., assume that $|\psi_k(t_0)| \geqslant a$. Consider first the case of $k \leqslant r$. It is then clear that $|\psi_k(t)|$ increases when $t \geqslant t_0$ and, consequently, the equation $\psi_k(t_0+\omega) = \psi_k(t_0)$ can not hold. Now consider the case of $k > r$. Then, for $t \leqslant t_0$, $|\psi_k(t)|$ increases as time decreases, and the equation $\psi_k(t_0-\omega) = \psi_k(t_0)$ can not hold. In either case, the function $\psi_k(t)$ is not periodic. The contradiction thus obtained shows that $|\psi_i(t)| < a$ $(i=1, \ldots, n)$. But system (6.11) coincides with (6.1) when $|x_i| \leqslant a$. Consequently, $x_i = \psi_i(t)$ is an ω-periodic solution of system (6.1). Q.E.D.

3. We will now prove one more theorem about the existence of harmonic oscillations. Consider the system of differential equations

$$\frac{dX}{dt} = AX + F(X, t) \tag{6.18}$$

where X and $F(X, t)$ are real n-dimensional vectors with components $x_1, \ldots, x_n$ and $f_1, \ldots, f_n$, respectively, and $A = \{a_{ij}\}$ is a real, $n \times n$ constant matrix.

We will assume that the function $F(X, t)$ is continuous, has a period 2π relative to the argument t, and satisfies the conditions required in order that the solutions for all X and t be unique.

Theorem 6.3. If the matrix A has no characteristic roots of the form ki (k is a natural number or zero, i is the square root of -1) and if the function F(X, t) satisfies the condition

$$\|F(X,\ t)\| < L\|X\| \tag{6.19}$$

for sufficiently large $\|X\|$, where the positive constant L is sufficiently small, then system (6.18) has at least one 2π-periodic solution.

Proof. As usual, let $X(t,\ X_0,\ t_0)$ be the solution of system (6.18). It follows [1] from inequality (6.19) that all solutions of system (6.18) can be extended to all times between $-\infty$ and $+\infty$. Let $V(X) = TX - X$ be the displacement vector of the transformation T, and let $v_1,\ \ldots,\ v_n$ be the components of the vector V.

Consider the linear system

$$\frac{dX}{dt} = AX. \tag{6.20}$$

Without loss of generality, we can assume that the matrix A is in canonical form. For system (6.20), define T_0, a transformation of the space X into itself which is analogous to the transformation T for system (6.18). Denote the displacement vector of the transformation T_0 by $W = \{w_1,\ \ldots,\ w_n\}$, i.e., $W = T_0X - X$. Assume that matrix A has characteristic roots $\lambda_1 \pm i\mu_1,\ \ldots,\ \lambda_s \pm i\mu_s,\ \varkappa_1,\ \ldots,\ \varkappa_{n-2s}$, among which some may repeat. It is clear that

$$\frac{D(w_1,\ \ldots,\ w_n)}{D(x_1,\ \ldots,\ x_n)} =$$

$$= \begin{vmatrix} e^{2\pi\lambda_1}\cos 2\pi\mu_1 - 1, & -e^{2\pi\lambda_1}\sin 2\pi\mu_1, & 0,\ \ldots,\ 0 \\ e^{2\pi\lambda_1}\sin 2\pi\mu_1, & e^{2\pi\lambda_1}\cos 2\pi\mu - 1, & 0,\ \ldots,\ 0 \\ \cdots & \cdots & \cdots \\ 0, & 0, & e^{2\pi\varkappa_{n-2s}} - 1 \end{vmatrix},$$

and, by Laplace's expansion theorem,

$$\frac{D(w_1,\ \ldots,\ w_n)}{D(x_1,\ \ldots,\ x_n)} =$$

$$= \prod_{m=1}^{s}\left(1 - 2e^{2\pi\lambda_m}\cos 2\pi\mu_m + e^{4\pi\lambda_m}\right)\prod_{m=1}^{n-2s}\left(e^{2\pi\varkappa_m} - 1\right).$$

By virtue of the hypothesis of the theorem, $\varkappa_m \neq 0$, and if $\lambda_m = 0$, then $\mu_m \neq k$ (k is a natural number). Thus, we find that

$$\frac{D(w_1,\ \ldots,\ w_n)}{D(x_1,\ \ldots,\ x_n)} \neq 0. \tag{6.21}$$

This shows that the point $x_1 = x_2 = \ldots = x_n = 0$ is a singular point whose index is ± 1 with respect to the vector field $W(X)$.

Moreover, inequality (6.21) implies that there exists a constant $K > 0$ such that

$$\|W(X)\| \geqslant K\|X\|. \tag{6.22}$$

We will now estimate the norm of the difference $V(X_0) - W(X_0)$ for sufficiently large $\|X_0\|$. It is clear that

$$V(X_0) - W(X_0) = X(2\pi, X_0, 0) - \Psi(2\pi, X_0, 0), \tag{6.23}$$

where $\Psi(t, X_0, t_0)$ denotes the solution of system (6.20) with initial data $t = t_0$, $X = X_0$. Let $Y(t)$ be a solution of the matrix equation

$$\frac{dY}{dt} = AY \tag{6.24}$$

with $Y(0) = I$.

Then it is known (see, for example, [3]) that the solution $X(t, X_0, 0)$ of system (6.18) satisfies the integral equation

$$X(t, X_0, 0) = \Psi(t, X_0, 0) + \int_0^t Y(t-\tau) F(X, \tau)\, d\tau. \tag{6.25}$$

Let the elements of matrix Y be y_{ij} and set

$$\|Y\| = \sum_{i,j=1}^{n} |y_{ij}| \text{ and } c_1 = \max_{0 \leqslant t \leqslant 2\pi} \|\Psi(t, X_0, 0)\|.$$

Since Ψ is the solution of linear system (6.20), there exists a positive constant M such that $c_1 \leqslant M\|X_0\|$. Moreover, assume that $c_2 = \max\limits_{0 \leqslant t \leqslant 2\pi} \|Y(t)\|$.

Equation (6.25) yields

$$\|X(t, X_0, 0)\| \leqslant c_1 + c_2 \int_0^t \|F(X(\tau, X_0, 0), \tau)\|\, d\tau \text{ for } 0 \leqslant t \leqslant 2\pi.$$

Assuming that $\|X_0\|$ is sufficiently large, we have, by virtue of condition (6.19),

$$\|X\| < c_1 + c_2 L \int_0^t \|X(\tau, X_0, 0)\|\, d\tau \text{ for } 0 \leqslant t \leqslant 2\pi. \tag{6.26}$$

Therefore, by a well-known lemma (see [1]), we have

$$\|X(t, X_0, 0)\| < c_1 e^{c_2 L t} \quad (0 \leqslant t \leqslant 2\pi). \tag{6.27}$$

On the other hand, Eq. (6.25) provides the estimate

$$\|X(t, X_0, 0) - \Psi(t, X_0, 0)\| \leqslant c_2 \int_0^t \|F(X, \tau)\| d\tau \quad (0 \leqslant t \leqslant 2\pi),$$

and, therefore, taking into account (6.19) and (6.27) yields

$$\|X(t, X_0, 0) - \Psi(t, X_0, 0)\| < c_2 L c_1 \int_0^t e^{c_2 L \tau} d\tau = c_1 (e^{c_2 L t} - 1)$$

for sufficiently large $\|X_0\|$. This last inequality, in combination with (6.23) and noting that $c_1 \leqslant M\|X_0\|$, yields

$$\|V(X_0) - W(X_0)\| < M(e^{2\pi c_2 L} - 1)\|X_0\| \tag{6.28}$$

for sufficiently large $\|X_0\|$.

Assume that the constant L is so small that the inequality

$$K \geqslant M(e^{2\pi c_2 L} - 1) \tag{6.29}$$

is satisfied, and let S be a sphere of sufficiently large radius with center at the origin. It follows from estimates (6.22) and (6.28) that the vectors V and W have opposite directions at no point on the sphere S, and that V vanishes nowhere on the same sphere. Thus, it follows that the net rotations of the vectors V and W on the sphere S coincide. But we have already shown that the index of the point $X = 0$, as a singular point of the field W, is equal to ± 1. By virtue of inequality (6.22), the sphere S contains no singular points of the field W aside from the origin, and, therefore, the net rotation of the vector W on the sphere S is ± 1. As a result, the net rotation of V on the sphere S is also ± 1, and this means that the sphere S contains at least one singular point for the vector V. This point is clearly a stationary point of the transformation T. Q.E.D.

This theorem was apparently first proved by Barbalat [33]. Here we have given the proof published in [34].

Note that, as the very proof of Theorem 6.3 implies, an effective estimate of the constant L in inequality (6.19) can be obtained by means of matrix A.

In conclusion, we should note that results similar in content to those given above were published recently by Krasnosel'skiy [32].

7. CONVERGENT SYSTEMS

1. Here and in the following sections we will study systems with a unique harmonic oscillation that is stable in the large.

As usual, assume that the right sides of the system

$$\frac{dX}{dt} = F(X, t) \tag{7.1}$$

are continuous, ω-periodic with respect to t, and satisfy uniqueness conditions for all (X, t).

Definition 7.1. System (7.1) will be said to be convergent if
1) all solutions $X(t, X_0, t_0)$ can be extended to all times $t \geqslant t_0$;
2) system (7.1) has a unique ω-periodic solution $X = \Phi(t)$;
3) this solution is Lyapunov-stable;
4) the following relationship is satisfied by any solution $X(t, X_0$ $t_0)$:

$$\lim_{t \to +\infty} \|X(t, X_0, t_0) - \Phi(t)\| = 0. \tag{7.2}$$

Thus, a convergent system is a dissipative system in which the set I (see Paragraph 3, Section 2) degenerates to a point. The following theorem states a characteristic property of convergent systems.

Theorem 7.1. System (7.1) will be convergent if and only if there exists a solution that is bounded when $t \geqslant t_0$ and any solution $X(t, X_0, t_0)$ of system (7.1) is uniformly asymptotically stable when $t \geqslant t_0$, i.e., for any $\varepsilon > 0$ there exists a $\delta(X_0, t_0)$ such that if $\|X^* - X(t^*, X_0, t_0)\| < \delta$, then, for $t \geqslant t^* \geqslant t_0$,

$$\|X(t, X_0, t_0) - X(t, X^*, t^*)\| < \varepsilon \tag{7.3}$$

and there exists a $\Delta(X_0, t_0)$ such that if

$$\|X^* - X(t^*, X_0, t_0)\| < \Delta$$

then

$$\lim_{t \to \infty} \|X(t, X_0, t_0) - X(t, X^*, t^*)\| = 0. \tag{7.4}$$

Proof. Necessity [35]. Assume that system (7.1) is convergent; then it has an ω-periodic solution $X = \Phi(t)$, which, by definition, is asymptotically stable. But it is well known (see, for example, [15]) that an asymptotically stable ω-periodic solution of system (7.1) is also uniformly asymptotically stable. Thus, the solution $X = \Phi(t)$ is uniformly asymptotically stable. We will now show that, in addition, any solution $X(t, X_0, t_0)$ is uniformly asymptotically stable when $t \geqslant t_0$. Choose an arbitrary $\varepsilon > 0$. Since the solution $X = \Phi(t)$ is uniformly asymptotically stable, there exists for this ε a δ such that if $\|\bar{X}_0 - \Phi(\bar{t}_0)\| < \delta$ then $\|X(t, \bar{X}_0, \bar{t}_0) - \Phi(t)\| < \varepsilon$ for $t \geqslant \bar{t}_0$. It follows from (7.2) that there exists a $\tau \geqslant t_0$ such that

$$\|X(t, X_0, t_0) - \Phi(t)\| < \frac{\delta}{2}$$

for $t \geqslant \tau$. By the theorem on integral continuity, there exists a $\delta_1 \in (0, \delta/2)$, such that if $\|X^* - X(t^*, X_0, t_0)\| < \delta_1$ and $t_0 \leqslant t^* \leqslant \tau$, then $\|X(t, X^*, t^*) - X(t, X_0, t_0)\| < \delta/2$ for all $t_0 \leqslant t \leqslant \tau$. Inequality (7.3) then follows.

Necessity is proved.

Sufficiency [36]. We assume that system (7.1) has a solution $X = \Psi(t)$ that is bounded when $t \geqslant \bar{t}_0$ and we will show that for any t_0 and X

$$\lim_{t \to +\infty} \|X(t, X_0, t_0) - \Psi(t)\| = 0. \tag{7.5}$$

Assume the contrary, i.e., assume that there exists a t^* and X_0^* for which the solution $X(t, X_0^*, t^*)$ does not satisfy (7.5). By hypothesis, any solution $X(t, X_0, t_0)$ of system (7.1) can be extended to $t \geqslant t_0$, so that, without loss of generality, we can assume that $t^* \geqslant \bar{t}_0$. Let G be the set of points in the hyperplane $t = t^*$ through which the solutions with property (7.5) pass. The set G is nonempty, since it is clear that $\Psi(t^*) \in G$. On the other hand, by hypothesis, the set G does not coincide with the entire hyperplane $t = t^*$. Let X^* be a boundary point of the set G. Relationship (7.5) is not satisfied for the solution $X(t, X^*, t^*)$, because if it were satisfied, the fact that the solution $\Psi(t)$ is uniformly asymptotically stable would require that relationship (7.5) be satisfied for all solutions in a neighborhood of $X(t, X^*, t^*)$, and the point X^* would not be a boundary point of G.

Since relationship (7.5) is not satisfied for the solution $X(t, X^*, t^*)$, and any neighborhood of the point X^* contains points of the domain G, it is clear that the solution $X(t, X^*, t^*)$ can not be stable. This contradicts the hypothesis of the theorem, and the contradiction proves relationship (7.5). This relationship implies that system (7.1) is dissipative; consequently, it has a solution with period $k\omega$ and a solution with period $(k+1)\omega$, where k is a sufficiently large natural number. By virtue of (7.5), the difference between these solutions should approach zero when $t \to +\infty$; it thus follows that these solutions simply coincide. But if a solution has period $k\omega$ and $(k+1)\omega$, it must have period ω as well.

Thus, system (7.1) has an ω-periodic solution, which is approached by all the remaining solutions. It thus follows that the hypothesis of the theorem is sufficient.

2. As before, assume that T is the topological transformation of the hyperplane $t=0$ into itself which associates the point X with the point $X(\omega, X_0, 0)$. We will prove the following theorem [37].

Theorem 7.2. If system (7.1) is dissipative and there exists a continuous function $v(X, Y)$ of the points X and Y in the hyperplane $t=0$ with the properties:

1) *$v(X, Y) \geqslant 0$ and $v(X, Y)=0$ if and only if $X=Y$;*

2) *$v(TX, TY) \leqslant v(X, Y)$ and $X=Y$ when $v(TX, TY)=v(X, Y)$,*

then system (7.1) is convergent.

Proof. The set I is defined for a dissipative system (7.1). We will show that, under the conditions of the theorem, this set degenerates into a point. We assume, on the contrary, that this is not so; then

$$\alpha = \sup_{X, Y \in I} v(X, Y) > 0. \tag{7.6}$$

As shown in Section 2, the set I is closed, so that there exist points $\overline{X} \in I$ and $\overline{Y} \in I$ such that $v(\overline{X}, \overline{Y}) = \alpha$. The equation $TI=I$ implies that $T^{-1}\overline{X} \in I$ and $T^{-1}\overline{Y} \in I$.

The hypothesis of the theorem then implies the inequality

$$v(T^{-1}\overline{X}, T^{-1}\overline{Y}) > v(\overline{X}, \overline{Y}) = \alpha.$$

But this contradicts the definition of α, and this contradiction shows that the set I is a point Z in the hyperplane $t=0$. This and Theorem 2.3 imply that the solution $X(t, Z, 0)$ is an ω-periodic solution of system (7.1) that is stable in the large. Q.E.D.

It turns out that the hypothesis of this theorem is also necessary for convergence.

Theorem 7.3. If system (7.1) is convergent, then there exists a function $v(X, Y)$ that satisfies the hypothesis of Theorem 7.2.

Proof. Assume that system (7.1) is convergent and let $X=\Phi(t)$ be a harmonic oscillation. The set of points constituting this solution is the set S for dissipative system (7.1) (set S was defined on p. 24, Paragraph 3, Section 2). Let $a>0$ be such that $\|\Phi(0)\| < a$.

Consider the function $\alpha(t)$ defined in Paragraph 4 of Section 2. It follows from inequality (2.34) that

$$\|X(t, X_0, t_0) - \Phi(t)\| < \alpha(t) \tag{7.7}$$

for $t_0 \leqslant t < +\infty$, $t_0 \in [0, \omega]$, $\|X_0\| \leqslant a$.

It then follows that if $\|X\| \leqslant a$, $\|Y\| \leqslant a$, then

$$\|T^k X - T^k Y\| < 2\alpha(k) \tag{7.8}$$

for $k > 0$. By inverting the function $\beta = 2\alpha(t)$, we obtain the function $t = t(\beta)$, which is defined and continously differentiable when $0 < \beta < +\infty$. For such β, we have $t'(\beta) < 0$ and $t(\beta) \to 0$ when $\beta \to \infty$, and $t(\beta) \to \infty$ for $\beta \to 0$.

Define

$$v(X, Y) = \begin{cases} \sum_{k=0}^{\infty} \frac{1}{t^2(\|T^k X - T^k Y\|)} & \text{for } X \neq Y \\ 0 & \text{for } X = Y. \end{cases} \tag{7.9}$$

We will show that the series defining the function v for $X \neq Y$ converges uniformly when $\|X\| \leqslant b$, $\|Y\| \leqslant b$, where b is an arbitrary positive constant. As proved in Section 2, since system (7.1) is dissipative, there exists a $k(b)$ such that $\|T^k X\| \leqslant a$ when $k \geqslant k(b)$ and $\|X\| \leqslant b$. Thus, it follows from inequality (7.8) that

$$\|T^k X - T^k Y\| < 2\alpha(k - k(b))$$

when $k > k(b)$. Since the function $t(\beta)$ is monotonic, this inequality gives us

$$t(\|T^k X - T^k Y\|) > t(2\alpha(k - k(b))) = k - k(b)$$

and, consequently,

$$\frac{1}{t^2(\|T^k X - T^k Y\|)} < \frac{1}{[k - k(b)]^2} \tag{7.10}$$

when $\|X\| \leqslant b$, $\|Y\| \leqslant b$. As a result, the series under discussion converges uniformly when $\|X\| \leqslant b$, $\|Y\| \leqslant b$. From the foregoing, in conjunction with the fact that $t(\beta) \to \infty$ when $\beta \to 0$ and the continuity of the transformation T, it follows that the function v is continuous for all X and Y.

In order to prove the theorem, it remains to be proved that $v(TX, TY) < v(X, Y)$ when $X \neq Y$. We have

$$v(TX, TY) = \sum_{k=0}^{\infty} \frac{1}{t^2(\|T^{k+1}X - T^{k+1}Y\|)} =$$

$$= \sum_{k=1}^{\infty} \frac{1}{t^2(\|T^k X - T^k Y\|)} = v(X, Y) - \frac{1}{t^2(\|X - Y\|)}.$$

Since $[1/t^2(\|X - Y\|)] > 0$ when $X \neq Y$, the required follows. Q.E.D.

The following theorem, which is a simple corollary of the preceding theorem [38, 39], is frequently found useful in practice.

Theorem 7.4. Assume that system (7.1) is dissipative and that there exists a function $v(X, Y, t)$ *with the following properties:*

1) $v(X, Y, t) = v(X, Y, t+\omega)$,
2) $v(X, Y, t) \geqslant 0$, *with* $v(X, Y, t) = 0$ *if and only if* $X = Y$,
3) $\dot{v} = \frac{\partial v}{\partial t} + \sum_{k=1}^{n} \frac{\partial v}{\partial x_k} f_k(X, t) + \sum_{k=1}^{n} \frac{\partial v}{\partial y_k} f_k(Y, t) \leqslant 0$, *with* $\dot{v} = 0$ *if and only if* $X = Y$ *(as usual,* x_k, y_k, *and* f_k *denote the components of the vectors* X, Y, *and* F, *respectively). Then system (7.1) is convergent.*

Proof. Consider two solutions, $X(t, X_0, 0)$ and $X(t, Y_0, 0)$, of system (7.1), assuming that $X_0 \neq Y_0$. The third property of the function v gives us the inequality

$$\frac{d}{dt} v(X(t, X_0, 0), X(t, Y_0, 0), t) < 0$$

from which we obtain the relationships $v(X_0, Y_0, 0) > v(TX_0, TY_0, \omega) = v(TX_0, TY_0, 0)$. It is now clear that the function $v(X, Y, 0)$ satisfies the conditions of Theorem 7.2, which completes the proof of the present theorem.

It is not difficult to use the considerations presented in the proof of Theorem 2.6 to show that the converse of Theorem 7.4 is true, but we will not dwell on this point.

3. We will now give several sufficient conditions for the convergence of certain systems. Consider the system [40]

$$\frac{dX}{dt} = AX + G(X, t) \tag{7.11}$$

where A is a constant square matrix with elements a_{ij} $(i, j = 1, \ldots, n)$, while X and G are n-dimensional vectors with components x_i and g_i, respectively. Assume that the function $G(X, t)$ is continuous, guarantees that the solutions of system (7.11) are unique, and is ω-periodic with respect to t. Moreover, assume that, for all X, Y, and t, the following inequalities hold:

$$|g_i(x_1, \ldots, x_n, t) - g_i(y_1, \ldots, y_n, t)| \leqslant \varkappa \sum_{k=1}^{n} |x_k - y_k|$$
$$i = 1, \ldots, n. \tag{7.12}$$

Theorem 7.5. If all of the characteristic roots of matrix A *have negative real parts and the constant* $\varkappa$ *is sufficiently small, then system (7.11) is convergent.*

Proof. Consider the following "first-approximation" system

$$\frac{dX}{dt} = AX. \tag{7.13}$$

It is well known [41] that this system has a Lyapunov function in the form of a quadratic form, i.e., there exists a positive definite form

$$W(x_1, \ldots, x_n) = \sum_{i, j=1}^{n} b_{ij} x_i x_j \tag{7.14}$$

whose time derivative [by virtue of the differential equations of system (7.13)]

$$\dot{W} = \sum_{i,j=1}^{n} c_{ij} x_i x_j \tag{7.15}$$

is negative definite.

Set

$$v(X, Y) = W(x_1 - y_1, \ldots, x_n - y_n) = \\ = \sum_{i, j=1}^{n} b_{ij}(x_i - y_i)(x_j - y_j). \tag{7.16}$$

We now use the differential equations of system (7.11) to compute the time derivative of the function $v(X, Y)$:

$$\dot{v} = \sum_{i, j=1}^{n} c_{ij}(x_i - y_i)(x_j - y_j) + \\ + \sum_{i, j=1}^{n} b_{ij}[g_i(x_1, \ldots, x_n, t) - g_i(y_1, \ldots, y_n, t)](x_j - y_j) + \\ + \sum_{i, j=1}^{n} b_{ij}(x_i - y_i)[g_j(x_1, \ldots, x_n, t) - g_j(y_1, \ldots, y_n, t)]. \tag{7.17}$$

But the form (7.15) is negative definite. Therefore it follows from inequalities (7.12) that, for sufficiently small $\varkappa$, the inequality $\dot{v}(X, Y) \leqslant 0$ is satisfied, with $\dot{v}(X, Y) = 0$ if and only if $X = Y$; and since the form (7.14) is positive definite, $v(X, Y) \geqslant 0$, with $v(X, Y) = 0$ if and only if $X = Y$.

Thus, the function $v(X, Y)$ satisfies the hypothesis of Theorem 7.14. Moreover, as previously shown (see Theorem 3.0), system (7.11) is dissipative. Consequently, system (7.11) is convergent. Q.E.D.

Note that, as the proof of Theorem 7.5 implies, the constant $\varkappa$ in inequality (7.12) may be effectively estimated by means of matrix A.

4. We now consider the following system [42]:

$$\frac{dX}{dt} = F(X) + G(t) \tag{7.18}$$

where X, F, and G are n-dimensional vectors with components x_i, f_i, and g_i, respectively. Assume that the vector function G is continuous and ω-periodic, and assume that the functions $f_i(x_1, \ldots, x_n)$ are continuously differentiable with respect to all of their arguments. Consider the Jacobian matrix of the vector function $F(X)$

$$J(X) = \begin{pmatrix} \frac{\partial f_1}{\partial x_1}, & \frac{\partial f_1}{\partial x_2}, & \ldots, & \frac{\partial f_1}{\partial x_n} \\ \cdot & \cdot & \cdot & \cdot \\ \frac{\partial f_n}{\partial x_1}, & \frac{\partial f_n}{\partial x_2}, & \ldots, & \frac{\partial f_n}{\partial x_n} \end{pmatrix} \tag{7.19}$$

and set

$$W(X) = \frac{1}{2}(J + J^*) \tag{7.20}$$

where J^* is the transpose of matrix J. We will now prove the following theorem.

Theorem 7.6. If the characteristic roots of matrix W are less than some negative constant for all X, then system (7.18) is convergent.

Proof. Let $\lambda_k(X)$ be the characteristic roots of matrix $W(X)$. By hypothesis, there exists a $\delta > 0$ such that the inequalities $\lambda_k(X) < -\delta$ are satisfied for all X. Denote the scalar product of the vectors X and Y by $X \cdot Y$. We will show that the inequality

$$W(Y)X \cdot X < -\delta \|X\|^2 \tag{7.21}$$

holds for all X and Y.

Treating the function $W(Y)X \cdot X$ as a quadratic form in the components of the vector X, we can use an orthogonal transformation $X = PZ$ to reduce it to canonical form:

$$W(Y)X \cdot X = \sum_{k=1}^{n} \lambda_k(Y) z_k^2 \tag{7.22}$$

where the z_k are the components of the vector Z. It follows from Eq. (7.22) and the inequalities $\lambda_k(Y) < -\delta$ that

$$W(Y)X \cdot X < -\delta \|Z\|^2.$$

But the transformation $X = PZ$ is orthogonal, so that $\|Z\| = \|X\|$. Hence, inequality (7.21) follows.

Set $v(X) = \|X\|^2$ and differentiate this function with respect to t, utilizing system (7.18). Thus,

$$\dot{v} = 2F(X) \cdot X + 2G(t) \cdot X$$

or

$$\dot{v}=2[F(X)-F(0)]\cdot X+2[G(t)+F(0)]\cdot X. \tag{7.23}$$

Furthermore,

$$F(X)-F(0)=\int_0^1 J(uX)\,X\,du. \tag{7.24}$$

It is easily seen that

$$\int_0^1 J(uX)\,X\,du\cdot X=\int_0^1 W(uX)\,X\,du\cdot X. \tag{7.25}$$

Equations (7.23)-(7.25) yield the relationship

$$\dot{v}=2\int_0^1 W(uX)\,X\cdot X\,du+2[G(t)+F(0)]\cdot X, \tag{7.26}$$

which, in conjunction with (7.21), yields

$$\dot{v}<-2\delta\|X\|^2+2[G(t)+F(0)]\cdot X. \tag{7.27}$$

The function $G(t)$ is continuous and periodic, and therefore bounded; as a result, $\dot{v}<0$ for sufficiently large $\|X\|$. It then follows from Theorem 2.5 that system (7.18) is dissipative.

Now consider the function $v_1(X, Y)=\|X-Y\|^2$ and write the derivative of this function with respect to t with the aid of system (7.18):

$$\dot{v}_1=2[X-Y]\cdot[F(X)-F(Y)].$$

Proceeding as above, we use (7.24) and the identity (7.25) to show that

$$\dot{v}_1=2\int_0^1 W(Y+u(X-Y))(X-Y)\,du\cdot(X-Y).$$

Then inequality (7.21), which is valid for all values of the argument of matrix W, yields

$$\dot{v}_1<-2\delta\|X-Y\|^2. \tag{7.28}$$

It follows from this inequality that the function v_1 satisfies the hypothesis of Theorem 7.4, from which the theorem follows.

5. In this paragraph we will consider a system for direct automatic control with one nonlinearity and periodic disturbing forces [37]:

$$\frac{dx_k}{dt}=\sum_{\nu=1}^{n} b_{k\nu}x_\nu+h_k f(\sigma)+p_k(t), \quad \sigma=\sum_{i=1}^{n}\alpha_i x_i \; (k=1, \ldots, n), \quad (7.29)$$

where $b_{k\nu}$, h_k, and α_k are real constants, the functions $p_k(t)$ are continuous and ω-periodic, and $f(\sigma)$ is a continuously differentiable function for all σ.

Assume that all characteristic roots of the matrix composed of the coefficients $b_{k\nu}$ are simple and have negative real parts.

Following Lur'ye [43], system (7.29) will be reduced to canonical form. Assume that the resultant reduced system is given by

$$\frac{dz_\rho}{dt}=\lambda_\rho z_\rho+f(\sigma)+q_\rho(t), \quad \sigma=\sum_{k=1}^{n}\gamma_k z_k \quad (\rho=1, \ldots, n). \quad (7.30)$$

For the sake of definiteness, we will assume that the first s roots λ_k are real, and that the remaining roots comprise $(n-s)/2$ pairs of complex conjugate roots. It is then clear that $z_1, \ldots, z_s$ are real and that $z_{s+1}, \ldots, z_n$ consist of $(n-s)/2$ pairs of complex conjugates.

We will attempt to find a Lyapunov function for the system

$$\frac{dz_\rho}{dt}=\lambda_\rho z_\rho+f(\sigma), \quad \sigma=\sum_{k=1}^{n}\gamma_k z_k \quad (\rho=1, \ldots, n) \quad (7.31)$$

in the form of a quadratic in the variables z_ρ (see [43], Chapter II, Section 4).

Set

$$F(z_1, \ldots, z_n)=\sum_{\alpha, \beta=1}^{n}\frac{z_\alpha z_\beta}{\lambda_\alpha+\lambda_\beta}. \quad (7.32)$$

The quadratic form $F(z_1, \ldots, z_n)$ takes on only real values. This is a consequence of the fact that the terms in this form are either real or pairs of complex conjugates.

We will show that the form F is negative definite. Taking note of the identity

$$\frac{1}{\lambda_1+\lambda_\beta}=-\int_0^\infty e^{(\lambda_\alpha+\lambda_\beta)\tau}\,d\tau$$

we have

$$F = -\int_0^\infty \sum_{\alpha, \beta=1}^{n} z_\alpha z_\beta e^{(\lambda_\alpha+\lambda_\beta)\tau} d\tau = -\int_0^\infty \left(\sum_{\alpha=1}^{n} z_\alpha e^{\lambda_\alpha \tau} \right)^2 d\tau.$$

But the sum $\sum_{\alpha=1}^{n} z_\alpha e^{\lambda_\alpha \tau}$ is real (every complex term in the sum occurs with its conjugate), and thus its square is positive. Furthermore, the indicated sum can vanish for different λ_α and for all τ if and only if each of the variables z_α vanishes. Thus, F is a negative definite form.

We now use the differential equations

$$\dot{z}_\alpha = \lambda_\alpha z_\alpha \; (\alpha = 1, \ldots, n) \tag{7.33}$$

to find the total derivative of F with respect to time, obtaining

$$\dot{F} = \sum_{\alpha=1}^{n} \frac{\partial F}{\partial z_\alpha} \lambda_\alpha z_\alpha = 2 \sum_{\alpha=1}^{n} \lambda_\alpha z_\alpha \sum_{\beta=1}^{n} \frac{z_\beta}{\lambda_\alpha + \lambda_\beta}$$

or

$$\dot{F} = 2 \sum_{\alpha=1}^{n} \sum_{\beta=1}^{n} \frac{\lambda_\alpha}{\lambda_\alpha + \lambda_\beta} z_\alpha z_\beta = \sum_{\alpha=1}^{n} \frac{\lambda_\alpha}{\lambda_\alpha + \lambda_\beta} z_\alpha z_\beta +$$
$$+ \sum_{\beta=1}^{n} \sum_{\alpha=1}^{n} \frac{\lambda_\beta}{\lambda_\beta + \lambda_\alpha} z_\alpha z_\beta = \sum_{\alpha=1}^{n} \sum_{\beta=1}^{n} z_\alpha z_\beta = \sum_{\alpha=1}^{n} z_\alpha \sum_{\beta=1}^{n} z_\beta.$$

Thus,

$$\dot{F} = \left(\sum_{\alpha=1}^{n} z_\alpha \right)^2. \tag{7.34}$$

For positive $A_1, \ldots, A_s, C_1, \ldots, C_{n-s-1}$, the quadratic form

$$\Phi(z_1, \ldots, z_n) = \frac{1}{2}(A_1 z_1^2 + \ldots + A_s z_s^2) +$$
$$+ (C_1 z_{s+1} z_{s+2} + C_3 z_{s+3} z_{s+4} + \ldots + C_{n-s-1} z_{n-1} z_n) \tag{7.35}$$

is clearly positive definite. By virtue of system (7.33), its time derivative has the form

$$\dot{\Phi} = A_1 \lambda_1 z_1^2 + A_2 \lambda_2 z_2^2 + \ldots + A_s \lambda_s z_s^2 +$$
$$+ C_1 (\lambda_{s+1} + \lambda_{s+2}) z_{s+1} z_{1+2} + \ldots + C_{n-s-1} (\lambda_{n-1} + \lambda_n) z_{n-1} z_n \tag{7.36}$$

and, therefore, is a negative definite quadratic form.

We will now attempt to find a Lyapunov function for system (7.31) in the form

$$v(z_1, \ldots, z_n) = \Phi(z_1, \ldots, z_n) - F(a_1 z_1, \ldots, a_n z_n). \qquad (7.37)$$

By virtue of the differential equations of system (7.31), the time derivative of this function is, as (7.34) and (7.36) imply,

$$\begin{aligned}\dot{v} = -\left(\sum_{\rho=1}^{n} a_\rho z_\rho\right)^2 &+ A_1\lambda_1 z_1^2 + \ldots + A_s\lambda_s z_s^2 + \\ &+ C_1(\lambda_{s+1} + \lambda_{s+2}) z_{s+1} z_{s+2} + \ldots \\ &\ldots + C_{n-s-1}(\lambda_{n-1} + \lambda_n) z_{n-1} z_n + f(\sigma) \times \\ &\times \left\{ \sum_{\rho=1}^{s} z_\rho \left[A_\rho - 2a_\rho \sum_{\alpha=1}^{n} \frac{a_\alpha}{\lambda_\alpha + \lambda_\rho} \right] + \right. \\ &\left. + \sum_{\rho=1}^{n-s} z_{s+\rho} \left[C_\rho - 2a_{s+\rho} \sum_{\alpha=1}^{n} \frac{a_\alpha}{\lambda_\alpha + \lambda_{s+\rho}} \right] \right\}; \end{aligned} \qquad (7.38)$$

where, in order to simplify the notation of the last sum, we have substituted the constants $C_2, C_4, \ldots, C_{n-s}$ for the constants $C_1, C_3, \ldots, C_{n-s-1}$, respectively.

Now assume that the function $f(\sigma)$ is such that

$$f(\sigma)\sigma > 0 \text{ for } \sigma \neq 0. \qquad (7.39)$$

Add $\mu\sigma f(\sigma)$ to the right side of Eq. (7.38) and subtract $\mu f(\sigma) \sum_{\rho=1}^{n} \gamma_\rho z_\rho$, which is equal to $\mu\sigma f(\sigma)$. Then, if we subject the constants $a_1, \ldots, a_n, A_1, \ldots, A_s, C_1, \ldots, C_{n-s}$, and μ to the conditions

$$A_\rho - 2a_\rho \sum_{\alpha=1}^{n} \frac{a_\alpha}{\lambda_\alpha + \lambda_\rho} + \mu\gamma_\rho = 0 \qquad (\rho = 1, \ldots, s) \qquad (7.40)$$

$$C_\rho - 2a_\rho \sum_{\alpha=1}^{n} \frac{a_\alpha}{\lambda_\alpha + \lambda_{s+\rho}} + \mu\gamma_{s+\rho} = 0 \quad (\rho = 1, 2, \ldots, n-s) \qquad (7.41)$$

the expression for $\dot{v}$ will take the form

$$\begin{aligned} v = -\mu\sigma f(\sigma) - \left(\sum_{\rho=1}^{n} a_\rho z_\rho\right)^2 &+ A_1\lambda_1 z_1^2 + \ldots + A_s\lambda_s z_s^2 + \\ &+ C_1(\lambda_{s+1} + \lambda_{s+2}) z_{s+1} z_{s+2} + \ldots \\ &\ldots + C_{n-s-1}(\lambda_{n-1} + \lambda_n) z_{n-1} z_n, \end{aligned} \qquad (7.42)$$

and the function $\dot{v}$ will be negative definite when $\mu \geqslant 0$.

It is not difficult to use the function $\dot{v}$ to prove the following theorem.

Theorem 7.7. If (7.39) is satisfied and there exist constants $A_1>0, \ldots, A_s>0$, $C_1=C_2>0, \ldots, C_{n-s-1}=C_{n-s}>0$ *and* $\mu>0$ *such that the system of quadratic equations (7.40) and (7.41) has real roots* $a_1, \ldots, a_s$ *and* $(n-s)/2$ *pairs of complex conjugate roots* $a_{s+1}, \ldots, a_n$, *then system (7.29) is dissipative.*

Proof. Using the differential equations of system (7.30) to obtain the derivative of v with respect to t, we obtain

$$\begin{aligned}\dot{v}=\mu f(\sigma)\sigma-\left(\sum_{\rho=1}^{n} a_\rho z_\rho\right)^2+A_1\lambda_1 z_1^2+\ldots\\ \ldots+A_s\lambda_s z_s^2+C_1(\lambda_{s+1}+\lambda_{s+2})z_{s+1}z_{s+2}+\ldots\\ \ldots+C_{n-s-1}(\lambda_{n-1}+\lambda_n)z_{n-1}z_n+L(t, z_1, \ldots, z_n),\end{aligned} \tag{7.43}$$

where $L(t, z_1, \ldots, z_n)$ is a linear form in the variables $z_1, \ldots, z_n$ with coefficients periodic in t. It is clear that the function (7.43) will be negative definite for sufficiently large values of the sum $|z_1|+\ldots+|z_n|$. The theorem then follows from Theorem 2.5.

Theorem 7.8. If the hypothesis of the preceding theorem is satisfied, and if, moreover, $f'(\sigma)>0$ *for all* σ, *then system (7.29) is convergent.*

Proof. In order to prove this theorem, define the function

$$\begin{aligned}V\left(z_1^{(1)}, \ldots, z_n^{(1)}, z_1^{(2)}, \ldots, z_n^{(2)}\right)=\\ =v\left(z_1^{(1)}-z_1^{(2)}, \ldots, z_n^{(1)}-z_n^{(2)}\right).\end{aligned} \tag{7.44}$$

Using the differential equations of system (7.30), we find the total derivative of V with respect to t. In order to do this, we first find the derivatives of the differences $z_\rho^{(1)}-z_\rho^{(2)}$:

$$\dot{z}_\rho^{(1)}-\dot{z}_\rho^{(2)}=\lambda_\rho\left(z_\rho^{(1)}-z_\rho^{(2)}\right)+f(\sigma^{(1)})-f(\sigma^{(2)}) \quad (\rho=1, \ldots, n).$$

By the law of the mean,

$$\dot{z}_\rho^{(1)}-z_\rho^{(2)}=\lambda_\rho\left(z_\rho^{(1)}-z_\rho^{(2)}\right)+f'(\tilde{\sigma})(\sigma^{(1)}-\sigma^{(2)}) \quad (\rho=1, \ldots, n). \tag{7.45}$$

where $\tilde{\sigma}$ is between $\sigma^{(1)}$ and $\sigma^{(2)}$.

It follows from Eqs. (7.31), (7.42), and (7.45) that

$$\begin{aligned}\dot{V}=-\mu f'(\tilde{\sigma})(\sigma^{(1)}-\sigma^{(2)})^2-\left[\sum_{\rho=1}^{n} a_\rho\left(z_\rho^{(1)}-z_\rho^{(2)}\right)\right]^2+\\ +A_1\lambda_1\left(z_1^{(1)}-z_1^{(2)}\right)^2+\ldots+A_s\lambda_s\left(z_s^{(1)}-z_s^{(2)}\right)^2+\\ +C_1(\lambda_{s+1}+\lambda_{s+2})\left(z_{s+1}^{(1)}-z_{s+1}^{(2)}\right)\left(z_{s+2}^{(1)}-z_{s+2}^{(2)}\right)+\ldots\\ \ldots+C_{n-s-1}(\lambda_{n-1}+\lambda_n)\left(z_{n-1}^{(1)}-z_{n-1}^{(2)}\right)\left(z_n^{(1)}-z_n^{(2)}\right).\end{aligned}$$

It is clear that when the hypothesis of the theorem is satisfied, $\dot{V} \leqslant 0$ with $\dot{V}=0$ if and only if $z_\rho^{(1)}=z_\rho^{(2)}$ $(\rho=1, \ldots, n)$.

Thus, the hypothesis of Theorem 7.4 is satisfied and the theorem is proved.

8. PROBLEMS ON CONVERGENCE FOR SECOND-ORDER EQUATIONS

In this section we will consider the equation

$$\ddot{x}+f(x)\dot{x}+g(x)=p(t) \tag{8.1}$$

and the equation with a parameter

$$\ddot{x}+kf(x)\dot{x}+g(x)=kp(t). \tag{8.2}$$

1. Equation (8.1) will be studied under the assumption that $g(x)$ is linear, i.e., we will consider the equation

$$\ddot{x}+f(x)\dot{x}+ax=p(t). \tag{8.3}$$

The functions $f(x)$ and $p(t)$ are assumed to be continuous, and $p(t)$ is assumed to be ω-periodic.

Theorem 8.1. Let $a>0$ and assume, in addition, that there exists a $K>0$ such that the inequality $f(x)\geqslant K$ is satisfied for all x. Then Eq. (8.3) is convergent.

Proof. From Theorem 4.2 it follows that Eq. (8.3) belongs to the class of D-systems. Set $y=\dot{x}+F(x)$, where, as usual, $F(x)=\int\limits_0^x f(x)\,dx$; then we obtain the system

$$\frac{dx}{dt}=y-F(x), \quad \frac{dy}{dt}=-ax+p(t). \tag{8.4}$$

Define

$$v(x_1, y_1, x_2, y_2)=a(x_1-x_2)^2+(y_1-y_2)^2. \tag{8.5}$$

Now compute the total derivative of this function with respect to time, assuming that x_1, y_1 and x_2, y_2 are solutions of system (8.4). In order to do so, we first compute the derivatives of the differences x_1, y_1 and x_2, y_2 :

$$\dot{x}_1-\dot{x}_2=y_1-y_2+F(x_2)-F(x_1), \quad \dot{y}_1-\dot{y}_2=a(x_2-x_1).$$

Then, by the law of the mean,

$$\dot{x}_1 - \dot{x}_2 = y_1 - y_2 + f(\tilde{x})(x_2 - x_1). \qquad (8.6)$$

We can therefore write

$$\dot{v} = -f(\tilde{x})(x_1 - x_2)^2. \qquad (8.7)$$

Now let $x_1(t),\ y_1(t)$ and $x_2(t),\ y_2(t)$ be two arbitrary solutions of system (8.4). If $x_1(0) = x_2(0),\ y_1(0) = y_2(0)$ then $v(x_1(t),\ y_1(t),\ x_2(t),\ y_2(t)) \equiv 0$; moreover, let $[x_1(0) - x_2(0)]^2 + [y_1(0) - y_2(0)]^2 > 0$. Then we will show that the difference $x_1(t) - x_2(t)$ may vanish only at isolated points. Let $x_1(t^*) - x_2(t^*) = 0$; then, by virtue of the uniqueness theorem, $y_1(t^*) - y_2(t^*) \neq 0$. When $t = t^*$, we find from the first equation in system (8.4) that

$$\dot{x}_1 - \dot{x}_2 = y_1 - y_2 \neq 0.$$

Thus, it follows that the difference $x_1 - x_2$ vanishes only at isolated points. Therefore, the $\dot{v}$ also vanishes on the solutions $x_1(t),\ y_1(t)$ and $x_2(t),\ y_2(t)$ only at isolated points. Since $\dot{v} < 0$ when $x_1 \neq x_2$, it is clear that the function $v(x_1(t),\ y_1(t),\ x_2(t),\ y_2(t))$ decreases as time increases. Consequently, we have

$$v(x_1(0),\ y_1(0),\ x_2(0),\ y_2(0)) > v(x_1(\omega),\ y_1(\omega),\ x_2(\omega),\ y_2(\omega)). \qquad (8.8)$$

Our theorem then follows from Theorem 7.2.

2. Consider Eq. (8.2) under the following assumptions:

1) the functions f, g, and p are continuous, g satisfies a Lipschitz condition in the neighborhood of each point x, and $p(t)$ has the period ω.

2) There exist positive numbers a, α, and β such that $f(x) \geqslant \alpha$ for $|x| \geqslant a$, $g(x) \geqslant \beta$ for $x \geqslant a$, $g(x) \leqslant -\beta$ for $x \leqslant -a$.

3) the function $P(t) = \int\limits_0^t p(t)\,dt$ is bounded for all t.

From the above conditions it follows that a can be assumed sufficiently large to satisfy the following condition as well:

4) There exists a positive γ such that

$$F(x) - E \geqslant \gamma \text{ for } x \geqslant a,\ F(x) + E \leqslant -\gamma \text{ for } x \leqslant -a;$$
$$G(x) > 0 \text{ for } |x| \geqslant a,$$

where $F(x) = \int\limits_0^x f(x)\,dx$, $G(x) = \int\limits_0^x g(x)\,dx$, and $E > 0$ is such that $|P(t)| < E$ for all t.

It follows from Theorem 4.1 that under the previously stated conditions, Eq. (8.2) is a D-system. In order to establish convergence, we must obtain a more accurate estimate of the region in which the solutions of Eq. (8.2) fall. This type of estimate has been made by Cartright and Littlewood [44]. Here we will obtain these estimates by the method given by Lefschetz [45].

Note that, as in Section 4, Eq. (8.2) is equivalent to the system

$$\frac{dx}{dt} = y - k(F(x) - P(t))$$
$$\frac{dy}{dt} = -g(x). \tag{8.9}$$

Henceforth we will assume that $k \geqslant 1$.

Let λ_0 be such that $|F| + E \leqslant \lambda_0$ for $|x| \leqslant a$, and let λ_1 be a positive constant that will be determined below. Consider the rectangle R defined by the inequalities

$$|x| \leqslant a, \quad |y| \leqslant k\lambda_0 + \lambda_1. \tag{8.10}$$

We will now show that, as time increases, any solution of system (8.9) will fall within the rectangle R.

Lemma 8.1. Let $|x_0| \leqslant a$ *and* $|y_0| > k\lambda_0 + \lambda_1$. *Then the solution passing through the point* $(t = t_0)$ *at* x_0, y_0 *will either enter the rectangle* R *as* t *increases or leave the strip* $|x| \leqslant a$.

Proof. Divide the second equation of the system (8.9) by the first, obtaining

$$\frac{dy}{dx} = \frac{-g(x)}{y - k(F(x) - P(t))}. \tag{8.11}$$

Inside the strip $|x| \leqslant a$ we have $|F(x) - E| \leqslant \lambda_0$, so that inside this strip, but outside R, we have $|y - k(F(x) - P(t))| \geqslant \lambda_1$. Moreover, $|g(x)| \leqslant \delta$. As a result,

$$\left|\frac{dy}{dx}\right| \leqslant \frac{\delta}{\lambda_1} = m_0. \tag{8.12}$$

Thus, it follows that, as time increases, the solution under discussion will leave the strip $|x| \leqslant a$ if it remains outside R. Here it is clear that, above the rectangle R, all solutions pass across the strip $|x| \leqslant a$ as x increases, while below the rectangle, this passage occurs as x decreases.

Remark. The time required for solutions to pass across the strip $|x| \leqslant a$ outside the rectangle R has a positive upper bound τ_1.

Indeed, assume that, for example, the solution passes across the strip $|x| \leqslant a$ above R; then the first equation of the system yields

$$dx = [y - k(F(x) - P(t))]\,dt > \lambda_1\,dt.$$

Consequently,

$$t_1 - t_2 \leqslant \frac{2a}{\lambda_1} = \tau_1.$$

where t_1 and t_2 denote the times at which the solution under discussion intersects the lines $x = \pm a$.

Lemma 8.2. Any solution beginning outside the strip $|x| \leqslant a$ *reaches it in a finite time.*

Proof. Consider the function

$$v(x, y) = \frac{1}{2}y^2 + G(x). \tag{8.13}$$

Using the differential equations of system (8.9) to obtain the derivative of Eq. (8.13) with respect to t, we find

$$\dot{v} = -kg(x)[F(x) - P(t)]. \tag{8.14}$$

Choose an arbitrary point (x_0, y_0) outside the strip $|x| \leqslant a$ and, for definiteness, assume that $x_0 > a$. Consider the solution $x(t)$, $y(t)$ with initial data $x = x_0$, $y = y_0$ at $t = t_0$. As long as this solution remains outside the strip $|x| \leqslant a$ the inequalities $g(x) \geqslant \beta$ and $[F(x) - P(t)] \geqslant \gamma$ are satisfied along it. Thus, the inequality

$$\frac{dv}{dt} < -k\beta\gamma \tag{8.15}$$

is satisfied on this solution.

As long as the solution under discussion is outside the strip $|x| \leqslant a$, the inequality $v > 0$ will be satisfied along it. Thus, the solution must leave the half-plane $x \geqslant a$ at time $t = \tau$ and $\tau - t_0 < (1/k\beta\gamma)\,v(x_0, y_0)$.

The lemma is proved.

Lemma 8.3. If λ_1 *is sufficiently large, then any solution of system (8.9) will enter the rectangle* R *as time increases.*

Proof. Consider a solution $x(t)$, $y(t)$ of system (8.9) and assume, contrary to the assertion of the lemma, that it remains outside the rectangle R for all t. Then it follows from Lemmas 8.1 and 8.2 that this solution will intersect each of the lines $x = \pm a$

an infinite number of times. Let t_1 and t_2 be two successive times of intersection of the solution and the line $x = -a$. We will show that there exists a q such that

$$y^2(t_1) - y^2(t_2) \geqslant kq.$$

For definiteness, assume that $y(t_1) > 0$. As t increases (from t_1), the solution under discussion will be in the strip $|x| \leqslant a$ and then, at $t = \theta_1$, will intersect the line $x = a$ and enter the half-plane $x > a$.

It follows from Lemma 8.2 that, upon further increase in t, the solution will intersect the line $x = a$ when $t = \theta_2 > \theta_1$. Here it is clear that $y(\theta_2) < 0$, because $x = a$ when $\dot{x} > 0$ and $y > \lambda_0 k + \lambda_1$. Further, the solution will intersect the line $x = -a$ when $t = \theta_3$, and then intersect this same line again when $t = t_2 > \theta_3$.

We will now find the increment $\Delta_1 v$ experienced by the function v along the solution when t changes from t_1 to θ_1. Equation (8.14) yields

$$|\Delta_1 v| = k \left| \int_{t_1}^{\theta_1} g(x)[F(x) - P(t)]\, dt \right| =$$

$$= k \left| \int_{-a}^{+a} [F(x) - P(t)] \frac{dy}{dx}\, dx \right| \leqslant$$

$$\leqslant k \int_{-a}^{+a} (|F| + E) \left| \frac{dy}{dx} \right| dx \leqslant 2ak\lambda_0 m_0 = \frac{2ak\lambda_0\delta}{\lambda_1}.$$

This estimate is clearly also valid for the increment $\Delta_3 v$ of the function v on the interval $\theta_2 \leqslant t \leqslant \theta_3$. Consequently, the total increment v on these two intervals satisfies the inequality

$$\Delta_1 v + \Delta_3 v \leqslant \frac{4ak\lambda_0\delta}{\lambda_1}. \tag{8.16}$$

On the other hand, on the time interval between θ_1 and θ_2 the function v decreases, and y decreases at the same time. Let $\Delta_2 v$ be the increment of v along one solution for $\theta_1 \leqslant t \leqslant \theta_2$. Then

$$\Delta_2 v = -k \int_{\theta_1}^{\theta_2} g(x)[F(x) - P(t)]\, dt = k \int_{y(\theta_1)}^{y(\theta_2)} [F(x) - P(t)]\, dy. \tag{8.17}$$

But $x \geqslant a$ when $\theta_1 \leqslant t \leqslant \theta_2$ and, therefore, $[F(x) - E] \geqslant \gamma$. Moreover, it is clear that $y(\theta_1) > \lambda_1$ and $y(\theta_2) < -\lambda_1$, because the vertical sides of the rectangle R are longer than $2\lambda_1$. Consequently, (8.17) gives us the estimate $\Delta_2 v < -2k\lambda_1\gamma$.

Of course, the same estimate holds for the increment $\Delta_4 v$ of the function v on the interval $\theta_3 \leqslant t \leqslant t_2$, so that

$$\Delta_2 v + \Delta_4 v < -4k\lambda_1\gamma. \tag{8.18}$$

Let Δv be the increment experienced by v along the solution under discussion over the interval $t_1 \leqslant t \leqslant t_2$. Combining (8.16) and (8.18), we find that

$$v(t_1) - v(t_2) \geqslant 4k\left(\lambda_1\gamma - \frac{\lambda_0}{\lambda_1} a\delta\right).$$

Choose $\lambda_1 > \sqrt{(\lambda_0 a\delta/\gamma)}$ and set $q = 8\,[\lambda_1\gamma - (\lambda_0/\lambda_1)\,a\delta] > 0$, thus obtaining

$$y^2(t_1) - y^2(t_2) = 2(v(t_1) - v(t_2)) \geqslant kq. \tag{8.19}$$

But then it is clear that after a sufficiently large number of intersections with the line $x = -a$, the solution under discussion will enter the rectangle R. This contradicts the assumption that our solution will remain outside R for all t, which proves the lemma.

We will now prove the following theorem, which will prove important in future use.

Theorem 8.2. Assume that Conditions 1-3 of the present section are satisfied, and let $k > 1$. *Then there exists an* $M > 0$ *such that any solution of system (8.9) will enter the region* $|x| < M$, $|y| < M(1+k)$ *as time increases and, henceforth, remain there.*

Proof. If the solution remains in the rectangle R, the theorem is proved. By Lemma 8.3, every solution will reach this rectangle. Assume that it also leaves it, say, at $x = a$ and time $t = t_0$, at which point dx/dt is equal to $\dot{x}_0$. The trajectory turns around at time t, at which point $dx/dt = 0$. By integrating Eq. (8.2), we find that

$$-\dot{x}_0 + k(F(x) - F(a)) + \beta(t - t_0) \leqslant k(P(t) - P(t_0)) \leqslant 2kE,$$

because $g > \beta$ for $x \geqslant a$ and $|P(t)| \leqslant E$. Consequently,

$$k(F(x) - F(a)) \leqslant 2kE + \dot{x}_0. \tag{8.20}$$

It follows from the first equation of system (8.9) that, at $x = a$, the largest possible value of $\dot{x}_0$ is of the form $kC + D \leqslant k(C + D)$ (where C and D are positive constants that are independent of k). Consequently, for $x \geqslant a$ inequality (8.20) yields

$$F(x) \leqslant F(a) + 2E + C + D = K > 0.$$

Since the function $F(x)$ increases monotonically when $x \geqslant a$, the inequality gives us $x \leqslant \varepsilon$, where $\varepsilon \geqslant a$. Now it is not difficult to complete the proof.

Theorem 8.3. Assume that the conditions of the preceding theorem are satisfied. If, in addition, $f(x) \geqslant A > 0$ for all x, then for sufficiently large t, the inequality $|dx/dt| < N$, where N is a sufficiently large constant independent of k, is satisfied for all solutions.

Proof. For any given $\varepsilon > 0$ and for sufficiently large t, it is impossible for $\dot{x}(t) > \varepsilon$, because $|x(t)|$ is bounded. As a result, either $\dot{x}(t) \to 0$ for $t \to \infty$, and then the theorem is proved, or $\dot{x}(t)$ oscillates infinitely as t increases.

If t_1 is one of the maximum points of $\dot{x}(t)$, then $\ddot{x}(t_1) = 0$. Equation (8.2) therefore yields

$$\dot{x}(t_1) = \frac{kp(t_1) - g(x(t_1))}{kf(x(t_1))}.$$

Since, by the preceding theorem, $|x|$ is bounded by a constant not depending on k, then $|g(x)| < L$, where L is also independent of k. Hence, since $k > 1$, we have

$$\dot{x}(t_1) < \frac{k \max p(t) + L}{kA} \leqslant \frac{k(\max p(t) + L)}{kA} = K,$$

where K is independent of k. Thus, $\dot{x}(t)$ has a fixed upper bound independent of k for all its maximum points, and, consequently, for all sufficiently large t. A similar argument holds for the minima. Q.E.D.

Now we turn our attention to the following cases. Assume that the point (x_0, y_0) lies in the rectangle R; then, as an immediate consequence of the proof of Theorem 8.2, we have the inequalities

$$|x(t)| < M, \quad |y(t)| < M(1 + k) \tag{8.21}$$

for all $t \geqslant t_0$, where $(x(t), y(t))$ is the solution with initial data t_0, x_0, y_0.

From the proof of Theorem 8.3 it follows that there exists a $\tau_1 \geqslant 0$, such that the inequalities

$$|x(t)| < M, \quad \frac{dx}{dt} < N \tag{8.22}$$

are satisfied on our solution for all $t \geqslant t_0 + \tau_1$, where τ_1 is independent of both the parameter k and the point (x_0, y_0, t_0). Indeed, the inequality $|x| < M$ follows immediately from (8.21). We will show that the inequality $|dx/dt| < N$ is also satisfied for $t \geqslant t_0 + \tau_1$. If this inequality is satisfied for $t = t_0$, then the considerations given in the proof of Theorem 8.3 imply that it is also satisfied for all $t \geqslant t_0$. Now assume that $(dx/dt) \geqslant N$ for $t = t_0$. Since $|x| < M$ for all $t \geqslant t_0$, it is clear that the inequality $dx/dt \geqslant N$ can be satisfied only when $t - t_0 < 2M/N = \tau_1$. When $t \geqslant t_0 + \tau_1$, both inequalities in (8.22) will be satisfied.

As Lemma 8.3 implies, system (8.9) is dissipative (this follows from Theorem 4.1). For this system, we define the sets I and S (I and S are defined on pages 21 and 24, respectively).

It follows from the foregoing discussion that the inequalities

$$|x| \leqslant M, \quad \left|\frac{dx}{dt}\right| = |y - k(F(x) - P(t))| < N \tag{8.23}$$

are satisfied for any point in the set S. Moreover, in virtue of Theorem 2.3, the set S is stable. We can therefore find a sufficiently small neighborhood U of the set I so that inequalities (8.23) will be satisfied on any solution passing through U when $t = 0$.

3. We will now consider Eq. (8.2) under more rigid restrictions, assuming that the following conditions are satisfied:

1) The functions f, g, and p are continuous: g satisfies a Lipschitz condition in the neighborhood of each point x, and $p(t)$ has period ω.

2) There exists a positive constant α such that $f(x) \geqslant \alpha$ for all x.

3) The function $g(x)$ is twice continuously differentiable in the interval $|x| \leqslant M$, where M is as defined by Theorem 8.2. When $|x| \leqslant M$, we have $g'(x) > 0$. There exists a $\beta > 0$ such that $g(x) \operatorname{sign} x \geqslant \beta$ for $|x| \geqslant M$.

4) There exists a positive E such that

$$|p(t)| \leqslant E, \quad |P(t)| = \left|\int_0^t p(t)\,dt\right| \leqslant E \text{ for all } t.$$

Under these conditions, we will prove the following convergence theorem about the system in Eq. (8.2) [46].

Theorem 8.4. Assume that Conditions 1-4 of the present Paragraph are satisfied; then for $k > k_0$, *where*

$$k_0 = \frac{1}{2} N \max_{|x| \leqslant M} \frac{g''(x)}{f(x)\, g'(x)} \tag{8.24}$$

and the constants M *and* N *are defined by Theorems 8.2 and 8.3, the system is convergent.*

Proof. Fix $k > k_0$. We will show that, under the previously stated assumptions, the set I of dissipative system (8.9) degenerates into a point thus proving the theorem.

Assume the opposite, i.e., assume that the set I contains two distinct points, separated by a distance $d > 0$. Take any two points (x_{10}, y_{10}) and (x_{20}, y_{20}) in I and connect them by a smooth arc γ that has no self-intersections and is contained entirely in U (U is the neighborhood of the set I that is defined at the end of the preceding paragraph). Let $x=\varphi(u)$, $y=\psi(u)$, $0 \leqslant u \leqslant 1$ be the parametric equations of the arc γ, so that $\varphi(0)=x_{10}$, $\psi(0)=y_{10}$, $\varphi(1)=x_{20}$, $\psi(1)=y_{20}$. It is not difficult to see that the curves γ can be selected so that there will be q constant Γ which will depend neither on the choice of points on I nor on the particular choice of curve γ and will be such that the inequality $[\varphi'(u)]^2+[\psi'(u)]^2 \leqslant \Gamma$ is satisfied for all points on I and for any $u \in [0, 1]$.

Extend the solution $(x(t, u), y(t, u))$ of system (8.9) through all points of the arc γ so that $x(0, u)=\varphi(u)$, $y(0, u)=\psi(u)$. The arc γ is in U. By the definition of U, we have, for all

$$|x(t, u)| < M, \quad |\dot{x}(t, u)| = |y(t, u) - k(F(x) - P(t))| < N. \tag{8.25}$$

Let $C(t)(t \geqslant 0)$ denote the curve defined by the parametric equations

$$x = x(t, u), \; y = y(t, u) \quad (0 \leqslant u \leqslant 1). \tag{8.26}$$

Since the distance between the points $(x(t, 0), y(t, 0))$ and $(x(t, 1), y(t, 1))$ is less than or equal to the length of the curve $C(t)$, we have

$$\{[x(t, 0) - x(t, 1)]^2 + [y(t, 0) - y(t, 1)]^2\}^{\frac{1}{2}} \leqslant \leqslant \int_0^1 \left\{\left[\frac{\partial x(t, u)}{\partial u}\right]^2 + \left[\frac{\partial y(t, u)}{\partial u}\right]^2\right\} du. \tag{8.27}$$

Set

$$v_1(t, u) = \frac{\partial x(t, u)}{\partial u}, \quad v_2(t, u) = \frac{\partial y(t, u)}{\partial u}. \tag{8.28}$$

It is not difficult to prove that the functions $v_1(t, u)$ and $v_2(t, u)$ satisfy the following system of linear differential equations:

$$\frac{dv_1}{dt} = v_2 - kf(x(t, u))v_1, \quad \frac{dv_2}{dt} = -g'(x(t, u))v_1. \tag{8.29}$$

Consider the function

$$W(t, u) = g'(x(t, u))v_1^2 + v_2^2 - 2\eta v_1 v_2 \quad (t \geqslant 0, \; 0 \leqslant u \leqslant 1). \tag{8.30}$$

W is a quadratic form in the variables v_1 and v_2 and has coefficients depending on t and u. Select a positive constant η such that the form W will be positive definite uniformly with respect to $|x| \leqslant M$. In order to do this, it is clearly sufficient to choose the number η so as to satisfy the inequality

$$\eta^2 < \min_{|x| \leqslant M} g'(x). \tag{8.31}$$

Now find the total time derivative of the function W by means of the differential equations of systems (8.9) and (8.29):

$$\frac{\partial W}{\partial t} = (g''(x)\dot{x} - 2kg'(x)f(x) + 2\eta g'(x))v_1^2 - \\ - 2\eta v_2^2 + 2k\eta f(x)v_1v_2. \tag{8.32}$$

The arc γ is contained in U, and k is fixed so that $k > k_0$, as a result of which $|x| \leqslant M$, $|\dot{x}| \leqslant N$ of all $t \geqslant 0$. Consequently, we have the following inequality for $t \geqslant 0$:

$$g''(x)\dot{x} - 2kg'(x)f(x) \leqslant -\mu < 0, \tag{8.33}$$

where μ is some sufficiently small constant. Let $\varkappa > 0$ be such that $g'(x) < \varkappa$ and $f(x) < \varkappa$ for $|x| \leqslant M$. Then (8.32) and (8.33) yield the inequality

$$\frac{\partial W}{\partial t} \leqslant (-\mu + 2\eta\varkappa)v_1^2 + 2k\eta f(x)v_1v_2 - 2\eta v_2^2. \tag{8.34}$$

For sufficiently small η, the form in the right side of the last inequality is negative definite. Fix η so that the right side of inequality (8.34) is negative definite, and so that inequality (8.31) is satisfied. Then the function W will be a form that is uniformly positive definite for $|x| \leqslant M$. Then there exists a $\lambda > 0$ such that the inequality

$$\frac{\partial W(t, u)}{\partial t} \leqslant -\lambda W(t, u) \tag{8.35}$$

is satisfied for all $t \geqslant 0$. Therefore, for $t \geqslant 0$,

$$W(t, u) \leqslant W(0, u)e^{-\lambda t}.$$

From the form of the function W and the inequality $[\varphi'(u)]^2 + [\psi'(u)]^2 = v_1^2(0, u) + v_2^2(0, u) < \Gamma$, it follows that there exists a number $\overline{W}$ which depends neither on the choice of points in I nor on the curve γ, and is such that

$$W(t, u) \leqslant \overline{W}e^{-\lambda t}. \tag{8.36}$$

Since, for $t \geqslant 0$, the function $W(t, u)$ is a uniformly positive definite form in the variables v_1 and v_2, inequality (8.36) implies the existence of a τ, such that for $t \geqslant \tau$ and any choice of two points in I the inequality

$$\{v_1^2(t, u) + v_2^2(t, u)\}^{\frac{1}{2}} < \frac{d}{2} \tag{8.37}$$

holds.

Now choose a natural number n so large that $n\omega > \tau$.

It follows from inequality (8.27) that

$$\{[x(n\omega, 0) - x(n\omega, 1)]^2 + [y(n\omega, 0) - y(n\omega, 1)]^2\}^{\frac{1}{2}} < \frac{d}{2}. \tag{8.38}$$

Since (x_{10}, y_{10}) and (x_{20}, y_{20}) are two arbitrary points in I, and the set I is invariant under the transformation T^n, the points $(x(n\omega, 0), y(n\omega, 0))$ and $(x(n\omega, 1), y(n\omega, 1))$ are also arbitrary points of the set I. Then inequality (8.38) implies that the distance between two distinct points in the set I is less than $d/2$. But, by definition, the set I contains two points separated by a distance d. The contradiction which we have thus obtained proves the theorem.

2

First- and Second-Order Periodic Systems

9. FIRST-ORDER EQUATIONS

Here we will consider Eq. (1.1) for the case of $n = 1$, i.e., x is a scalar,

$$\frac{dx}{dt} = F(x, t). \tag{9.1}$$

As usual, we will assume that $F(x, t)$ is defined, continuous, satisfies the uniqueness condition for all x and t, and that $F(x, t+\omega) \equiv F(x, t)$.

1. Assume that Eq. (9.1) has a solution $x = \varphi(t)$ that is bounded when $t \geqslant t_0$. Because the function $F(x, t)$ is periodic, we can assume without loss of generality that the solution $x = \varphi(t)$ is given for $t = 0$. Consider the sequence $x_k = \varphi(k\omega)$ $(k = 0, 1, \ldots)$. If $\varphi(0) = \varphi(\omega)$, then the solution $x = \varphi(t)$ is ω-periodic and we have $\varphi(k\omega) = \varphi(l\omega)$ for any integral k and l. Suppose $\varphi(0) \neq \varphi(\omega)$. We will show that, in that case, the sequence x_k is monotonic. For definiteness, assume that $\varphi(0) < \varphi(\omega)$, and we will show that then

$$\varphi(\omega) < \varphi(2\omega). \tag{9.2}$$

Assume the contrary, i.e., that

$$\varphi(\omega) \geqslant \varphi(2\omega). \tag{9.3}$$

Consider the solution $x = \psi(t)$ of Eq. (9.1) with initial data $\psi(\omega) = \varphi(0)$. Because $F(x, t)$ is periodic, $\psi(t) = \varphi(t - \omega)$. As a result, $\psi(2\omega) = \varphi(\omega)$ and we have $\psi(\omega) = \varphi(0) < \varphi(\omega)$. On the other hand, Eq. (9.3) implies the inequality $\psi(2\omega) \geqslant \varphi(2\omega)$. The foregoing inequalities imply that there exists a t^* in the interval $\omega < t \leqslant 2\omega$ such that

$\varphi(t^*) = \psi(t^*)$. But this is impossible, because the solutions of Eq. (9.1) are unique. The contradiction proves inequality (9.2).

Similarly, we can show that for any natural k we have the inequality

$$\varphi(k\omega) < \varphi((k+1)\omega). \tag{9.4}$$

Assume that the solution $x = \varphi(t)$ is bounded when $t \geqslant 0$. The sequence $\varphi(k\omega)$ is therefore bounded, and the limit

$$\lim_{k \to \infty} \varphi(k\omega) = a \tag{9.5}$$

exists.

We will consider the solution $x = \chi(t)$ with initial data $\chi(0) = a$, and show that it is periodic. Set $\varphi_k(t) = \varphi(t + k\omega)$. Since the right side of Eq. (9.1) is ω-periodic with respect to t, each of the functions $\varphi_k(t)$ is a solution. Moreover, it follows from the definition of $\varphi_k(t)$ together with (9.5) that $\varphi_k(0) \to a$ as $k \to \infty$. Consequently, by the theorem on integral continuity, $\varphi_k(\omega) \to \chi(\omega)$ as $k \to \infty$. But $\varphi_k(\omega) = \varphi((k+1)\omega) \to a$ as $k \to \infty$. Thus, it follows that $\chi(\omega) = a = \chi(0)$. The solution $x = \chi(t)$ therefore has period ω.

We will show that the solution $x = \varphi(t)$ asymptotically approaches the solution $x = \chi(t)$, i.e., that

$$\lim_{t \to \infty} (\varphi(t) - \chi(t)) = 0. \tag{9.6}$$

Choose an $\varepsilon > 0$; for any solution $x = x(t)$ there exists, for this ε, a $\delta > 0$ such that, if $|x(0) - a| < \delta$, then

$$|x(t) - \chi(t)| < \varepsilon \quad \text{for} \quad 0 \leqslant t \leqslant \omega. \tag{9.7}$$

Assume that k_1 is so large that $|\varphi(k\omega) - a| < \delta$ when $k > k_1$. Then it is clear that $|\varphi(t) - \chi(t)| < \varepsilon$ when $t \geqslant k\omega$, which proves (9.6).

We have therefore proved the following:

Theorem 9.1. If a solution $x = \varphi(t)$ is bounded then $t \geqslant t_0$ (when $t \leqslant t_0$), then either it is ω-periodic or it asymptotically approaches some ω-periodic solution as $t \to +\infty$ (as $t \to -\infty$).

2. Isolated periodic solutions of Eq. (9.1) possess certain remarkable properties.

Definition 9.1. A periodic solution $x = \chi(t)$ is said to be isolated if there exists an $h > 0$ such that there are no periodic solutions other than $x = \chi(t)$ in the region

$$\chi(t) - h \leqslant x \leqslant \chi(t) + h. \tag{9.8}$$

Theorem 9.2. If an isolated periodic solution, $x = \chi(t)$, of Eq. (9.1) is Lyapunov-stable, then it is asymptotically stable.

Proof. Corresponding to the h given in the definition of isolated periodic solutions, choose a $\delta > 0$ such that all solutions with initial data $|x(0)-\chi(0)|<\delta$ satisfy inequalities (9.8) when $t \geqslant 0$. Let $x=\varphi(t)$ be a solution of Eq. (9.1) such that $|\varphi(0)-\chi(0)|<\delta$. This solution can not be periodic, because $x=\chi(t)$ is isolated. Consequently, $\varphi(t)$ must asymptotically approach a periodic solution in the strip (9.8). But the only such periodic solution is $\chi(t)$. As a result, all solutions of Eq. (9.1) whose initial data for $t=0$ differ but slightly from $\chi(0)$ approach $\chi(t)$ as $t\to+\infty$, which proves the theorem.

Again, let $x=\chi(t)$ be an isolated periodic solution. We will show that any solution that is sufficiently close to $x=\chi(0)$ when $t=0$ asymptotically approaches $x=\chi(t)$ either when $t\to+\infty$ or when $t\to-\infty$. Corresponding to h in (9.8), choose a $\delta>0$ such that if $|x(0)-\chi(0)|<\delta$ then the solution $x(t)$ lies in the strip (9.8) when $-\omega\leqslant t\leqslant+\omega$. Let $x=\varphi(t)$ be a solution of Eq. (9.1) such that $|\varphi(0)-\chi(0)|<\delta$ for definiteness, assume that $\varphi(0)<\chi(0)$. Since $x=\chi(t)$ is an isolated periodic solution, it is clear that $\varphi(0)\neq\varphi(\omega)$. First, let $\varphi(0)<\varphi(\omega)$. In that case, the sequence $\varphi(k\omega)$ is defined and increases with k. If we set $a=\lim\limits_{k\to\infty}\varphi(k\omega)$, it is not difficult to see that $a\leqslant\chi(0)$. But the solution with initial data $t=0$, $x=a$ is periodic, and since there is only one periodic solution in the strip (9.8), this solution is $x=\chi(t)$, so that $a=\chi(0)$. Hence, it follows that

$$\lim_{t\to\infty}[\varphi(t)-\chi(t)]=0. \tag{9.9}$$

Now let $\varphi(0)>\varphi(\omega)$. As the preceding considerations imply, we now have $\varphi(-\omega)>\varphi(0)$. But then the sequence $\varphi(-k\omega)$ is defined and increases. Let $a=\lim\varphi(-k\omega)$. As in the case $\varphi(0)<\varphi(\omega)$, it turns out that $a=\chi(0)$ and

$$\lim_{t\to-\infty}[\varphi(t)-\chi(t)]=0.$$

3. We will now demonstrate an interesting property of the solutions of Eq. (9.1).

Theorem 9.3. Any solution $\varphi(t)$ of Eq. (9.1) is bounded either above or below as t increases.

Proof. There are two possibilities: The solution $x=\varphi(t)$ either can or cannot be extended to all $t\geqslant t_0$. First, assume that there exists a $\tau>t_0$ such that the solution $x=\varphi(t)$ becomes infinite when $t\to\tau$. By a well-known theorem on continuation of solutions, we have $\lim\limits_{t\to\tau}|\varphi(t)|=\infty$. But then it is clear that one of the following two equations holds:

$$\lim_{t\to\tau}\varphi(t)=+\infty,\quad \lim_{t\to\tau}\varphi(t)=-\infty.$$

From which it follows that $\varphi(t)$ is bounded either above or below when $t \geqslant t_0$.

Now assume that the solution $x=\varphi(t)$ can be extended to the entire half-axis $t \geqslant t_0$. If $\varphi(t_0)=\varphi(t_0+\omega)$ then the solution $x=\varphi(t)$ is periodic and therefore bounded. Let $\varphi(t_0) \neq \varphi(t_0+\omega)$; for definiteness assume that $\varphi(t_0) < \varphi(t_0+\omega)$. We set $m=\min\{\varphi(t)\}$ for $t_0 \leqslant t \leqslant t_0+\omega$, and we will show that $\varphi(t) \geqslant m$ when $t \geqslant t_0$.

Assume to the contrary that there exists a $t^* > t_0$ such that

$$\varphi(t^*) < m. \tag{9.10}$$

Let $k \geqslant 1$ be such that $k\omega + t_0 < t^* \leqslant (k+1)\omega + t_0$ and consider the solution $x=\varphi_1(t)$, $\varphi_1(t_0)=\varphi(t_0+k\omega)$. Since $\varphi(t_0) < \varphi(t_0+\omega)$, it is clear that

$$\varphi(t_0) < \varphi_1(t_0) = \varphi(k\omega + t_0). \tag{9.11}$$

The periodicity of the right side of the equation, combined with inequality (9.10), leads to

$$\varphi_1(t^* - t_0 - k\omega) < m \leqslant \varphi(t^* - t_0 - k\omega).$$

This last inequality, together with inequality (9.11), contradicts the uniqueness theorem, which proves the theorem.

4. We will now consider the case where F is analytic with respect to x. Assume that the function $F(x, t)$ may be written, for all $x_0 \in [a, b]$, in the form

$$F(x, t) = \sum_{n=0}^{\infty} L_n(t)(x - x_0)^n \tag{9.12}$$

and that the series on the right is absolutely and uniformly convergent for all $t \in (-\infty, +\infty)$ and $|x - x_0| < \alpha$, where α is a positive constant.

We now introduce the function $p(c)$. Let, as usual, $x(t, c, 0)$ be the solution of (9.1) with initial data $t=0$, $x=c$, and assume that $x(t, c, 0)$ is defined and continues for $0 \leqslant t \leqslant \omega$; then the function p is defined at the point c, $p(c)=x(\omega, c, 0)$. It is well known that the function $p(c)$ is analytic at a point c if $x(t, c, 0) \in [a, b]$ for $t \in [0, \omega]$.

Theorem 9.4. If the function $F(x, t)$ is representable in the form (9.12) in the neighborhood of any point $x_0 \in [a, b]$, then either all solutions entirely contained in the strip $a \leqslant x \leqslant b$ are periodic, or there is no more than a finite number of periodic solutions in this strip.

Proof. Assume that there is a sequence of different periodic solutions $x_k = \psi_k(t)$ $(k=1, 2, \ldots)$ entirely contained in this strip. The sequence of points $\psi_k(0)$ is contained in the interval $[a, b]$, and it can therefore be assumed to be convergent (otherwise we would choose a convergent subsequence). Set $\lim_{k\to\infty}\psi_k(0)=\eta$ and $\chi(t)=x(t,\eta,0)$. The solution $x=\chi(t)$ lies in the strip $a\leqslant x\leqslant b$ when $0\leqslant t\leqslant\omega$, because otherwise the solutions $\psi_k(t)$ would not satisfy the inequalities $a\leqslant\psi_k(t)\leqslant b$ for sufficiently large k and all $0\leqslant t\leqslant\omega$; this would contradict the definition of $\psi_k(t)$.

As a result, the analytic function $p(c)$ is defined at the point $c=\eta$. Construct the difference $q(c)=p(c)-c$, which, by the very definition of the function $p(c)$, vanishes when $c=\psi_k(0)$. Thus, it follows that the point η is a cluster point of the zeros of the analytic function $q(c)$, but then $q(c)\equiv 0$. Consequently, all solutions entirely contained in the strip $a\leqslant x\leqslant b$ are periodic. Q.E.D.

5. Hereinafter we will be concerned with the behavior of the solutions of Eq. (9.1) when the function $F(x,t)$ is a polynomial in the unknown function. Consider the equation

$$\frac{dx}{dt}=x^n+p_1(t)x^{n-1}+\ldots+p_{n-1}(t)x+p_n(t), \tag{9.13}$$

assuming that the functions $p_k(t)$ are continuous and ω-periodic.

Let $n\geqslant 2$. It is not difficult to see that there exists an $a_1>0$ such that the inequality

$$|x^n|-|p_1(t)x^{n-1}|-\ldots-|p_n(t)|>\frac{1}{2(n-1)}|x^n| \tag{9.14}$$

is satisfied when $|x|\geqslant a_1$.

Set $a=\max\left\{a_1,\left(\frac{2}{\omega}\right)^{\frac{1}{n-1}}\right\}$ and consider the equation

$$\frac{dx}{dt}=\frac{1}{2(n-1)}x^n. \tag{9.15}$$

It is not difficult to see that the function

$$x=\frac{2^{\frac{1}{n-1}}}{(2a^{1-n}-t)^{\frac{1}{n-1}}} \tag{9.16}$$

is the solution of Eq. (9.15) with initial data $t=0$, $x=a$. As we can easily see, this solution is defined only when $t=2a^{1-n}\leqslant\omega$. If $x_0\geqslant a$, it follows from (9.14) that

$$x(t,x_0,0)\geqslant\frac{2^{\frac{1}{n-1}}}{(2a^{1-n}-t)^{\frac{1}{n-1}}}\quad\text{for}\quad t\geqslant 0. \tag{9.17}$$

Thus, it follows that the solution $x(t, x_0, 0)$ is not continuable to the time interval $0 \leqslant t \leqslant \omega$.

It also follows from what we have said that if $x_0 \geqslant a$, then the solution $x(t, x_0, t_0)$ is not continuable to the entire time interval $t_0 \leqslant t \leqslant t_0 + \omega$ and $x(t, x_0, t_0) > a$ when $t > t_0$. Furthermore, when n is even and $x_0 \leqslant -a$, we have $x(t, x_0, t_0) < -a$ when $t < t_0$, and the solution $x(t, x_0, t_0)$ is not continuable to $t_0 - \omega \leqslant t \leqslant t_0$; when n is odd and $x_0 \leqslant -a$ $x(t, x_0, t_0) < -a$, for $t > t_0$, the solution $x(t, x_0, t_0)$ is not continuable to $t_0 \leqslant t \leqslant t_0 + \omega$.

Theorem 9.5. Equation (9.13) can have only a finite number of periodic solutions.

Proof. Let a be defined as above. Then if $|x| \geqslant a$ along all solutions, x varies monotonically. Consequently, if $|x_0| \geqslant a$, the solution $x(t, x_0, t_0)$ will remain outside the strip $|x| < a$ either when $t \geqslant t_0$ or $t \leqslant t_0$, and will become infinite. Therefore, all periodic solutions will lie entirely within the strip $|x| \leqslant a$. By Theorem 9.4, Eq. (9.13) either has a finite number of periodic solutions, or all solutions contained entirely in a strip when $0 \leqslant t \leqslant \omega$ are periodic. But if all solutions in the strip $|x| \leqslant a$ are periodic, then there exists a periodic solution having a point on the line $x = a$. This is impossible, because such a solution becomes infinite. Therefore, Eq. (9.13) has only a finite number of periodic solutions.

The location of the solution curves of Eq. (9.13) depends essentially on whether or not n is even. Assume, at first, that $n > 2$ is odd, and, as before, let a_1 be the number determined by inequality (9.14). Then it is clear that when $|x| \geqslant a_1$ $|x|$ increases as t increases and decreases as t decreases along all solutions. It follows from what we have said above that any solution $x(t, x_0, t_0)$ for which $|x_0| \geqslant a_1$ remains in the set $|x| \geqslant a_1$ as time increases, and becomes infinite at some finite value of the argument t. When t decreases, however, such a solution enters the strip $|x| < a_1$ and remains there. This implies, in particular, that, for odd n, Eq. (9.13) has at least one periodic solution. Of course, it may turn out that there is more than one periodic solution; then among them there will be a "largest" $x = \varphi(t)$ and a "smallest" $x = \psi(t)$. Let $x = x(t, x_0, t_0)$ be a solution of Eq. (9.13). Then, if $\psi(t_0) \leqslant x_0 \leqslant \varphi(t_0)$, this solution will remain in the strip $\psi(t) \leqslant x \leqslant \varphi(t)$ for all t and will either be itself periodic or approach some periodic solution when $t \to +\infty$ as well as $t \to -\infty$. If, however, $x_0 > \varphi(t_0)$ (or $x_0 < \psi(t_0)$), then $x(t, x_0, t_0)$ [asymptotically approaches the solution $x = \varphi(t)$ (or $x = \psi(t)$)] as $t \to -\infty$, and becomes infinite as t increases a certain finite value.

Now let $n \geqslant 2$ be an even number. If $x_0 \geqslant a_1$, then when t increases, the solution $x(t, x_0, t_0)$ becomes infinite at some finite value of t. If, however, $x_0 \leqslant -a_1$, the solution $x(t, x_0, t_0)$ becomes infinite when t decreases. When n is even, Eq. (9.1) need not have periodic solutions. For instance, the equation

$$\frac{dx}{dt} = x^n + p_n(t) \tag{9.18}$$

has only increasing functions for solutions when $p_n(t) > 0$. For such equations, all solutions become infinite as time increases as well as when it decreases.

Now assume that Eq. (9.13) has periodic solutions for even n; let $x = \varphi(t)$ be the "largest" solution, and let $x = \psi(t)$ be the "smallest." Then any solution beginning in the strip $\psi(t) \leqslant x \leqslant \varphi(t)$ remains in this strip for all t and is either periodic itself, or approaches some periodic solution when $t \to -\infty$, as well as when $x_0 > \varphi(t_0)$. If $t \to +\infty$, the solution $x(t, x_0, t_0)$ asymptotically approaches $x = \varphi(t)$ as $t \to -\infty$, and becomes infinite as time increases. If, however, $x_0 < \psi(t_0)$, the solution $x = x(t, x_0, t_0)$ approaches $x = \psi(t)$ as $t \to +\infty$, and becomes infinite when time decreases.

The qualitative pattern of behavior of the solution curves of Eq. (9.13) therefore depends entirely on the periodic solutions.

6. In what follows we will be concerned with the determination of the maximum number of periodic solutions possible for Eq. (9.13) for a fixed n.

If $n = 1$, then Eq. (9.13) is linear:

$$\dot{x} = x + p_1(t),$$

$$x = e^t \left[x_0 + \int_0^t p_1(t) e^{-t} dt \right]. \tag{9.19}$$

It is clear that Eq. (9.19) has one and only one periodic solution:

$$x = e^t \left[\frac{e^\omega}{1 - e^\omega} \int_0^\omega p_1(t) e^{-t} dt + \int_0^t p_1(t) e^{-t} dt \right]. \tag{9.20}$$

Let $n = 2$, i.e., let Eq. (9.13) be a form of Riccati's equation:

$$\dot{x} = x^2 + p_1(t) x + p_2(t). \tag{9.21}$$

It is not difficult to find equations of the form (9.21) that have exactly two periodic solutions. For example, the equation

$$\dot{x} = x^2 - 1. \tag{9.22}$$

has exactly two periodic solutions, $x = 1$ and $x = -1$. All of the remaining solutions are monotonically varying functions.

Theorem 9.6. Equation (9.21) can not have more than two periodic solutions.

Proof. Assume, contrary to our assertion, that Eq. (9.21) has three different periodic solutions x_1, x_2, and x_3. In virtue of uniqueness, we can assume that the inequalities $x_1(t) < x_2(t) < x_3(t)$ are satisfied for all t. Substituting the solutions x_1, x_2, and x_3 into Eq. (9.21), we obtain the identities

$$\dot{x}_1 = x_1^2 + p_1(t)\, x_1 + p_2(t),$$
$$\dot{x}_2 = x_2^2 + p_1(t)\, x_2 + p_2(t),$$
$$\dot{x}_3 = x_3^2 + p_1(t)\, x_3 + p_2(t).$$

Subtracting the first and second identities from the third, we find that

$$\dot{x}_3 - \dot{x}_1 = (x_3 - x_1)(x_3 + x_1) + p_1(t)(x_3 - x_1),$$
$$\dot{x}_3 - \dot{x}_2 = (x_3 - x_2)(x_3 + x_2) + p_1(t)(x_3 - x_2).$$

By hypothesis, $x_3 > x_2$ and $x_3 > x_1$, so that the two preceding equations yield

$$\frac{\dot{x}_3 - \dot{x}_2}{x_3 - x_2} - \frac{\dot{x}_3 - \dot{x}_1}{x_3 - x_1} = x_2 - x_1.$$

By integrating the preceding identity with respect to t over the interval $0 \leqslant t \leqslant \omega$, we obtain

$$\ln(x_3 - x_2)\big|_0^{\omega} - \ln(x_3 - x_1)\big|_0^{\omega} = \int_0^{\omega} (x_2 - x_1)\, dt.$$

But the functions x_1, x_2, and x_3 are ω-periodic, so that the left side of the last equation is equal to zero. On the other hand, $x_2 - x_1 > 0$ by hypothesis, so that the right side of the last equation is positive. The contradiction which we have obtained shows that Eq. (9.21) can not have more than two different periodic solutions.

Finally, consider the case of $n = 3$, i.e., the case in which Eq. (9.13) is Abel's equation:

$$\dot{x} = x^3 + p_1(t)\, x^2 + p_2(t)\, x + p_3(t). \tag{9.23}$$

It is easy to find examples of equations of the form (9.23) with exactly three different periodic solutions, e.g.,

$$\dot{x} = x^3 - x. \tag{9.24}$$

This equation has three periodic solutions: $x = 1$, $x = 0$, and $x = -1$. The remaining solutions are monotonic functions.

Theorem 9.7. Equation (9.23) can have no more than three periodic solutions.

Proof. Assume that this is not so, i.e., assume that Eq. (9.23) has four different periodic solutions: x_1, x_2, x_3, and x_4. In virtue of uniqueness, the inequality $x_i \neq x_k$ (for $i \neq k$) is satisfied for all t. Substituting the solutions $x_i(t)$ into Eq. (9.23), we obtain the following identities:

$$\dot{x}_i = x_i^3 + p_1(t)\,x_i^2 + p_2(t)\,x_i + p_3(t) \qquad (i = 1,\ 2,\ 3,\ 4).$$

Substracting the second and third identities from the first, and dividing by the nonzero differences $x_1 - x_2$ and $x_1 - x_3$, we obtain the expressions

$$\frac{\dot{x}_1 - \dot{x}_2}{x_1 - x_2} = x_1^2 + x_1 x_2 + x_2^2 + p_1(t)(x_1 + x_2) + p_2(t)$$

and

$$\frac{\dot{x}_1 - \dot{x}_3}{x_1 - x_3} = x_1^2 + x_1 x_3 + x_3^2 + p_1(t)(x_2 + x_3) + p_2(t).$$

Subtracting the last equation from the preceding one, we obtain

$$\frac{\dot{x}_1 - \dot{x}_2}{x_1 - x_2} - \frac{\dot{x}_1 - \dot{x}_3}{x_1 - x_3} = x_1(x_2 - x_3) + x_2^2 - x_3^2 + p_1(t)(x_2 - x_3)$$

and, similarly, substituting x_1 for x_4,

$$\frac{\dot{x}_4 - \dot{x}_2}{x_4 - x_2} - \frac{\dot{x}_4 - \dot{x}_3}{x_4 - x_3} = x_4(x_2 - x_3) + x_2^2 - x_3^2 + p_1(t)(x_2 - x_3).$$

Subtracting this equation from the preceding one, we then obtain

$$\frac{\dot{x}_1 - \dot{x}_2}{x_1 - x_2} - \frac{\dot{x}_1 - \dot{x}_3}{x_1 - x_3} - \frac{\dot{x}_4 - \dot{x}_2}{x_4 - x_2} + \frac{\dot{x}_4 - \dot{x}_3}{x_4 - x_3} = (x_1 - x_4)(x_2 - x_3).$$

Integrating this identity over the interval $[0, \omega]$, we have

$$\ln \frac{(x_1 - x_2)(x_4 - x_3)}{(x_1 - x_3)(x_4 - x_2)} \Bigg|_0^{\omega} = \int_0^{\omega} (x_1 - x_4)(x_2 - x_3)\,dt.$$

Since the x_i are periodic functions, the left side of this equation is equal to zero. The integrand on the right, however, contains a continuous nonvanishing function. Consequently, the right side of the equation is nonzero. This contradiction shows that Abel's equation can not have more than three different periodic solutions.

It is not difficult to construct an example of Eq. (9.13) with exactly n periodic solutions. In order to do so, it is sufficient to have the right side consist of a polynomial with constant coefficients and n different real roots. These roots will be periodic solutions of the equation. As we have just proved, Eq. (9.13) can not have more than n different periodic solutions when $n \leqslant 3$ (the author obtained these ingenious proofs from N. V. Adamov). It is natural to assume that the same is also true for Eq. (9.13) for any n. This assumption, however, proves to be false. Later, we will examine an equation of the form (9.13) with $n=4$ and having six different periodic solutions. We will also find conditions sufficient for Eq. (9.13) to have no more than n periodic solutions. Moreover, we will attempt to find a theoretical basis for the fact that, beginning with $n=4$, there are equations with more than n different periodic solutions [47].

7. Let us again consider the previously introduced functions $p(c)= x(\omega, c, 0)$ and $q(c)=p(c)-c$. These functions are defined and analytic at those points c at which the solutions $x(t, c, 0)$ can be extended to the interval $0 \leqslant t \leqslant \omega$. As Theorem 9.1 implies, any periodic solution of Eq. (9.13) has period ω, so that the zeros of the function $q(c)$ (and only they) constitute the initial data for the periodic solutions of (9.13). The problem concerning the number and distribution of periodic solutions is, therefore, reduced to the problem of finding the number and distribution of zeros of the analytic function $q(c)$. As a result, it is natural to consider not only the real values of c, but the complex values as well, and to admit complex-valued functions of the real argument t as the solutions. Set $x=u+iv=re^{i\varphi}$. Then (9.13) yields the equation

$$\dot{r}e^{i\varphi}+ir\dot{\varphi}e^{i\varphi}=r^n e^{in\varphi}+p_1(t)\,r^{n-1}e^{i(n-1)\varphi}+\ldots$$
$$\ldots+p_{n-2}(t)\,r^2e^{2i\varphi}+p_{n-1}(t)\,re^{i\varphi}+p_n(t).$$

Dividing by $e^{i\varphi}$ and separating the real and imaginary parts, we obtain equations for the argument and modulus of x:

$$\dot{r}=r^n\cos(n-1)\varphi+\ldots+p_{n-2}(t)\,r^2\cos\varphi+ \\ +p_{n-1}(t)\,r+p_n(t)\cos\varphi, \tag{9.25}$$

$$r\dot{\varphi}=r^n\sin(n-1)\varphi+\ldots+p_{n-2}(t)\,r^2\sin\varphi-p_n(t)\sin\varphi. \tag{9.26}$$

As before, define the function $q(c)$ by means of the equation $q(c)=x(\omega, c, 0)$, and assume that it is defined only at those points in the complex c-plane through which solutions that can be continued to the segment $0\leqslant t\leqslant\omega$ pass. The zeros of $q(c)$ determine the

ω-periodic solutions of Eq. (9.13) for complex c as well. Conversely, any ω-periodic solution passes through a zero of the function $q(c)$ at $t=0$.

If x can take on complex values, Eq. (9.13) may have periodic solutions with the periods not equal to ω. For example, the equation

$$\dot{x}=x^2+1, \quad \omega=1 \tag{9.27}$$

has the general solution

$$x=\operatorname{tg}(t+B).$$

None of the solutions of Eq. (9.27) has a period equal to unity. At the same time, note that any solution with $\operatorname{Im}\{B\}\neq 0$ is continuous and has period π; the solutions of (9.27) for $\operatorname{Im}\{B\}=0$, on the other hand, become infinite both when t increases and when t decreases.

Hereafter we will be mainly concerned with ω-periodic solutions, and, therefore, these are the only solutions which we will call periodic.

If the coefficients of Eq. (9.13) are changed, then the function $q(c)$ and its zeros will change. As the coefficients are continuously varied, the zeros may "disappear," merging into singular points. The singular points of $q(c)$ are the points of the complex c-plane through which solutions that cannot be continued to the segment $0\leqslant t\leqslant\omega$ pass. We will now study the behavior of such solutions.

We will first investigate the qualitative pattern of behavior of the solutions of Eq. (9.13) in the neighborhood of the point at infinity. Hereafter, we will assume that the coefficients of Eq. (9.13) satisfy a Lipschitz condition

$$|p_i(t_1)-p_i(t_2)|\leqslant L\,|t_1-t_2| \qquad (i=1,\,2,\,\ldots,\,n). \tag{9.28}$$

The functions $p_i(t)$ are periodic and thus bounded; let M_i be a number such that the inequalities

$$|p_i(t)|\leqslant M_i \quad (i=1,\,2,\,\ldots,\,n) \tag{9.29}$$

are satisfied for all t, and set $a=\max\{6,\,6M_1\}$. Choose a number $\rho>0$ sufficiently large so that the following relations are satisfied:

$$\frac{\pi}{4(n-1)}>\frac{a}{\rho}, \tag{9.30}$$

$$\sin\frac{(n-1)\,a}{r}>\frac{5}{6}\,\frac{(n-1)\,a}{r} \quad \text{for} \quad r\geqslant\rho \tag{9.31}$$

$$\sum_{k=2}^{n} M_k r^{n-k} < \frac{a}{6} r^{n-1} \quad \text{for} \quad r \geqslant \rho, \tag{9.32}$$

$$r^n > 4 \sum_{k=1}^{n} M_k r^{n-k} \quad \text{for} \quad r \geqslant \rho. \tag{9.33}$$

We now introduce domains G_k defined by the inequalities

$$\left\{ r > \rho, \ \frac{k\pi}{n-1} - \frac{a}{r} < \varphi < \frac{k\pi}{n-1} + \frac{a}{r} \right\} \ (k = 0, 1, \ldots, 2n-3),$$

and domains H_k that complete the system of domains G_k to the entire exterior of the cylinder $r = \rho$. The H_k are defined by means of the relations $\{r > \rho \ \ (k\pi)/(n-1) + a/r < \varphi < (k+1)\pi/(n-1) - a/r\}$. It follows from relation (9.30) that the closures of the domains G_k do not intersect. We will show that the boundaries of the domains G_k have no points of contact with the field of lines defined by systems (9.25)-(9.26). Consider the region $\{r = \rho, \ (k\pi)/(n-1) - a/\rho \leqslant \varphi \leqslant (k\pi)/(n-1) + a/\rho\}$, which we will call the bottom wall of the domain G_k. It follows from inequality (9.30) that the inequalities

$$\frac{dr}{dt} > \frac{r^n}{\sqrt{2}} + p_1(t) r^{n-1} \cos(n-2)\varphi + \ldots$$
$$\ldots + p_{n-1}(t) r + p_n(t) \cos\varphi$$

are satisfied on this wall when k is even, and

$$\frac{dr}{dt} < -\frac{r^n}{\sqrt{2}} + p_1(t) r^{n-1} \cos(n-2)\varphi + \ldots$$
$$\ldots + p_{n-1}(t) r + p_n(t) \cos\varphi$$

where k is odd. These inequalities and (9.33) imply that the following inequalities are satisfied in the closures of the domains G_k:

$$\frac{dr}{dt} > \frac{2-\sqrt{2}}{2\sqrt{2}} r^n, \tag{9.34}$$

for even k, and

$$\frac{dr}{dt} < -\frac{2-\sqrt{2}}{2\sqrt{2}} r^n \tag{9.35}$$

for odd k.

The surfaces $\{r \geqslant \rho, \ (k\pi)/(n-1) - a/r = \varphi\}$ and $\{r \geqslant \rho, \ \varphi = (k\pi)/(n-1) + a/r\}$ will be called, respectively, the first and second side walls of the domain G_k. It follows from (9.26), (9.31), and (9.32), that the inequality

$$r\dot{\varphi} > \frac{1}{2} ar^{n-1} \tag{9.36}$$

is satisfied on the first side wall of the domain G_k for odd k, and on the second side wall of the domain G_k for even k. On the other hand,

$$r\dot{\varphi} < -\frac{1}{2} ar^{n-1} \tag{9.37}$$

on the second side wall of the domain G_k for odd k, and on the first side wall of the domain G_p for even k.

From relations (9.34)-(9.37) it follows that the side and bottom walls of the domain G_k are surfaces with no points of contact. Thus, for k even, all solutions enter the domain G_k, through the bottom wall, and leave through the side walls as time increases. A similar pattern holds for decreasing time when k is odd, i.e., if k is odd, solutions leave G_k through the bottom wall, and they enter G_k through the side walls as time increases.

We will now conduct a detailed study of the behavior of solutions in the domain G_k. It follows from inequality (9.33) and Eq. (9.25) that r varies monotonically in the domains G_k along all solutions, and we can therefore take r as the independent variable.

$$R = \cos(n-1)\varphi + \frac{1}{r} p_1 \cos(n-2)\varphi + \dots$$
$$\dots + \frac{1}{r^{n-1}} p_{n-1} + \frac{1}{r^n} p_n \cos\varphi. \tag{9.38}$$

$$\Phi = \sin(n-1)\varphi + \frac{1}{r} p_1 \sin(n-2)\varphi + \dots$$
$$\dots + \frac{1}{r^{n-2}} p_{n-2} \sin\varphi - \frac{1}{r^n} p_n \sin\varphi. \tag{9.39}$$

Then (9.25) and (9.26) yield the system of equations

$$\frac{dt}{dr} = \frac{1}{r^n R(r, \varphi, t)}, \tag{9.40}$$

$$\frac{d\varphi}{dr} = \frac{\Phi(r, \varphi, t)}{rR(r, \varphi, t)}. \tag{9.41}$$

Consider two solutions of this system: $t_1(r), \varphi_1(r)$ and $t_2(r), \varphi_2(r)$ with the initial data $r = \rho$, $t = t_{10}$, $\varphi = \varphi_{10}$, and $t = t_{20}$, $\varphi = \varphi_{20}$, respectively. Here we will assume that $\varphi_{20} > \varphi_{10}$ and $|t_{20} - t_{10}| \leqslant \varphi_{20} - \varphi_{10}$. Then Eq. (9.40) yields

$$\frac{dt_2}{dr} - \frac{dt_1}{dr} = \frac{R(r, \varphi_1, t_1) - R(r, \varphi_2, t_2)}{r^n R(r, \varphi_1, t_1) R(r, \varphi_2, t_2)}.$$

It follows from the form of the function $R(r, \varphi, t)$ and condition (9.28) that for sufficiently large ρ the inequality

$$\left| \frac{dt_2}{dr} - \frac{dt_1}{dr} \right| < \frac{L_1}{r^{n+1}} (|t_2 - t_1| + |\varphi_2 - \varphi_1|) \tag{9.42}$$

where L_1 is some positive constant, will be satisfied inside the region G_k.

Equation (9.41) yields

$$\frac{d\varphi_2}{dr} - \frac{d\varphi_1}{dr} = \frac{1}{r} \left(\frac{\Phi_2}{R_2} - \frac{\Phi_1}{R_1} \right)$$

where $\Phi_i = \Phi(r, \varphi_i, t_i)$, $R_i = R(r, \varphi_i, t_i)$ $(i = 1, 2)$ or

$$\frac{d\varphi_2}{dr} - \frac{d\varphi_1}{dr} = \frac{1}{r} \frac{R_1\Phi_2 - R_2\Phi_1}{R_1 R_2}. \tag{9.43}$$

Write

$$\begin{aligned} R_1\Phi_2 - R_2\Phi_1 = R_1\Phi_2 - R_1\Phi(r, \varphi_1, t_2) + R_1\Phi(r, \varphi_1, t_2) - \\ - R_1\Phi_1 + R_1\Phi_1 - R(r, \varphi_2, t_1)\Phi_1 + R(r, \varphi_2, t_1)\Phi_1 - R_2\Phi_1. \end{aligned} \tag{9.44}$$

By the law of the mean, we can write

$$\begin{aligned} &\Phi(r, \varphi_2, t_2) - \Phi(r, \varphi_1, t_2) = \\ &= \cos[(n-1)(\varphi_1 + \eta(\varphi_2 - \varphi_1))](\varphi_2 - \varphi_1) + O\left(\frac{1}{r}\right)(\varphi_2 - \varphi_1). \end{aligned}$$

Since the inequality $\left|\varphi_i - k\pi/n-1\right| \leqslant a/r$ holds in the domain G_k, the last relation gives us the following estimate:

$$\begin{aligned} &\Phi(r, \varphi_2, t_2) - \Phi(r, \varphi_1, t_2) = \\ &\qquad = (\cos k\pi)(\varphi_2 - \varphi_1) + O\left(\frac{1}{r}\right)(\varphi_2 - \varphi_1). \end{aligned} \tag{9.45}$$

Using the law of the mean and condition (9.28), we obtain the following estimates:

$$\Phi(r, \varphi_1, t_2) - \Phi(r, \varphi_1, t_1) = O\left(\frac{1}{r}\right)(t_2 - t_1) \tag{9.46}$$

$$R(r, \varphi_2, t_1) - R(r, \varphi_1, t_1) = O\left(\frac{1}{r}\right)(\varphi_2 - \varphi_1) \tag{9.47}$$

$$R(r, \varphi_2, t_2) - R(r, \varphi_2, t_1) = O\left(\frac{1}{r}\right)(t_2 - t_1). \tag{9.48}$$

Moreover, it is immediately clear from the form of the function R that the following equation holds inside G_k:

$$R(r, \varphi, t) = \cos k\pi + O\left(\frac{1}{r}\right). \tag{9.49}$$

It follows from (9.43), (9.44) and the previously obtained estimates that

$$\frac{d\varphi_2}{dr} - \frac{d\varphi_1}{dr} = \frac{1}{r}(\varphi_2 - \varphi_1) + O\left(\frac{1}{r^2}\right)(|\varphi_2 - \varphi_1| + |t_2 - t_1|) \tag{9.50}$$

in the domain G_k.

We will now show that when both solutions t_1, φ_1 and t_2, φ_2 are in the domain G_k, the inequality

$$\varphi_2 - \varphi_1 \geqslant |t_2 - t_1| \tag{9.51}$$

holds for sufficiently large ρ.

Assume to the contrary that there exists an r^* such that for $\rho \leqslant r \leqslant r^*$ the solutions $t_1(r), \varphi_1(r)$ and $t_2(r), \varphi_2(r)$ are located in $\bar{G}_k$ and $\varphi_2(r^*) - \varphi_1(r^*) = |t_2(r^*) - t_1(r^*)|$, while for $r > r^*$ but sufficiently close to r^* inequality (9.51) is violated. From (9.42) and (9.50) it follows that when $r = r^*$ we have the inequality

$$\frac{d(\varphi_2 - \varphi_1)}{dr} > \left|\frac{d(t_2 - t_1)}{dr}\right|$$

if ρ is sufficiently large. This last inequality also proves inequality (9.51) for the domain G_k provided ρ is sufficiently large, which we will assume to be the case.

It follows from (9.50) and (9.51) that we have the following inequality in the domain G_k:

$$\frac{d(\varphi_2 - \varphi_1)}{dr} > \frac{1}{2r}(\varphi_2 - \varphi_1).$$

Integrating the last inequality, we obtain

$$\ln(\varphi_2 - \varphi_1) - \ln(\varphi_{20} - \varphi_{10}) > \frac{1}{2}(\ln r - \ln \rho)$$

or

$$\frac{\varphi_2 - \varphi_1}{\varphi_{20} - \varphi_{10}} > \sqrt{\frac{r}{\rho}} \quad \text{for} \quad r > \rho. \tag{9.52}$$

Thus it follows that at least one of the solutions under discussion will leave G_k when r increases.

We now consider a region G with the index k even. On the bottom wall of the region G_k, choose an arc of the circle $\gamma_k(t_0)$:

$$\left\{t=t_0,\ r=\rho,\ \frac{k\pi}{n-1}-\frac{a}{\rho}\leqslant\varphi\leqslant\frac{k\pi}{n-1}+\frac{a}{\rho}\right\}.$$

It is not difficult to see that solutions beginning sufficiently close to $\varphi=k\pi/n-1 - a/\rho$ on the curve $\gamma_k(t_0)$ will, when t increases, leave the domain G_k, intersecting the first side wall. On the other hand, solutions beginning sufficiently close to the point $\varphi=k\pi/n-1 + a/\rho$ on the curve $\gamma_k(t_0)$ will, when t increases, leave the domain G_k through the second side wall. Let $\varphi=f_k(t_0)$ be the least upper bound of those points on the arc $\gamma_k(t_0)$ through which the solutions intersecting the first side wall with increasing t pass. It follows from continuity considerations that the solution with initial data $t=t_0$, $r=\rho$, $\varphi=f_k(t_0)$ remains in G_k for all $t>t_0$ for which it is defined. We will show that the arc $\gamma_k(t_0)$ has only one point with such properties. Assume to the contrary that there exist φ_{10} and φ_{20} on $\gamma_k(t_0)$ such that the solutions $t=t_1(r)$, $\varphi=\varphi_1(r)$ and $t=t_2(r)$, $\varphi=\varphi_2(r)$ of system (9.40, (9.41) with initial data $r=\rho$, $t=t_0$, $\varphi=\varphi_{10}$ and $r=\rho$, $t=t_0$, $\varphi=\varphi_{20}$, respectively, lie in G_k for all $r>\rho$. As we have just proved, this is impossible.

Thus, on the arc $\gamma_k(t_0)$ there is one and only one point $\varphi=f_k(t_0)$ such that the solution system (9.25), (9.26) lies in G_k for all $t>t_0$ for which it is defined.

The function $\varphi=f_k(t)$ satisfies a Lipschitz condition:

$$|f_k(t_1)-f_k(t_2)|<|t_1-t_2|. \tag{9.53}$$

Indeed, as we proved above, two solution of systems (9.40), (9.41) with initial data $r=\rho$, $t=t_1$ $\varphi=f_k(t_1)$ and $r=\rho_1$, $t=t_2$, $\varphi=f_k(t_2)$ can not remain in G_k as t increases if inequality (9.53) is not satisfied. It follows from the periodicity of the coefficients $p_j(t)$ that the function $f_k(t)$ is ω-periodic.

Let $r=r(t)$, $\varphi=\varphi(t)$ be the solution of systems (9.25), (9.26) with initial data $t=t_0$, $r=\rho$, $\varphi=f_k(t_0)$. It is then clear that inequality (9.34) is satisfied for this solution when t increases. Integrating (9.34), we obtain

$$\frac{1}{\rho^{n-1}}-\frac{1}{r^{n-1}}>\frac{(2-\sqrt{2})(n-1)}{2\sqrt{2}}(t-t_0).$$

It thus follows that $r(t)\to\infty$ as $t\to t_1>t_0$.

Now assume that G_k has an odd index k. As above, it turns out that on the bottom wall of this region there exists a curve $\varphi=f_k(t)$

with the following properties: The function $f_k(t)$ is ω-periodic and satisfies a Lipschitz condition. The solution curve with initial data $t=t_0$, $r=\rho$, $\varphi=f_k(t_0)$ becomes infinite as $t\to t_1$, where $t_1<t_0$, and is contained in G_k when $t_1<t<t_0$.

Consider the surface composed of the solution curves that pass through the curve $r=\rho$, $\varphi=f_k(t)$, and let Γ_k be the part of this solution surface that is located in G_k (for even k, Γ_k corresponds to increasing values of t, while for odd k, it corresponds to decreasing values). It follows from the preceding discussion that any solution beginning in G_k outside the surface Γ_k leaves G_k both when t increases and when t decreases.

We will now study the behavior of the solutions in the regions

$$H_k\left\{r>\rho,\ \frac{k\pi}{n-1}+\frac{a}{r}<\varphi<\frac{(k+1)\pi}{n-1}-\frac{a}{r}\right\}$$

that complement G_k in the exterior of the cylinder $r=\rho$. It follows from Eq. (9.26) and conditions (9.31), (9.32) that $\dot{\varphi}>0$ for even k, while for odd k we have $\dot{\varphi}<0$. We will show that every solution leaves the region H_k when time increases as well as when it decreases. In H_k, when $(k\pi/n-1)+(a/r)\leqslant\varphi\leqslant(\pi/n-1)(k+1/4)$, we have the inequality

$$\frac{dr}{d\varphi}<2r\,\frac{\cos(n-1)\varphi}{\sin(n-1)\varphi}.$$

Integrating this inequality, we obtain

$$\ln\frac{r}{r_0}<\frac{2}{n-1}\ln\frac{\sin(n-1)\varphi}{\sin(n-1)\varphi_0}.$$

Thus, r remains finite when φ increases from φ_0 to $(\pi/n-1)$ $(k+1/4)$. When $(\pi/n-1)(k+1/4)\leqslant\varphi\leqslant(k+1)/(n-1)\pi-a/r$, we have

$$\frac{dr}{d\varphi}<2r.$$

This inequality implies that when φ increases from $(\pi/n-1)$ $(k+1/4)$ to the boundary of H_k, r remains finite. A similar argument shows that r also remains finite when φ decreases in H_k. It follows from inequalities (9.31) and (9.32) that $|d\varphi/dt|>a/2$ in H_k. This shows that every solution leaves the region H_k when time increases as well as when it decreases.

Now we will estimate r on solutions contained inside H_k. When $(k\pi/n-1)+a/r\leqslant\varphi\leqslant(\pi/n-1)(k+3/4)$ we have the inequality

$$\frac{dr}{d\varphi} > -2r,$$

and, therefore, for such φ

$$r \geqslant r_0 e^{-2(\varphi-\varphi_0)} > r_0 e^{-2\pi} \tag{9.54}$$

in H_k. When $(\pi/n-1)(k+3/4) \leqslant \varphi \leqslant (k+1/n-1)\pi - a/r$ we have

$$\frac{dr}{d\varphi} > 2r \frac{\cos(n-1)\varphi}{\sin(n-1)\varphi},$$

which leads to

$$\ln \frac{r}{r_1} > \frac{2}{n-1} \ln \frac{\sin(n-1)\varphi}{\sin(n-1)\varphi_1}.$$

But $\varphi \leqslant (k+1)/(n-1)\pi - a/r$, so that, in virtue of (9.31), we can write $|\sin(n-1)\varphi| > 5(n-1)a/6r$. Further, $\varphi_1 \geqslant (\pi/n-1)(k+3/4)$ so that $|\sin(n-1)\varphi_1| \leqslant 1/\sqrt{2}$. Using these inequalities, we find that

$$r > r_1 \left[\frac{5(n-1)a}{6\sqrt{2}r}\right]^{\frac{2}{n-1}}.$$

It follows from this and (9.54) that, as φ increases inside H_k,

$$r > h \cdot r_0^{\frac{n-1}{n+1}} \tag{9.55}$$

where h is some constant independent of r_0. It is easily seen that this inequality also holds when φ decreases. Inequality (9.55) is therefore satisfied on any solution in H_k.

It follows from Eq. (9.26) and condition (9.32) that in the domain H_k with even k we have the inequality

$$\frac{dt}{d\varphi} < \frac{2}{r^{n-1}\sin(n-1)\varphi} \tag{9.56}$$

whereas for odd k

$$\frac{dt}{d\varphi} > \frac{2}{r^{n-1}\sin(n-1)\varphi}. \tag{9.57}$$

Let k be an even number and consider the solution of our system with the initial data $t=t_0$, $\varphi=\varphi_0$, $r=r_0$ in H_k. Inequality (9.55) is satisfied for the entire time that this solution remains in H_k. Set $r_m = hr_0^{\frac{n-1}{n+1}}$; then (9.56) yields the inequality

$$\frac{dt}{d\varphi} < \frac{2}{r_m^{n-1} \sin(n-1)\varphi}$$

Integrating this inequality, we obtain

$$t - t_0 < \frac{2}{r_m^{n-1}} \ln \frac{\tan(n-1)\frac{\varphi}{2}}{\tan(n-1)\frac{\varphi_0}{2}}. \tag{9.58}$$

But in H_k we have $\varphi_0 \geqslant (k\pi/n-1) + a/r_0$, so that $\tan(n-1)(\varphi_0/2) \geqslant (n-1)a/2r_0$. In this region $\varphi \leqslant (k+1)\pi/n-1 - a/r$. Assuming that ρ is sufficiently large, we can write $\tan(n-1)(\varphi/2) \leqslant 4r_0/a(n-1)$. It follows then from (9.58) that

$$t - t_0 < \frac{2}{r_m^{n-1}} \ln \frac{8r_0^2}{a(n-1)} \tag{9.59}$$

From this inequality it follows that if $r_0 \to \infty$, the time that the solution remains in H_k will approach zero. Similarly, inequality (9.57) can be used to prove the same statement for H_k with odd k.

Summarizing what we have said about the behavior of solutions of systems (9.25), (9.26) in the neighborhood of the point at infinity, we can say: On the bottom wall of each domain G_k there exists a curve $r=\rho$, $\varphi=f_k(t)$ (f_k satisfies a Lipschitz condition and is ω-periodic) through which the solution surface Γ_k, entirely contained in G_k, passes. Any solution on Γ_k becomes infinite at some finite value of t; if k is even, this occurs when t increases, while if k is odd, it occurs when t decreases. If the solution has a point in the region $r \geqslant \rho$ that does not lie on one of the solution surfaces Γ_k, then it leaves the region $r \geqslant \rho$ both, upon increase and decrease in t. Any solution that becomes infinite at a finite value of t passes through one of the curves $\varphi=f_k(t)$, and, consequently, is located on one of the surfaces Γ_k. If the point (t_0, φ_0, r_0) is in H_k, then the time during which the solution with initial data (t_0, φ_0, r_0) remains in H_k approaches zero as $r_0 \to \infty$.

8. Herein, we will compare different equations of the form (9.13) having complex x with a view to determining the number of periodic (with period ω) solutions. In connection with this, it is desirable to introduce the space of such equations. Consider the space R_n of vector functions $P(t)=\{p_1(t), \ldots, p_n(t)\}$. We will frequently refer to the points of this space as equations, because the vector $P(t)$ defines Eq. (9.13). We will characterize the space R_n by the following symbols: ω—the period of all points P of this space, L—the Lipschitz constant of condition (9.28), and the numbers $M_1, \ldots, M_n$ appearing in estimates (9.29). Thus, by $R_n(\omega, L, M_1, \ldots, M_n)$ we will mean the space of all ω-periodic vector functions $P(t)$ satisfying

conditions (9.28) and (9.29). By the distance between two points $P_1 = \{p_1^{(1)}(t), \ldots, p_n^{(1)}(t)\}$ and $P_2 = \{p_1^{(2)}(t), \ldots, p_n^{(2)}(t)\}$ we will mean the quantity

$$\|P_2 - P_1\| = \max_{\substack{i=1,\ldots,n \\ 0 \leqslant t \leqslant \omega}} \{ | p_i^{(2)}(t) - p_i^{(1)}(t) | \}. \tag{9.60}$$

We begin with a point-by-point discussion of the points in the space R_n. The periodic solutions and their initial data will, generally speaking, vary. These periodic solutions may even vanish, if the corresponding zeros of the function $q(c)$ approach singular points of this function, i.e., approach points through which solutions that cannot be continued to the entire period pass. In such cases the periodic solutions will approach certain systems of solutions that become infinite both, when t increases and when it decreases. The systems of solutions approached by vanishing periodic solutions will be called singular periodic solutions. The following definition provides a rigorous statement of this notion.

Definition 9.1. Assume that there exists $s+1\,(s \geqslant 1)$ numbers $t_0 < t_1 < \ldots < t_s$ such that $t_s - t_0 = \omega$ and such that a solution $x = x_i(t)$ which becomes infinite both when $t \to t_{i-1}$, and $t \to t_i$ is defined in each of the intervals (t_{i-1}, t_i); in that case, if $x_i(t)$ becomes infinite when $t \to t_i$ and remains in G_k (i.e., lies on Γ_k) for t sufficiently close to t_i, then $x_{i+1}(t)$ becomes infinite for $t \to t_i$ and remains in G_{k-1} or G_{k+1} (either on Γ_{k-1} or Γ_{k+1}) for t sufficiently close to t_i; when $i = s$, x_1 plays the role of $x_{s+1}(t)$. Because the coefficients $p_j(t)$ of Eq. (9.13) are periodic, it follows that the system of solutions $x_i(t)$ $(i = 1, \ldots, s)$ repeats when $t_0 + l\omega \leqslant t \leqslant t_0 + (l+1)\omega$ where l is an integer. The system of solutions which we have described will be called singular periodic solutions of Eq. (9.13).

We will now show that when a periodic solution of Eq. (9.13) vanishes as the coefficients $p_j(t)$ are varied, it approaches a singular periodic solution.

Theorem 9.8. Let $P_0 \in R_n$; if for any ε and N there exists a $P \in R_n$ satisfying the inequality $\|P - P_0\| < \varepsilon$ and having a periodic solution $x = x(t)$ such that $\max |x(t)| > N$, then P_0 has a singular periodic solution.

Proof. Select a sequence of equations P_k such that

$$\lim_{k\to\infty} \|P_k - P_0\| = 0 \tag{9.61}$$

and each of the equations P_k has a periodic solution $x_k(t)$; here

$$\lim_{k\to\infty} \max |x_k(t)| = \infty. \tag{9.62}$$

It follows from the preceding discussion that each of these periodic solutions has a point in the cylinder $|x| \leqslant \rho$. But then, in virtue of the Bolzano-Weierstrass theorem, we can assume that for $k \to \infty$ and $0 \leqslant t_0 < \omega$ there exists a sequence $t_k \to t_0$ such that $\lim_{k \to \infty} x_k(t_k) = x_0$, $|x_0| \leqslant \rho_1$. Then from the continuity of solutions with respect to initial data and with respect to the coefficients of Eq. (9.13), combined with the preceding considerations, it follows that a singular periodic solution of the equation P_0 passes through the point (t_0, x_0).

The follcwing statement also follows from the preceding considerations.

Theorem 9.9. If $P_\nu \in R_n$, $P_\nu \to P_0$ as $\nu \to \infty$, and P_ν has a singular periodic solution for all ν, then P_0 also has a singular periodic solution.

Theorem 9.10. If an equation P has an infinite number of periodic solutions, then it also has a singular periodic solution.

Proof. It is not difficult to see that if P has infinitely many periodic solutions, the moduli of all periodic solutions of this equation can not be bounded by the same number. Consequently, the hypothesis of Theorem 9.8 is satisfied, and our assertion follows.

Let $A \subset R_n$ denote the set of solutions without singular periodic solutions, and let B denote its complement in R_n. It follows from Theorem 9.9 that set B is closed in R_n, and A is open.

Definition 9.2. By the multiplicity of a periodic solution of Eq. (9.13) we will mean the multiplicity of its values with $t = 0$ as zeros of the function $q(c)$.

Theorems 9.8–9.10 make it possible to prove the following statement about the number of periodic solutions of "neighboring" equations.

Theorem 9.11. Let $P_0 \in A$; then there exists an $\varepsilon > 0$ such that, if $\|P - P_0\| < \varepsilon$, the equations P and P_0 have the same number of periodic solutions, taking into account the multiplicity of each solution.

Proof. From Theorem 9.5 it follows that there exists an $\varepsilon > 0$ and an $N > 0$ such that for all periodic solutions $x(t)$ of all equations in the set $\|P_0 - P\| < \varepsilon$ we have the inequality

$$|x(t)| < N. \tag{9.63}$$

Let $q_P(c)$ be the function q for the equation P. It follows from inequality (9.63) that every zero of each of the functions $q_P(c)$ is located in the region $|c| \leqslant N$. Moreover, it follows from this inequality that there exists a $\delta > 0$ such that all zeros of each function $q_P(c)$ are at a distance greater than δ from the boundary of the domain of definition of the function $q_P(c)$. It then follows from Rouché's theorem that all functions $q_P(c)$ with $\|P - P_0\| < \varepsilon$ have the same number of zeros if the multiplicity of each zero is taken into account, which proves Theorem 9.11.

Corollary. Every component of the set A consists of equations having the same number of periodic solutions if the multiplicity of each is taken into account.

When the set A coincides with the entire space R_n, i.e., if more of the equations in the space R_n has a singular periodic solution, all equations of the space have the same number of periodic solutions. But the space R_n must contain the equation

$$\frac{dx}{dt} = x^n \tag{9.64}$$

which has one periodic solution $x = 0$ of multiplicity n. In this case, therefore, all equations of R_n have n periodic solutions, if the multiplicity of each solution is taken into account. This argument makes it possible to prove the following two theorems.

Theorem 9.12. Assume that the space R_n is such that none of its equations has solutions which become infinite for increasing as well as for decreasing time in the course of a period, i.e., assume that there are no solutions $x(t)$ such that $x(t) \to \infty$ as $t \to t_1$ $x(t) \to \infty$ when $t \to t_2$, and $0 < t_2 - t_1 \leqslant \omega$. Then all equations of the space R_n have exactly n periodic solutions, if the multiplicity of each solution is taken into account.

In order to prove this proposition, we need only remark that, in the case under discussion, none of the equations in the space R_n has singular periodic solution, i.e., $R_n = A$.

It is not difficult to see Theorem 9.12 (we will not dwell on this) to prove the following proposition. Assume that in Eq. (9.13) we have $|p_i(t)| \leqslant M$ $(i = 1, \ldots, n)$

$$\omega \leqslant \frac{2\sqrt{2}}{(n-1)(1+\sqrt{2})\beta^{n-1}}$$

where β is the positive root of the equation

$$\beta^n = M\sqrt{2}(\beta^{n-1} + \beta^{n-2} + \ldots + \beta + 1).$$

Then Eq. (9.13) has exactly n periodic solutions, taking into account the multiplicity of each.

Theorem 9.13. Abel's equation ($n = 3$) *with real coefficients has exactly three periodic solutions, taking into account the multiplicity of each.*

Proof. We will show that the conditions of the preceding theorem are satisfied in the present case. Assume that a solution $x(t)$ becomes infinite as time increases. Then, as previously shown, $x(t)$

has points either on Γ_0 or Γ_2. But Γ_0 and Γ_2, as we can readily see, constitute part of the plane of real x. Consequently, the solution $x(t)$ is real, and, therefore, since k is odd, it can not become infinite as time decreases. Q.E.D.

9. We will now give an example of an equation with $n=4$ that has no less than five different periodic solutions. Consider the equation

$$\frac{dx}{dt}=x^4+[(2+\mu_1)\cos t+\cos 2t+\mu_2]\,x^3+ \\ +(\sin t+\mu_3)\,x^2+\mu_4 x, \qquad (9.65)$$

where μ_1, μ_2, μ_3 and μ_4 are parameters; for this equation $\omega=2\pi$. Equation (9.65) has $x=0$ as a solution and, therefore, its solutions can be represented in the form

$$x=\sum_{\nu=1}^{\infty}\varphi_\nu(t,\ \mu_1,\ \mu_2,\ \mu_3,\ \mu_4)\,c^\nu \qquad (9.66)$$

where the $\varphi_\nu(t,\ \mu_1,\ \mu_2,\ \mu_3,\ \mu_4)$ are analytic functions of μ_1, μ_2, μ_3, and μ_4 are continuous functions of t such that $\varphi_1(0,\ \mu_1,\ \mu_2,\ \mu_3,\ \mu_4)=1$ and $\varphi_\nu(0,\ \mu_1,\ \mu_2,\ \mu_3,\ \mu_4)=0$ when $\nu\geqslant 2$. The series in the right side of (9.66) converges uniformly when $0\leqslant t\leqslant 2\pi$ and provided $|\mu_i|$ and $|c|$ are sufficiently small.

It follows from (9.66) that the function $q(c)$ for (9.65) can be represented in the form

$$q(c,\ \mu_1,\ \mu_2,\ \mu_3,\ \mu_4)=\sum_{\nu=1}^{\infty}h_\nu(\mu_1,\ \mu_2,\ \mu_3,\ \mu_4)\,c^\nu, \qquad (9.67)$$

where

$$h_1(\mu_1,\ \mu_2,\ \mu_3,\ \mu_4)=\varphi_1(2\pi,\ \mu_1,\ \mu_2,\ \mu_3,\ \mu_4)-1,$$
$$h_\nu(\mu_1,\ \mu_2,\ \mu_3,\ \mu_4)=\varphi_\nu(2\pi,\ \mu_1,\ \mu_2,\ \mu_3,\ \mu_4)\ (\nu\geqslant 2).$$

Substituting series (9.66) into Eq. (9.65), we find that

$$\varphi_1(t,\ 0,\ 0,\ 0,\ 0)=1,$$
$$\varphi_2(t,\ 0,\ 0,\ 0,\ 0)=1-\cos t,$$
$$\varphi_3(t,\ 0,\ 0,\ 0,\ 0)=(1-\cos t)^2+2\sin t+\frac{1}{2}\sin 2t,$$
$$\varphi_4(t,\ 0,\ 0,\ 0,\ 0)=(1-\cos t)^3-\sin 2t+\frac{8}{3}\sin^3 t+3\sin t,$$
$$\varphi_5'(t,\ 0,\ 0,\ 0,\ 0)=2\sin t\left[(1-\cos t)^3-\sin 2t+\frac{8}{3}\sin^3 t+\right. \\ \left.+3\sin t\right]+2\sin t(1-\cos t)\left[(1-\cos t)^2+2\sin t+\right. \\ \left.+\frac{1}{2}\sin 2t\right]+3(2\cos t+\cos 2t)(1-\cos t)^2+ \\ +3(2\cos t+\cos 2t)\left[(1-\cos t)^2+2\sin t+\frac{1}{2}\sin 2t\right]+ \\ +4(1-\cos t).$$

It thus follows that $h_1(0, 0, 0, 0)=h_2(0, 0, 0, 0)=h_3(0, 0, 0, 0)=h_4(0, 0, 0, 0)=0$, $h_5(0, 0, 0, 0)=\pi/2$.

Equation (9.65) therefore has $x=0$ as a solution of multiplicity five. We will show that the parameters μ_1, μ_2, μ_3 and μ_4 can be ordered so that Eq. (9.65) has at least five different real periodic solutions. Direct computation easily shows that $h_1(\mu_1, 0, 0, 0)=h_2(\mu_1, 0, 0, 0)=h_3(\mu_1, 0, 0, 0)=0$ and $h_4(\mu_1, 0, 0, 0)=-\mu_1\pi$. The function $q(c, \mu_1, 0, 0, 0)$ therefore has a zero of multiplicity four at the point $c=0$ and a simple zero at the point $c=c_1$, $c_1=2\mu_1+O(\mu_1^2)$.

Fix some sufficiently small μ_1. It is easily seen that $h_1(\mu_1, \mu_2, 0, 0)=h_2(\mu_1, \mu_2, 0, 0)=0$ and $h_3(\mu_1, \mu_2, 0, 0)=\mu_2$. If we choose a sufficiently small μ_2, it turns out that the function $q(c, \mu_1, \mu_2, 0, 0)$ has a zero of multiplicity three at $c=0$, a simple zero in the neighborhood of the point c_1, and one more simple zero in the neighborhood of the point $\mu_2/\mu_1\pi$. If we now fix a sufficiently small μ_2 and choose μ_3 and μ_4 similarly, we obtain an equation of the form (9.65) with four different nonzero periodic solutions. Since $x=0$ is a solution of Eq. (9.65) for all μ_1, μ_2, μ_3 and μ_4, it follows that, when the parameters are appropriately chosen, Eq. (9.65) has no less than five different real periodic solutions.

10. FIRST-ORDER EQUATIONS PERIODIC WITH RESPECT TO BOTH ARGUMENTS

In this section we will consider the first-order equation

$$\frac{d\theta}{d\varphi}=f(\varphi, \theta) \tag{10.1}$$

whose right side is periodic with respect to both arguments.

Without loss of generality, we can assume that the function $f(\varphi, \theta)$ is 2π-periodic with respect to φ and θ. Moreover, we will assume that the function f satisfies the condition required for uniqueness of solutions of Eq. (10.1).

The right side of Eq. (10.1) is periodic with respect to both arguments, and is therefore bounded, so that all solutions continue to all values of the argument between $-\infty$ and $+\infty$. Thus, any solution curve is defined for $\varphi=0$ and it is natural to consider solutions for which the initial value of one of the arguments is zero. Let $\theta=F(\varphi, \theta_0)$ be the solution of Eq. (10.1) with initial data $\varphi=0$ $\theta=\theta_0$.

We will treat the variables φ and θ as Cartesian coordinates in the plane. The direction field defined by Eq. (10.1) is 2π-periodic with respect to both arguments, and if the field is given in the square $0\leqslant\varphi<2\pi$, $0\leqslant\theta<2\pi$, then it is known in the remainder of the plane because of periodicity. It is therefore natural to interpret the variables φ and θ as angles; hence we have an identity among points of the form $(\varphi+2k\pi, \theta+2n\pi)$, where k and n are integers. Geometrically, such a mutual identification can be accomplished by superposition of the corresponding sides of the basic square $0\leqslant\varphi\leqslant 2\pi$, $0\leqslant\theta\leqslant 2\pi$. In consequence of such a superposition, we obtain a toroidal surface, i.e., a surface resulting from the revolution of a circle about a nonintersecting axis. Draw through this axis of revolution a pencil of planes, and choose one of these planes as the origin. We will characterize each cross section of the torus on a half-plane by the angle φ (the longitude of a point on the torus). On each cross section of the torus, choose the point farthest from the axis of rotation as the origin from which to measure the angle θ for the given cross section (the angle θ is the latitude of a point on the torus). One and only one point of the torus corresponds to each pair (φ, θ). On the other hand, each point on the torus corresponds to a set of pairs of numbers of the form $(\varphi+2k\pi, \theta+2n\pi)$ with integral k and n.

We will treat the variables φ and θ as the coordinates of points on the torus. It is then clear that one and only one solution curve passes through each point of the torus.

1. Draw some solution curve, $\theta=F(\varphi, \theta_0)$, through the zero meridian. It is possible that there exist integers p and q such that

$$F(2q\pi, \theta_0)=\theta_0+2p\pi, \tag{10.2}$$

i.e., that in completing exactly q revolutions longitudinally, the solution curve will complete exactly p-revolutions in latitude and close. In that case, we have a $2q\pi$-periodic solution. It may, of course, occur that no such integers p and q exist, and in that case the solution curve $\theta=F(\varphi, \theta_0)$ is not closed.

Example. Let $f(\varphi, \theta)=\alpha$, i.e., assume that we have the equation

$$\frac{d\theta}{d\varphi}=\alpha. \tag{10.3}$$

In the Cartesian coordinate-plane of the variables φ and θ, the solution curves of Eq. (10.3) form a system of parallel lines with slope α.

Two cases are possible:

I. $\alpha=p/q$ is a rational number. The equation of the solution curve has the form

$$\theta=\alpha\varphi+\theta_0. \tag{10.4}$$

Let $\varphi=2q\pi$; then (10.4) yields

$$\theta=\theta_0+2p\pi, \tag{10.5}$$

i.e., we have Eq. (10.2), and, consequently, all solution curves of Eq. (10.3) are closed.

II. α is an irrational number.

Consider the curve $\theta = \alpha\varphi$, i.e., the solution curve of Eq. (10.3) that passes through the point $\varphi = \theta = 0$. We will show that this curve is everywhere dense on the torus, i.e., that it passes through every neighborhood of every point on the torus.

We will first show that the set of points of the intersection between the curve $\theta = \alpha\varphi$ and the zero meridian is everywhere dense on it. Choose an arbitrary point on the zero meridian, $\varphi = 0$, $\theta = \beta$ $(0 \leqslant \beta < 2\pi)$. The points with coordinates $(2q\pi,\ 2p\pi + \beta)$ on the plane all correspond to this point on the torus. Now choose an arbitary $\varepsilon > 0$ and consider the latitude of the intersection between the trajectory $\theta = \alpha\varphi$ and the zero meridian: This intersection will occur at $0,\ 2\pi\alpha,\ 4\pi\alpha,\ \ldots$. In addition, consider the system of numbers denoting the latitude of the point $(0,\ \beta)$: $\beta,\ \beta + 2\pi,\ \beta + 4\pi,\ \ldots$. We have therefore two arithmetic progressions with the ratio of their common differences equal to an irrational number α. By Lemma 1.1, there exists two numbers M and N, such that

$$|\beta + 2M\pi - 2N\pi\alpha| < \varepsilon \qquad (10.6)$$

this also means that after N longitudinal revolutions, the solution curve $\theta = \alpha\varphi$ intersects an ε-neighborhood of the point $(0,\ \beta)$.

The point $(0,\ \beta)$ was taken on the zero meridian. Now consider an arbitrary point $(\gamma,\ \beta)$. Assume that the solution of our equation that passes through this point is $\theta = \alpha\varphi + \beta - \gamma\alpha$. It has been shown that the trajectory $\theta = \alpha\varphi$ passes through any neighborhood of every point on the zero meridian, in particular, through an ε-neighborhood of the point $(0,\ \beta - \gamma\alpha)$. It is therefore clear that the solution curve $\theta = \alpha\varphi$ passes through an ε-neighborhood of $(\alpha,\ \beta)$.

We have thus shown that the curve $\theta = \alpha\varphi$ is everywhere dense on the torus.

2. We now turn to the study of Eq. (10.1) in general form. Points in the plane $(\varphi,\ \theta)$ with coordinates which are integral multiples of 2π will be called corner points. The corner point $(2q\pi,\ 2p\pi)$ will be characterized by the pair $(q,\ p)$.

Consider the solution curve of Eq. (10.1) that passes through the origin, i.e., the curve $\theta = F(\varphi,\ 0)$. We will investigate the position of the corner points of the plane relative to the curve $\theta = F(\varphi,\ 0)$. If this curve passes through at least one corner point besides the origin, then the curve is closed on the torus, since we have

$$F(2q\pi,\ 0) = 2p\pi. \qquad (10.7)$$

If (10.7) is satisfied, then the solution curve $\theta = F(\varphi,\ 0)$ passes through any corner point with coordinates $(2nq\pi,\ 2np\pi)$, since the direction field is periodic.

Assume that the point $P_1(q, p)$ is above the curve $\theta = F(\varphi, 0)$. We will show that in such a case the point $P_2(2q, 2p)$ also lies above this curve. Draw through the point P_1 a solution curve of Eq. (10.1) $\theta = \theta(\varphi)$; because of the uniqueness of solutions, this curve is above the curve $\theta = F(\varphi, 0)$, i.e., we have the inequality $\theta(\varphi) > F(\varphi, 0)$ and, in particular,

$$\theta(4q\pi) > F(4q\pi, 0). \tag{10.8}$$

But the curve $\theta = \theta(\varphi)$ passes through a corner point, and, because the direction field is periodic with respect to both arguments, it is congruent to the curve $\theta = F(\varphi, 0)$. Consequently, the point $P_2(2q, 2p)$ is above the curve $\theta = \theta(\varphi)$, i.e.,

$$4p\pi > \theta(4q\pi). \tag{10.9}$$

Thus it follows from (10.8) that

$$4p\pi > F(4q\pi, 0). \tag{10.10}$$

Inequality (10.10) means that the point P_2 is above the curve $\theta = F(\varphi, 0)$. By repeating this argument, we can show that for all natural n, the point $P_n(nq, np)$ lies above the curve $\theta = F(\varphi, 0)$.

By reversing the inequality sign in the preceding argument and replacing the word "above" by the word "below," we can show that if a point $P_1(q, p)$ lies below the curve $\theta = F(\varphi, 0)$, then for any natural n, the point $P_n(nq, np)$ also lies below this curve.

Now let the numbers q and p be representable in the form $q = kq_1$, $p = kp_1$, where k is a natural number, and assume that the point $P(q\ \ p)$ is above the curve $\theta = F(\varphi, 0)$; then the point $P_1(q_1, p_1)$ will also be above this curve. Indeed, assume that this is not so; then one of two cases must occur:

I. P_1 lies below the curve $\theta = F(\varphi, 0)$. But then, according to what we have proved, $P(kq_1, kp_1)$ also lies below this curve, which contradicts the hypothesis.

II. P_1 lies on the curve $\theta = F(\varphi, 0)$. But then, on account of periodicity, P also lies on $\theta = F(\varphi, 0)$, which also contradicts the hypothesis.

Thus, if $P(q, p)$ is above the curve $\theta = F(\varphi, 0)$, then $P_1(q_1, p_1)$ is also above this curve.

Similarly, we can show that if $P(q, p)$ is below the curve $\theta = F(\varphi, 0)$ or on it, the point $P(q_1, p_1)$ has the same disposition.

Thus, whether or not a point $P(q, p)$ is above, below or on the curve $\theta = F(\varphi, 0)$ depends only on the ratio p/q.

Partition the rational numbers into two classes as follows:

I. A rational number p/q will be placed in the first class if the point $P(q, p)$ lies above the curve $\theta = F(\varphi, 0)$ or on it.

II. A rational number p/q will be placed in the second class if the point $P(q, p)$ lies below the curve $\theta = F(\varphi, 0)$.

Both of these classes are nonempty, and every rational number belongs to either one or the other. We will show that every number in the first class is larger than every number in the second. In order to do so, it is sufficient to show that if $p/q < p'/q'$ and $2p\pi \geqslant F(2q\pi, 0)$, then $2\pi p' > F(2q'\pi, 0)$. On the basis of what we have proved above, the corner point (qq', pq') is above the curve $\theta = F(\varphi, 0)$ or on it, but the point $(qq', p'q)$ has the same abcissa and a larger ordinate, so that it lies above the curve $\theta = F(\varphi, 0)$. Hence, $2p'\pi > F(2q'\pi, 0)$.

Thus, we have a Dedekind cut in the rational numbers. Denote the number which it defines by μ. This number will be called the turning point of Eq. (10.1).

Theorem 10.1. The following limit relation holds for any θ_0:

$$\lim_{\varphi \to +\infty} \frac{F(\varphi, \theta_0)}{\varphi} = \mu. \tag{10.11}$$

Proof. We will first prove the following special case of relation (10.11):

$$\lim_{n \to \infty} \frac{F(2n\pi, 0)}{2n\pi} = \mu. \tag{10.12}$$

Choose an $\varepsilon > 0$, a natural number N such that $2/N < \varepsilon$, and an integer m such that the following inequalities are satisfied:

$$\frac{m-1}{N} < \mu < \frac{m+1}{N}. \tag{10.13}$$

By the definition of μ, the corner point $P_1(N, m-1)$ is below the curve $\theta = F(\varphi, 0)$, and $P_2(N, m+1)$ is above the curve. Thus, we have the inequalities

$$2(m-1)\pi < F(2N\pi, 0) < 2(m+1)\pi.$$

By dividing these inequalities by $2N\pi$ and subtracting the result from (10.13), we obtain

$$-\frac{2}{N} < \mu - \frac{F(2N\pi, 0)}{2N\pi} < \frac{2}{N}. \tag{10.14}$$

Then, by the definition of N, we obtain the inequality

$$\left| \mu - \frac{F(2N\pi, 0)}{2N\pi} \right| < \varepsilon. \tag{10.15}$$

Since N is an arbitrary sufficiently large natural number, the last inequality proves (10.12).

We will now prove that

$$\lim_{\varphi\to+\infty}\frac{F(\varphi,\ 0)}{\varphi}=\mu. \tag{10.16}$$

Choose an arbitrary number φ, which can be written in the form $\varphi=2\pi n+\varphi'$, where $\varphi'\in[0,\ 2\pi)$. Integrating Eq. (10.1), we find that

$$\theta=F(\varphi,\ 0)=F(2n\pi,\ 0)+\int_{2n\pi}^{\varphi}f(\varphi,\ \theta)\,d\varphi. \tag{10.17}$$

Since $f(\varphi,\ \theta)$ is periodic with respect to both arguments, there exists an integer M such that $|f(\varphi,\ \theta)|<M$. If we set

$$\theta'=\int_{2n\pi}^{\varphi}f(\varphi,\ \theta)\,d\varphi$$

then it is clear that $|\theta'|<M\varphi'<M2\pi$;

$$\frac{F(\varphi,\ 0)}{\varphi}=\frac{F(2n\pi,\ 0)+\theta'}{2n\pi+\varphi'}=\frac{\dfrac{F(2n\pi,\ 0)}{2n\pi}+\dfrac{\theta'}{2n\pi}}{1+\dfrac{\varphi'}{2n\pi}}. \tag{10.18}$$

If we let $\varphi\to+\infty$, then n will also approach $+\infty$, but φ' and θ' will remain bounded. Expression (10.16) then follows from (10.12).

Now consider the three solution curves $\theta=F(\varphi,\ 0)$, $\theta=F(\varphi,\ \theta_0)$, and $\theta=F(\varphi,\ 2k\pi)$, where k is a natural number such that $0\leqslant\theta_0\leqslant 2k\pi$.

Because the direction field is periodic, we have

$$F(\varphi,\ 2k\pi)=F(\varphi,\ 0)+2k\pi.$$

Since the solution curves of Eq. (10.1) do not intersect, we have the inequalities

$$F(\varphi,\ 0)\leqslant F(\varphi_0,\ 0)\leqslant F(\varphi,\ 2k\pi)=F(\varphi,\ 0)+2k\pi.$$

Dividing these by φ and letting $\varphi\to+\infty$, we obtain (10.11), with the aid of (10.16). Q.E.D.

3. The behavior of the solutions of Eq. (10.1) depends largely on the turning point, and a very important role is played by the arithmetic nature of this number. We will show that if Eq. (10.1) has a closed solution curve on the torus, then the turning point is rational.

Theorem 10.2. If Eq. (10.1) has a closed solution curve on the torus and this curve, prior to closure, makes q longitudinal and p latitudinal rotations, i.e., if

$$F(2q\pi, \theta_0) = \theta_0 + 2p\pi, \tag{10.19}$$

then the turning point $\mu = p/q$.

Proof. From (10.19) and the periodicity of the direction field it follows that

$$F(2qn\pi, \theta_0) = \theta_0 + 2pn\pi \tag{10.20}$$

for any integer n. Dividing Eq. (10.20) by $2qn\pi$ and passing to the limit as $n \to +\infty$, we obtain

$$\lim_{n \to \infty} \frac{F(2qn\pi, \theta_0)}{2qn\pi} = \frac{p}{q}. \tag{10.21}$$

It follows then from (10.11) that $\mu = p/q$. Q.E.D.

This theorem implies:

Corollary 10.1. Assume that Eq. (10.1) has two periodic solutions, i.e., let

$$F(2q_1\pi, \theta_1) = 2p_1\pi + \theta_1, \quad F(2q_2\pi, \theta_2) = 2p_2\pi + \theta_2,$$

then $p_1/q_1 = p_2/q_2 = \mu$.

Theorem 10.2 shows that if Eq. (10.1) has a closed solution curve, then its turning point is rational. We will now prove the converse.

Theorem 10.3. If the turning point μ is rational, i.e., if $\mu = p/q$, where p and q are relatively prime, then there exists at least one solution curve which is closed on the torus and which prior to closure, completes q longitudinal and p latitudinal rotations.

Proof. We begin by introducing the function

$$v(\theta_0) = F(2q\pi, \theta_0) - 2p\pi - \theta_0.$$

It follows from the definition of the function v that the zeros of this function determine the closed solution curves. Because the solutions depend continuously on the initial data, the function $v(\theta_0)$ is continuous. From the periodicity of f, it follows that this function is 2π-periodic.

Contrary to the assertion of the theorem, assume that Eq. (10.1) has no solution curves which are closed on the torus and which prior to closure, complete q longitudinal and p latitudinal rotations, i.e., assume that for any θ_0

$$v(\theta_0) = F(2q\pi, \theta_0) - 2p\pi - \theta_0 \neq 0. \tag{10.22}$$

Because $v(\theta_0)$ is continuous, it follows from (10.22) that $v(\theta_0)$ maintains constant sign. For definiteness, assume that $v(\theta_0) > 0$ and set $\alpha = \inf v(\theta_0)$. Since $v(\theta_0)$ is a continuous periodic function, $\alpha > 0$. By the definition of α, we have

$$v(\theta_0) \geqslant \alpha > 0. \tag{10.23}$$

By the definition of $v(\theta_0)$, inequality (10.23) yields

$$F(2q\pi, \theta_0) > 2p\pi + \theta_0 + \alpha. \tag{10.24}$$

Set $F(2q\pi, \theta_0) = \theta_1$. Then we can write

$$F(2q\pi, \theta_1) > 2p\pi + \theta_1 + \alpha, \tag{10.25}$$

since θ_0 in inequality (10.24) is arbitrary. It follows from the periodicity of the right side of Eq. (10.1) that

$$F(2q\pi, \theta_1) = F(4q\pi, \theta_0). \tag{10.26}$$

Substituting for θ_1 and $F(2q\pi, \theta_1)$ in inequality (10.25), we find that

$$F(4q\pi, \theta_0) > 2p\pi + F(2q\pi, \theta_0) + \alpha.$$

Combining this with (10.24) yields

$$F(4q\pi, \theta_0) > 4p\pi + 2\alpha + \theta_0. \tag{10.27}$$

We will now show that for any n

$$F(2nq\pi, \theta_0) > 2np\pi + n\alpha + \theta_0. \tag{10.28}$$

Assume that this inequality is satisfied for some n, and set $F(2nq\pi, \theta_0) = \theta_n$. Then it follows from (10.24) that

$$F(2q\pi, \theta_n) > 2p\pi + \theta_n + \alpha.$$

But $F(2q\pi, \theta_n) = F(2q(n+1)\pi, \theta_0)$. Consequently,

$$F(2(n+1)q\pi, \theta_0) > 2p\pi + F(2qn\pi, \theta_0) + \alpha$$

This, combined with (10.28), implies that

$$F(2(n+1)q\pi, \theta_0) > 2(n+1)p\pi + (n+1)\alpha + \theta_0.$$

By the principle of mathematical induction, this last inequality proves inequality (10.28).

Divide inequality (10.28) by $2nq\pi$:

$$\frac{F(2nq\pi, \theta_0)}{2nq\pi} > \frac{p}{q} + \frac{\alpha}{2q\pi} + \frac{\theta_0}{2qn\pi}.$$

Passing to the limit as $n \to +\infty$, we obtain

$$\mu \geqslant \frac{p}{q} + \frac{\alpha}{2q\pi}.$$

This inequality contradicts the hypothesis that $\mu = p/q$, and the contradiction proves the theorem.

Equation (10.1) therefore has closed solution curves on the torus if and only if its turning point is rational.

4. Assume that Eq. (10.1) has a rational turning point $\mu = p/q$; then it has a closed solution curve $\theta = F(\varphi, \theta_0)$ on which the equation $F(2q\pi, \theta_0) = 2p\pi + \theta_0$ is satisfied. Consider the set K of points on the zero meridian ($\varphi = 0$) of the torus through which closed solution curves pass. As noted, this set is the set of zeros of the continuous function $v(\theta_0) = F(2q\pi, \theta_0) - 2p\pi - \theta_0$, and is therefore closed. Let M be the complement of K on the zero meridian. It is well known that the set M is the union of a finite or countable number of disjoint intervals, which will be called the co-sets of the set K. Every periodic solution intersects at least one of these intervals.

Theorem 10.4. Assume that Eq. (10.1) has a rational turning point $\mu = p/q$. Then any nonperiodic solution approaches a periodic solution as $\varphi \to +\infty$, and some (possibly different) periodic solution as $\varphi \to -\infty$.

Proof. If we consider a periodic solution $\theta = F(\varphi, \theta')$ of our equation, then $\theta' \in M$. Let $\theta' \in (\theta_1, \theta_2)$ where (θ_1, θ_2) is a co-set of the set K, i.e., no point inside this interval belongs to K, but its ends, the points θ_1 and θ_2, belong to K. Above, introduce the following function of the points on the zero meridian:

$$v(\theta_0) = F(2q\pi, \theta_0) - 2p\pi - \theta_0.$$

For definiteness, assume that $v(\theta_0) > 0$ when $\theta_0 \in (\theta_1, \theta_2)$. Then we will show that

$$\lim_{\varphi \to -\infty} [F(\varphi, \theta_1) - F(\varphi, \theta')] = 0 \tag{10.29}$$

and

$$\lim_{\varphi \to +\infty} [F(\varphi, \theta_2) - F(\varphi, \theta')] = 0 \tag{10.30}$$

this will prove the theorem.

Choose an arbitrary point $\bar{\theta} \in (\theta_1, \theta_2)$. We will show that $F(2q\pi, \bar{\theta})$ belongs to the interval (θ_1, θ_2). Indeed, because of the uniqueness of solutions, the inequalities

$$\theta_1 < \bar{\theta} < \theta_2$$

imply that

$$F(\varphi, \theta_1) < F(\varphi, \bar{\theta}) < F(\varphi, \theta_2) \tag{10.31}$$

and, in particular, that

$$F(2q\pi, \theta_1) < F(2q\pi, \bar{\theta}) < F(2q\pi, \theta_2).$$

But, by hypothesis, θ_1 and θ_2 belong to K, so that

$$F(2q\pi, \theta_i) = 2p\pi + \theta_i \quad (i = 1, 2).$$

We thus obtain the inequalities

$$\theta_1 + 2p\pi < F(2q\pi, \bar{\theta}) < \theta_2 + 2p\pi \tag{10.32}$$

which show that the point $F(2q\pi, \bar{\theta})$ belongs to the interval (θ_1, θ_2).

We will now show that

$$F(2qn\pi, \theta') - 2pn\pi \xrightarrow[n \to +\infty]{} \theta_2. \tag{10.33}$$

The solutions $F(\varphi, \theta_1)$ and $F(\varphi, \theta_2)$ are periodic, so that for any integral n $F(2qn\pi, \theta_i) = 2pn\pi + \theta_i$ $(i = 1, 2)$. Then it follows from **(10.31)** that

$$\theta_1 < F(2qn\pi, \theta') - 2pn\pi < \theta_2. \tag{10.34}$$

By the definition of the function v, we have

$$\begin{aligned} v(F(2qn\pi, \theta')) &= F(2q(n+1)\pi, \theta') - F(2qn\pi, \theta') - 2p\pi = \\ &= [F(2q(n+1)\pi, \theta') - 2p(n+1)\pi] - \\ &\quad - [F(2qn\pi, \theta') - 2pn\pi] > 0. \end{aligned} \tag{10.35}$$

Thus it follows from **(10.34)** that the limit

$$\lim_{n \to \infty} [F(2qn\pi, \theta') - 2pn\pi] = \theta^* \in [\theta_1, \theta_2] \tag{10.36}$$

exists.

We will now show that $\theta^* = \theta_2$. Assume to the contrary that $\theta^* < \theta_2$; it is then clear that $[\theta', \theta^*] \subset (\theta_1, \theta_2)$. But the function v is continuous, so that $v \geqslant \alpha > 0$ on the segment $[\theta', \theta^*]$. Let $N > (\theta^* - \theta')/\alpha$. It follows from relations (10.35) and (10.36) that for all integral $n \geqslant 0$ the following inequalities hold:

$$\theta' \leqslant F(2qn\pi, \theta') - 2pn\pi < \theta^*. \tag{10.37}$$

Consequently,

$$F(2q(n+1)\pi, \theta') - F(2qn\pi, \theta') - 2p\pi \geqslant \alpha > 0.$$

Summing this inequality over all n from 0 to N, we find that

$$F(2q(N+1)\pi, \theta') - 2p(N+1)\pi - \theta' \geqslant N\alpha,$$

which, in virtue of the definition of N, contradicts inequality (10.37). This contradiction thus obtained shows that $\theta^* = \theta_2$, and, therefore, relation (10.33) is proved.

Now choose an arbitrary $\varepsilon > 0$. Because the right side of Eq. (10.1) is periodic and the solutions are continuous functions of the initial data, there exists for this ε a $\delta > 0$ such that if $|\theta^{(1)} - \theta^{(2)}| < \delta$ then $|F(\varphi, \theta^{(1)}) - F(\varphi, \theta^{(2)})| < \varepsilon$ when $\varphi \in [0, 2q\pi]$. In virtue of expression (10.33), we can find for this δ a k_0 such that when $k > k_0$

$$\theta_2 - F(2qk\pi, \theta_0) + 2pk\pi < \delta. \tag{10.38}$$

Then it follows from the definition of δ that

$$|F(\varphi, \theta') - F(\varphi, \theta_2)| < \varepsilon \quad \text{for} \quad \varphi \in [2qk\pi, 2q(k+1)\pi].$$

But in (10.38), k is an arbitrary integer larger than k_0; thus, the last inequality also indicates that (10.30) is satisfied. Equation (10.29) can be proved similarly. Q.E.D.

We note the following two corollaries of Theorem 10.4.

Corollary 10.2. If an isolated periodic solution of Eq. (10.1) is Lyapunov-stable, then it is asymptotically stable.

Corollary 10.3. An isolated periodic solution is the limit either as $\varphi \to +\infty$ or $\varphi \to -\infty$ of all solutions beginning in a sufficiently small neighborhood of it.

5. In defining the turning point, we discussed the distribution of ntegral (mod 2π) points relative to the initial trajectory $\theta = F(\varphi, 0)$. This distribution can be used to study the relationship between p/q and the turning point μ. It turns out that the distribution of points of the form $(2q\pi, 2p\pi + \theta_0)$ relative to the solution curve $\theta = F(\varphi, \theta_0)$ can also be used to study this relation. We will prove:

Lemma 10.1. Let μ be the turning point of Eq. (10.1). If the point $(2q\pi, 2p\pi + \theta_0)$ is below the solution curve $\theta = F(\varphi, \theta_0)$ or on it, then

$p/q \leqslant \mu$, and, conversely, if the point $(2q\pi, 2p\pi+\theta_0)$ *is above the curve* $\theta=F(\varphi, \theta_0)$ *or on it, then* $p/q \geqslant \mu$.

Proof. In Eq. (10.1), make the substitution $\vartheta=\theta-\theta_0$; then it takes the form

$$\frac{d\vartheta}{d\varphi}=f(\varphi, \vartheta+\theta_0). \tag{10.39}$$

The function $\vartheta=F(\varphi, \theta_0)-\theta_0$ is a solution of Eq. (10.39). It follows then from Theorem 10.1 that the turning points of Eqs. (10.1) and (10.39) coincide. But the curve $\vartheta=F(\varphi, \theta_0)-\theta_0$ is the initial solution curve of Eq. (10.39), because $F(0, \theta_0)=\theta_0$. Then, by the definition of the turning point μ, we have: If $2p\pi \leqslant F(2q\pi, \theta_0)-\theta_0$, then $p/q \leqslant \mu$, while if $2p\pi \geqslant F(2q\pi, \theta_0)-\theta_0$, then $p/q \geqslant \mu$. Q.E.D.

We will now study the case in which Eq. (10.1) has an irrational turning point. As Theorem 10.2 implies, all solution curves on the torus are open.

Hereafter, we will use the following terminology. Through a point θ_0 of the zero meridian, draw the solution $\theta=F(\varphi, \theta_0)$. After each rotation, this solution curve will intersect the zero meridian at the points $F(2n\pi, \theta_0)$. Let θ_n be the reduced coordinate of the points $F(2n\pi, \theta_0)$, i.e., the coordinate of the points $F(2n\pi, \theta_0)$ that lies in the half-open interval $[0, 2\pi)$. We will call the points $\theta_1, \theta_2, \ldots$ successive points of θ_0. Because we have assumed that the turning point μ is irrational, the solution curve $\theta=F(\varphi, \theta_0)$ is open, and all of the points θ_k are different.

Take the point θ_0 and two of its successive points θ_{q_1} and θ_{q_2} $(0<q_1<q_2)$ on the zero meridian. We will say that θ_{q_2} follows θ_{q_1} and write $\theta_0 \prec \theta_{q_1} \prec \theta_{q_2}$ if in moving along the zero meridian in the positive direction from θ_0 we first encounter the point θ_{q_1} and then the point θ_{q_2}. Otherwise, we will say that θ_{q_1} follows θ_{q_2} and write $\theta_0 \prec \theta_{q_2} \prec \theta_{q_1}$.

It turns out that the relative locations of the points θ_0, θ_{q_1}, and θ_{q_2} depend only on the turning point and the values of q_1 and q_2. We will prove the following:

Theorem 10.5. If $(\mu q_1)<(\mu q_2)$, *then* $\theta_0 \prec \theta_{q_1} \prec \theta_{q_2}$, *and, similarly, if* $(\mu q_2)<(\mu q_1)$, *then* $\theta_0 \prec \theta_{q_2} \prec \theta_{q_1}$ [(a) *is the fractional part of the number* a].

This theorem can be formulated somewhat differently as follows: The cyclic order of the points θ_0, θ_{q_1}, and θ_{q_2} coincides with the order of the numbers 0, (μq_1), and (μq_2).

Proof. Without loss of generality, we can assume $\theta_0=0$. Generality is not disturbed by this assumption, because if $\theta_0 \neq 0$ then it is sufficient to carry out the substitution $\vartheta=\theta-\theta_0$. As shown in the proof Lemma 10.1, the turning point does not change when such a substitution is made. Moreover, because such a substitution changes only the coordinate origin, it is clear that the cyclic order of the points will not change, except that we will have $\vartheta = 0$ instead of $\theta = \theta_0$.

Thus, we must prove that if $(\mu q_1) < (\mu q_2)$, then $0 < \theta_{q_1} < \theta_{q_2}$ and, conversely, if $(q_1 \mu) > (\mu q_2)$, then $0 < \theta_{q_2} < \theta_{q_1}$.

Take a point θ_0' on the zero meridian; let $\theta_1', \theta_2', \ldots,$ be its successive points, and let p denote a number such that $F(2q\pi, \theta_0') = 2p\pi + \theta_q'$. Since μ is irrational, only one of two cases is possible: Either $\theta_0' < \theta_q'$ or $\theta_0' > \theta_q'$. First, assume that $\theta_0' < \theta_q'$. Then, by the definition of p, we have $F(2q\pi, \theta_0') > 2p\pi + \theta_0'$. In virtue of Lemma 10.1, this implies that

$$\frac{p}{q} \leqslant \mu.$$

On the other hand, by the definitions of $\theta_q' < 2\pi$ and p, we have

$$\frac{p+1}{q} \geqslant \mu.$$

Since μ is irrational, these two inequalities yield the relation

$$p < \mu q < p + 1$$

or

$$p = [\mu q]. \tag{10.40}$$

([a] is the integral part of the number a)

Now assume that the second possibility is realized: $\theta_0' > \theta_q'$. Then by the definition of p, we have $p > \mu q$ and $p - 1 < \mu q$. Consequently, in this case

$$p - 1 = [\mu q]. \tag{10.41}$$

Now let p_1 and p_2 be integers such that $F(2q_1\pi, 0) = \theta_{q_1} + 2p_1\pi$ and $F(2q_2\pi, 0) = \theta_{q_2} + 2p_2\pi$. Through the point $(0, \theta_{q_1})$, draw the solution curve $\theta = F(\varphi, \theta_{q_1})$. Since the direction field is periodic, it coincides with the segments of the curve $\theta = F(\varphi, 0)$ as φ varies between $2q_1\pi$ and $2q_2\pi$. We thus obtain the equation

$$F(2(q_2 - q_1)\pi, \theta_{q_1}) = \theta_{q_2} + 2(p_2 - p_1)\pi. \tag{10.42}$$

Now assume that $\theta_{q_2} > \theta_{q_1}$. Then, in virtue of Eq. (10.40), we have

$$p_2 - p_1 = [\mu(q_2 - q_1)]. \tag{10.43}$$

Moreover, because $\theta_{q_1} > 0$ and $\theta_{q_2} > 0$, Eq. (10.40) leads to the equations

$$p_1 = [\mu q_1], \quad p_2 = [\mu q_2]. \tag{10.44}$$

We will now estimate (μq_2). We have

$$(\mu q_2) = \mu q_2 - [\mu q_2] = \mu q_2 - p_2 = \\ = \mu (q_2 - q_1) - (p_2 - p_1) + \mu q_1 - p_1.$$

This, together with Eqs. (10.43) and (10.44), gives us

$$(\mu q_2) = \mu (q_2 - q_1) - [\mu (q_2 - q_1)] + (\mu q_1);$$

since μ is irrational, we have

$$\mu (q_2 - q_1) - [\mu (q_2 - q_1)] > 0,$$

which leads to the inequality

$$(\mu q_2) > (\mu q_1). \tag{10.45}$$

Let $\theta_{q_1} > \theta_{q_2}$. Then the relation (10.41) yields

$$p_2 - p_1 - 1 = [\mu (q_2 - q_1)]. \tag{10.46}$$

But then we have, as above,

$$(\mu q_2) = \mu q_2 - [\mu q_2] = \mu q_2 - p_2 = \mu (q_2 - q_1) - (p_2 - p_1) + \\ + \mu q_1 - p_1 = \mu (q_2 - q_1) - (p_2 - p_1) + (\mu q_1).$$

This and (10.46) imply the inequality

$$(\mu q_2) < (\mu q_1). \tag{10.47}$$

The inequality $\theta_{q_2} > \theta_{q_1}$ therefore implies (10.45), while the inequality $\theta_{q_2} < \theta_{q_1}$ implies (10.47). But then it is also clear that, conversely, inequality (10.45) implies that $\theta_{q_2} > \theta_{q_1}$, while (10.47) implies the inequality $\theta_{q_2} < \theta_{q_1}$. Q.E.D.

6. We will now introduce a transformation of the zero meridian onto itself, which we will denote by T: With each point of the zero meridian we associate the point $F(2\pi, \theta_0)$. As implied by the uniqueness and integral continuity theorems, the transformation T is one-to-one and continuous in both directions. Uniqueness also implies that this transformation preserves orientation.

Lemma 10.2. Assume that we have on the zero meridian an arc $\alpha(\theta_1 \leqslant \theta \leqslant \theta_2)$ *with the property that* $T^q\alpha \subset \alpha$, *where* q *is a natural number. Then a closed solution curve passes through some point of* α.

Proof. Since $T^q\alpha \subset \alpha$, the transformation T^q has a stationary point $\theta_0 \in \alpha$. By the definition of T, this means that there exists an integer p such that $F(2q\pi, \theta_0) = 2p\pi + \theta_0$. Consequently, the solution curve $\theta = F(\varphi, \theta_0)$ is closed.

Assuming, as before, that the turning point μ of Eq. **(10.1)** is irrational, we will now study the behavior of the trajectory $\theta = F(\varphi, 0)$. Let θ_k be the successive points of $\theta = 0$, and let P be the limit set of the sequence θ_k.

Theorem 10.6. The set P is perfect.

Proof. Because it is a limit set, P is closed. We will show that it is dense in itself. Let P' be the derived set of P, i.e., the set of all limit points in the set P. We will show that $P \subset P'$. Let $\vartheta_0 \in P$, and choose an arbitrary $\varepsilon > 0$. With regard to ε, assume that

$$\varepsilon < \min\left\{\frac{1}{3}\vartheta_0, \ \frac{1}{3}(2\pi - \vartheta_0)\right\}.$$

Since ϑ_0 is the limit of the sequence θ_k, there exist numbers $m<k<m_1<k_1$ such that $|\theta_m - \vartheta_0| < \varepsilon$, $|\theta_k - \vartheta_0| < \varepsilon$, $|\theta_{m_1} - \vartheta_0| < \varepsilon$ and $|\theta_{k_1} - \vartheta_0| < \varepsilon$. Since the turning point μ is irrational, all of the points θ_k are different, so that at least three of the four points $\theta_m, \theta_k, \theta_{m_1}$ and θ_{k_1} do not coincide with ϑ_0. Assume that these three points are θ_m, θ_k, and θ_{m_1}. Of these three points, at least two lie within one of the intervals $(\vartheta_0 - \varepsilon, \vartheta_0)$ or $(\vartheta_0, \vartheta_0 + \varepsilon)$, and, for definiteness, we will assume that θ_k and θ_m are in the interval $(\vartheta_0, \vartheta_0 + \varepsilon)$. Consider the numbers $(m\mu)$ and $(k\mu)$, and, for definiteness, assume that $(m\mu) < (k\mu)$. Then, by Theorem **10.5**, $0 \prec \theta_m \prec \theta_k$, and, in virtue of our notation, we have $\vartheta_0 < \theta_m < \theta_k < \vartheta_0 + \varepsilon$. Now choose an arbitrary number b satisfying the inequalities $(m\mu) < b < (k\mu)$, and a positive δ such that $(m\mu) < b - \delta < b + \delta < (k\mu)$. Consider the two progressions $\{b, b+1, b+2, \dots\}$ and $\{\mu, 2\mu, 3\mu, \dots\}$. By Lemma **1.1**, there exists an infinite sequence of pairs $(M_i, N_i)(i=1, 2, \dots)$ such that

$$|b + M_i - N_i\mu| < \delta.$$

It is then clear that $|(N_i\mu) - b| < \delta$, whereupon we will have, for any i, the inequalities $(m\mu) < (N_i\mu) < (k\mu)$. By Theorem **10.5**, for any i we have $\vartheta_0 < \theta_m < \theta_{N_i} < \theta_k$. Thus, in the interval $\theta_m \leqslant \theta \leqslant \theta_k$ there exists at least one point that is a limit point for the sequence θ_k. Assume that this point is ϑ_1; by definition, $\vartheta_1 \in P$. But the point ϑ_1 is in an ε-neighborhood of the point ϑ_0. Since ε is an arbitrary sufficiently small number, it follows that the point ϑ_0 is a limit point of P; but ϑ_0 is an arbitrary point of P, so that any point of P is a limit point, i.e., $P \subset P'$. Thus, the set P is dense in itself, and since it is also closed, it is perfect.

It is well known that a perfect set on a circle can only be one of the following three types: a) It coincides with the entire circle;

b) the set is nowhere dense on the circle; c) the set does not cover the entire circle, but it does contain at least one segment.

Theorem 10.7. The set P can not contain an entire segment, and it can not cover the entire circle.

Proof. Assume, contrary to the assertion of the theorem, that there exists a segment $\alpha \subset P$, and assume that α is a large segment, i.e., any neighborhood of its boundary points contains points that do not belong to P. Since $\alpha \subset P$, α contains at least two points of the sequence θ_n: θ_k and θ_m; let $m < k$. As before, let T denote the transformation that associates the point $F(2\pi, \theta_0)$ with the point θ_0. It is then clear that $T^{(k-m)}\theta_m = \theta_k$. But $\theta_m \in \alpha$ and $\theta_k \in \alpha$; consequently, $T^{(k-m)}\theta_m \in \alpha$. Consider the intersection $T^{(k-m)}\alpha \cdot \alpha$; it is nonempty because $\theta_k \in \alpha$, $\theta_k \in T^{(k-m)}\alpha$. Consider the segment consisting of the union $T^{(k-m)}\alpha + \alpha$. If this segment coincides with α, then $T^{(k-m)}\alpha \subset \alpha$. It follows then from Lemma 10.2 that there is a closed solution curve on the torus. But this is impossible, because the turning point μ is irrational. Now assume that the segment $T^{(k-m)}\alpha + \alpha$ contains α as a proper subset. It is not difficult to see that the set P is invariant under the transformation T; consequently, $T^{(k-m)}\alpha \subset P$ which means that $T^{(k-m)}\alpha \cup \alpha \subset P$. This is impossible, since we have assumed that α is a large segment. The contradiction which we have obtained proves that P can not contain an entire arc of the zero meridian without covering it entirely.

Denjoy [48] proved that if the only restriction on the function $F(2\pi, \theta_0)$ is continuity, then P can be any perfect no where dense set. If, however, we require that $F(2\pi, \theta_0)$ be sufficiently smooth, then P covers the entire zero meridian. That is, we have the following theorem, which was proved by Denjoy.

Theorem 10.8. If the function $f(\varphi, \theta)$ is continuously differentiable with respect to θ, and if the derivative $d/d\theta_0\, F(2\pi, \theta_0)$ is a function of bounded variation, then the set P covers the entire zero meridian.

Before we prove Theorem 10.8, we will prove the following lemma.

Lemma 10.3. Let μ be an irrational number; then for any n_0 there exist integers $n > n_0$ and l such that

$$|n\mu - l| < |b\mu - a| \tag{10.48}$$

for an integer b satisfying the inequality $0 < b < n$ and any integral a.

Proof of Lemma 10.3. Consider the set of numbers of the form $|b\mu - a|$, where a and b are integers and $0 < b \leqslant n_0$. It is not difficult to see that there exist only $2n_0$ pairs of integers (a, b), $0 < b \leqslant n_0$, for which the inequality $|b\mu - a| < 1$ holds. Therefore, for $0 < b \leqslant n_0$, there is an $\varepsilon = \min|b\mu - a|$, and since μ is irrational, it is clear that $\varepsilon > 0$. In virtue of Lemma 1.1, there exists for this ε a pair of integers M and N such that

$$|M\mu - N| < \varepsilon. \tag{10.49}$$

It follows from the definition of ε that $M > n_0$. Now let $\delta = \min |b\mu - a|$ for integral a and b and $0 < b \leqslant M$. Since μ is irrational, it is clear that there exists only one pair of numbers (n, l) such that $\delta = |n\mu - l|$. Clearly, these integers n and l are the ones desired.

Proof of Theorem 10.8. Contrary to the assertion of the theorem, assume that P does not cover the entire zero meridian, i.e., that it is a perfect nowhere dense set. Let α_0 be some co-set of the set P, and let ϑ_0 be a point in this co-set. As already noted, the set P is invariant under the transformation T, so that any interval of the form $T^k\alpha_0$ is a co-set of P. Therefore it follows that two intervals of the form $T^k\alpha_0$ and $T^l\alpha_0$ are disjoint if $l \neq k$. Indeed, if the intervals $T^k\alpha_0$ and $T^l\alpha_0$ were not disjoint, then the intervals α_0 and $T^{k-l}\alpha_0$ would intersect. But then the interval $\alpha_0 + T^{k-l}\alpha_0$ would coincide with α_0, because otherwise α_0 would not be a co-set of P. Thus it follows that $T^{k-l}\alpha_0 \subset \alpha_0$, and, by Lemma 10.2, Eq. (10.1) has a closed solution curve on the torus, which contradicts the assumption that the turning point is irrational.

Let n be any natural number for which inequality (10.48) is satisfied, and consider the points

$$\vartheta_{-n} = T^{-n}\vartheta_0,\ \vartheta_{-n+1} = T^{-n+1}\vartheta_0,\ \ldots,\ \vartheta_0,\ \vartheta_1 = T\vartheta_0,\ \ldots,\ \vartheta_{2n} = T^{2n}\vartheta_0$$

and the corresponding co-sets of P:

$$\alpha_{-n} = T^{-n}\alpha_0,\ \alpha_{-n+1} = T^{-n+1}\alpha_0,\ \ldots,\ \alpha_0,\ \alpha_1 = T\alpha_0,\ \ldots,\ \alpha_{2n} = T^{2n}\alpha_0.$$

For definiteness, assume that $n\mu - l > 0$. We will show that the interval between ϑ_0 and ϑ_n (with motion from ϑ_0 to ϑ_n being in the positive direction) contains no point in the form ϑ_k with $-n < k < 2n$, $k \neq 0$, $k \neq n$. Initially, assume that $0 < k < n$ and that, contrary to our assertion, $\vartheta_0 \prec \vartheta_k \prec \vartheta_n$. Then, by Theorem 10.5, we have the inequality

$$(\mu k) < (\mu n),$$

which means that there exists an integer m such that

$$0 < \mu k - m < \mu n - l,$$

and this contradicts the choice of n, because $k < n$.

Now let $k = n + q$, where $0 < q < n$. Again assuming that $\vartheta_0 \prec \vartheta_k \prec \vartheta_n$, we obtain, because of Theorem 10.5,

$$(\mu n + \mu q) < (\mu n).$$

Thus it follows that there exists an integer m such that

$$0 < \mu n + \mu q - m - l < \mu n - l$$

or

$$-\mu n + l < \mu q - m < 0.$$

This inequality also contradicts the choice of n.

Finally, let $-n < k < 0$. The assumption that $\vartheta_0 \prec \vartheta_k \prec \vartheta_n$ leads to the conclusion that $\vartheta_k \prec \vartheta_n \prec \vartheta_0$ and, if we take the point ϑ_k as the origin, Theorem 10.5 yields the inequality

$$(\mu n - \mu k) < (-\mu k),$$

which means that there exists a number m such that

$$0 < \mu n - \mu k - l - m < (-\mu k)$$

or

$$-\mu n + l < -\mu k - m < (-\mu k) - \mu n + l.$$

If $-\mu k - m < 0$, the last inequality gives us

$$-\mu n + l < -\mu k - m < 0$$

which contradicts the choice of n, because $-n < k < 0$. If, on the other hand, $-\mu k - m > 0$, we obtain the inequality

$$0 < -\mu k - m < (-\mu k) - \mu n + l,$$

and, since we have assumed that $\mu n - l > 0$, we have

$$0 < -\mu k - m < (-\mu k).$$

Clearly, the last inequality can not hold. Thus, the assumption that $\vartheta_0 \prec \vartheta_k \prec \vartheta_n$, leads to a contradiction, which proves our assertion.

Now consider two intervals α_{-n+p} and α_p, where p is an integer satisfying the inequalities $0 \leqslant p \leqslant n-1$. We will show that between them (if we move from the interval α_{-n+p} to the interval α_p in the positive direction) there is no interval α_k $(-n \leqslant k \leqslant n-1,\ k \neq -n+p,\ k \neq p)$. In order to prove this assertion, it is sufficient to show that between the points ϑ_{-n+p} and ϑ_p there is no point ϑ_k $(-n \leqslant k \leqslant n-1,\ k \neq -n+p,\ k \neq p)$. Assume that this is not so, i.e., that $\vartheta_{-n+p} \prec \vartheta_k \prec \vartheta_p$. Applying the transformation T^{n-p} to this relation, we find that $\vartheta_0 \prec \vartheta_{k+n-p} \prec \vartheta_n$. This contradicts the statement which we have just proved, since, by the choice of k and p, we have the inequalities $-n < k+n-p < n,\ k+n-p \neq 0,\ k+n-p \neq n$.

Now consider the system of intervals $\alpha_{-n}, \alpha_{-n+1}, \ldots, \alpha_0, \ldots, \alpha_{n-1}$, and choose, from within it, an interval α_{-n+p} $(0 \leqslant p \leqslant n-1)$. Then the interval closest to it (in the direction of increasing polar angles) and belonging to the system under consideration will be α_p.

Let $u(\varphi,\ \theta_0)$ denote the function $u = \partial/\partial\theta_0\, F(\varphi,\ \theta_0)$. It is well known that, under our assumptions, the function u satisfies the equation

$$\frac{du}{d\varphi} = f'_\theta(\varphi,\ F(\varphi,\ \theta_0))\, u.$$

Since $u(0,\ \theta_0) = \partial/\partial\theta_0\, F(0,\ \theta_0) = 1$, integration of the last equation yields

$$u = e^{\int_0^\varphi f'_\theta(\varphi,\ F(\varphi,\ \theta_0))\, d\varphi}$$

and, in particular,

$$u(2\pi,\ \theta_0) = e^{\int_0^{2\pi} f'_\theta(\varphi,\ F(\varphi,\ \theta_0))\, d\varphi}$$

By hypothesis, f'_θ is continuous, so that the last equation implies the existence of numbers H_1 and H_2 such that

$$0 < H_1 \leqslant u(2\pi,\ \theta_0) \leqslant H_2.$$

Consider the function

$$h(\theta_0) = \ln u(2\pi,\ \theta_0). \tag{10.50}$$

This function is bounded and, because the logarithmic function is monotonic has bounded variation. By definition, the total variation of the function $h(\theta_0)$ is

$$V = \sup \sum_{k=0}^{n-1} \left| h\left(\theta_0^{(k+1)}\right) - h\left(\theta_0^{(k)}\right) \right| \tag{10.51}$$
$$\left(\theta_0^{(0)} < \theta_0^{(1)} < \ldots < \theta_0^{(n)} = \theta_0^{(0)} + 2\pi\right).$$

Consider an interval β of length s on the zero meridian, and let the length of the interval $T\beta = \beta'$ be s'. It is then clear that

$$s' = \int_{\beta} u(2\pi, \theta_0)\, d\theta_0 = s e^{h(\tau)}, \tag{10.52}$$

where τ is some point in the interval β. In other words, for the point τ

$$h(\tau) = \ln \frac{s'}{s}. \tag{10.53}$$

Assume that the interval α_q has length s_q. Consider the point α_q lying in τ_q and having properties analogous to those of the point τ in β. We will then have

$$s_{q+1} = s_q e^{h(\tau_q)}, \quad h(\tau_q) = \ln \frac{s_{q+1}}{s_q}. \tag{10.54}$$

Now consider the amplitude of oscillation of the function $h(\theta_0)$ between the points τ_{-n+p} and τ_p; this oscillation will be equal to $[h(\tau_p) - h(\tau_{-n+p})]$. Since, as previously shown, there are no intervals of the system $\alpha_q (q = -n, -n+1, \ldots, 0, \ldots, n-1)$ between the intervals α_{-n+p} and α_p, it is clear that the sum of the absolute values of the amplitudes of such oscillations will be no greater than the total variation of the function h; consequently, we can write

$$\left| \sum_{p=0}^{n-1} h(\tau_p) - \sum_{p=0}^{n-1} h(\tau_{-n+p}) \right| \leqslant \sum_{p=0}^{n-1} |h(\tau_p) - h(\tau_{-n+p})| \leqslant V.$$

It follows then from (10.54) that

$$\left| \ln \frac{s_n}{s_0} - \ln \frac{s_0}{s_{-n}} \right| \leqslant V$$

or

$$e^{-V} \leqslant \frac{s_k s_{-n}}{s_0^2} \leqslant e^V. \tag{10.55}$$

We have shown that intervals of the form $T^k\alpha_0$ and $T^l\alpha_0$ are disjoint, so that the length s_k of the interval $T^k\alpha_0$ approaches zero as $k \to \pm\infty$. Consequently, the first of inequalities (10.55) can not be satisfied when n is sufficiently large. Since the value of n in the preceding considerations may, in accord with Lemma 10.3, be arbitrarily large, we obtain a contradiction, which proves the theorem.

Note that the function $d/d\theta_0\, F(2\pi, \theta_0)$ is of bounded variation if the variation of the function $\partial f/\partial\theta$ is uniformly bounded with respect to φ. Indeed,

$$h(\theta_0^{(k+1)}) - h(\theta_0^{(k)}) = \int_0^{2\pi} [f'_\theta(\varphi, \theta_0^{(k+1)}) - f'_\theta(\varphi, \theta_0^{(k)})]\, d\varphi.$$

Thus, if the total variation of the function $\partial f/\partial\theta$ with respect to the variable θ is less than W for all φ, we have

$$\sum_{k=0}^{n-1} |h(\theta_0^{(k+1)}) - h(\theta_0^{(k)})| < 2\pi W,$$

i.e., the variation of the function $h(\theta_0)$, and, consequently, the function $d/d\theta_0\, F(2\pi, \theta_0)$, is finite.

Hence, if the right side of Eq. **(10.1)** is sufficiently smooth, then the set P coincides with the entire zero meridian. In connection with this, it is of value to note the following theorem [1].

Theorem 10.9. Assume that the turning point μ *is irrational, and that the set* P *coincides with the entire zero meridian. Then there exists a homeomorphism* S *of the torus onto itself such that the solution curves of Eq.(10.1) are carried into the solution curves of the equation*

$$\frac{d\theta}{d\varphi} = \mu. \tag{10.56}$$

Proof. As before, let θ_k be the successive points of $\theta = 0$, and let P be the limit set for the sequence θ_k. By hypothesis, the set θ_k is everywhere dense. On the sequence θ_k, define a function Φ, given by the formula

$$\Phi(\theta_k) = (\mu k)\, 2\pi. \tag{10.57}$$

The function Φ is monotonic in its domain, since, by Theorem 10.5, if

$$\theta_{k_1} < \theta_{k_2}, \quad \text{then} \quad (\mu k_1) < (\mu k_2). \tag{10.58}$$

Since the set θ_k is everywhere dense on the zero meridian, we can, by taking any point $\bar{\theta}$ on it, find two sequences θ_{k_i} and θ_{k_j} such that

$$\lim_{i\to\infty} \theta_{k_i} = \bar{\theta}, \quad \lim_{j\to\infty} \theta_{k_j} = \bar{\theta}, \tag{10.59}$$

$$\theta_{k_i} \leqslant \bar{\theta} \leqslant \theta_{k_j}. \tag{10.60}$$

Since the function Φ is monotonic in its domain, we have

$$\lim_{l\to\infty} \Phi(\theta_{k_l}) = \Phi(\bar{\theta}-0), \tag{10.61}$$

$$\lim_{j\to\infty} \Phi(\theta_{k_j}) = \Phi(\bar{\theta}+0), \tag{10.62}$$

where the numbers $\Phi(\bar{\theta}-0)$ and $\Phi(\bar{\theta}+0)$ are independent of the choice of the sequences θ_{k_l} and θ_{k_j}.

We will now show that, for any $\bar{\theta}$,

$$\Phi(\bar{\theta}-0) = \Phi(\bar{\theta}+0). \tag{10.63}$$

Assume to the contrary that

$$\Phi(\bar{\theta}-0) < \Phi(\bar{\theta}+0).$$

Since the set (μk) is everywhere dense on the segment [0, 1], there exist two numbers $m \neq l$ such that

$$\Phi(\bar{\theta}-0) < (m\mu)\,2\pi < \Phi(\bar{\theta}+0),$$
$$\Phi(\bar{\theta}-0) < (l\mu)\,2\pi < \Phi(\bar{\theta}+0).$$

Consider the points θ_m and θ_l, assuming for definiteness that $\theta_m < \theta_l$. Then by Theorem 10.5, we have $\theta_{k_l} \leqslant \theta_m < \theta_l \leqslant \theta_{k_j}$. This is impossible, because of (10.59), which proves Eq. (10.63).

We now extend the function Φ to the entire meridian in the natural way: If $\bar{\theta} \neq \theta_k$, then $\Phi(\bar{\theta}) = \Phi(\bar{\theta}+0)$. It follows from (10.63) that Φ is continuous.

Since the function φ is monotonic, it has a continuous and monotonic inverse Φ^{-1}. Let A be a point on the torus, and let Φ and θ be its reduced coordinates. Through this point, draw the solution curve $\theta = F(\varphi, \theta_0)$. We associate the point A with point B having coordinates $(\theta = \mu\varphi + \Phi(\theta_0),\ \varphi = \varphi)$. This mapping will be the one required. It is not difficult to see that this mapping is one-to-one when $0 \leqslant \varphi < 2\pi$ and continuous in both directions. We will now show that it is also one-to-one for $0 \leqslant \varphi \leqslant 2\pi$, i.e., we will show that the points with coordinates $(\varphi = 2\pi,\ \theta = 2\mu\pi + \Phi(\theta_0))$ and $(\varphi = 0,\ \theta = \Phi(F(2\pi, \theta_0)))$ coincide. In view of continuity, it is sufficient to show that this is true for the case $\theta_0 = \theta_k$, because the points θ_k are everywhere dense on the zero meridian. $F(2\pi, \theta_k)$ has the reduced coordinate θ_{k+1}; as a result, $\mu 2\pi + \Phi(\theta_k)$ is, up to an integral multiple of 2π, coincident with $\Phi(\theta_{k+1})$. We have

$$\Phi(\theta_k) = (k\mu)\,2\pi, \quad \Phi(\theta_{k+1}) = ((k+1)\mu)\,2\pi$$

from which the theorem follows. Q.E.D.

7. At the beginning of Paragraph 6 we introduced a transformation T of the zero meridian of the torus onto itself generated by the general solution $\theta = F(\varphi, \theta_0)$ of Eq. (10.1).

We now assume that we have defined a direction-preserving homeomorphism T of the circle C onto itself, and we will show that this transformation is subject to the same laws as the transformation generated by Eq. (10.1). In order to do so, we will introduce a family of curves analogous to the family of solution curves of Eq. (10.1).

On the circle C, introduce an angular coordinate θ_0 with origin at the point $M^{(0)}$, so that the coordinates of the point $M^{(0)}$ are integral multiples of 2π. Let $TM^{(0)} = M_1^{(0)}$ and $\theta_1^{(0)}$ be the reduced coordinate of the point $M_1^{(0)} (0 \leqslant \theta_1^{(0)} < 2\pi)$. We define a function $\theta_1(\theta_0)$ by means of the following rule: Let θ_0 be the coordinate of the point $M \in C$; then $\theta_1(\theta_0)$ is the coordinate of the point TM, with $\theta_1(0) = \theta_1^{(0)}$. Since the transformation T is continuous, we can and will assume that the function θ_1 is continuous. Then it is not difficult to see that the function $\theta_1(\theta_0) - \theta_0$ is 2π-periodic. Consider the function

$$F(\varphi, \theta_0) = \frac{\theta_1(\theta_0) - \theta_0}{2\pi}\varphi + \theta_0 \text{ for } 0 \leqslant \varphi \leqslant 2\pi, \; -\infty < \theta_0 < +\infty. \tag{10.64}$$

The curves $\theta = F(\varphi, \theta_0)$ constitute a family of line segments connecting the verticals $\theta = 0$ and $\theta = 2\pi$ in the plane (φ, θ). These segments do not intersect, since, by hypothesis, the transformation T preserves orientation. Construct similar families of line segments in the strips of the form $2n\pi \leqslant \varphi \leqslant 2(n+1)\pi$, and "attach" corresponding segments at points along the vertical lines $\theta = 2n\pi$, thus obtaining a family of broken lines. More precisely, we extend the function $F(\varphi, \theta_0)$ to the entire plane in the following manner. Assume that the function $F(\varphi, \theta_0)$ is defined for all $0 \leqslant \varphi \leqslant 2n\pi \, (n \geqslant 1)$, and extend F in the following manner to strip $2n\pi \leqslant \varphi \leqslant 2(n+1)\pi$. Set

$$F(\varphi, \theta_0) = \frac{\theta_1(F(2n\pi, \theta_0)) - F(2n\pi, \theta_0)}{2\pi}(\varphi - 2n\pi) + F(2n\pi, \theta_0). \tag{10.65}$$

Thus, the function $F(\varphi, \theta_0)$ will be defined for all $\varphi \geqslant 0$. Similarly, $F(\varphi, \theta_0)$ is defined for $\varphi \leqslant 0$. In the plane (φ, θ), $\theta = F(\varphi, \theta_0)$ is represented by a family of broken lines that are continuous functions of the parameter θ_0 and do not intersect anywhere. One and only one broken line passes through each point of the plane.

It is not difficult to see that the family $\theta = F(\varphi, \theta_0)$ is subject to the same laws as the family of solution curves of Eq. (10.1).

Definition 10.1. By the turning point μ of the transformation T we will mean the turning point of the family $\theta = F(\varphi, \theta_0)$, defined above.

If the turning point μ of the transformation T is irrational, then the family of curves $\theta = F(\varphi, \theta_0)$ has no closed curves on the torus and, in turn, this means that there is no q for which the transformation T^q of the circle C has any stationary points. On the other hand, if the transformation T^q has stationary point M such that $T^q M = M$ and $T^r M \neq M$ for $1 \leqslant r < q$, then the transformation T has a rational turning point p/q, where p and q are relatively prime.

Conversely, if the transformation T has a rational turning point $\mu = p/q$ (assuming that the fraction p/q is irreducible), then the transformation T^q has a stationary point. In that case, if the relation $T^r M = M$ (where r is a natural number) is satisfied for some point $M \in C$, then we must have $r = kq$, where k is a natural number.

These assertions follow directly from Theorems **10.2–10.4**, which, as noted, hold in the case under discussion.

11. THE COARSENESS OF DIFFERENTIAL EQUATIONS DEFINED ON A TORUS

In this section we will again consider a first-order equation with the right side periodic with respect to both arguments:

$$\frac{d\theta}{d\varphi} = f(\varphi, \theta). \tag{11.1}$$

We will assume as before, that the function $f(\varphi, \theta)$ is 2π-periodic in both arguments, continuous, and that the solutions are unique for all φ and θ.

1. Here we will be concerned with the relationship between the turning point and parameters that may enter into the right side of the equation.

Consider the equation

$$\frac{d\theta}{d\varphi} = f(\varphi, \theta, \alpha), \tag{11.2}$$

where the function $f(\varphi, \theta, \alpha)$ is continuous at the point $(\varphi, \theta, \alpha_0)$ and, in the neighborhood of this point, has the same properties as the right side of Eq. **(11.1)**. It is clear that the turning point $\mu = \mu(\alpha)$ of Eq. **(11.2)** depends on α.

Theorem 11.1. The function $\mu(\alpha)$ *is continuous at the point* α_0.

Proof. Let $\theta = F(\varphi, \theta_0, \alpha)$ denote the solution of Eq. **(11.2)** for which $\theta_0 = F(0, \theta_0, \alpha)$. Choose an arbitrary $\varepsilon > 0$ and a sufficiently large natural number q so that $2/q < \varepsilon$. For this q, there is clearly an integer p such that

$$2\pi(p-1) < F(2\pi q, 0, \alpha_0) < 2\pi(p+1). \tag{11.3}$$

Because the solutions of Eq. (11.2) are continuous functions of the parameter α at the point α_0, there exists a $\delta > 0$ such that, for $|\alpha - \alpha_0| < \delta$, we have

$$2\pi(p-1) < F(2\pi q, 0, \alpha) < 2\pi(p+1). \tag{11.4}$$

It follows from inequalities (11.3) and (11.4), and the definition of the turning point, that

$$\frac{p-1}{q} < \mu(\alpha_0) < \frac{p+1}{q} \tag{11.5}$$

and

$$\frac{p-1}{q} < \mu(\alpha) < \frac{p+1}{q} \quad \text{for} \quad |\alpha - \alpha_0| < \delta. \tag{11.6}$$

Substracting inequality (11.5) from inequality (11.6), we obtain

$$-\frac{2}{q} < \mu(\alpha) - \mu(\alpha_0) < \frac{2}{q}.$$

Then it follows from the choice of the number q that

$$|\mu(\alpha) - \mu(\alpha_0)| < \varepsilon \quad \text{for} \quad |\alpha - \alpha_0| < \delta,$$

which proves the theorem.

Theorem 11.1 shows that the turning point depends continuously on the parameter if the right side of the equation is a continuous function of the parameter. This raises the question of whether or not the function $\mu(\alpha)$ is smooth to some extent if the right side is a sufficiently smooth function of its arguments. The following example shows that the function $\mu(\alpha)$ need not satisfy a Lipschitz condition even if the right side is an entire function.

Example.

$$\frac{d\theta}{d\varphi} = \sin^2\theta + \alpha.$$

When $\alpha \in [-1, 0]$, this equation admits constants as its solutions and, consequently, the turning point is equal to zero, i.e., $\mu(\alpha) = 0$ when $\alpha \in [-1, 0]$. Integrating the differential equation at hand with $\alpha > 0$ and initial data $\varphi = \theta = 0$, obtain

$$\int_0^\theta \frac{d\theta}{\alpha + \sin^2\theta} = \varphi.$$

It then follows that

$$\varphi = \frac{1}{\sqrt{\alpha^2+\alpha}} \operatorname{Arctan} \frac{\sqrt{\alpha+1}\tan\theta}{\sqrt{\alpha}}.$$

By Theorem 10.1,

$$\mu(\alpha) = \lim_{\varphi\to+\infty} \frac{F(\varphi, 0, \alpha)}{\varphi},$$

and hence

$$\mu(\alpha) = \lim_{\theta\to+\infty} \frac{\sqrt{\alpha^2+\alpha}\cdot\theta}{\operatorname{Arctan}\dfrac{\sqrt{\alpha+1}\cdot\tan\theta}{\sqrt{\alpha}}} = \sqrt{\alpha^2+\alpha}.$$

Thus, for the equation under discussion, $\mu(\alpha)$ does not satisfy a Lipschitz condition in the neighborhood of the point $\alpha = 0$.

2. As will be seen later, in certain cases the turning point μ of Eq. (11.1) remains constant despite arbitrary but sufficiently small pertubations of the right side. First, we will find the conditions under which such a phenomenon occurs. Consider, in conjunction with Eq. (11.1), the equation

$$\frac{d\theta}{d\varphi} = f(\varphi, \theta) + f_1(\varphi, \theta), \tag{11.7}$$

where the function $f_1(\varphi, \theta)$ is continuous, 2π-periodic with respect to both arguments, and is such that the solutions of Eq. (11.7) are unique.

Definition 11.1. We will say that Eq. (11.1) has a stable turning point if there exists an $\varepsilon > 0$ such that, for any function $f_1(\varphi, \theta)$ satisfying the condition $|f_1(\varphi, \theta)| \leqslant \varepsilon$, Eq. (11.7) has the same turning point as Eq. (11.1).

Otherwise we will say that Eq. (11.1) has an unstable turning point.

Lemma 11.1. If the turning point μ of Eq. (11.1) is irrational, then it is unstable.

Proof. In the case under discussion there are no closed solution curves on the torus and there exists a Poisson-stable trajectory. For definiteness, assume that the trajectory $L\{\theta = F(\varphi, 0)\}$ is Poisson-stable (otherwise we would make the substitution $\vartheta = \theta - \theta_0$). Now consider an arbitrary positive ε. Because the function $f(\varphi, \theta)$ is continuous and periodic, there exists for this ε a $\delta \in (0, \varepsilon/2)$ such that $|f(\varphi_1, \theta_1) - f(\varphi_2, \theta_2)| < \varepsilon/2$ and $|\varphi_1 - \varphi_2| < \delta$, $|\theta_1 - \theta_2| < \delta$. Because the trajectory L is Poisson-stable on the torus, there exists an integer

p and a natural number q such that $|2p\pi - F(2q\pi, 0)| < \delta$. For definiteness, assume that $2p\pi > F(2q\pi, 0)$ ($2p\pi = F(2q\pi, 0)$ is impossible because μ is, by hypothesis, irrational). Then, from the definition of μ and the fact that it is irrational it follows that

$$\frac{p}{q} > \mu. \tag{11.8}$$

Now set $f_1(\varphi, \theta) = \varepsilon$; then Eq. (11.7) takes the form

$$\frac{d\theta}{d\varphi} = f(\varphi, \theta) + \varepsilon. \tag{11.9}$$

Let $\theta = F_1(\varphi, \theta_0)$ denote a solution of Eq. (11.9), and let μ_1 denote its turning point. It follows from the definition of δ that the curve $M\{\theta = F(\varphi, 0) + \delta\}$ has no contact with the field of line elements of Eq. (11.9). Moreover, it follows from the form of Eq. (11.9) and the definition of δ that until the curve $\theta = F_1(\varphi, 0)$ enters the closed region $G\{F(\varphi, 0) \leqslant \theta \leqslant F(\varphi, 0) + \delta\}$ the inequality

$$F_1'(\varphi, 0) - F'(\varphi, 0) > \frac{\varepsilon}{2} \tag{11.10}$$

is satisfied. By integrating this inequality, we can see that the curve $\theta = F_1(\varphi, 0)$ lies outside of G when $0 < \varphi < 2\pi$. Since the curve M has no contact with the field of line elements of Eq. (11.9), it is clear that, when $\varphi \geqslant 2\pi$, $F_1(\varphi, 0) > F(\varphi, 0) + \delta$, from which it follows, by the definition of p and q, that $F_1(2q\pi, 0) > 2p\pi$. Then, by the definition of the turning point, we have

$$\mu_1 \geqslant \frac{p}{q};$$

this, in combination with (11.8), implies that $\mu_1 > \mu$, which proves the lemma.

Now assume that the turning point of Eq. (11.1) is rational, $\mu = p/q$. Consider the function

$$g(\theta_0) = F(2q\pi, \theta_0) - 2p\pi - \theta_0, \tag{11.11}$$

which we will call the determining function. It follows from Theorem 10.2 that the determining function has zeros when $\theta_0 \in [0, 2\pi)$. Periodic solutions of Eq. (11.1) (closed cycles on the torus) correspond to the zeros of this function.

Lemma 11.2. If the turning point of Eq. (11.1) is rational ($\mu = p/q$), *and if the determining function* $g(\theta_0)$ *does not change sign, then the turning point of Eq. (11.1) is unstable.*

Proof. For definiteness, assume that $g(\theta_0) \geqslant 0$ for all θ_0. In conjunction with (11.1), consider Eq. (11.9) with ε an arbitrary positive number. It is then clear that $F_1(2q\pi, \theta_0) > F(2q\pi, \theta_0)$ for all θ_0. But then it follows that

$$F_1(2q\pi, \theta_0) - 2p\pi - \theta_0 > F(2q\pi, \theta_0) - 2p\pi - \theta_0 = g(\theta_0) \geqslant 0,$$

which shows that Eq. (11.9) has no closed cycles that make q longitudinal and p latitudinal rotations prior to closure. Then it follows that the turning point of Eq. (11.9) is not p/q, which proves the lemma.

Lemma 11.3. If the turning point μ *of Eq. (11.1) is rational* ($\mu = p/q$), *and is the determining function* $g(\theta_0)$ *changes sign, then the turning point of Eq. (11.1) is stable.*

Proof. Let $\theta = F_2(\varphi, \theta_0)$ be a solution of Eq. (11.7). By hypothesis, the function $g(\theta_0)$ changes sign. Then, since solutions of differential equations are continuous functions of their right sides, it follows that there exists an $\varepsilon > 0$ such that the function $g_2(\theta_0) = F_2(2q\pi, \theta_0) - 2p\pi - \theta_0$ changes sign if $|f_1(\varphi, \theta)| < \varepsilon$ for all θ and φ. But then it follows from the continuity of the function $g_2(\theta_0)$ that there exists a θ_0' such that $g_2(\theta_0') = 0$. Consequently, a closed-cycle solution of Eq. (11.7) passes through the point ($\varphi = 0$, $\theta = \theta_0$), from which it follows that the turning point of Eq. (11.7) is equal to p/q. This proves the lemma.

The lemmas which we have proved make it possible to state the following theorem.

Theorem 11.2. Equation (11.1) has a stable turning point if and only if μ *is rational and the determining function* $g(\theta_0)$ *changes sign.*

When the right side of Eq. (11.1) is analytic with respect to θ, Theorem 11.2 may be stated differently.

Theorem 11.3. If the function $f(\varphi, \theta)$ *has a series expansion in powers of* θ *in the neighborhood of every point* $\theta \in [0, 2\pi]$, *the series converging uniformly when* $\varphi \in [0, 2\pi]$, *then the turning point* μ *of Eq. (11.1) is stable if and only if Eq. (11.1) has at least one asymptotically Lyapunov-stable periodic solution.*

Proof. Sufficiency is a consequence of Theorem 11.2 and the facts that, under the conditions of the theorem, the turning point is rational and the determining function changes sign.

Necessity. Assume that the hypothesis of Theorem 11.3 is not satisfied. If Eq. (11.1), has no periodic solutions in general, then its turning point is irrational and, by Lemma 11.1, unstable. Now assume that Eq. (11.1) has periodic solutions; then its turning point is rational. Consider the determining function $g(\theta_0)$; because the right side of Eq. (11.1) is analytic, the function $g(\theta_0)$ is also analytic. Then it follows that any equation $g(\theta_0) = 0$ has a finite number of roots in the interval $0 \leqslant \theta_0 \leqslant 2\pi$ or else $g(\theta_0) \equiv 0$. In the second case, it follows from Lemma 11.2 that the turning point of Eq. (11.1) is unstable. In the first case, the absence of stable periodic solutions prevents the function $g(\theta_0)$ from taking on values of either one sign or the other and, in virtue of Lemma 11.2, Eq. (11.1) has an unstable turning point. Q.E.D.

3. Here we will study the problem of the coarseness of Eq. (11.1). We will define coarseness for Eq. (11.1), given on a torus. This definition is, essentially, analogous to the definition of coarseness for plane dynamical systems [51, 52]. Assume that the function $f(\varphi, \theta)$ has continuous partial derivatives with respect to θ, and denote the Euclidean distance between points M and N of the torus R by $\rho(M, N)$.

Definition 11.2. We will say that Eq. (11.1) is coarse if for any $\varepsilon > 0$ there exists a $\delta(\varepsilon) > 0$ such that for any continuous $f_1(\varphi, \theta)$ that has a continuous partial derivative $\partial f_1/\partial\theta$, is 2π-periodic with respect to both arguments, and satisfies the inequalities

$$|f_1(\varphi, \theta)| < \delta, \quad \left|\frac{\partial f_1}{\partial\theta}\right| < \delta, \tag{11.12}$$

there exists a topological mapping S of the torus R onto itself with the following properties:

1) $\rho(M, SM) < \varepsilon$;

2) S transforms the solution curves of Eq. (11.1) into the solution curves of Eq. (11.7).

Lemma 11.4. If Eq. (11.1) is coarse, then it has a rational turning point $\mu = p/q$ and the determining function $g(\theta_0)$ changes sign.

Proof. We will prove the lemma indirectly. Initially, assume that the turning point μ of Eq. (11.1) is irrational and choose an $\varepsilon > 0$. We subject the solution $\theta = F(\varphi, 0)$ of Eq. (11.1) to the same assumptions as those made in the proof of Lemma 11.1. Then, as proved, the turning point μ_1 of Eq. (11.9) is larger than the turning point μ of Eq. (11.1). In virtue of Theorem 11.1, the turning point $\mu_1(\varepsilon)$ of Eq. (11.9) depends continuously on ε and, therefore, there exists an $\varepsilon_0 < \varepsilon$ such that the turning point $\mu_1(\varepsilon_0)$ is rational. But then it is clear that there is no topological mapping of the torus R onto itself which will transform the solution curves of Eq. (11.1) into the solution curves of Eq. (11.9) with $\varepsilon = \varepsilon_0$, because otherwise an open curve would be mapped by such a transformation into a closed cycle, which is impossible. But then, Definition 11.2 implies that Eq. (11.1) is not coarse. This contradicts the hypothesis, which shows that the turning point of Eq. (11.1) can not be irrational.

We now assume that $\mu = p/q$, and that the determining function does not change sign. For definiteness, assume that $g(\theta_0) \geqslant 0$. Then, as shown in the proof of Lemma 11.2, the turning point μ_1 of Eq. (11.9) is different from the turning point μ of Eq. (11.1) for any $\varepsilon > 0$.

Consequently, there exists a sufficiently small ε_0 such that, when $\varepsilon = \varepsilon_0$, the turning point of Eq. (11.9) is irrational. But then it is clear that Eq. (11.1) is not coarse. The contradiction thus obtained proves the lemma.

Lemma 11.5. If Eq. (11.1) is coarse, then it has only a finite number of closed cycles.

Proof. Choose an arbitrary $\delta > 0$. For this δ, there is a function $\bar{f}(\varphi, \theta)$ that is 2π-periodic with respect to both arguments, continuous with respect to φ, and has the following properties: 1) it can be expanded in a power series in θ, the series converging uniformly with $\varphi \in [0, 2\pi]$ and $|\theta| < A$, where A is an arbitrary positive number; 2) the following inequalities hold:

$$|f(\varphi, \theta) - \bar{f}(\varphi, \theta)| < \delta, \quad \left|\frac{\partial f}{\partial \theta} - \frac{\partial \bar{f}}{\partial \theta}\right| < \delta. \tag{11.13}$$

Consider the equation

$$\frac{d\theta}{d\varphi} = \bar{f}(\varphi, \theta). \tag{11.14}$$

In virtue of (11.13), this equation is an admissible perturbation for (11.1). Then, by the hypothesis of the lemma, there exists a topological mapping S of the torus R onto itself that maps the solution curves of Eq. (11.1) into the solution curves of Eq. (11.4). We now assume, contrary to assertion of the lemma, that Eq. (11.1) has an infinite number of closed cycles. Then Eq. (11.14)also has an infinite number of closed cycles. Since Eq. (11.14) has periodic solutions, its turning point is rational, and its determining function $\bar{g}(\theta_0)$ is defined. Since the function $\bar{f}(\varphi, \theta)$ is analytic by assumption, the function $\bar{g}(\theta_0)$ is also analytic. But the periodic solutions of Eq. (11.14) correspond to the zeros of the function $\bar{g}(\theta_0)$. Consequently, the function $\bar{g}(\theta_0)$ has infinitely many zeros and, since $\bar{g}(\theta_0)$ is an analytic function, this implies $\bar{g}(\theta_0) \equiv 0$. Thus it follows that all solutions of Eq. (11.14) are periodic. But then all solutions of Eq. (11.1) are also periodic, from which it follows that the determining function $g(\theta_0)$ of Eq. (11.1) is identically equal to zero. This contradicts the assumption that Eq. (11.1) is coarse, as well as Lemma 11.4. The contradiction proves the lemma.

Assume that Eq. (11.1) has a rational turning point $\mu = p/q$, and let θ_1 denote the latitude of a point on the zero meridian of the torus R through which a periodic solution of Eq. (11.1) passes. Associate with a periodic solution $\theta = F(\varphi, \theta_1)$ the characteristic exponent

$$h(\theta_1) = \frac{1}{2q\pi} \int_0^{2q\pi} \left.\frac{\partial f}{\partial \theta}\right|_{\theta = F(\varphi, \theta_1)} d\varphi. \tag{11.15}$$

It is not difficult to see that, under the preceding assumptions about the right side of Eq. (11.1), we have

$$\frac{d}{d\theta_0} F(2q\pi, \theta_0)\bigg|_{\theta_0=\theta_1} = e^{2q\pi h(\theta_1)}. \tag{11.16}$$

Let $g(\theta_0)$ be the determining function for Eq. (11.11); then it follows from (11.16) and the form of the function $g(\theta_0)$ that

$$\frac{dg}{d\theta_0}\bigg|_{\theta_0=\theta_1} = e^{2q\pi h(\theta_1)} - 1. \tag{11.17}$$

We will now state one more lemma concerning the coarseness of Eq. (11.1).

Lemma 11.6. If Eq. (11.1) is coarse, then any of its periodic solutions $\theta = F(\varphi, \theta_1)$ has a nonzero characteristic exponent.

Proof. Assume, contrary to the assertion of the lemma, that passing through a point θ_1 on the zero meridian there is a periodic solution $\theta = F(\varphi, \theta_1)$ and $h(\theta_1) = 0$. In virtue of Lemma 11.5, Eq. (11.1) has only a finite number of periodic solutions, so that there is a point θ_2 $(\theta_2 > \theta_1)$ on the zero meridian such that the solution $\theta = F(\varphi, \theta_2)$ is periodic, and no periodic solutions of Eq. (11.1) pass through the interval (θ_1, θ_2). Note that θ_2 is geometrically distinct from θ_1, because otherwise the function $g(\theta_0)$ would have only one zero in the interval $0 \leqslant \theta_0 < 2\pi$ and, being periodic, would not change sign, which would contradict Lemma 11.4. By the definition of the point θ_2, the function $g(\theta_0)$ does not change sign for $\theta_0 \in (\theta_1, \theta_2)$; for definiteness, assume that $g(\theta_0) > 0$ when $\theta_0 \in (\theta_1, \theta_2)$. Now choose a sufficiently small $\delta > 0$ so that the δ-neighborhood $\{F(\varphi, \theta_1) - \delta \leqslant \theta \leqslant F(\varphi, \theta_1) + \delta\}$ of the solution $\theta = F(\varphi, \theta_1)$ does not intersect any of the periodic solutions of Eq. (11.1) which are different from $\theta = F(\varphi, \theta_1)$. Choose an arbitrary $\varepsilon > 0$, and define a function $f_1(\varphi, \theta)$ with the following properties: a) $f_1(\varphi, \theta)$ belongs to the class C_2 and is 2π-periodic with respect to both arguments; b) $|f_1(\varphi, \theta)| \leqslant \varepsilon$; c) $f_1(\varphi, \theta) = 0$ on the curve $\theta = F(\varphi, \theta_1)$ and outside the δ-neighborhood of this curve; $\partial f_1/\partial\theta = -\varepsilon$ for $\theta = F(\varphi, \theta_1)$.

Consider Eq. (11.7) with $f_1(\varphi, \theta)$ having the properties listed above. It is clear that all periodic solutions of Eq. (11.1) will also be periodic solutions of Eq. (11.7). We will now find the characteristic exponent $h_1(\theta_1)$ of the solution $\theta = F(\varphi, \theta_1)$ of Eq. (11.7). By definition, we have

$$h_1(\theta_1) = \frac{1}{2\pi q}\int_0^{2q\pi}\left(\frac{\partial f}{\partial\theta} + \frac{\partial f_1}{\partial\theta}\right)\bigg|_{\theta=F(\varphi, \theta_1)} d\varphi$$

or

$$h_1(\theta_1)=\frac{1}{2q\pi}\int_0^{2q\pi}\frac{\partial f}{\partial\theta}\bigg|_{\theta=F(\varphi,\,\theta_1)}d\varphi+$$
$$+\frac{1}{2q\pi}\int_0^{2q\pi}\frac{\partial f_1}{\partial\theta}\bigg|_{\theta=F(\varphi,\,\theta_1)}d\varphi. \tag{11.18}$$

The first of the integrals in the right side of this equation coincides with the characteristic exponent $h(\theta_1)$ of the solution $\theta=F(\varphi,\ \theta_1)$ of Eq. (11.1), and, by hypothesis, is equal to zero. It follows then from the properties of the function $f_1(\varphi,\ \theta)$ that

$$h_1(\theta_1)=-\varepsilon. \tag{11.19}$$

Let $g_1(\theta_0)$ be the determining function for Eq. (11.7). Using Eq. (11.17), we obtain

$$g_1'(\theta_1)=e^{-2q\pi\varepsilon}-1<0. \tag{11.20}$$

By the definition of δ, the curve $\theta=F(\varphi,\ \theta_2)$ and the closed region $\{F(\varphi,\ \theta_1)-\delta\leqslant\theta\leqslant F(\varphi,\ \theta_1)+\delta\}$ do not intersect. Thus, there exists a $\delta_2>0$ such that the closed regions $\{F(\varphi,\ \theta_2)-\delta_2\leqslant\theta\leqslant F(\varphi,\ \theta_2)+\delta_2\}$ and $\{F(\varphi,\ \theta_1)-\delta\leqslant\theta\leqslant F(\varphi,\ \theta_1)+\delta\}$ do not intersect.

By the theorem on integral continuity, there exists an $l>0$ such that all solutions $\theta=F_1(\varphi,\ \theta_0)$ of Eq. (11.7) with $|\theta_2-\theta_0|<l$, are in the region $|\theta-F(\varphi,\ \theta_2)|<\delta_2$, in the interval $0\leqslant\varphi\leqslant 2q\pi$. But, in view of the properties of the function $f_1(\varphi,\ \theta)$, these solutions will simply coincide with the corresponding solutions of Eq. (11.1), and then because of our hypothesis we will have

$$g_1(\theta_0)=g(\theta_0)>0 \tag{11.21}$$

for $\theta_2-l\leqslant\theta_0\leqslant\theta_2$. As noted above, the function $\theta=F(\varphi,\ \theta_1)$ is a periodic solution of Eq. (11.7) and, therefore, $g_1(\theta_1)=0$. Then relations (11.20) and (11.21) imply the existence of $\theta_3\in(\theta_1,\ \theta_2)$ such that $g_1(\theta_3)=0$. This means that the solution $\theta=F_1(\varphi,\ \theta_3)$ of Eq. (11.7) is periodic. Thus, it turns out that Eq. (11.7) has more periodic solutions than Eq. (11.1). But then there can not be a transformation R of the torus onto itself that satisfies the definition of coarseness. This contradicts the hypothesis and thus proves the lemma.

Theorem 11.4. Equation (11.1) is coarse if and only if it has a rational turning point and all of its periodic solutions have nonzero characteristic exponents.

Proof. Necessity follows from Lemmas 11.4 and 11.6. We will now prove sufficiency. First, note that Eq. (11.1) has only a finite number of periodic solutions. Indeed, if there were infinitely many, then among them there would be one that is not isolated, and its characteristic exponent would be equal to zero. Choose an arbitrary positive number ε, and compare Eq. (11.1) with Eq. (11.7) with $|f_1| < \delta$, $|\partial f_1/\partial\theta| < \delta$. Let θ_1 and θ_2 be two points on the zero meridian through which periodic solutions of Eq. (11.1) pass. Here we assume that these solutions are adjacent, i.e., no closed cycle solutions of Eq. (11.1) pass through the interval (θ_1, θ_2). Denote the region between the closed curves $\theta = F(\varphi, \theta_1)$ and $\theta = F(\varphi, \theta_2)$ by A. Since the solutions $\theta = F(\varphi, \theta_1)$ and $\theta = F(\varphi, \theta_2)$ have nonzero characteristic exponents, they can be placed in arbitrarily narrow strips U_1 and U_2 bounded by closed smooth curves with no contact. Let L_1 and N_1 be the boundaries of U_1, and let L_2 and U_2 be the boundaries of N_2. Assume that the width of the strips U_1 and U_2 is less than $\varepsilon/2$, and that these strips do not intersect each other or periodic solutions of (11.1) different from $\theta = F(\varphi, \theta_1)$ and $\theta = F(\varphi, \theta_2)$. It follows from formula (11.17) that δ can be chosen sufficiently small so that Eq. (11.7) has as many periodic solutions as Eq. (11.1). It is possible to choose δ so small that the curves L_1, N_1, L_2, and N_2 have no contact with the field of Eq. (11.7), that each of the strips U_1 and U_2 contain exactly one periodic solution of Eq. (11.7) [$\theta = F_1(\varphi, \theta_1')$ and $\theta = F_1(\varphi, \theta_2')$, respectively], and that the region $A - U_1 - U_2$ have no periodic solutions. In addition, we will assume δ to be sufficiently small so that solutions of Eqs. (11.1) and (11.7) that begin at the same point in the region $A - U_1 - U_2$ differ from each other by a sufficiently small quantity as long as they are both within the region $A - U_1 - U_2$.

Assume that the curve L_1 lies in the region A. With each point of this curve we associate a point as follows: With each point p of the trajectory K of Eq. (11.1) passing through the point q of the curve L_1 we associate the point having the same longitude as p and lying on that trajectory of Eq. (11.7) which passes through q. It is clear that this correspondence defines a homeomorphism S_1 of the region A into the torus R. We now associate the points with the same longitude on the curves $\theta = F(\varphi, \theta_1)$ and $\theta = F_1(\varphi, \theta_1')$; we do likewise for the curves $\theta = F(\varphi, \theta_2)$ and $\theta = F_1(\varphi, \theta_2')$. Because the characteristic exponents of all of these curves are nonzero and, for corresponding pairs of curves, have the same sign, we obtain a homeomorphism of the closed region $\bar{A}$ into the torus R.

Extension of these considerations to all regions between adjacent periodic solutions makes it clear that there exists a $\delta > 0$ such that, for $|f_1| < \delta$ $|\partial f_1/\partial\theta| < \delta$, there exists a homeomorphism of the torus R onto itself with the properties required by the definition of coarseness. Q.E.D.

12. GENERAL THEOREMS ON THE BEHAVIOR OF SOLUTIONS OF SECOND-ORDER SYSTEMS

In this section we will study the behavior of second-order systems of equations

$$\frac{dX}{dt} = F(X, t), \tag{12.1}$$

where $X = \{x_1, x_2\}$ and $F = \{f_1, f_2\}$ are two-dimensional vectors. As usual, we will assume that the vector function F is defined, continuous, and guarantees that the solutions of system (12.1) are unique for all X and t. Moreover, we will assume, as before, that F has period ω with respect to t, i.e., $F(X, t+\omega) = F(X, t)$.

1. For system (12.1) the hyperplane $t = 0$ is simply the Euclidean plane E. As a result, when all solutions $X(t, X_0, 0)$ of system (12.1) extend to all times in the interval $0 \leqslant t \leqslant \omega$, the transformation T defined in Section 1 is a transformation of the Euclidean plane into itself. This circumstance makes it possible to state the following very important proposition [53] about system (12.1).

Theorem 12.1. If all solutions $X(t, X_0, 0)$ of system (12.1) continue to all times $0 \leqslant t \leqslant \omega$, and if there exists a solution that is bounded when $t \geqslant 0$, then there also exists an ω-periodic solution.

Before proving Theorem 12.1, we will prove the following important propositions concerning the theory of topological transformations of a plane. (The propositions proved below are due to Brouwer [54], but the reader can also find proofs of them in the article [55] by A. A. Andronov and A. G. Mayer.)

Let T be a direction-preserving homeomorphism of the Euclidean plane E into itself, and consider the following notations. Let X be a point in the plane E, let $X_1 = TX$, and let γ be a simple arc between the points X and X_1, with the property that the arc $\gamma_1 = T\gamma$ has the one point X_1 in common with γ. The arc γ will be called a transportation arc, and the set of points

$$\Gamma = \sum_{k=0}^{\infty} T^k \gamma \tag{12.2}$$

will be called a transportation ray.

Theorem 12.2. Assume that the transformation T has no stationary points; then the transportation ray can not have any double points, (i.e., points belonging to $\gamma_n = T^n\gamma$ and $\gamma_m = T^m\gamma$, $n \neq m$, and different from their common end points if $|m-n| = 1$).

Proof. Consider the transportation ray Γ of an arc γ beginning at a point X, and assume, contrary to the assertion of the theorem, that it has a double point. Attach the simple arc $\gamma_1 = T\gamma$ to the simple arc γ. By the definition of a transportation arc, we again obtain a simple arc $\gamma+\gamma_1$. To this simple arc, we attach the arc $\gamma_2=T^2\gamma$; the resultant curve $\gamma+\gamma_1+\gamma_2$ may prove to be a simple arc; in that case, we attach to it the arc $\gamma_3=T^3\gamma$, etc. By hypothesis, this process must terminate (since otherwise the transportation Γ would not have double points). Assume that a nonsimple arc is obtained for the first time upon the attachment of $\gamma_k (k>1)$ to the simple arc $\gamma+\gamma_1+\cdots+\gamma_{k-1}$, and denote by q_1 the first point of intersection between γ_k and $\gamma+\gamma_1+\cdots+\gamma_{k-1}$, encountered when starting at $X_k=T^kX$, thus the simple arc $\gamma+\gamma_1+\cdots+\gamma_{k-1}$ has no points of intersection with the arc $q_1\in\gamma$ other than q_1. We will show that X_kq_1. Assume to the contrary that $q_1\in\gamma_r (1\leqslant r\leqslant k-1)$. It is then clear that $T^{-r}q_1\in T^{-r}\gamma_r=T^{-r}T^r\gamma=\gamma$; but $q_1\in\gamma_k$, so that $T^{-r}q_1\in T^{-r}\gamma_k=\gamma_{k-r}$, which means that γ intersects γ_{k-r} at the point $T^{-r}q_1$, and this contradicts the definition of k. Let C denote the simple closed curve composed of the simple arcs q_1X_1 (part of γ), $\gamma_1, \gamma_2, \ldots, \gamma_{k-1}$, and X_kq_1 (part of γ_k). The points $q_2=Tq_1$ and $q=T^{-1}q_1$ belong to C ($q_2\in\gamma_1$, $q\in\gamma_{k-1}$). The simple arc $q_1X_{k+1}q_2$, composed of parts of γ_k and γ_{k+1}, can intersect only the arc q_1X_1 (part of γ), because otherwise γ_{k-1} would intersect, contrary to the hypothesis, one of the arcs $\gamma_1, \gamma_2, \ldots, \gamma_{k-2}$. As a result, the simple arc $q_2X_2q_1$ consisting of parts of the arcs γ_1, γ_k and the simple arcs $\gamma_2, \ldots, \gamma_{k-1}$ can be extended to a simple closed curve either by means of the simple arc $q_1X_1q_2$, which would give us C, or the simple arc $q_1X_{k+1}q_2$, which would give us the simple closed curve $C_1=TC$. Note that the region bounded by the simple arcs $q_1X_1q_2$ and $q_1X_{k+1}q_2$ can not contain the simple arc qX_kq_1, because otherwise the transformation T would change the orientation of the contour C.

Let $v(X)$ be the shift vector of the transformation T, i.e., the vector from the point X to the point TX. Since the region bounded by the arcs $q_1X_1q_2$ and $q_1X_{k+1}q_2$ does not contain qX_kq_1, the angle through which the vector v rotates when its initial point moves along the simple arc qX_kq_1 (and, consequently, the endpoint moves along the arc $q_1X_{k+1}q_2$) will be the same as the angle of rotation of a nonvanishing vector whose origin moves along the simple arc qX_kq_1 and whose end has a continuous but otherwise arbitrary motion along the simple arc $q_1X_1q_2$.

Thus it follows that the angle through which the vector v rotates as the initial point traverses the curve C will be the same as the angle of rotation of a nonvanishing vector such that, as its initial point traverses the curve C, its end point also traverses C; this angle is therefore $+2\pi$. Thus, the index of the closed curve C in the field of v is $+1$; consequently, in the region bounded by the curve C, the vector v vanishes at least at one point X_0. But then $X_0=TX_0$, i.e., the point X_0 is a stationary point of the transformation T. This contradicts the hypothesis, and proves the theorem.

Let E_1 denote the image of the plane E under the transformation T.

Theorem 12.3. If the transformation T has no stationary points, then a transportation ray may be passed through each point of E_1.

Proof. We will consider an arbitrary point $X \in E_1$ and show that it can be connected to $X_1 = TX$ by a transportation arc, which will prove the theorem.

Connect X to X_1 by a simple arc γ in E_1 and set $\gamma_1 = T\gamma$. If γ and γ_1 do not intersect, the theorem is proved. Assume that the curves γ and γ_1 do intersect.

Let q_1 denote a point of intersection of γ and γ_1 with the following property: if $q = T^{-1}q_1$, $q_2 = Tq_1$, then

a) either Xq_1 does not intersect X_1q_2 anywhere else,

b) or X_1q_1 does not intersect Xq anywhere else.

We will now prove that a point q_1 with such a property exists. Let a point s move along γ from X to X_1; then $s_1 = Ts$ moves along γ_1 from X_1 to X_2. There are two possibilities:

a) Either the point s moving along γ intersects γ_1 at q_1 along a section already covered by s_1 prior to the instant at which s_1 intersects a part of γ already covered by s; the point q_1 will be the one desired;

b) or the point s_1 moving along γ_1 intersects γ at q_1 along a section already covered by s prior to the instant at which s intersects a part of the arc γ_1 already covered by s_1; then this point q_1 will be the one desired.

We will consider only case (a); case (b) can be converted into case (a) by substituting T^{-1} for T.

Choose a sufficiently small positive ε, and denote the ε-neighborhood of the arc X_1q_1 (part of γ_1) by U_1. Assume that ε is so small that $U_1 \subset E_1$, and set $U = T^{-1}U_1$; assume that U does not intersect the ε-neighborhood of X_1q_2 (part of γ_1). In the ε-neighborhood of q_1, on Xq_1, take a point r_1 and connect it to X_1 by an arc β_1 that is contained in U_1 and intersects neither X_1q_2 (except at the point X_1) nor Xq_1 (except at the point r_1).

The arc $\beta = T^{-1}\beta_1$, connecting the points $r = T^{-1}r_1$ and X will then intersect neither Xr_1 (since β_1 does not intersect X_1q_1) nor X_1r_2, where $r_2 = Tr_1$ (clearly, $r_2 \in X_1q_2$)). Thus, the simple arc rXr_1 consisting of parts of β and γ is a transportation arc. Since, by Theorem 11.2, a transportation ray passed through the arc rXr_1 has no double points, the arc Xr_1X_1 of this ray is also a transportation arc. Q.E.D.

Theorem 12.4. Assume that T has no stationary points and that the sequence $Q_1, Q_2, \ldots, Q_k, \ldots \in E_1$ has $X \in E_1$ as its limit. Then a transportation arc containing at least two points of the sequence Q_k. can be passed through the point X.

Proof. Let $X_1 = TX$ and let γ be the transportation arc connecting these points. Theorem 12.3 guarantees that such an arc exists.

Now let U be a sufficiently small neighborhood of the point X so that: 1) It contains neither inside nor on the boundary points of the arc $\gamma_1 = T\gamma$; 2) the closures of the sets U, $U_1 = TU$ and $U_2 = TU_1$ are disjoint; 3) $\bar{U}_2$ has no points in common with the arc γ.

Let Y be the last (counting from X) point of γ in the intersection of γ and the boundary of U, i.e., the arc YX_1 (part of γ) lies entirely outside U and Y is on the boundary of U.

Let Z be the first (counting from Y) point in the intersection of γ and the boundary of U_1, i.e., the arc YZ (part of γ) lies entirely outside $U + U_1$ and Z is on the boundary of U_1. Connect the points X and Y by an arbitrary simple arc λ which, except for its end Y, lies entirely in U. Let $\lambda_1 = T\lambda$. It is then clear that, except for the point $Y_1 = TY$, λ_1 lies entirely in U_1. Connect the points Z and X_1 by a simple arc μ which, except for the end Z, lies entirely in U_1 and does not intersect λ_1 except at the point X_1. Let β denote the arc XX_1 consisting of the arc λ, the arc YZ (part of γ), and the arc μ. We will now show that β is a transportation arc. Let $\mu_1 = T\mu$; it is then clear that μ_1 lies entirely in U_2, except for the point $Z_1 = TZ$. The arc μ_1 intersects neither λ nor μ, because, by the choice of $\bar{U}, U_2$ intersects neither $\bar{U}$ nor $\bar{U}_1$, and μ_1 does not intersect YZ (part of γ), because $\bar{U}_2$ does not intersect γ. The arc Y_1Z_1 does not intersect λ, because $\bar{U}$ has no points in common with γ_1; the arcs Z_1Y_1 (part of γ_1) and YZ (part of γ) are disjoint, because γ is a transportation arc and, consequently, γ and γ_1 have no common points; the arc Y_1Z_1 does not intersect μ, because μ lies inside U_1, whereas Y_1Z_1 lies outside U_1 (since the image of the arc YZ is outside U). Finally, the arc λ_1 does not intersect λ, because $\lambda \subset U$, $\lambda_1 \subset U_1$; the arc λ_1 does not intersect YZ (part of γ), since the latter is outside U_1; the arcs λ_1 and μ, however, intersect only at the one point X_1, by the construction of μ. Thus, the arc β intersects its image only at the one point X_1, i.e., it is a transportation arc.

Because λ is arbitrary, it can always be passed between two points of the sequence Q_k, which proves the theorem.

Theorem 12.5. Let T be a direction preserving homeomorphism of the Euclidean plane E into itself, and assume that there exists a point Y of the plane such that the sequence Y, $Y_1 = TY$, $Y_2 = T^2Y, \ldots$ has a convergent subsequence; then the transformation T has a stationary point.

Proof. Assume that the sequence Y_k has X as a limit point. It follows from the continuity of the transformation T that the point TX is also a limit of this sequence and, therefore, we can assume that $X \in E_1$.

Now assume, contrary to the assertion of the theorem, that T has no stationary points. Then, by Theorem 12.4, we can pass through X a transportation arc γ containing two points of the sequence Y_k. Assume that these two points are Y_m and Y_n, $n > m$, and consider the transportation ray $\Gamma = \sum_{l=0}^{\infty} T^l \gamma$. Since $T^{(n-m)} Y_m = Y_n$, the arc γ intersects $T^{(n-m)}\gamma$, i.e., the transportation ray Γ has a double point, which contradicts Theorem 12.2. Q.E.D.

Theorem 12.1 follows from this last theorem. Indeed, let T be the transformation of the plane E that associates the point $X(\omega, X_0, 0)$ with the point X_0, i.e., let T be the transformation introduced in Section 1. This transformation preserves orientation. Indeed, consider an arbitrary closed contour C, and assign to it some arbitrary orientation. Through C, pass all of the solution curves possible for $t=0$, extending the curves up to their intersection with the plane $t=\omega$. These solution curves form a surface L whose intersection with the plane $t=\omega$ is the contour TC. The orientation of the contour TC will differ from the orientation of C only if solution curves intersect on the surface L, which, because of uniqueness, can not occur.

By the hypothesis of Theorem 12.1, there exists a solution that is bounded when $t \geqslant 0$. Let Y be the value of the solution at $t=0$. It follows from the definition of T that the sequence $T^k Y$ is bounded. Thus, the hypothesis of Theorem 12.5 holds, and Theorem 12.1 follows.

2. In Section 9, it was proved (Theorem 9.1) that if a first-order equation has a bounded solution, then it has an ω-periodic solution, i.e., Theorem 12.1 about continuability of all solutions to a period is unnecessary for the case of first-order equations. Massera [53] proved that this condition is essential for second-order systems. We will quote an example given by Massera.

Example. Consider the system

$$\begin{aligned} \frac{dx}{dt} &= f(u, v)\cos^2 \pi t - g(u, v)\sin \pi t \cos \pi t - \pi y, \\ \frac{dy}{dt} &= g(u, v)\cos^2 \pi t + f(u, v)\sin \pi t \cos \pi t + \pi x, \end{aligned} \qquad (12.3)$$

where u and v are given by the formulas

$$u = x\cos \pi t + y \sin \pi t, \quad v = y \cos \pi t - x \sin \pi t. \qquad (12.4)$$

Assume that the functions f and g satisfy the following conditions:

1) f and g are continuously differentiable with respect to their arguments;

2) $f(-u, -v) = f(u, v)$, $g(-u, -v) = g(u, v)$;

3) $f(1, 0) = g(1, 0) = 0$, $f(0, v) = 0$, $g(0, v) > 0$ for all v;

4) $\int_{-\infty}^{+\infty} \frac{dv}{g(0, v)} < \frac{2}{\pi}$.

It follows from Condition 2 that the right sides of the system under discussion have periods equal to unity.

In terms of the variables u and v, system (12.3) takes the form

$$\frac{du}{dt} = f(u, v)\cos \pi t, \quad \frac{dv}{dt} = g(u, v)\cos \pi t. \tag{12.5}$$

It follows from Conditions 2 and 3 that $u = \pm 1$, $v = 0$ are two solutions of system (12.5); consequently, $x = \pm \cos \pi t$, $y = \pm \sin \pi t$ are two periodic solutions of system (12.3) with period equal to 2. From the first equation of system (12.5) it follows that if $u = 0$ for $t = t_0$ on some solution, then, for this solution, $u = 0$ for all t. Thus it follows that, for the solutions of the system under discussion, the function u does not change sign. Now assume that system (12.3) has a solution with unit period, and assume that, for this solution, $t = t_0$ for $u \neq 0$; then it follows from the first of Eqs. (12.4) that u does change sign on this solution, which is impossible. Consequently, if system (12.3) has a solution with period equal to unity, $u \equiv 0$ on this solution. For this solution, the second of Eqs. (12.5) yields

$$\int_{v_0}^{v} \frac{dv}{g(0, v)} = \int_{t_0}^{t} \cos \pi t \, dt = \frac{1}{\pi}(\sin \pi t - \sin \pi t_0).$$

Assume that t varies between $-\frac{1}{2}$ and $+\frac{1}{2}$; then the last equation yields

$$\int_{v\left(-\frac{1}{2}\right)}^{v\left(+\frac{1}{2}\right)} \frac{dv}{g(0, v)} = \frac{2}{\pi},$$

which contradicts Condition 4.

Thus, system (12.3), which has two solutions with period equal to 2, has no solutions with unit period. This occurs, because it has no solution for which $u = 0$ that can be extended to a period, which can easily be seen by direct integration of the second of Eqs. (12.5) with $u = 0$.

3. Now assume that system (12.1) is dissipative. Then, by definition, all of its solutions $X(t, X_0, 0)$ are bounded for all $t \geqslant 0$; consequently, by Theorem 12.1, a dissipative system of two differential equations has a harmonic oscillation. The following more precise statement holds: there exists a closed region that is mapped into itself under transformation T and is bounded by a closed Jordan curve.

Before we prove this assertion, we will prove the following geometric lemmas.

Lemma 12.1. Let J_1 *and* J_2 *be two closed Jordan curves, and let* D_1 *and* D_2 *be their interior (bounded) regions. Moreover, let* D *be the unbounded component of the complement of the set* $J_1 \cup J_2$ *in the plane, and let* Γ *be its boundary. If the intersection* $D_1 \cap D_2$ *is non-empty, then* Γ *is a closed Jordan curve contained in the set* $J_1 + J_2$*. The region* Δ*, the interior of* Γ*, contains* D_1 *and* D_2*.*

Proof. One of three cases must occur: Either

$$D_1 \subset D_2 \tag{12.6}$$

or

$$D_2 \subset D_1 \tag{12.7}$$

or neither (12.6) nor (12.7) is satisfied. In case (12.6) we have $\Gamma = J_2$, $\Delta = D_2$; in case (12.7) we have $\Gamma = J_1$, $\Delta = D_1$. The case in which neither (12.6) nor (12.7) holds remains to be considered. In this case D_2 has points both inside and outside D_1, so that J_2 has points both inside and outside D_1. Indeed, if J_2 had no points outside D_1, then the points of D_2 outside D_1 could be connected to the point at infinity without encountering the curve J_2, which is impossible; and if the curve J_2 had no point inside D_1, then D_1 would be inside D_2, which, by hypothesis, is also impossible. It is also clear that Γ is contained in $J_1 + J_2$, and if Γ is a closed Jordan curve, then the domain Δ contains $D_1 + D_2$. It remains to be shown that Γ is a closed Jordan curve.

We will define the mapping S of the set Γ onto J_1, and show that this mapping is a homeomorphism. Let $X \in \Gamma$, $X \in J_1$; then set $SX = X$.

Now let $X \in \Gamma$, but $X \notin J_1$, so that $X \in J_2$. Then there exists a unique arc A_X of the curve J_2 that contains X as an interior point and is such that the interior points of this arc are in Γ but not in J_1. The end points a and b of the arc A_X lie in J_1. Then the set $A_X + J_1$ consists of three arcs that intersect only in their end points (the set has the form of the letter θ). The set $A_X + J_1$ divides the plane into three sections, two of which are bounded and do not intersect U. One of these bounded sections is clearly D_1. Denote the other by R_X. The region R_X is bounded by A_X and the arc B_X, which is in J_1 and has the same end points a and b as A_X.

We define S on A_X to be a homeomorphism of the arc A_X onto the arc B_X that leaves the points a and b of these arcs stationary. This completes the definition of the mapping S.

We will now show that a point $X \in J_1$ on Γ corresponds to each point $S^{-1}X$. This is obvious if $X \in J_1$ and $X \in \Gamma$. If $X \in J_1$ but $X \notin \Gamma$, then we can construct an arc C_X connecting the point X with the point at infinity and intersecting J_1 only at the point X. Let Y be the first point of intersection of this arc with the set Γ. Then the region R_X defined above contains the part of the arc C_X between X and Y and, consequently, X is the image of one of the points of the arc A_X under the mapping S.

We will now show that the transformation S is one-to-one. Assume the contrary, i.e., assume that there exist two points $X_1 \in \Gamma$ and $X_2 \in \Gamma$ such that $SX_1 = SX_2$. It is clear that if $X \in \Gamma$ and X is not in J_1, then SX will not be in Γ; consequently, if $SX_1 \in \Gamma$, then X_1 belongs to Γ and J_1 and, therefore, $X_1 = X_2 = SX_1 = SX_2$. Now assume that SX_1 is not in Γ; then the arcs A_{X_1} and A_{X_2} may intersect only, possibly, at their ends. The point SX_1 is then a boundary point of both R_{X_1} and R_{X_2}; it is not a terminal point of A_{X_1} or A_{X_2}. Thus, the regions R_{X_1} and R_{X_2} have common points. This is impossible, because if a point of X belongs to both R_{X_1} and R_{X_2}, it can be connected to the point at infinity by an arc intersecting only A_{X_2}, and not intersecting either A_{X_1} or B_{X_1}.

That S is continuous follows immediately from the fact that there may be no more than a countable number of domains R_X and only a finite number of them can have diameter larger than a given position number ε. Q.E.D.

Lemma 12.2. Let T be a homeomorphism of the plane into itself, and let D be the domain bounded by a closed Jordan J. Denote the unbounded component of the complement of the set $J \cup TJ \cup \ldots \cup T^N J$ in the plane by U_N, and denote its boundary by Γ_N. If the intersection $D \cap TD$ is nonempty, then Γ_N is a closed Jordan curve in $J \cup TJ \cup \ldots \cup T^N J$. The interior, Δ_N, of Γ_N contains the union $D \cup TD \cup \ldots \cup T^N D$.

Proof. For $N=1$, the theorem follows from the preceding lemma if we set $D_1 = D$ and $D_2 = TD$. Assume that the lemma is true for $N-1$, then we will prove that it is also true for N. Set $D_1 = \Delta_{N-1}$ $D_2 = T^N D$; then $J_1 = \Gamma_{N-1}$ and $J_2 = T^N J_1$ are closed Jordan curves, and, because Δ_{N-1} contains $D \cup TD \cup \ldots \cup T^N D$, the unbounded component of the complement of $\Gamma_{N-1} + T^N J$ will coincide with the unbounded component U_N of the complement of $J \cup TJ \cup \ldots \cup T^N J$. Since $D \cap TD$ is nonempty, so is $T^{N-1} D \cap T^N D$; but $T^{N-1} D \subset \Delta_{N-1}$ so that the intersection $\Delta_{N-1} \cdot T^N D$ is also nonempty. The hypothesis of the preceding lemma is therefore satisfied, and the present lemma then follows.

These two lemmas make it possible to prove the following theorem.

Theorem 12.6. Assume that system (12.1) is dissipative; then there exists a region Δ bounded by a closed Jordan curve Γ and such that

$$T\bar{\Delta} \subset \bar{\Delta} \tag{12.8}$$

where, as usual, $TX_0 = X(\omega, X_0, 0)$.

Proof. Consider the disk $H\{\|X\|<h\}$ defined by Theorem 2.2, and choose some disk $D\supset H$. By Theorem 2.2, there exists an N such that for $k\geqslant N$

$$T^kD\subset H. \tag{12.9}$$

Moreover, it follows from (2.28) that the set I corresponding to dissipative system (12.1) is contained in H. Since the set I is invariant under the transformation T, it is clear that $I\subset D\cap TD$ and, consequently, the intersection $D\cap TD$ is nonempty. Let J denote the circle bounding the disk D, and, as in Lemma 12.2, let U_N denote the unbounded component of the complement of the set $J\cup TJ\cup\ldots\cup T^NJ$ in the entire space under consideration; let Γ_N denote its boundary, and let ${}^N\nabla$ be the interior of Γ_N. We will now show that

$$T\bar{\Delta}_N\subset\bar{\Delta}_N. \tag{12.10}$$

In order to do so, it is clearly sufficient to prove that

$$T\Gamma_N\subset\bar{\Delta}_N. \tag{12.11}$$

By Lemma 12.2, we know that Γ_N is contained in the set $J\cup TJ\cup\ldots\cup T^NJ$. It follows from the definition of Δ_N that

$$J\cup TJ\cup\ldots\cup T^NJ\subset\bar{\Delta}_N. \tag{12.12}$$

Let X be an arbitrary point of Γ_N; then there exists an integer k, $0\leqslant k\leqslant N$, such that $X\in T^kJ$. If $k<N$, then $TX\in T^{k+1}J$ and, consequently, it follows from (12.12) that $TX\in\bar{\Delta}_N$. Now let $X\in T^NJ$,; then $T^{-N}X\in J$ and, by (12.9),

$$TX=T^{N+1}T^{-N}X\in\bar{H}.$$

By the choice of D, we have $\bar{H}\subset\bar{D}$ and, by the definition of Δ_N, we have $\bar{D}\subset\bar{\Delta}_N$ so that $TX\in\bar{\Delta}_N$. Inclusion (12.11) then follows, which proves the theorem.

This theorem was first published in [44], but the reader can find a proof in Russian in [45].

We now introduce the shift vector of the transformation T: $V=\overrightarrow{X,TX}$. The following proposition is a consequence of Theorem 12.6:

Corollary 12.1. The index of any closed Jordan curve located outside a disk of sufficiently large radius with center at the coordinate origin is equal to $+1$ in the field of the shift vector of the transformation T.

Indeed, the index of the curve Γ_N in the field of V is equal to $+1$, which follows immediately from Theorem 12.6. Now consider an arbitrary closed Jordan curve γ enclosing the region Δ_N. Clearly, in the annulus enclosed by the curves γ and Γ_N there are no singular points of the vector V and, therefore, the indices of the curves γ and Γ_N in the field of V coincide.

4. Again assume that system (12.1) is dissipative, and consider the set I corresponding to this system. If I degenerates into a point, we have the case of convergence. We therefore assume that I does not degenerate into a point. By definition, I is the intersection of embedded regions, and is therefore a continuum that does not split the plane.*

Let G be the complement of I in the plane, and let Γ be its boundary. By hypothesis, Γ does not consist of one point, so that the region G can be conformally mapped onto the exterior of the unit circle C.

Now, let G lie in the plane of the complex variable z ($z = x_1 + ix_2$); let the unit disk C lie in the plane of the complex variable w, and let D be the unbounded component of the complement of C in the w plane. It follows from Riemann's theorem that there exists a conformal mapping S of the domain G onto the domain D such that the point at infinity is carried into the point at infinity. This transformation maps the boundary Γ into the circle C in such a way that a boundary element corresponds to each point of the circle C (in the terminology of Caratheodory, such boundary elements are called prime ends [57]; for a detailed discussion about the boundary properties of conformal mappings, cf. also [58]; moreover, this correspondence is one-to-one.

Consider the mapping STS^{-1} of the exterior D of circle C into itself. This mapping is a homeomorphism in D. From the properties of the mapping S of the boundary Γ onto the circle C it follows that this mapping is also homeomorphic in the closed domain $\bar{D}$. It is not difficult to see that the mapping STS^{-1} of the closed region $\bar{D}$ onto itself preserves directions. Thus, STS^{-1} is a one-to-one continuous direction-preserving mapping of the circle C onto itself. Let μ be the turning point of this transformation (see the end of Section 10 with regard to the turning point of a mapping of a circle onto itself). Assume that $\mu = p/q$, where q is a natural number and p is an integer; then C has points that are stationary under the transformation $(STS^{-1})^q = ST^qS^{-1}$. Consequently, there exist in this case boundary elements in Γ that are stationary under the transformation T^q. If such a stationary boundary element is an element of the first kind, i.e., consists of one point z_0, then this point is a stationary point of the transformation T^q, and has a solution with period $q\omega$ passing through it.

Now assume that a boundary element that is stationary under T^q is a continuum K_1 that does not degenerate into a point. Let K denote the continuum that is the union of K_1 and all bounded components of

*As usual, we use the word continuum in the sense of a connected closed set.

the complement of K_1 in the plane (when K_1 does not split the plane, K coincides with K_1). The continuum K does not split the plane. Since $T^q K_1 = K_1$, it is clear that $T^q K = K$, i.e., the continuum T^q is invariant under the transformation T^q. We will show below that the transformation K has a stationary point in K. Thus, a T^q-periodic solution of system (12.1) corresponds to every boundary element that is stationary under $q\omega$.

We will now show that the transformation T^q has a stationary point in K. This theorem was proved by Cartwright and Littlewood [59], but we will give a later and simpler proof due to Reifenberger [60].

Theorem 12.7. Let T be a direction-preserving homeomorphism of the plane into itself. If T has an invariant bounded continuum I that does not split the plane, then I contains a stationary point of the transformation T.

Proof. Contrary to the assertion of the theorem, assume that T has no stationary points in I, and consider the shift vector $V = \overrightarrow{X, TX}$ of the transformation T. By hypothesis, this vector has no singular points in I, so that, because I is closed and bounded, there exists a $b > 0$ such that the length of the vector V in I is larger than 2b. Because V is continuous, there exists an $\varepsilon > 0$ such that the length of the shift vector is larger than b in the ε-neighborhood of I.

Now construct a polygon π with the following properties: The polygon π and its interior π_i lie in the ε-neighborhood of the continuum I; π_i contains I, and any point of π can be connected to some point of I by an arc contained in π_i and having a diameter less than $b/4$.

As usual, let $U(I, \varepsilon/2)$ denote the $(\varepsilon/2)$-neighborhood of the continuum I; let $\overline{U}(I, \varepsilon/2)$ denote its closure, and consider the complement of the set $\overline{U}(I, \varepsilon/2)$ in the entire space. It is not difficult to see that there can be only a finite number of bounded components of this complement that contain points outside the $(\varepsilon/2)$-neighborhood of the set $(U(I, \varepsilon/2)$. Denote these components by $A_1, A_2, \ldots, A_n$, and connect these regions to the point at infinity by curves $l_1, l_2, \ldots, l_n$ that do not intersect the set I. Let ε_1 be the distance from the continuum I to $l_1 + l_2 + \ldots + l_n$. It is clear that if at least one domain A_i actually exists, then $\varepsilon_1 < \varepsilon/2$; otherwise, set $\varepsilon_1 = \varepsilon/2$. Divide the plane into equal squares with sides parallel to the coordinate axes; the length of a side of each such square will be taken equal to $\min \{b/8, \varepsilon_1/2\}$. Now consider the set B of all squares that have at least one point in common with the continuum I (naturally, the squares in question are closed). Any bounded component of the complement of the set B belongs to $U(I, \varepsilon)$. Indeed, it is not difficult to see that $B \subset U(I, \varepsilon/2)$; consequently, if some bounded component A of the complement of B had points outside the ε-neighborhood of I, we would have $A \supset A_i$ for some i. Then the curve l_i would connect A

with the point at infinity without intersecting B, which is precluded by the definition of A. The polygon π, which is a part of the boundary of the set B (or coincides with this boundary if it is connected), also contains the set B in its interior π_i and is clearly the set desired.

On the polygon π, select a finite number of points $p_1, p_2, \ldots p_n$ such that their index increases in the positive direction of rotation and the diameter of the arcs $p_k p_{k+1} (k=1, 2, \ldots, n, p_{n+1}=p_1)$ is less than $b/4$. We can take, for example, all corner points of the polygon π, labeling them in order in the positive direction of rotation.

By the choice of the polygon π, for each point p_k there is a corresponding accessible point r_k of the continuum I and an arc that connects p_k to r_k and lies, except for its end points, in the region $\pi_i - I$. The diameter of the arcs $p_k r_k$ is less than $b/4$. Let L_k denote the arc $r_k p_k p_{k+1} r_{k+1}$. The diameter of L_k is less than b, so that

$$L_k \cdot TL_k = 0. \tag{12.13}$$

Let D_k be the region bounded by the arc L_k and the continuum I. It follows from (12.13) that either the regions D_k and TD_k are disjoint or one of them contains the other.

Since $T^{-1}\pi$ lies at a positive distance from I, there exists an arc Λ_k that connects r_k to r_{k+1}, lies in D_k, and does not intersect $T^{-1}\pi$. Clearly, $T\Lambda_k$ lies inside π_i.

Consider the angular change of the shift vector V of the transformation T as the point p moves in the positive direction along the polygon π. Denote the total angular change of the vector V after one entire passage around the polygon π by Δ. Let α_k be the angular change of the vector V due to motion along the arc $p_k p_{k+1}$; then

$$\Delta = \sum_{k=1}^{n} \alpha_k. \tag{12.14}$$

Let β_k be the angular change of a continuous vector whose origin moves along the arc $p_k p_{k+1}$ of the polygon π and whose end moves from the point Tr_k to the point Tr_{k+1} along the arc TL_k. We will show that

$$\sum_{k=1}^{n} \beta_k = \sum_{k=1}^{n} \alpha_k. \tag{12.15}$$

This relation is obvious if, in the definition of β_k, we choose a vector that first moves along the arc $Tr_k Tp_k$ with its origin fixed at p_k, then becomes the shift vector on the arc $p_k p_{k+1}$, and, finally, moves along the arc $Tp_{k+1} Tr_{k+1}$ with origin fixed at the point p_{k+1}.

Now let γ_k be the angular change of a vector whose end point moves along the arc $T\Lambda_k$ and whose initial point moves along the arc $p_k p_{k+1}$ of the polygon π. The sum $\sum_{k=1}^{n} \gamma_k$ represents the total angular change of a vector whose origin tranverses π in the positive direction and whose end always lies in π_l. Therefore, we have

$$\sum_{k=1}^{n} \gamma_k = +2\pi. \tag{12.16}$$

We now compare β_k and γ_k. Since $T\Lambda_k$ does not intersect π and TL_k does not intersect L_k, the union $T\Lambda_k \cup TL_k$ is a closed Jordan curve that does not intersect the arc $p_k p_{k+1}$ of the polygon π.

The following three cases are possible:

I. $D_k \cdot TD_k = 0$.

The region bounded by the curve $T\Lambda_k + TL_k$ lies in TD_k, which does not contain points of $\bar{D}_k$, and, consequently, $p_k p_{k+1}$ lies outside $T\Lambda_k + TL_h$, so that

$$\beta_k - \gamma_k = 0 \tag{12.17}$$

II. $TD_k \subset D_k$.

Here the region bounded by the curve $T\Lambda_k \cup TL_k$ lies in $TD_k \subset D_k$, and, therefore, $p_k p_{k+1}$ again lies outside the curve $T\Lambda_k \cup TL_k$, i.e., Eq. (12.17) is again satisfied.

III. $D_k \subset TD_k$.

The arc $p_k p_{k+1}$ of the polygon π does not intersect $TL_k \cup l$, but it is contained in the region $\bar{D}_k \subset \overline{TD}_k$, and, consequently, is contained in the region bounded by the arc TL_k and the continuum l. On the other hand, because $T\Lambda_k \subset \pi_l$, the arc $p_k p_{k+1}$ is outside of the region bounded by the arc $T\Lambda_k$ and the continuum l. Consequently, the arc $p_k p_{k+1}$ is inside the region bounded by the closed Jordan curve $T\Lambda_k \cup TL_k$; in the case under discussion we therefore have

$$\beta_k - \gamma_k = \pm 2\pi. \tag{12.18}$$

The sign in Eq. (12.18) is selected in the following manner. If the path—initial along the arc TL_k from the point Tr_k to the point Tr_{k+1} and then along $T\Lambda_k$ in the opposite direction—is in the positive direction, the "plus" sign must be chosen; otherwise, the "minus" sign is used. Since the arc $p_k p_{k+1}$ is positive on the polygon π and the arc $p_{k+1} r_{k+1} + \Lambda_k + r_k p_k$ lies in π_l, the path—initially along L_k from r_k to r_{k+1} and then along Λ_k in the opposite direction—is positive. But T preserves orientation, so that the path moving initially along the arc TL_k from Tr_k to Tr_{k+1} and then along $T\Lambda_k$ in the opposite direction is positive. Thus it follows that the "plus" sign must always be used in (12.18), and, therefore,

$$\beta_k - \gamma_k = 2\pi. \tag{12.19}$$

It follows from (12.14)-(12.17) and (12.19) that

$$\Delta = 2\pi m \quad (m \geqslant 1).$$ (12.20)

This equation shows that the shift vector of the transformation $\overline{\pi}_i$ has a singular point in T. But π_i is a proper subset of $U(I, \varepsilon)$, so that, by the choice of ε, the length of the vector V in $\overline{\pi}_i$ is at least $b > 0$. We thus obtain a contradiction, which proves the theorem.

Thus, a qth order subharmonic corresponds to every boundary element of the domain G that is stationary under the transformation T^q.

In the following two sections we will discuss dissipative systems whose sets I are closed regions bounded by closed Jordan curves; then, in Section 15 we will study a dissipative system with a more complex set I.

13. THE EXISTENCE OF INVARIANT SURFACES

Again consider a system of two equations that are periodic with respect to their arguments:

$$\frac{dx}{dt} = X(x, y, t), \quad \frac{dy}{dt} = Y(x, y, t).$$ (13.1)

In conjunction with this system, consider the following "neighboring" system:

$$\left.\begin{array}{l} \dfrac{dx}{dt} = X(x, y, t) + \varepsilon X_1(x, y, t), \\[2mm] \dfrac{dy}{dt} = Y(x, y, t) + \varepsilon Y_1(x, y, t). \end{array}\right\}$$ (13.2)

Assume that the functions X, X_1, Y, and Y_1 are continuously differentiable with respect to all of their arguments and have period ω with respect to t. In addition, assume that the functions $X(x, y, t)$ and $Y(x, y, t)$ have continuous second derivatives with respect to x and y; ε is a small parameter.

1. Assume that system (13.1) has a smooth toroidal invariant surface; we will show that, when certain additional conditions are satisfied, system (13.2) also has such an invariant surface [61-65].

Thus, assume that system (13.1) has a smooth toroidal (if we identify with each other all planes of the form $t = n\omega$) invariant surface, and assume this surface to be represented in the form

$$x = \varphi(\theta, t), \quad y = \psi(\theta, t)$$ (13.3)

It is assumed that the functions φ and ψ are periodic with respect to t, and have period ω. Since surface (13.3) is invariant, the curves $x=\varphi(\theta, 0)$, $y=\psi(\theta, 0)$ and $x=\varphi(\theta, \omega)$, $y=\psi(\theta, \omega)$ must coincide, so that the assumptions made do not restrict the generality of the following discussion.

The intersection of surface (13.3) and the plane $t=0$ is a smooth closed curve which does not intersect itself; hence we can assume that the functions $\varphi(\theta, 0)$ and $\psi(\theta, 0)$ have some period ω_1, that the equations $\varphi(\theta_1, 0)=\varphi(\theta_2, 0)$, $\psi(\theta_1, 0)=\psi(\theta_2, 0)$ imply the equation $\theta_1-\theta_2=n\omega_1$ where n is an integer, and that $[\varphi_\theta'(\theta, 0)]^2+[\psi_\theta'(\theta, 0)]^2>0$. By hypothesis, surface (13.3) is invariant, i.e., consists of complete solution curves, so that the functions $x=\varphi(\theta, t)$, $y=\psi(\theta, t)$ yield smooth closed curves without self-intersections for every fixed t. Consequently, we can assume that the following equations hold for all t:

$$\varphi(\theta+\omega_1, t)=\varphi(\theta, t),\ \psi(\theta+\omega_1, t)= \\ =\psi(\theta, t),\ [\varphi'(\theta, t)]^2+[\psi'(\theta, t)]^2>0.$$

Since surface (13.3) is smooth, we can and will assume that the functions φ and ψ have continuous partial derivatives with respect to both of their arguments. Moreover, we will assume that $\varphi(\theta, t)$ and $\psi(\theta, t)$ have continuous second derivatives with respect to θ.

We will now introduce the following new coordinate system in the neighborhood of our invariant surface: The coordinate t is retained without variation. Fix some $t=\bar{t}$ and draw the normals to the curve $x=\varphi(\theta, \bar{t})$, $y=\psi(\theta, \bar{t})$ in the plane $t=\bar{t}$. Since the functions φ and ψ have continuous second derivatives, the periodicity of these functions with respect to both arguments implies that the radius of curvature of the curves $x=\varphi(\theta, t)$, $y=\psi(\theta, \bar{t})$ is bounded below by the same number for all θ and t. We can, therefore, find a sufficiently small neighborhood of surface (13.3) so that the above-noted normals do not intersect, provided that they correspond to geometrically different points of the curve $x=\varphi(\theta, \bar{t})$, $y=\psi(\theta, t)$. Now choose a point (x, y, t) in this neighborhood and pass through it a plane of constant t. In this plane, draw the normal n to the curve $x=\varphi(\theta, t)$, $y=\psi(\theta, t)$ at the chosen point. We take the new coordinates of the point (x, y, t) to be the coordinate θ of the point of intersection of the normal n with the curve $x=\varphi(\theta, t)$, $y=\psi(\theta, t)$ and the length z of the normal n from the point (x, y, t) to the point at which the normal intersects the curve. Here, z is taken to be positive if the points (x, y, t) is outside the region bounded by the curve $x=\varphi(\theta, t)$, $y=\psi(\theta, t)$, and negative if it is inside.

The coordinate system which we have thus selected is frequently called a normal coordinate system. It is not difficult to see that the new coordinates are related to the old ones by the following formulas:

$$\left.\begin{aligned} x &= \varphi(\theta, t) - \frac{\partial\psi}{\partial\theta} z, \\ y &= \psi(\theta, t) + \frac{\partial\varphi}{\partial\theta} z, \end{aligned}\right\} \tag{13.4}$$

where the functions $\alpha = -\partial\psi/\partial\theta$ and $\beta = \partial\varphi/\partial\theta$, like φ and ψ, have continuous partial derivatives with respect to both arguments, period ω with respect to t, and period ω_1 with respect to θ.

In terms of the new variables, system (13.1) can be written, for a neighborhood of surface (13.3), in the form

$$\left.\begin{aligned} \frac{d\theta}{dt} &= G(\theta, t) + zF(\theta, t, z), \\ \frac{dz}{dt} &= A(\theta, t) z + z^2 H(\theta, t, z). \end{aligned}\right\} \tag{13.5}$$

Henceforth, we will assume that the functions $F(\theta, t, z)$, $A(\theta, t)$ and $H(\theta, t, z)$ have continuous partial derivatives with respect to all of their arguments.

We will now make one more extremely important assumption: $G(\theta, t) \equiv 1$. This assumption deserves further analysis: Of course, system (13.5) has an invariant surface $z = 0$ coinciding with surface (13.3). If we assume that $G(\theta, t) \equiv 1$, then the coordinate θ on this surface is subject to the condition

$$\frac{d\theta}{dt} = 1.$$

Using the formulas $\tau = t\,(2\pi/\omega)$, $\vartheta = \theta\,(2\pi/\omega_1)$ to change the variables in this last equation, we obtain the equation

$$\frac{d\vartheta}{d\tau} = \frac{\omega}{\omega_1}, \tag{13.6}$$

which has period 2π with respect to both arguments.

The assumption that $G(\varphi, \theta) \equiv 1$ therefore means that, on the solution surface itself, the solutions behave in the same way as the solutions of Eq. (13.6). As Theorem 10.7 of Section 10 shows, in certain cases this can be achieved by appropriate changes of variables.

Under the assumptions made above, in terms of the new variables, system (13.2) takes the form

$$\left.\begin{aligned} \frac{d\theta}{dt} &= 1 + zF(\theta, t, z) + \varepsilon P(\theta, t, z), \\ \frac{dz}{dt} &= A(\theta, t) z + z^2 H(\theta, t, z) + \varepsilon R(\theta, t, z), \end{aligned}\right\} \tag{13.7}$$

where, as before, ε is a small parameter. The functions A, F, H, P, and R are ω- and ω_1-periodic with respect to t and θ, respectively, and have continuous partial derivatives with respect to all of their arguments.

In what follows, we will also assume that the inequality

$$-M(a)=\int_0^\omega A(t+a,\ t)\,dt<0 \tag{13.8}$$

holds. Set $\inf M(a)=M$. It is not difficult to see that $M(a)$ is an ω_1-periodic function, and therefore we can assert that $M>0$.

Let a and c denote the initial values of the functions θ and z when $t=0$, i.e., if $\theta(t,\ a,\ c,\ \varepsilon)$, $z(t,\ a,\ c,\ \varepsilon)$ is a solution of system (13.7), then $\theta(0,\ a,\ c,\ \varepsilon)=a$, $z(0,\ a,\ c,\ \varepsilon)=c$. Consider the following transformation T_ε of the Cartesian plane $(\theta,\ z)$ into itself: With a point $(\theta=a,\ z=c)$ we associate the point $\theta=\theta(\omega,\ a,\ c,\ \varepsilon)$, $z=z(\omega,\ a,\ c,\ \varepsilon)$. In view of the continuous dependence of solutions on initial data and parameters, this transformation is defined for $|\varepsilon|\leqslant\varepsilon_0$ and $|c|\leqslant h$, where ε_0 and $h>0$ are sufficiently small.

It follows from the second equation of system (13.7) that, when $\varepsilon=0$, the line $z=0$ is invariant under transformation T_0.

We will show that under the previously made assumptions there exists, for a sufficiently small ε, a curve $\gamma\,(z=z(\theta))$ which is ω_1-periodic with respect to θ, maps into itself under the transformation T_ε and approaches the line $\varepsilon\to 0$ as $z=0$.

First, note that the ω_1-periodicity of the right sides of system (13.7) with respect to θ implies that

$$\left.\begin{aligned}\theta(t,\ a+\omega_1,\ c,\ \varepsilon)&=\theta(t,\ a,\ c,\ \varepsilon)+\omega_1,\\ z(t,\ a+\omega_1,\ c,\ \varepsilon)&=z(t,\ a,\ c,\ \varepsilon).\end{aligned}\right\} \tag{13.9}$$

Consider the curve γ: $c=g(a)$, in the plane $t=0$; we assume that $g(a+\omega_1)=g(a)$ for all a and $|g(a)|\leqslant h$ for all a, where h is the constant given above. We will now study the curve $\bar\gamma=T_\varepsilon\gamma$, where $|\varepsilon|\leqslant\varepsilon_0$ and we will show that if the point $(\bar a,\ \bar c)$ is on $\bar\gamma$, then the point $(\bar a+\omega_1,\ c)$ is also on this curve. Indeed, let $(a,\ c)$ be the preimage of the point $(\bar a,\ \bar c)$ under the transformation T_ε, i.e., let $T_\varepsilon^{-1}(\bar a,\ \bar c)=(a,\ c)$; then, by the definition of T_ε, $\bar a=\theta(\omega,\ a,\ c,\ \varepsilon)$, $\bar c=z(\omega,\ a,\ c,\ \varepsilon)$. It follows from (13.9) that, when $t=\omega$,

$$\begin{aligned}\theta(\omega,\ a+\omega_1,\ c,\ \varepsilon)&=\theta(\omega,\ a,\ c,\ \varepsilon)+\omega_1=\bar a+\omega_1,\\ z(\omega,\ a+\omega_1,\ c,\ \varepsilon)&=z(\omega,\ a,\ c,\ \varepsilon)=\bar c,\end{aligned}$$

i.e., $T_\varepsilon(a+\omega_1,\ c)=(\bar a+\omega_1,\ \bar c)$. But, by hypothesis, the point $(a+\omega_1,\ c)$ is on γ, so that the point $T_\varepsilon(a+\omega_1,\ c)$ is on $\bar\gamma$; hence, the point $(\bar a+\omega_1,\ \bar c)$ is on $\bar\gamma$.

Thus, we have an operator Φ_ε that associates the curve $\bar{\gamma}$ with the ω_1-periodic curve $\gamma\,(c=g\,(a),\ |g\,(a)|\leqslant h)$. In what follows we will show that this operator has a stationary point for any sufficiently small ε.

Introduce the notation:

$$\bar{a}\,(a,\ c,\ \varepsilon)=\theta\,(\omega,\ a,\ c,\ \varepsilon),\ \bar{c}\,(a,\ c,\ \varepsilon)=z\,(\omega,\ a,\ c,\ \varepsilon). \tag{13.10}$$

We will now estimate the partial derivatives

$$\frac{\partial\bar{a}}{\partial a},\quad \frac{\partial\bar{a}}{\partial c},\quad \frac{\partial\bar{c}}{\partial a},\quad \frac{\partial\bar{c}}{\partial c}.$$

Set $\varepsilon=c=0$. Then system (13.7) has the solution $\theta=a+t,\ z=0$. Consequently, $\bar{a}=a+\omega$ and, therefore, for $\varepsilon=c=0$ we have

$$\frac{\partial\bar{a}}{\partial a}=1,\quad \frac{\partial\bar{a}}{\partial c}=0. \tag{13.11}$$

We will now evaluate the derivatives $\partial\bar{c}/\partial a$ and $\partial\bar{c}/\partial c$ for $\varepsilon=c=0$. Let u be either a or c. As usual, we will denote partial differentiation by the corresponding subscript; then the second equation of system (13.7) yields, for $\varepsilon=0$,

$$\frac{dz_u}{dt}=A\,(\theta,\ t)\,z_u+zA_\theta\theta_u+2zz_uH+z^2H_\theta\theta_u+z^2H_zz_u.$$

Setting $c=0$, we find that $z=0$ for all t; therefore, for $c=\varepsilon=0$, the last equation yields

$$\frac{dz_u}{dt}=A\,(\theta,\ t)\,z_u.$$

Then for $c=\varepsilon=0,\ \theta=t+a$, integration yields

$$z_u\,(\omega)=z_u\,(0)\,e^{\int\limits_0^\omega A\,(t+a,\ t)\,dt}$$

By (13.8),

$$z_u\,(\omega)=z_u\,(0)\,e^{-M\,(a)} \tag{13.12}$$

Further, it is clear that

$$z_a\,(0)=\frac{\partial c}{\partial a}=0,$$
$$z_c\,(0)=\frac{\partial c}{\partial c}=1.$$

Then it follows from (13.12) that

$$\frac{\partial \bar{c}}{\partial a} = 0, \quad \frac{\partial \bar{c}}{\partial c} = e^{-M(a)} < 1 \tag{13.13}$$

for $\varepsilon = c = 0$.

The partial derivatives $\partial\bar{a}/\partial a$, $\partial\bar{a}/\partial c$, $\partial\bar{c}/\partial a$, and $\partial\bar{c}/\partial c$ are continuous with respect to their arguments, and it follows from (13.9) that they have period ω_1 with respect to a, so that all of these partial derivatives are uniformly continuous for $|c| \leqslant h$, $|\varepsilon| \leqslant \varepsilon_0$, $-\infty < a < +\infty$. The following lemma is a consequence of (13.11), (13.13), and the above results:

Lemma 13.1. For any $\delta > 0$ there exists an $\varepsilon_0 > 0$ and an $h > 0$ such that the following inequalities are satisfied when $|c| \leqslant h$ and $|\varepsilon| \leqslant \varepsilon_0$:

$$\left|\frac{\partial \bar{a}}{\partial a} - 1\right| < \delta, \quad \left|\frac{\partial \bar{a}}{\partial c}\right| < \delta,$$
$$\left|\frac{\partial \bar{c}}{\partial a}\right| < \delta, \quad 0 \leqslant \frac{\partial \bar{c}}{\partial c} < e^{-M} + \delta,$$

where $M = \inf M(a) > 0$.

The following lemma is a corollary of Lemma 13.1:

Lemma 13.2. If ε_0 and h are sufficiently small, then, when $|\varepsilon| \leqslant \varepsilon_0$, the inequality $|c| \leqslant h$ implies the inequality $|\bar{c}| < h$.

Proof. It follows from the preceding lemma that $h\,|\,\partial\bar{c}/\partial c\,| \leqslant \beta < 1$ for sufficiently small ε_0. Choose h and ε_0 so that the hypothesis of the preceding lemma is satisfied. Because the solutions depend continuously on the parameter ε, there exists an $\varepsilon_0' > 0$ such that the inequality

$$|\bar{c}(a, 0, \varepsilon)| < h(1-\beta)$$

is satisfied when $|\varepsilon| \leqslant \varepsilon_0'$. Integration of the inequality $|\,\partial\bar{c}/\partial c\,| \leqslant \beta$ from 0 to $c \leqslant h$ now yields the assertion of the lemma.

Lemma 13.3. Let ε_0 and h be sufficiently small positive constants so that the preceding lemma holds, and let $\gamma\,(c = g(a),\ a_1 \leqslant a \leqslant a_2)$ be a segment of a curve such that $|g| \leqslant h$, $|g'(a)| \leqslant 1$ for $a_1 \leqslant a \leqslant a_2$. Then $\bar{\gamma} = T_\varepsilon\gamma$ for $|\varepsilon| \leqslant \varepsilon_0$ is a differentiable curve, and if $\bar{a}$ and $\bar{c}$ are the running coordinates of $\bar{\gamma}$, then $|\,d\bar{c}/d\bar{a}\,| \leqslant 1$.

Proof. The derivative $d\bar{c}/d\bar{a}$ exists on the curve $\bar{\gamma}$ and is given by the fraction

$$\frac{d\bar{c}}{d\bar{a}} = \frac{\dfrac{\partial\bar{c}}{\partial a} + \dfrac{\partial\bar{c}}{\partial c}\dfrac{dc}{da}}{\dfrac{\partial\bar{a}}{\partial a} + \dfrac{\partial\bar{a}}{\partial c}\dfrac{dc}{da}} \tag{13.14}$$

provided that the denominator is not equal to zero. But, by Lemma 13.1,

$$\left|\frac{\partial \bar{a}}{\partial a}-1\right|<\delta, \quad \left|\frac{\partial \bar{a}}{\partial c}\right|<\delta$$

and, by hypothesis, $|dc/da| \leqslant 1$; so that if δ is sufficiently small, the denominator of (13.14) is nonzero. The inequalities established in Lemma 13.1 imply that

$$\left|\frac{d\bar{c}}{d\bar{a}}\right| \leqslant \frac{\delta+(e^{-M}+\delta)\left|\frac{dc}{da}\right|}{1-\delta-\delta\left|\frac{dc}{da}\right|} \leqslant \frac{e^{-M}+2\delta}{1-2\delta}$$

because $|dc/da| \leqslant 1$. If h and ε_0 are so small that $4\delta \leqslant 1-e^{-M}$, we will have $|d\bar{c}/d\bar{a}| \leqslant 1$. Q.E.D.

Lemma 13.4. Let ε_0 and h be sufficiently small, and choose two points p_1 [with coordinates (a_1, c_1)] and p_2 [with coordinates (a_2, c_2)] in the plane $t=0$; let $|c_1|<h$ $|c_2|<h$ and $|c_2-c_1| \leqslant |a_2-a_1|$; then the following inequality is valid for the points $\bar{p}_i=T_\varepsilon p_i$ $(i=1, 2, |\varepsilon| \leqslant \varepsilon_0)$ with coordinates $(\bar{a}_i, \bar{c}_i)$:

$$|\bar{c}_2-\bar{c}_1| \leqslant |\bar{a}_2-\bar{a}_1|. \tag{13.15}$$

Proof. Connect the points p_1 and p_2 by means of a segment of the line $\gamma: c-c_1=(c_2-c_1/a_2-a_1)(a-a_1)$. Since, by hypothesis, $|c_2-c_1| \leqslant |a_2-a_1|$, the inequality $|dc/da| \leqslant 1$ is satisfied on γ. Now consider the curve $\bar{\gamma}=T_\varepsilon\gamma$; by Lemma 13.3, the inequality $|d\bar{c}/d\bar{a}| \leqslant 1$ will hold on this curve. Then Lagrange's mean-value theorem gives us (13.15), which proves the lemma.

As before, assume that ε_0 and h are so small that the above lemmas are satisfied when $|\varepsilon| \leqslant \varepsilon_0$ and $|c|<h$. Now choose $\delta>0$ sufficiently small so that

$$e^{-M}+2\delta=q<1. \tag{13.16}$$

In the plane $t=0$, consider the two curves $\gamma_1(c=g_1(a))$ and $\gamma_2(c=g_2(a))$. Assume that the functions g_1 and g_2 are ω_1-periodic, $|g_i(a)|<h$ $(i=1, 2)$ for all a, and that $|g_i(a_1)-g_i(a_2)|<|a_1-a_2|$ $(i=1, 2)$. Let $\bar{\gamma}_i=T_\varepsilon\gamma_i$ $(i=1, 2, |\varepsilon| \leqslant \varepsilon_0)$ be the images of the curves γ_i under the mapping T_ε. It follows from Lemma 13.4 that the curves $\bar{\gamma}_1$ and $\bar{\gamma}_2$ may be represented in the form $c=f_1(a)$ and $c=f_2(a)$, respectively, and the functions f_1 and f_2 satisfy a Lipschitz condition:

$$|f_i(a_1)-f_i(a_2)| \leqslant |a_1-a_2| \quad (i=1, 2). \tag{13.17}$$

As shown above, the functions $f_1(a)$ and $f_2(a)$ are ω_1-periodic. Introduce the notation:

$$\rho = \max |g_1(a) - g_2(a)|; \tag{13.18}$$

$$\bar{\rho} = \max |f_1(a) - f_2(a)|. \tag{13.19}$$

Lemma 13.5.

$$\bar{\rho} \leqslant q\rho. \tag{13.20}$$

Proof. Contrary to the assertion of the lemma, assume that $\bar{\rho} > q\rho$. Then there exists an a' such that $|f_1(a') - f_2(a')| > q\rho$. Assume that the point $\bar{p}_1$ has coordinates $(a', f_1(a'))$, and that its preimage p_1 under the transformation T_ε has coordinates $(a, g_1(a) = c_1)$. Let p_2 be a point with coordinates $(a, g_2(a) = c_2)$. By definition,

$$|c_2 - c_1| \leqslant \rho. \tag{13.21}$$

Let $\bar{p}_2 = T_\varepsilon p_2$. It follows from (13.10) that $\bar{p}_1$ has coordinates $\bar{a}(a, c_1, \varepsilon) = a'$, $\bar{c}(a, c_1, \varepsilon) = f_1(a')$ while $\bar{p}_2$ has coordinates $\bar{a}(a, c_2, \varepsilon)$, $\bar{c}(a, c_2, \varepsilon)$. By Lagrange's mean-value theorem, we have

$$|\bar{c}(a, c_2, \varepsilon) - \bar{c}(a, c_1, \varepsilon)| = \left|\frac{\partial \bar{c}}{\partial c}\right| |c_2 - c_1|$$

where the derivative $\partial\bar{c}/\partial c$ is taken at some intermediate point. Then by Lemma 13.1,

$$|\bar{c}(a, c_2, \varepsilon) - \bar{c}(a, c_1, \varepsilon)| \leqslant (e^{-M} + \delta) |c_2 - c_1| \tag{13.22}$$

Moreover,

$$|\bar{a}(a, c_2, \varepsilon) - \bar{a}(a, c_1, \varepsilon)| \leqslant \left|\frac{\partial \bar{a}}{\partial c}\right| |c_2 - c_1|$$

from which it follows that

$$|\bar{a}(a, c_2, \varepsilon) - \bar{a}(a, c_1, \varepsilon)| \leqslant \delta |c_2 - c_1|. \tag{13.23}$$

By inequality (13.17),

$$|f_2(\bar{a}(a, c_2, \varepsilon)) - f_2(\bar{a}(a, c_1, \varepsilon))| \leqslant \\ \leqslant |\bar{a}(a, c_2, \varepsilon) - \bar{a}(a, c_1, \varepsilon)| \leqslant \delta |c_2 - c_1|. \tag{13.24}$$

Also,

$$f_2(\bar{a}(a, c_1, \varepsilon)) - f_1(\bar{a}(a, c_1, \varepsilon))| \leqslant |f_2(\bar{a}(a, c_2, \varepsilon)) - \\ - f_1(\bar{a}(a, c_1, \varepsilon))| + |f_2(\bar{a}(a, c_2, \varepsilon)) - f_2(\bar{a}(a, c_1, \varepsilon))|. \tag{13.25}$$

By the definition of the points $\bar{p}_1$ and $\bar{p}_2'$, we can write

$$f_2(\bar{a}(a, c_2, \varepsilon))=\bar{c}(a, c_2, \varepsilon), \quad f_1(\bar{a}(a, c_1, \varepsilon))=\bar{c}(a, c_1, \varepsilon).$$

It follows from these last equations, as well as (13.24) and (13.25), that

$$|f_2(\bar{a}(a, c_1, \varepsilon))-f_1(\bar{a}(a, c_1, \varepsilon))| \leqslant \\ \leqslant (e^{-M}+\delta)|c_2-c_1|+\delta|c_2-c_1|.$$

But because of our notation, $\bar{a}(a, c_1, \varepsilon)=a'$; then it follows from (13.16) that

$$|f_2(a')-f_1(a')| \leqslant q|c_2-c_1|. \tag{13.26}$$

This last, together with (13.21), contradicts the hypothesis, which proves the lemma.

The lemmas which we have just proved make it possible to prove the following theorem:

Theorem 13.1. If system (13.2) takes the form (13.7) upon substitution of variables (13.4), and if condition (13.8) is satisfied, then if $|\varepsilon| \leqslant \varepsilon_0$, *where* $\varepsilon_0 > 0$ *is sufficiently small, there exists an invariant toroidal surface that approaches the surface (13.3) as* $\varepsilon \to 0$.

Proof. In order to prove the theorem, it is sufficient to show that for an arbitrarily small h and a sufficiently small ε_0 there exists an ω_1-periodic curve γ ($c=g(a)$ $|g(a)| \leqslant h$ for all a) such that $T_\varepsilon\gamma=\gamma$ if $|\varepsilon| \leqslant \varepsilon_0$, and this is the approach we will use.

Assume that h is sufficiently small. In fact, we will assume that it is so small that the previously proved lemmas hold, and consider the space Ω of all curves γ with the indicated properties. The curves γ are representable in the form $c=g(a)$, where the functions $g(a)$ are ω_1-periodic and satisfy a Lipschitz condition with the Lipschitz constant equal to unity:

$$|g(a_1)-g(a_2)| \leqslant |a_1-a_2|; \tag{13.27}$$

the functions g are bounded in absolute value by h: $|g(a)| \leqslant h$. We introduce the natural metric in the space Ω

$$\rho(\gamma_1, \gamma_2)=\max|g_1(a)-g_2(a)|. \tag{13.28}$$

It follows from Lemmas 13.2 and 13.4 that the operator Φ_ε maps the space Ω into itself. Lemma 13.5 shows that the operator Φ_ε is a contraction operator on this space. It then follows from Banach's theorem that the operator Φ_ε has on Ω the stationary point $\gamma=\Phi_\varepsilon\gamma$. Consequently, $\gamma=T_\varepsilon\gamma$, which proves the theorem.

2. Let Σ_ε be the invariant surface whose existence was proved in Paragraph 1. When $\varepsilon = 0$, this surface degenerates into the surface Σ_0 given by formulas (13.3) (in the (θ, t, z) coordinate system, the surface Σ_0 is the plane $z = 0$).

We will now examine the stability of the surface Σ_ε.

Let h and ε_0 be such that the theorems of Paragraph 1 are satisfied, and let γ be the intersection of the plane $t = 0$ and the surface Σ_ε, i.e., $T_\varepsilon \gamma = \gamma$. In the (x, y) plane, the curve γ is, as we can easily see, a closed curve lying arbitrarily close to the curve $x = \varphi(0, 0)$, $y = \psi(0, 0)$ when ε is sufficiently small. Denote the curves $z = -h$ and $z = h$ in the (x, y) plane by Γ_1 and Γ_2, and denote the annular region bounded by these curves by H. It follows from the proof of Theorem 13.1 that $\gamma \subset H$, and from Lemma 13.2 it follows that $T_\varepsilon H \subset H$, where, as usual, H is the closure of H.

Theorem 13.2. The invariant surface Σ_ε, whose existence was established by Theorem 13.1, is asymptotically Lyapunov-stable.

Proof. The existence of the curve γ was proved by means of Banach's theorem, so that the curve γ can be obtained by successive approximations, i.e., $T_\varepsilon^k \Gamma_1 \to \gamma$ and $T_\varepsilon^k \Gamma_2 \to \gamma$ as $k \to \infty$. Thus it follows that

$$\prod_{k=0}^{\infty} T_\varepsilon^k H = \gamma.$$

Choose an arbitrary positive number $\lambda > 0$. Denote the Euclidean distance between the points p and q by $\rho(p, q)$, and denote the solution vector of system (13.2), i.e., the vector with coordinates $x(t, x_0, y_0, t_0, \varepsilon)$, $y(t, x_0, y_0, t_0, \varepsilon)$, by $\chi(t, p, t_0)$. In virtue of the theorem on integral continuity, there exists, for the chosen λ, a $\delta_1 > 0$ such that $\rho(p, \gamma) < \delta_1$, then $\rho(\chi(t, p, 0), \Sigma_{\varepsilon t}) < \lambda$ for $0 \leqslant t \leqslant \omega$, where, as in definition 2.3, $\Sigma_{\varepsilon t}$ denotes the intersection of the invariant surface Σ_ε and the corresponding plane in the space (x, y, t).

Since $\gamma = \prod_{k=0}^{\infty} T_\varepsilon^k H$, there exists a K such that $\rho(T^K \Gamma_1, \gamma) < \delta_1$ $\rho(T^K \Gamma_2, \gamma) < \delta_1$. Set $\delta = \min\{\rho(T^K \Gamma_1, \gamma), \rho(T^K \Gamma_2, \gamma)\}$.

By the choice of δ, it follows that if $\rho(p, \gamma) < \delta$, then $\rho(\chi(t, p, 0), \Sigma_{\varepsilon t}) < \lambda$ for all $t \geqslant 0$, which proves that the invariant set Σ_ε is stable.

The relation $\gamma = \prod_{k=0}^{\infty} T_k H$ immediately implies that if $p \in H$, then $T^k p \to \gamma$ as $k \to \infty$. It follows then from the theorem on integral continuity that any solution beginning in H approaches Σ_ε as $t \to \infty$, which proves the theorem.

3. As an example, we will consider the case in which the right sides of system (13.1) are independent of time [66]. Consider the system

$$\left.\begin{aligned}\frac{dx}{dt} &= X(x, y) + \varepsilon X_1(x, y, t),\\ \frac{dy}{dt} &= Y(x, y) + \varepsilon Y_1(x, y, t).\end{aligned}\right\} \tag{13.29}$$

As before, assume that the right sides of this system are continuously differentiable with respect to all of their arguments and have period ω in t. Moreover, assume that X and Y have continuous second derivatives.

Assume that the trajectories of the system

$$\frac{dx}{dt} = X(x, y), \quad \frac{dy}{dt} = Y(x, y) \tag{13.30}$$

behave in the following manner. The origin O is an equilibrium state, and both roots of the characteristic equation corresponding to this equilibrium state are positive. There exists a periodic solution $(x = \varphi(t),\ y = \psi(t))$ with period ω_1. The characteristic exponent

$$\varkappa = \int_0^{\omega_1} [X'_x(\varphi(t), \psi(t)) + Y'_y(\varphi(t), \psi(t))]\,dt \tag{13.31}$$

of this periodic solution is negative. Except for the equilibrium state O, all trajectories of system (13.30) approach the limit cycle $\beta(x = \varphi(t),\ y = \psi(t))$ as $t \to \infty$. Then clearly, it follows that the limit cycle β includes the origin. Let Δ be the domain bounded by β. Any solution beginning in Δ approaches the origin as $t \to -\infty$. Any solution beginning outside Δ becomes infinite as time decreases.

We will now study the behavior of solutions of system (13.29) under these conditions with ε sufficiently small.

As above, introduce coordinates θ and z in the neighborhood of the limit cycle β by means of the formulas

$$x = \varphi(\theta) - \psi'(\theta)\,z, \quad y = \psi(\theta) + \varphi'(\theta)\,z. \tag{13.32}$$

The Jacobian of this transformation is

$$D = \frac{D(x, y)}{D(\theta, z)} = \begin{vmatrix} \varphi'(\theta) - \psi''(\theta)\,z, & -\psi'(\theta) \\ \psi'(\theta) + \varphi''(\theta)\,z, & \varphi'(\theta) \end{vmatrix} = \\ = \varphi'^2 + \psi'^2 + z(\psi'\varphi'' - \varphi'\psi''). \tag{13.33}$$

Clearly, $D > 0$ for sufficiently small z.

Differentiating Eq. (13.32) with respect to t, we obtain

$$\dot{x} = (\varphi' - z\psi'')\,\dot{\theta} - \psi'\dot{z},$$
$$\dot{y} = (\psi' + z\varphi'')\,\dot{\theta} + \varphi'\dot{z}.$$

Then it follows from system (13.30) that

$$(\varphi' - z\psi'')\dot{\theta} - \psi'\dot{z} = X(\varphi - \psi' z,\ \psi + \varphi' z),$$
$$(\psi' + z\varphi'')\dot{\theta} + \varphi'\dot{z} = Y(\varphi - \psi' z,\ \psi + \varphi' z).$$

Solving this system for $\dot{\theta}$ and $\dot{z}$, we obtain

$$\left.\begin{aligned} \dot{\theta} &= \{X(\varphi - \psi' z, \psi + \varphi' z)\varphi' + \\ &\qquad + Y(\varphi - \psi' z,\ \psi + \varphi' z)\psi'\}\frac{1}{D}, \\ \dot{z} &= \{-X(\varphi - \psi' z,\ \psi + \varphi' z)(\psi' + z\varphi'') + \\ &\qquad + Y(\varphi - \psi' z,\ \psi + \varphi' z)(\varphi' - z\psi'')\}\frac{1}{D}. \end{aligned}\right\} \tag{13.34}$$

The right side of the first of these equations becomes $\{X(\varphi,\ \psi)\varphi' + Y(\varphi,\ \psi)\psi'\}\ (1/\varphi'^2 + \psi'^2)$ when $z = 0$, but the pair of functions $(\varphi,\ \psi)$ is a solution of system (13.30), so that $X(\varphi,\ \psi) = \varphi'$, $Y(\varphi,\ \psi) = \psi'$ and, therefore, the right side of the first of Eqs. (13.34) is equal to 1 when $z = 0$. Thus, the first equation of system (13.34) may be written in the form

$$\frac{d\theta}{dt} = 1 + zF(\theta,\ z). \tag{13.35}$$

It is not difficult to see that when $z = 0$ the first part of the second equation of system (13.34) vanishes, so that the second equation may be written in the form

$$\frac{dz}{dt} = A(\theta)z + z^2 H(\theta,\ z). \tag{13.36}$$

We will now find $A(\theta)$. It follows immediately from the form of the right side of the second of Eqs. (13.34) that

$$\begin{aligned} A(\theta) &= \\ &= \frac{1}{\varphi'^2 + \psi'^2}\{X_x\psi'^2 - X_y\varphi'\psi' - X\varphi'' - Y_x\varphi'\psi' + Y_y\varphi'^2 - Y\psi''\} = \\ &= \frac{1}{\varphi'^2 + \psi'^2}\{(X_x + Y_y)(\varphi'^2 + \psi'^2) - \varphi'(X_x\varphi' + X_y\psi') - \\ &\qquad - \psi'(Y_x\varphi' + Y_y\psi') - \varphi'\varphi'' - \psi'\psi''\}. \end{aligned}$$

Differentiating the identities $\varphi' = X(\varphi,\ \psi)$ and $\psi' = Y(\varphi,\ \psi)$ with respect to θ, we find that $\varphi'' = X_x\varphi' + X_y\psi'$ and $\psi'' = Y_x\varphi' + Y_y\psi'$, consequently,

$$A(\theta)=X_x+Y_y-2\frac{\varphi'\varphi''+\psi'\psi''}{\varphi'^2+\psi'^2}$$

or

$$A(\theta)=X_x+Y_y-\frac{d}{d\theta}\ln(\varphi'^2+\psi'^2). \tag{13.37}$$

Since the functions φ and ψ have period ω_1, this equation yields

$$\int_0^{\omega_1} A(\theta)\,d\theta=\int_0^{\omega_1}[X_x(\varphi,\psi)+Y_y(\varphi,\psi)]\,d\theta=\varkappa. \tag{13.38}$$

In terms of variables θ, t, and z system (13.29) takes the form

$$\left.\begin{aligned} \frac{d\theta}{dt}&=1+zF(\theta,z)+\varepsilon P(\theta,t,z),\\ \frac{dz}{dt}&=A(\theta)z+z^2H(\theta,z)+\varepsilon R(\theta,t,z). \end{aligned}\right\} \tag{13.39}$$

This system satisfies all of the conditions of the foregoing discussion, so that the invariant surface Σ_ε exists.

Our assumptions concerning the behavior of solutions of system (13.30) imply that this system is dissipative. Since the right sides of this system are independent of time, it follows from Theorem 2.6 that there exists a function $v(x,y)$ with the following properties: The function v is defined and continuously differentiable with respect to both arguments when $x^2+y^2\geqslant a^2$ (where a is some positive number), $v(x,y)>0$ when $x^2+y^2\geqslant a^2$, $v(x,y)\to\infty$ when $x^2+y^2\to\infty$ and $(\partial v/\partial x)X+(\partial v/\partial y)Y<0$ when $x^2+y^2\geqslant a^2$.. It is not difficult to see that there exists a continuous positive-definite function $w(x,y)$ such that if

$$|X_1(x,y,t)|+|Y_1(x,y,t)|\leqslant w(x,y) \tag{13.40}$$

for $x^2+y^2\geqslant a^2$, the inequality

$$\frac{\partial v}{\partial x}(X+X_1)+\frac{\partial v}{\partial y}(Y+Y_1)<0 \tag{13.41}$$

will hold for all such x and y. Whence with the aid of Theorem 2.5 it follows that, for any $\varepsilon<1$, system (13.29) is dissipative, and moreover, there exists a number a_1 (that is independent of ε) such that any solution of system (13.29) enters the cylinder $x^2+y^2\leqslant a_1^2$ as time increases and does not leave it upon further increase in time.

It now follows from the asymptotic stability of the surface Σ_ε and the theorem on integral continuity that any solution beginning outside the cylinder bounded by Σ_ε approaches Σ_ε as $t \to +\infty$ if ε is sufficiently small.

It is known in the theory of perturbations of periodic solutions (see, for example, [67]) that if ε is sufficiently small, then system (13.29) has a unique periodic solution in the neighborhood of the coordinate origin and the characteristic exponents of this solution are positive. Then it follows from the theorem on integral continuity that all solutions beginning inside the surface Σ_ε, except for periodic solutions, approach Σ_ε as $t \to +\infty$.

Thus, if condition (13.40) holds and ε is sufficiently small system (13.29) is a dissipative system. The set I of this system is a closed region $\bar{G}$ bounded by a closed curve γ that satisfies a Lipschitz condition. Inside the region G, the transformation T_ε has a stationary point p_ε corresponding to a periodic solution with positive characteristic exponents. If p is a point different from p_ε, then $T_\varepsilon^k p \to \gamma$ as $k \to \infty$.

Of course, the disposition of solution curves on the surface Σ_ε and the behavior of the transformation T_ε on γ require a special investigation analogous to the one conducted in Section 10.

14. THE EXISTENCE OF AN INVARIANT SURFACE AND THE BEHAVIOR OF SOLUTIONS ON IT IN ONE SPECIAL CASE

In this section we will again study the problem of the existence of a toroidal invariant surface, and we again consider the system

$$\left.\begin{aligned} \frac{dx}{dt} &= X(x, y, t) + \varepsilon X_1(x, y, t, \varepsilon), \\ \frac{dy}{dt} &= Y(x, y, t) + \varepsilon Y_1(x, y, t, \varepsilon). \end{aligned}\right\} \tag{14.1}$$

where the functions X, X_1 Y, and Y_1 are assumed to be continuous with respect to all of their arguments, and continuously differentiable with respect to x and y. Moreover, as usual, we assume that these functions have period ω in t.

As in Section 13, we will assume that system (14.1) has, when $\varepsilon = 0$, an invariant surface Σ_0 that is homeomorphic to a torus. In the preceding section, however, we assumed that the solution curves on the surface Σ_0 itself behave like the solutions of Eq. (13.6).

Now we will assume that on the surface Σ_0 there are $k\omega$-periodic (k an integer) solutions of system (14.1) with $\varepsilon = 0$, and that both characteristic exponents of each of these solutions are nonzero. Moreover, we will assume that the invariant surface Σ_0 is asymptotically stable.

We now introduce the transformation T_ε of the plane (x, y) into itself in the usual way: If $x(t, x_0, y_0, t_0, \varepsilon)$, $y(t, x_0, y_0, t_0, \varepsilon)$ is a solution of (14.1), we associate the point (x_0, y_0) with the point $(x(\omega, x_0, y_0, 0, \varepsilon)$ $y(\omega, x_0, y_0, 0, \varepsilon))$.

Thus, it is assumed that there exists a closed Jordan curve γ_0, without self-intersections, that is invariant under the transformation T_0. The surface Σ_0 consists of the family of all solutions that pass through γ_0 when $t=0$.

Henceforth, we will consider system (14.1) in a toroidal phase space with all points of the form $(x, y, t+n\omega)$ $(n=0, \pm 1, \pm 2, \ldots)$ coinciding.

1. Here we will consider the structure of the surface Σ_0 in more detail. If S is a topological mapping of γ_0 onto the circle C, then ST_0S^{-1} is a topological direction-preserving mapping of the circle C onto itself. By hypothesis, when $\varepsilon=0$, system (14.1) has periodic solutions on Σ_0. Consequently, on γ_0, there exists a point p that is stationary under the transformation T_0^k. Assume that k is the smallest such number, i.e., assume that if $k \geqslant 2$, then $T_0^l p \neq p$ for $l=1, 2, \ldots, k-1$. We will show that the point Sp is stationary under the transformation $[ST_0S^{-1}]^k$. Indeed, it is not difficult to see that $[ST_0S^{-1}]^k = ST_0^kS^{-1}$ so that

$$[ST_0S^{-1}]^k Sp = ST_0^kS^{-1}Sp = ST_0^k p.$$

But the point p is stationary under the transformation T_0^k, i.e., $T_0^k p = p$, so that

$$[ST_0S^{-1}]^k Sp = Sp.$$

Let l be a natural number less than k, and consider the identity

$$[ST_0S^{-1}]^l Sp = ST_0^lS^{-1}Sp = ST_0^l p.$$

By hypothesis, $T_0^l p \neq p$, so that

$$[ST_0S^{-1}]^l Sp \neq Sp.$$

It follows from the considerations of Paragraph 7 of Section 10 that the turning point μ of the transformation ST_0S^{-1} is m/k, where m is a nonnegative integer. It also follows from these considerations that if a point P of the circle C is stationary under the transformation $[ST_0S^{-1}]^l$ (where l is a natural number), then $l=km_1$ (m_1 is an integer), and the point P is also stationary under $[ST_0S^{-1}]^k$. Thus it follows that if a point p_1 of the curve γ_0 is stationary under T_0^l, then $l=km_1$ (m_1 is an integer) and $T_0^k p_1 = p_1$.

Thus, all periodic solutions on Σ_0 have $k\omega$ as their smallest period.

The assumption that any periodic solution on Σ_0 has nonzero characteristic exponents implies that there is only a finite number of periodic solutions on Σ_0. Indeed, if the set of periodic solutions on Σ_0 were infinite, there would exist among them a periodic solution every neighborhood of which would also contain another periodic solution, different from the first. This contradicts the assumption that both characteristic exponents of such a solution are nonzero. Since the surface Σ_0 is asymptotically stable, at least one of the characteristic exponents of a periodic solution on Σ_0 must be negative. Indeed, if this were not so, i.e., if a periodic solution with both characteristic exponents positive existed, there would exist solutions that approached Σ_0 as $t \to -\infty$ and did not lie on Σ_0. This is impossible because Σ_0 is stable.

Let p be a stationary point of the transformation T_0^k. As we have just proved, there is only a finite number of stationary points of the transformation T_0^k; on Σ_0, so that p is an isolated stationary point of the transformation T_0^k. By Corollary **10.3**, one of the following relations holds for any point q in a sufficiently small neighborhood of the point p:

$$T_0^{nk} q \xrightarrow[n \to +\infty]{} p \tag{14.2}$$

$$T_0^{nk} q \xrightarrow[n \to -\infty]{} p. \tag{14.3}$$

In that case, if relation (14.2) holds for some point q on γ_0, then the same relation holds for all points on γ_0 between p and q, and conversely.

It is clear that if a periodic solution with negative characteristic exponents passes through the point p, relation (14.2) holds for any point q sufficiently close to p. Henceforth we will call such p stable.

Let $x = \bar{\varphi}_i(t)$, $y = \bar{\psi}_i(t)$ be a $k\omega$-periodic solution with negative characteristic exponents, and let p_{i0} denote the point with coordinates $\bar{\varphi}_i(0)$, $\bar{\psi}_i(0)$ it is then clear that the points $p_{il} = T_0^l p_{i0}$ $(l = 0, 1, \ldots, k-1)$ are geometrically different, stable, stationary points of the transformation T_0^k.

Consider a periodic solution $x = \varphi_j(t)$, $y = \psi_j(t)$ that lies on Σ_0 and has one positive characteristic exponent. Let q_{j0} be the point with coordinates $x = \varphi_j(0)$ $y = \psi_j(0)$; then the points $q_{jl} = T^l q_{j0}$ $(l = 0, 1, \ldots, k-1)$ are different stationary points of the transformation T_0^k. Substituting $\bar{x} = x - \varphi_j(t)$ $\bar{y} = y - \psi_j(t)$ into system (14.1) with $\varepsilon = 0$, we obtain

$$\left.\begin{aligned} \frac{d\bar{x}}{dt} &= a_{11}(t)\bar{x} + a_{12}(t)\bar{y} + \bar{X}(\bar{x}, \bar{y}, t), \\ \frac{d\bar{y}}{dt} &= a_{21}(t)\bar{x} + a_{22}(t)\bar{y} + \bar{Y}(\bar{x}, \bar{y}, t). \end{aligned}\right\} \tag{14.4}$$

In this system the functions $a_{ik}(t)$ $(i, k=1, 2)$, $\bar{X}(\bar{x}, \bar{y}, t)$, and $\bar{Y}(\bar{x}, \bar{y}, t)$ have period ω in t, and, furthermore, the functions $\bar{X}(\bar{x}, \bar{y}, t)$ and $\bar{Y}(\bar{x}, \bar{y}, t)$ vanish, together with their partial derivatives with respect to $\bar{x}$ and $\bar{y}$, when $\bar{x}=\bar{y}=0$.

It is well known [68] that by changing the variables with periodic coefficients, system (14.4) can be reduced to the form

$$\left.\begin{aligned}\frac{d\xi}{dt}&=\lambda_1\xi+X_1(\xi, \eta, t),\\ \frac{d\eta}{dt}&=\lambda_2\eta+Y_1(\xi, \eta, t).\end{aligned}\right\} \tag{14.5}$$

Here λ_1 and λ_2 are characteristic exponents, the functions X_1 and Y_1 are continuously differentiable with respect to ξ and μ and vanish together with their derivatives when $\xi=\eta=0$.

Consider the first-approximation system for (14.4):

$$\left.\begin{aligned}\frac{d\bar{x}}{dt}&=a_{11}(t)\,\bar{x}+a_{12}(t)\,\bar{y},\\ \frac{d\bar{y}}{dt}&=a_{21}(t)\,\bar{x}+a_{22}(t)\,\bar{y}\end{aligned}\right\} \tag{14.6}$$

and consider the characteristic equation of this system:

$$\begin{vmatrix}\bar{x}_1(k\omega)-\rho, & \bar{x}_2(k\omega)\\ \bar{y}_1(k\omega), & \bar{y}_2(k\omega)-\rho\end{vmatrix}=0, \tag{14.7}$$

where $\bar{x}_1(t)$, $\bar{y}_1(t)$ is the solution of system (14.6) with initial data $\bar{x}_1(0)=1$, $\bar{y}_1(0)=0$, and $\bar{x}_2(t)$, $\bar{y}_2(t)$ is the solution with initial data $\bar{x}_2(0)=0$, $\bar{y}_2(0)=1$. Since, by hypothesis, one of the characteristic exponents of the solution $x=\varphi_j(t)$, $y=\psi_j(t)$ is positive, it follows from what we have proved that the characteristic exponents λ_1 and λ_2 have different signs; consequently, the absolute value of one of the roots of Eq. (14.7) is greater than unity, while the absolute value of the other is less. Thus it follows that both roots of Eq. (14.7) are real. If the roots of Eq. (14.7) are positive, then the transformation mapping system (14.4) into system (14.5) has period $k\omega$ [68] and, consequently, the functions X_1 and Y_1 have the same period. If, however, the roots of the characteristic equation are negative, this transformation has period $2k\omega$, which is also the period of the functions X_1 and Y_1. Indeed, it is not difficult to show that the second case is impossible under the assumed conditions. We will therefore not dwell on the proof of this assertion, since in what follows it will not matter whether the functions X_1 and Y_1 have period $k\omega$ or $2k\omega$.

Since one of the coefficients, either λ_1 or λ_2, in system (14.5) is positive, the space (ξ, η, t) contains a two-dimensional continuously differentiable solution surface passing through the line

$\xi=\eta=0$. Solution curves approaching $\xi=\eta=0$ as $t\to-\infty$ lie on this surface, and any solution not on this surface will, as t decreases, leave a sufficiently small neighborhood of the solution $\xi=\eta=0$ (concerning the existence of such surfaces, see, for example, [3]). Thus it follows that there exists a smooth arc Λ_{j0} that passes through the point q_{j0} and has the property that if $q\in\Lambda_{j0}$, then $T_0^{nk}q\to q_{j0}$ as $k\to-\infty$.

From the stability of Σ_0, it follows that $\Lambda_{j0}\subset\gamma_0$, since otherwise there would exist solutions that did not lie on Σ_0 and approached Σ_0 as $t\to-\infty$, which is clearly impossible.

Thus, we have proved that if a periodic solution with a positive characteristic exponent passes through a point p that is stationary under T_0^k, relation (14.3) holds for any point q that is sufficiently close to p on γ_0. We will call such points p unstable.

From the foregoing, it follows that the points $q_{jl}=T_0^l q_{j0}$ $(l=0, 1, \ldots, k-1)$ are geometrically different unstable stationary points of the transformation T_0^k.

If we consider the transformation $ST_0^kS^{-1}$, then it easily follows from Theorem 10.4 that stable and unstable points alternate on γ_0.

Assume that there are on Σ_0 m different periodic solutions with negative characteristic exponents; then, on γ_0, there are km stable stationary points p_{il} $(l=1, 2, \ldots, m,\ l=0, 1, \ldots, k-1)$, plus the same number of unstable stationary points q_{il} $(l=1\ 2, \ldots, m,\ l=0, 1, \ldots, k-1)$.

Consider some unstable stationary point q_{jl}, the arc Λ_{jl} corresponding to it, and the open arc

$$H_{jl}=\sum_{s=0}^{\infty} T^{sk}\Lambda_{jl}. \tag{14.8}$$

This arc is invariant under the transformation T_0^k and the relation $T^{sk}q\to q_{jl}$ as $s\to-\infty$ holds for any $q\in H_{jl}$, so that $H_{jl}\subset\gamma_0$.

It follows from Theorem 10.4 that the ends of the arc H_{jl} lie next to stable stationary points, Thus, the curve γ_0 is the union of all arcs H_{jl} and the adjoined stable stationary points p_{jl} $(j=1, 2, \ldots, m,\ l=0, 1, \ldots, k-1)$.

2. In the (x, y) plane, enclose the points p_{jl} and q_{jl} in circular neighborhoods U_{jl} and V_{jl}, respectively, having small radii so that each contains only one stationary point of the transformation T_0^k, and so that they do not intersect.

It is a well-known fact in the theory of perturbations of periodic systems that each of the neighborhoods U_{jl} and V_{jl} contains one and only one stationary point of the transformation T_ε^k for $|\varepsilon|\leqslant\varepsilon_0$, where $\varepsilon_0>0$ is sufficiently small. Denote these points by $p_{jl}^{(\varepsilon)}$ and $q_{jl}^{(\varepsilon)}$. The roots of the characteristic equation corresponding to the solution which passes through the point $p_{jl}^{(\varepsilon)}$ or $q_{jl}^{(\varepsilon)}$ depend continuously on ε, so that, for sufficiently small ε, a periodic solution with negative characteristic exponents passes through $p_{jl}^{(\varepsilon)}$, and a solution having one positive and one negative characteristic exponent passes through the point $q_{jl}^{(\varepsilon)}$. In connection with this, we will call the points $p_{jl}^{(\varepsilon)}$ stable, and the points $q_{jl}^{(\varepsilon)}$ unstable.

As in the case of the point q_{jl}, so also for the point $q_{jl}^{(\varepsilon)}$ there exists a smooth arc $\Lambda_{jl}^{(\varepsilon)}$ that passes through $q_{jl}^{(\varepsilon)}$ and has the property that if $q \in \Lambda_{jl}^{(\varepsilon)}$, then $T_\varepsilon^{nk} q \to q_{jl}^{(\varepsilon)}$ as $n \to -\infty$. For any point q sufficiently close to $q_{jl}^{(\varepsilon)}$, but on $\Lambda_{jl}^{(\varepsilon)}$, the sequence $T_\varepsilon^{nk} q$ leaves a sufficiently small neighborhood of the point $q_{jl}^{(\varepsilon)}$, from which it follows that $\Lambda_{jl}^{(\varepsilon)} \subset T_\varepsilon^k \Lambda_{jl}^{(\varepsilon)}$. Moreover, it is not difficult to see that the arcs $\Lambda_{jl}^{(\varepsilon)}$ and $T_\varepsilon^l \Lambda_{j0}^{(\varepsilon)}$ $(l = 0, 1, \ldots, k-1)$ either coincide or can be superimposed on each other so that their union is again a smooth arc.

It follows from the proof of the above-noted (see again [3]) theorem on the existence of integral manifolds that the arc $\Lambda_{j\varepsilon}^{(\varepsilon)}$ is a continuous function of ε. Consider the open arc

$$H_{jl}^{(\varepsilon)} = \sum_{s=0}^{\infty} T_\varepsilon^{sk} \Lambda_{jl}^{(\varepsilon)}.$$

From the continuous dependence of solutions on parameters and initial data, it follows that the ends of this arc lie in certain sufficiently small neighborhoods of stable stationary points of the transformation T_0^k. If we denote these points by p_{jl} and $p_{(j+1)l}$, then it is clear that they also lie within sufficiently small neighborhoods of the stable stationary points of $p_{jl}^{(\varepsilon)}$ and $p_{(j+1)l}^{(\varepsilon)}$. But then the arc $H_{jl}^{(\varepsilon)}$ simply adjoins the points $p_{jl}^{(\varepsilon)}$ and $p_{(j+1)l}^{(\varepsilon)}$.

Consider the curve γ_ε consisting of all the open arcs $H_{jl}^{(\varepsilon)}$ and the stable points $p_{jl}^{(\varepsilon)}$. By construction, this curve is a closed Jordan curve, and it is invariant under the transformation T_ε: $T_\varepsilon \gamma_\varepsilon = \gamma_\varepsilon$.

The following theorem is a consequence of the foregoing discussion [69].

Theorem 14.1. Under the assumptions made above, if ε is sufficiently small, system (14.1) has an invariant surface Σ_ε that is homeomorphic to a torus.

15. INVESTIGATION OF A DISSIPATIVE SYSTEM WHOSE SET *I* IS OF SINGULAR STRUCTURE

In this section we will study a dissipative system whose solutions and set I are strongly singular. Consider the equation

$$\ddot{x} + k(x^2 - 1)\dot{x} + x = b\lambda k \cos \lambda t \tag{15.1}$$

and its generalization

$$\ddot{x} + kf(x)\dot{x} + g(x) = kp(t) \tag{15.2}$$

where k is a large parameter and b and λ are constants. Cartwright and Littlewood [71-73] have subjected these equations to detailed study, which brought to light, among other things, the following remarkable remarks.

When $b > 2/3$ and $k > k_0(\lambda, b)$ Eq. (15.1) is convergent. The most detailed analysis is has been carried for the case of $1/100 < b < (2/3) - (1/100)$. From within this interval for b, a set of subintervals whose total length is small is excluded, i.e., for sufficiently large k_0 there exists an arbitrarily small ε that has the following properties: If $k \geqslant k_0$, then there exists a set of excluded intervals with total length less than ε. The remaining set B is also a system of intervals, which varies with k, but, for $k \geqslant k_0$, its measure is not less than $(2/3) - (2/100) - \varepsilon$. B is divided into two parts, B_1 and B_2, of comparable measure.

If b is in the interval $I_1 \subset B_1$, then Eq. (15.1) has a system of stable subharmonics of order $2n+1$, and the "majority" of other solutions approach one of these subharmonics as $t \to +\infty$. The number n is constant in I_1 and is of the order of $[(2/3) - b]k$. If b lies in $I_1 \subset B_1$, then there exists a system of unstable subharmonics of order $(2n+1)$.

If b belongs to an interval I_2 of B_2, then Eq. (17.1) has two systems of stable harmonics of order $2n+1$ and $2n-1$; the "majority" of the remaining solutions approach one of these subharmonics. Moreover, there is an infinite set Σ of unstable periodic solutions, and there exists a set X of nonperiodic recurrent solutions, the set X having the cardinality of a continuum. The number n, as in the first case, is constant in I_2. The sets X and Σ remain topologically equivalent as b varies in I_2.

For all b in the interval $1/100 < b < (2/3) - (1/100)$ and for sufficiently large k, there exists a single totally unstable (asymptotically stable as $t \to -\infty$) periodic solution with period $2\pi/\lambda$.

Similar results are obtained for Eq. (15.2) under certain conditions.

The proofs of these assertions are very lengthy and complex, apparently not admitting any substantial simplification, so that it will not be possible to prove them here, and we refer the reader to the original works.

Levinson [74] considered a simpler equation whose solutions exhibit the same peculiar behavior as those of Eqs. (15.1) and (15.2). Here we will repeat Levinson's discussion. Familiarity with this material will considerably ease the task of studying the difficult works of Cartwright and Littlewood.

1. Consider the equation

$$\varepsilon \ddot{x} + \varphi(x)\dot{x} + \varepsilon x = b \sin t \tag{15.3}$$

where $\varepsilon > 0$ is a small parameter, $\varphi(x) = 1$ when $|x| > 1$, $\varphi(x) = -1$ when $|x| < 1$ and the constant b is chosen in some system of intervals embedded in the interval (0, 1). As Theorem 4.1 implies, Eq. (15.3) is dissipative. Performing a change of variables by setting $x_1 = x$ and $x_2 = \varepsilon x + \Phi(x_1)$ where $\int_0^{x_1} \varphi(x)\,dx = \Phi(x_1)$, we obtain the system

$$\varepsilon \frac{dx_1}{dt} = x_2 - \Phi(x_1), \quad \frac{dx_2}{dt} = -\varepsilon x_1 + b \sin t. \tag{15.4}$$

Let $P(x)$ be a function that satisfies a Lipschitz condition and is such that $|P(x) - \Phi(x)| < \Delta$ when $|x| \leqslant 5$, where Δ is sufficiently small positive constant. Since $\Phi(x)$ is continuous, $P(x)$ may be a polynomial. Now, together with (15.4), consider the system

$$\varepsilon \frac{dy_1}{dt} = y_2 - P(y_1), \quad \frac{dy_2}{dt} = -\varepsilon y_1 + b \sin t. \tag{15.5}$$

This system is equivalent to the equation

$$\varepsilon \ddot{y} + P'(y)\, y + \varepsilon y = b \sin t. \tag{15.6}$$

The function $\Phi(x)$ satisfies a Lipschitz condition with the Lipschitz constant equal to unity, so that, if $y_i(t_0) = x_i(t_0)$ $(i = 1, 2)$, then

$$|y_1(t) - x_1(t)| + |y_2(t) - x_2(t)| \leqslant \frac{\Delta}{1+\varepsilon^2}\left[e^{\left(\frac{1}{\varepsilon}+\varepsilon\right)(t-t_0)} - 1\right] \tag{15.7}$$

as long as $|y_1| \leqslant 5$. This inequality follows from well-known theorems of the theory of differential equations (see, for example, [1]).

By choosing a sufficiently small Δ, we can make the differences $(y_1 - x_1)$ and $(y_2 - x_2)$ arbitrarily small over an arbitrary but fixed time interval. Thus, the behavior of the solutions of systems (15.4) and (15.5) is, for sufficiently small Δ, the same over a finite time interval. Hereinafter, we will show that the behavior of the solutions of system (15.5) is determined for $-\infty < t < +\infty$ by the behavior of its solutions in some finite time interval. Thus, the solutions of systems (15.4) and (15.5) will behave in the same way for all t if Δ is made sufficiently small.

Before we turn to a precise statement of the results, we will describe the behavior of the solutions of Eq. (15.3) approximately and without proofs. It turns out that among the solutions of this equation there is a family F with the following particular structure. A solution $x(t)$ in this family takes a maximal value equal to approximately 3, and if this maximum is achieved at $t = t_1$, then for $t > t_1$ and $x > 1$ the solution will behave in approximately the same way as the function

$$(3 - b)\, e^{-\rho(t-t_1)} - b \cos t, \tag{15.8}$$

where ρ is a small positive constant. For $t > t_1$, therefore, the first term of (15.8) decreases slowly. When x reaches a value equal to 1, the solution begins to decrease rapidly, and in a time of no more than 2π reaches a minimum approximately equal to -3. Then the pattern repeats: The solution slowly increases to $x = -1$, and then rapidly achieves a maximum equal to approximately 3. The solution continues to behave in this way as time continues to increase.

By an *even point of intersection* we will mean a value of t for which a solution $x(t)$ in the family F first achieves the value $x = 1$ as it decreases from its maximal value of approximately 3. By an *odd point of intersection* we will mean a value of t at which the solution $x(t)$ first achieves the value $x = -1$ as it increases from its minimal value. For each solution in the family F, even and odd points of intersection alternate as time increases, and we will call both even and odd points of intersection simply points of intersection.

Each even point of intersection always lies in some short interval $t = \tau \pmod{2\pi}$, $0 < \tau < \tau_1 < 1/10$, that is called an even base interval.

All odd points of intersection lie in some short interval $t = \pi + \tau \pmod{2\pi}$, $0 < \tau < \tau_1 < 1/10$, that is called an odd base interval.

We can associate with Eq. (15.3) a large integer n. The distance between two adjacent base intervals that contain points of intersection of the same solution in the family F is either close to $(2n-1)\pi$ or $(2n+1)\pi$. Choose an arbitrary sequence d_k $(-\infty < k < +\infty)$, where d_k is either $(2n-1)\pi$ or $(2n+1)\pi$; then the family F contains a solution whose points of intersection lie in base intervals with respective distances equal to d_k, and this solution has no other points of intersection.

Since the sequence d_k contains an infinite set of changes from +1 to -1, the set of such sequences has the cardinality of a continuum. A majority of the solutions in the family F are nonperiodic solutions, because the sequences d_k are generally not periodic themselves, although the set of all sequences d_k has a countable subset of periodic sequences. At least one periodic solution in F with intersection points in base intervals corresponds to each such periodic sequence, and the distances between them are determined by the corresponding sequence d_k. We will denote the family of such periodic motions by Σ.

Equation (15.3) has two systems of subharmonics of order $(2n-1)\pi$ and $(2n+1)\pi$, each of these subharmonics being asymptotically stable as $t \to +\infty$. There exists also a harmonic oscillation that is asymptotically stable as $t \to -\infty$.

2. Solutions of Eq. (15.3) can be found exactly: When $x \neq \pm 1$ Eq. (15.3) is a linear equation with constant coefficients. Let ρ be the smaller root of the equation

$$\varepsilon\rho^2 - \rho + \varepsilon = 0, \tag{15.9}$$

i.e.,

$$\rho = \frac{1 - \sqrt{1 - 4\varepsilon^2}}{2\varepsilon} = \varepsilon + \varepsilon^3 + \ldots, \quad \varepsilon = \frac{\rho}{1 + \rho^2}. \tag{15.10}$$

Since ε is small, so is ρ.

The solution of Eq. (15.3) is given by the formulas

$$x = A_1 e^{-(t-t_0)/\rho} + A_2 e^{-(t-t_0)\rho} - b\cos t \quad \text{for} \quad |x| > 1 \tag{15.11}$$

where A_1, A_2, and t_0 are constants and, similarly,

$$x = B_1 e^{(t-t_0)/\rho} + B_2 e^{(t-t_0)\rho} + b\cos t \quad \text{for} \quad |x| < 1. \tag{15.12}$$

In order to prove the existence of a family F containing at least one solution corresponding to each sequence d_k, we will prove several assertions concerning transformations of base intervals. Consider a continuous family of solutions with initial data in the odd base interval:

$$x_0 = -1, \; \dot{x}_0 = \rho(1 + b\cos\tau) - b\sin\tau + E, \quad t_0 = \pi + \tau, \tag{15.13}$$

where $0 \leqslant \tau \leqslant \tau_1 \leqslant 1/10$ and $|E| < e^{-\frac{10}{\rho}}$. We will call this family an odd base family, and we will show below that the solutions of an odd base family are close to 3 when $t = 3\pi$. When $t > 3\pi$ these solutions yield formula (15.11) with a negligibly small first term. Thus, these solutions are approximately equal to

$$x = Ae^{-\rho(t-3\pi)} - b\cos t, \tag{15.14}$$

where A is close to $(3 - b)$.

We will also show that for an odd base family, the value of A in formula (15.14) lies in the interval

$$3 - b - 2\pi(3 - b)\rho \leqslant A \leqslant 3 - b + 2\pi(1 - b)\rho. \tag{15.15}$$

The solutions (15.14) decrease and achieve the value $x = 1$ on some set of even points of intersection. The solution $x = x(t)$ first attains the value $x = 1$ when t is close to $2m\pi$, which follows from formula (15.14), since here cos (t) must be close to unity. The larger the value of $\bar{A}$, the larger the time required for attaining the value $x = 1$. An even point of intersection t_M corresponding to the maximal value of A in the interval (15.15) lies approximately 4π to the right of an odd point of intersection t_m corresponding to the minimal value of A, provided that b is appropriately selected. As we will see below, it follows from continuity considerations that the set of even points of intersection corresponding to the initial odd base family includes two even base intervals. They are in the interval (t_m, t_M) and are given by the formulas $t=2n\pi+\tau$ and $t=2(n+1)\pi+\tau$, $0\leqslant\tau\leqslant\tau_1$, where n is a large integer depending on b and ρ.

A similar pattern emerges upon examination of an even base family.

Let the solution curves of an initial odd base family define a transformation of the initial odd base interval into the set of even points of intersection on the line $x=1$; it is then clear that the image of the initial interval includes two even base intervals. Thus, the initial family of solutions contains two subfamilies each of which intersects the line $x=1$ when $\dot{x}<0$, so that the points of intersection cover the base interval; one of these intervals is $t=2\pi n+\tau$, the other $-t=2(n+1)\pi+\tau$. In exactly the same way, each family of trajectories beginning in an even base interval intersects $x=1$, $\dot{x}>0$, so that the points of intersection cover two odd base intervals, etc. The distance between a given interval and the two intervals in its image is $(2n-1)\pi$ and $(2n+1)\pi$.

Now consider the sequence of base intervals and the corresponding distances given by an arbitrary sequence d_k, $-\infty<k<+\infty$, where each d_k is either $(2n-1)\pi$ or $(2n+1)\pi$. Then it is possible to use the transformation which we have described to show that there exists at least one solution of Eq. (15.3) with points of intersection separated by distances corresponding to the sequence d_k.

3. We now turn to the precise statement of the above assertions and to their proofs. Consider the odd base interval given by the formula $t=\pi+\tau$, $0\leqslant\tau\leqslant\tau_1$, where $\tau_1<1/10$ is given by the equation

$$\sin\tau_1=\frac{\rho}{b}-\frac{q}{\varepsilon},\quad q=e^{-\frac{2\pi}{\rho}+2\rho}{}^{-\frac{3}{4}}. \tag{15.16}$$

Formula (15.13) for $\dot{x}_0$ is simply a corollary of (15.11). Indeed, by differentiating (15.11) and excluding A_2, we obtain

$$\dot{x}=-\rho(x+b\cos t)+b\sin t-\left(\frac{1}{\rho}-\rho\right)A_1e^{-(t-t_0)/\rho}. \tag{15.17}$$

If we set $x=-1$ and $t=\pi+\tau$, we obtain (15.13) with a very small exponential term E, provided that $t-t_0$ is sufficiently large.

When $|x|>1$ Eq. (15.3) becomes $\varepsilon\ddot{x}+\dot{x}+\varepsilon x=b\sin t$, consequently, its general solution is given by formula (15.11). If $x=x_0$ and $\dot{x}=\dot{x}_0$ when $t=t_0$, then

$$A_1=\frac{-\varepsilon\rho(x_0+b\cos t_0)-\varepsilon\dot{x}_0+\varepsilon b\sin t_0}{1-2\varepsilon\rho}, \tag{15.18}$$

$$A_2 = \frac{(1-\varepsilon\rho)(x_0 + b\cos t_0) + \varepsilon\dot{x}_0 - \varepsilon b \sin t_0}{1-2\varepsilon\rho}. \tag{15.19}$$

When $|x| < 1$, the general solution of Eq. (15.3) is given by formula (15.12), where the constants B_1 and B_2 are given by the following expressions in terms of x_0, $\dot{x}_0$, and t_0:

$$B_1 = \frac{-\varepsilon\rho(x_0 - b\cos t_0) + \varepsilon\dot{x}_0 + \varepsilon b \sin t_0}{1-2\varepsilon\rho} \tag{15.20}$$

$$B_2 = \frac{(1-\varepsilon\rho)(x_0 - b\cos t_0) - \varepsilon\dot{x}_0 - \varepsilon b \sin t_0}{1-2\varepsilon\rho}. \tag{15.21}$$

Assume that ε and ρ are sufficiently small positive constants, and that b lies between zero and one and is different from zero and one. For convenience, assume that $0.1 < b < 0.9$. Below we will need the following lemmas on the behavior of the solutions of Eq. (15.3).

Lemma 15.1. The solution of Eq. (15.3) beginning at the left end of the odd base interval $t = \pi$ *with initial data* $x_0 = -1$, $\dot{x}_0 = \rho(1+b) + E$, *where* $|E| < e^{-\frac{10}{\rho}}$ *satisfies the inequality*

$$x \leqslant 3 - 2\pi(3-b)\rho + \rho^{6/5} \quad \textit{for} \quad t = 3\pi. \tag{15.22}$$

Proof. Denote the solution under discussion by $x(t)$. Since $\dot{x}_0 > 0$, then for $t > \pi$ but sufficiently close to π we have $x > -1$, so that (15.12) yields

$$\ddot{x} = \frac{1}{\rho^2} B_1 e^{(t-\pi)/\rho} + \rho^2 B_2 e^{\rho(t-\pi)} - b\cos t.$$

It follows then from (15.20) and (15.21) that

$$\ddot{x} = \frac{\varepsilon}{\rho} \frac{2 + E/\rho}{1-2\varepsilon\rho} e^{(t-\pi)/\rho} + D(\rho) e^{\rho(t-\pi)} - b\cos t,$$

where $|D(\rho)| \leqslant 2\rho^2$. Since the coefficients of the first term in the right side of the last equation is positive, $\ddot{x} > 1/2$ as long as $|x| < 1$ and $\pi < t < 5\pi/4$. Thus, $\dot{x} > 0$ under these conditions, because $\dot{x}_0 > 0$. Moreover, $\ddot{x} > 3/2\, e^{(t-\pi)/\rho}$ as long as $|x| < 1$. Since $\dot{x}_0 > 0$, this inequality for $\ddot{x}$ implies that x becomes equal to unity when $t < \pi + 3\rho \ln 1/\rho$.

We now integrate differential equation (15.3), and label the point at which x reaches unity by the index 1; we thus find that

$$\varepsilon\dot{x}_1 - 2 + \varepsilon\int_{t_0}^{t_1} x\,dt = -b\cos t_1 + b\cos t_0 + \varepsilon\dot{x}_0. \tag{15.23}$$

Since $t_0 = \pi < t_1 < \pi + 3\rho \ln 1/\rho$, $|\dot{x}_0| < 2\rho$ and $|x| \leqslant 1$, we can write

$$\varepsilon \dot{x}_1 + b \cos t_1 = 2 - b + \gamma\varepsilon\rho \ln \frac{1}{\rho}, \tag{15.24}$$

where γ denotes a variable that is bounded as $\varepsilon \to 0$. It follows from (15.24) that $\dot{x}_1 > 0$, so that further investigation of the solution requires the use of formula (15.11). The constants A_1 and A_2 are found from (15.18) and (15.19) at the point t_1. For sufficiently small ε, Eq. (15.24) yields

$$x = \gamma_1 e^{-(t-t_1)/\rho} + (3 - b) e^{-\rho(t-t_1)} - b \cos t + \gamma\varepsilon\rho \ln \frac{1}{\rho}, \tag{15.25}$$

where γ is bounded as $\varepsilon \to 0$ and $|\gamma_1| < 2.05$, for sufficiently small ε. It is not difficult to use formula (15.25) to show that, if ε is sufficiently small, then $t_1 \leqslant t$ when $\leqslant 3\pi$ $x > 1$, and in setting $t = 3\pi$ in this formula, proves the lemma.

Lemma 15.2. The solution of Eq. (15.3) beginning at the right end of the odd base interval $t = \pi + \tau_1$ and satisfying (15.13) when $\tau = \tau_1$ satisfies the inequality

$$x \geqslant 3 + 2\pi(1 - b)\rho - \rho^{6/5} \quad \textit{for} \quad t = 3\pi. \tag{15.26}$$

Proof. In proving the lemma we will show that $x > -1 + 1/3\, b\rho^{1/2}$ for $5/4\,\pi < t < 3\pi$..

Consider the solution $x(t)$, beginning at $t_0 = \pi + \tau_1$, where τ_1 is given by formulas (15.16). In virtue of (15.13), we have $\dot{x}_0 > 0$, so that we can use expression (15.12) to find x. From conditions (15.16) it follows that the constant B_1 is small; indeed,

$$B_1 = \frac{2bq + \varepsilon E}{1 - 2\varepsilon\rho}, \quad B_2 = -(1 - b + \gamma\rho^2), \tag{15.27}$$

where, as before, γ denotes a variable that is bounded as $\varepsilon \to 0$. Thus,

$$x - \rho b \sin t - b \cos t + (1 - \rho^2)(1 - b + \gamma\rho^2) e^{(t-\pi-\tau_1)\rho}, \tag{15.28}$$

and it is clear that

$$\ddot{x} = D_1(\rho) - b \cos t \tag{15.29}$$

where $D_1(\rho) > -3\rho^2$ when $\pi + \tau_1 \leqslant t \leqslant 5\pi/4$. Thus, $\ddot{x} > 1/2\, b > 0$ on this interval, and, because $\dot{x}_0 > 0$, we have $x > -1$ up to $t = 5\pi/4$.

By the definition of E and q, the first term in the right side of Eq. (15.28) is small in the interval $\pi+\tau_1<t<3\pi-3\rho^{1/4}$. As a result, we have in this interval,

$$x=-1+b+b\cos t+\gamma\rho \tag{15.30}$$

(as before, γ is variable that is bounded as $\varepsilon\to 0$). In particular, then, $1>x>-1+b\rho^{\frac{1}{2}}$ for $5\pi/4<t<3\pi-3\rho^{\frac{1}{4}}$.

If we set $t=3\pi-s$, Eq. (17.28) yields

$$x=-1+\frac{2b}{1-2\varepsilon\rho}e^{-\frac{\tau_1}{\rho}+2\rho^{-\frac{3}{4}}-\frac{s}{\rho}}+\frac{1}{2}bs^2+\gamma\rho \tag{15.31}$$

for $\rho^{\frac{1}{4}}<s<3\rho^{\frac{1}{4}}$ as long as $|x|<1$. From this last equation it follows that, in the interval of s under discussion, the inequality $x>-1+1/3\,b\rho^{\frac{1}{2}}$ holds as long as $|x|<1$. Consequently, in this interval $x>-1$. When $s=\rho^{\frac{1}{4}}$ the second term in the right side of (15.28) is very large, so that x is larger than unity for some s in the interval $\rho^{\frac{1}{4}}<s<3\rho^{\frac{1}{4}}$.

Differentiating (15.28) and excluding the terms having $e^{(t-\pi-\tau_1)/\rho}$ as a factor from the equations for x and $\dot{x}$, we obtain

$$\rho\dot{x}=x-\rho b\sin t-b\cos t+(1-\rho^2)(1-b+\gamma\rho^2)\,e^{(t-\pi-\tau_1)\rho}. \tag{15.32}$$

Now assume that $t=t_1$ when $x=1$. As we have proved, $\rho^{\frac{1}{4}}<3\pi-t_1<3\rho^{\frac{1}{4}}$, so that (15.32) yields

$$\rho\dot{x}_1+b\cos t_1=2-b+2\pi(1-b)\rho+\gamma\varepsilon^{\frac{5}{4}}. \tag{15.33}$$

In particular, $\dot{x}_1>0$. Thus, in order to find x we can use formula (15.11), in which A_1 and A_2 are determined with the aid of (17.33). Thus,

$$\begin{aligned} x=-\left(2+\gamma\rho^{\frac{1}{2}}\right)e^{-(t-t_1)/\rho}+[(3-b)+\\ +2\pi(1-b)\rho+\gamma\rho^{5/4}]\,e^{-(t-t_1)/\rho}-b\cos t \end{aligned} \tag{15.34}$$

as long as $x>1$. This equation implies that $x>1$ for $t_1<t\leqslant 3\pi$. Now, setting $t=3\pi$ in (15.34), the lemma follows.

Lemma 15.3. All solutions of Eq. (15.3) that begin in the odd base interval $t=\pi+\tau_1$ and satisfy (15.13) satisfy the inequality

$$|\dot{x}(3\pi)|\leqslant\gamma\rho \tag{15.35}$$

where γ is bounded when ε is small. The inequality $-1 < x < 3.1$ *holds for such solutions when* $\pi + \tau < t < 3\pi$. *For these solutions* $\dot{x} > b\rho/2$ *when* $\pi + \tau \leqslant t < 5/4\,\pi$ *and* $x > -1 + (b/10)\,\rho^{\frac{1}{2}}$ *when* $(5/4)\pi \leqslant t \leqslant 3\pi$. *Moreover, each such solution intersects the line* $x = 1$ *only once as t increases in the interval* $\pi + \tau < t < 3\pi - (1/2)\,\rho^{\frac{1}{4}}$, *and each such solution remains above the line* $x = 1$ *until* $t = 3\pi$.

Proof. In the case under discussion, Eq. (15.28) holds if q is replaced by some large quantity and τ_1 is replaced by τ. As a result, Eq. (15.29) is satisfied for the solutions under discussion and, therefore, $\ddot{x} > 0$ when $\pi + \tau < t < (5/4)\,\pi$. Thus, we have $\dot{x} > \dot{x}_0 > (1/2)\,b\rho$ in this interval, and, therefore, either $x = 1$ for some t in this interval or Eq. (15.28) is satisfied, provided that q is, in this equation, replaced by some large quantity and τ_1 is replaced by τ. In the latter case, $x(t)$ may prove to be smaller than the right side of Eq. (15.28) by a quantity of the order of $\gamma\varepsilon^2$. Thus, $x = 1 - \gamma\varepsilon^2$ for some $t < 3\pi - \rho^{1/4}$. By integrating differential equation (15.3) from $t_0 = \pi + \tau$ to t in the same way as in the proof of Lemma 15.1, we find that $\varepsilon\dot{x} > 1$ for $0.9 < x \leqslant 1$. Thus, it turns out that $x = 1$ when $t = t_1 < 3\pi - (1/2)\,\rho^{\frac{1}{4}}$. Since $x(t)$ may prove to be smaller than the solution discussed in Lemma 15.2 by only $\gamma\varepsilon^2$, we find, moreover, that $x(t) > -1 + (1/4)\,b\rho^{1/2}$ when $(5/4)\,\pi \leqslant t$ as long as $x \leqslant 1$.

In every case, x achieves a value of unity. The point at which this occurs for the first time will be denoted by the index 1. Then $t_1 < 3\pi - (1/2)\,\rho^{\frac{1}{4}}$. If we use Eq. (15.32), which is satisfied under our conditions, and set $x = 1$, $t = t_1$, we obtain

$$\rho\dot{x}_1 = 2 - b - b\cos t_1 + \gamma\rho. \tag{15.36}$$

It follows then from (15.18) and (15.19) that $-3 < A_1 < 0$ and $A_2 = 3 - b + \gamma\rho$. By (15.11), we have

$$x = A_1 e^{-(t-t_1)/\rho} + A_2 e^{-(t-t_1)\rho} - b\cos t. \tag{15.37}$$

for $x \geqslant 1$. Differentiating with respect to t, we find that

$$\dot{x} = -\frac{A_1}{\rho}\,e^{-(t-t_1)/\rho} - \rho A_2 e^{-\rho(t-t_1)} + b\sin t.$$

Since $t_1 < 3\pi - (1/2)\,\rho^{\frac{1}{4}}$, it is clear that if $x \geqslant 1$ up to $t = 3\pi$, we actually have $\dot{x} = \gamma\rho$ when $t = 3\pi$.

It remains to be proved that $x > 1$ when $t_1 < t \leqslant 3\pi$. Assume to the contrary that $x = 1$ when $t = t_2 \in (t_1, 3\pi]$. Integrating Eq. (15.3) from t_1 to t_2, we find that

$$\varepsilon\dot{x}_2 = \varepsilon\dot{x}_1 - \varepsilon\int_{t_1}^{t_2} x\,dt + b\int_{t_1}^{t_2}\sin t\,dt. \tag{15.38}$$

From (15.37) it follows that $x < 3.1$, and, by (15.36) and (15.38), $\varepsilon\dot{x}_2 > 2 - 2b + \gamma\rho > 0$. But this is impossible, since we must have $t = t_2$ when $\dot{x} \leqslant 0$, which proves the lemma.

In Paragraph 2 we noted (albeit without proof) that the solutions of an odd base family are given, for $t \geqslant 3\pi$, by the approximate formula

$$x = (3 - b)\,e^{-(t-3\pi)\rho} - b\cos t.$$

It is clear that this solution first reaches unity for such t that $(3-b)\,e^{-(t-3\pi)\rho}$ is close to $1 + b$. In other words, this value of t depends on

$$\frac{1}{\rho}\ln\frac{3-b}{1+b}.$$

Consider the integer n defined by the relationship

$$\frac{1}{\rho}\ln\frac{3-b}{1+b} = (2n-1)\pi - \delta, \tag{15.39}$$

where $0 \leqslant \delta < 2\pi$. Since ρ is small, n is large. Moreover, if by changing b slightly, it can be arranged for δ to lie between 0 and $2\pi\ (1 - b/3 - b)$. Below, it will be convenient to assume that

$$\rho^{\frac{1}{10}} \leqslant \delta \leqslant 2\pi\frac{1-b}{3-b} - \rho^{\frac{1}{10}}. \tag{15.40}$$

Condition (15.40) yields values of b for which the image of a base interval includes two base intervals lying at distances of $(2n-1)\pi$ and $(2n+1)\pi$ from the initial base interval.

Since we have assumed that $0.1 < b < 0.9$, we can select b so that n satisfies the inequality

$$1 + \frac{1}{2\pi\rho}\ln\frac{2.1}{1.9} < n < \frac{1}{2\pi\rho}\ln\frac{2.9}{1.1} \tag{15.41}$$

Take some n that satisfies inequalities (15.41). The interval (0.1, 0.9) then contains a segment $I_n(\rho)$ such that, if $b \in I_n(\rho)$, relations (15.39) and (15.40) hold.

Hereafter, we will assume that b belongs to one of the segments $I_n(\rho)$.

We will now consider Eq. (15.6) with a function $P(y)$ that is sufficiently close to the function $\Phi(y)$, and will define more precisely the notion of a continuous odd base family for the solutions $y(t)$ of this equation. Let θ be a parameter, and let $\tau(\theta)$ and $E(\theta)$ be two continuous functions of θ that are defined on the interval $\theta_0 \leqslant \theta \leqslant \theta_1$ and are such that $\tau(\theta_0)=0$ $\tau(\theta_1)=\tau_1$, $0<\tau(\theta)<\tau_1$ for $\theta_0<\theta<\theta_1$, and $|E(\theta)| \leqslant e^{-\frac{10}{\rho}}$. Then the family of solutions of Eq. (15.6), $y(t, \theta)$, satisfying the initial conditions

$$\begin{gathered} y_0=-1, \quad t_0=(2m+1)\pi+\tau(\theta), \\ \dot{y}_0=\rho(1+b\cos\tau(\theta))-b\sin\tau(\theta)+E(\theta), \end{gathered} \tag{15.42}$$

where m is an integer and $\theta_0 \leqslant \theta \leqslant \theta_1$, is a continuous odd base family. A continuous even base family is defined analogously.

Choose a sufficiently small $\varepsilon>0$ and an integer n satisfying inequalities (15.41), and let $b \in I_n(\rho)$. We will now state the following fundamental result concerning Eq. (15.6) with a function $P(y)$ sufficiently close to $\Phi(y)$ (i.e., the constant Δ is sufficiently small).

Lemma 15.4. Let $y(t, \theta)$, $\theta_0 \leqslant \theta \leqslant \theta_1$ *be a continuous odd base family of the odd base interval* $t=\pi+\tau(\theta)$. *Then there exist two disjoint intervals* Θ_1 *and* Θ_2, *in* (θ_0, θ_1) *such that the solutions* $y(t, \theta)$ *beginning in* Θ_1 *intersect for the first time* $y=1$, $y<0$, *in the even base interval* $t=2n\pi+\tau$, $0<\tau<\tau_1$, *and, in addition, form a continuous even base family in this interval. Similarly, solutions beginning in the interval* Θ_2 *form a continuous even base family in the even base interval* $t=2(n+1)\pi+\tau$, $0<\tau<\tau_1$. *In exactly the same way, a continuous even base family has two disjoint subfamilies each of which forms a continuous odd base family in the odd base intervals at distances of* $(2n-1)\pi$ *and* $(2n+1)\pi$ *from the initial base interval.*

Proof. Let $y(t, \theta)$, $\theta_0 \leqslant \theta \leqslant \theta_1$, be a continuous odd base family in the odd base interval $t=\pi+\tau$, and consider the family of solutions of Eq. (15.3) with the same initial data as $y(t, \theta)$. Choose Δ in inequality (15.7) so that the solutions $y(t, \theta)$ and $x(t, \theta)$ of Eq. (15.6) and (15.3), respectively, differ by a sufficiently small quantity in the time interval $|t-\pi| \leqslant (2n+2)\pi$. Set

$$<\tau_1 \text{ for } \theta_0<\theta<. \tag{15.43}$$

Then, if $|x| \leqslant 5$ and $|y| \leqslant 5$, inequality (15.7) yields

$$|y(t)-x(t)| \leqslant e^{-\frac{11}{\rho}} \quad \text{for} \quad |t-\pi| \leqslant (2n+2)\pi. \tag{15.44}$$

Since $\varepsilon\dot{y}=y_2-P(y_1)$, $\varepsilon\dot{x}=x_2-\Phi(x_1)$ we can write

$$\begin{aligned} \varepsilon|\dot{y}-\dot{x}| &\leqslant |y_2(t)-x_2(t)|+|P(y_1)-\Phi(x_1)| \leqslant \\ &\leqslant |y_2-x_2|+|P(y_1)-\Phi(y_1)|+|\Phi(y_1)-\Phi(x_1)| \leqslant \\ &\leqslant |y_2-x_2|+\Delta+|y_1-x_1| \leqslant 2e^{-\frac{11}{\rho}} \end{aligned}$$

or

$$|\dot{y}(t)-\dot{x}(t)|\leqslant\frac{1}{20}e^{-\frac{10}{\rho}}\quad\text{for}\quad|t-\pi|\leqslant(2n+2)\pi. \tag{15.45}$$

It follows from Lemma 15.3 that $|x|<3.1$ when $\pi+\tau\leqslant t\leqslant 3\pi$. Then, in virtue of (15.44), the inequality $|y|<4$ holds in this interval. Also, by Lemma 15.3 and inequalities (15.44) and (15.45), we have $y(t)>-1$ when $\pi+\tau<t<3\pi$. Consider $x(t,\ \theta)$ with $t\geqslant 3\pi$, and set $t_0=3\pi$ in Eq. (15.11); we find that

$$x(t,\ \theta)=A_1e^{-(t-3\pi)/\rho}+A_2e^{-(t-3\pi)\rho}-b\cos t \tag{15.46}$$

and, by using Lemma 15.3, we can easily show that $|A_1|\leqslant\rho$.

It follows from the form of system (15.4) that x_1 and x_2 are continuous functions of the initial data, so that this is also true of $x(t)$ and $\dot{x}(t)$. In particular, $x(3\pi,\ \theta)$ and $\dot{x}(3\pi,\ \theta)$ continuously depend on the initial data on the line $x=-1$ and, consequently, are continuous functions of θ. Thus, $A_2(\theta)$ is a continuous function of θ, and $A_1(\theta)$, as we have just proved, satisfies the inequality $|A_1(\theta)|\leqslant\rho$.

It follows from relations (15.44)-(15.46) that the relations

$$y(t,\ \theta)=A_2e^{-\rho(t-3\pi)}-b\cos t+\frac{1}{10}G(\theta,\ t), \tag{15.47}$$

and

$$\dot{y}(t,\ \theta)=-\rho A_2e^{-\rho(t-3\pi)}+b\sin t+\frac{1}{10}G(\theta,\ t), \tag{15.48}$$

hold when $|G(\theta,\ t)|\leqslant e^{-\frac{10}{\rho}}$ in both cases. Eliminating A_2 from both of these equations, we find that

$$\dot{y}(t,\ \theta)=-\rho y(t,\ \theta)-\rho b\cos t+b\sin t+\frac{1}{5}G(\theta,\ t). \tag{15.49}$$

Setting $t_0=3\pi$ in (15.19), Lemmas 15.1-15.3 yield

$$A_2(\theta_0)\leqslant 3-b-2\pi(3-b)\rho+2\rho^{\frac{6}{5}},$$
$$A_2(\theta_1)\geqslant 3-b+2\pi(1-b)\rho-2\rho^{\frac{6}{5}}.$$

If we set $A_2(\theta)=3-b+r(\theta)$, it becomes clear that the function $r(\theta)$ is continuous when $\theta_0\leqslant\theta\leqslant\theta_1$, and that the set of values of $r(\theta)$ for $\theta\in[\theta_0,\ \theta_1]$ contains the segment

$$-2\pi(3-b)\rho+2\rho^{\frac{6}{5}}\leqslant r\leqslant 2\pi(1-b)\rho-2\rho^{\frac{6}{5}}. \tag{15.50}$$

If we now set $A_2 = 3 - b + r,\ t = 2n\pi + \sigma$ in (15.47) and use notation (15.39), we find that

$$y(t,\ \theta) = (1+b)\,e^{-\rho(\sigma+\delta-2\pi)} + r(\theta)\frac{1+b}{3-b}\,e^{-\rho(\sigma+\delta-2\pi)} - \\ - b\cos\sigma + \frac{1}{10}G.$$

It is clear that if inequalities (15.50) are satisfied, $y > 1$ when $\sigma < -10\pi$. For $|\sigma| \leqslant 10\pi$, we have

$$y(t,\ \theta) = 1 + b - b\cos\sigma - \\ - \left[\rho(1+b)(\sigma+\delta-2\pi) - r(\theta)\frac{1+b}{3-b}\right] + \gamma\rho^2, \qquad (15.51)$$

where, as usual, γ is a variable that is bounded for small ρ.

Let $t(\theta)$ denote the smallest values of t after $t = 3\pi$ at which $y(t,\theta) = 1$, and consider the right side of Eq. (15.51) with $0 \leqslant \sigma \leqslant \tau_1$. If $r = r_1 = -(3-b)\left(2\pi - \delta + \rho^{\frac{1}{2}}\right)\rho$ this right side is less than unity, which means that if $\theta = \theta_{10}$ is a root of the equation $r(\theta) = r_1$, then $t(\theta_{10}) < 2n\pi$. Similarly, let $r = r_2 = -(3-b)\left(2\pi - \delta - \rho^{\frac{1}{2}}\right)\rho$ and $r(\theta_{20}) = r_2$; then $> 2n\pi + \tau_1$. Since r_1 and r_2 are inside the segment (15.50), it is possible to choose θ_{10} and θ_{20} inside the interval $[\theta_0,\ \theta_1]$. The function $r(\theta)$ is continuous, and the inequalities $r(\theta_1) > r(\theta_{20}) > r(\theta_{10}) > r(\theta_0)$ hold. Hence, we can choose θ_{10} and θ_{20} so that $\theta_{10} < \theta_{20}$, and $r_1 < r(\theta) < r_2$ when $\theta_{10} < \theta < \theta_{20}$.

Since $r_1 \leqslant r \leqslant r_2$, Eq. (15.51) implies that $y > 1$ for $\sigma < (-1/4)\pi$. Thus, $t(\theta) > 2n\pi\,(-1/4)\pi$ when $\theta_{10} \leqslant \theta \leqslant \theta_{20}$. Since $t(\theta_{10}) < 2n\pi$ and $\dot{y}(t(\theta),\ \theta) < (-1/4)\,b\rho$ when $2n\pi\,(-1/4)\pi \leqslant t(\theta) \leqslant 2n\pi + \tau_1 + (1/4)\,b\rho$ because of (15.48), it is clear that when θ increases, $t(\theta)$ is a continuous function as long as $2n\pi\,(-1/4)\pi \leqslant t(\theta) \leqslant 2n\pi + + \tau_1\,(1/4)\,b\rho$. Since $t(\theta_{20}) > 2n\pi + \tau_1$, there exist θ_{11} and θ_{12} such that $\theta_{10} < \theta_{11} < \theta_{12} < \theta_{20}$, and for which $t(\theta_{11}) = 2n\pi,\ t(\theta_{12}) = 2n\pi + \tau_1$ and $t(\theta_{11}) < t(\theta) < t(\theta_{12})$ when $\theta_{11} < \theta < \theta_{12}$. Thus, we can see that $(\theta_{11},\ \theta_{12})$ is the interval Θ_1 mentioned in the lemma.

We can prove the existence of the interval Θ_2 in exactly the same way, by choosing $r_3 = (3-b)\left(\delta - \rho^{\frac{1}{2}}\right)\rho$ and $r_4 = (3-b)\left(\delta + \rho^{\frac{1}{2}}\right)\rho$.

The proof for even base families is analogous to that above. Q.E.D.

Remark. It follows from (15.49) that the inequality $|E| < \frac{1}{5}e^{-\frac{10}{\rho}}$ holds for even base families formed of the family $y(t,\ \theta)$ on the intervals $t = 2n\pi + \tau$ and $t = 2(n+1)\pi + \tau$.

We will now prove the existence of the family F.

Theorem 15.1. Given a sequence d_k, $-\infty < k < +\infty$, *where* d_k *is either* $(2n-1)\pi$ *or* $(2n+1)\pi$, *there exists a solution* $y(t)$ *of Eq.*

(15.6) with points of intersection lying in the base intervals with respective distances equal to d_k, $-\infty < k < +\infty$. *This solution has no other points of intersection.*

Proof. Consider a subsequence of base intervals with respective distances equal to d_k, $-N \leqslant k \leqslant +N$, where N is a natural number. By Lemma 15.4, any continuous base family beginning at the left end of these base intervals has a subfamily that is a continuous base family in the next of the selected base intervals. In turn, this family has a subfamily that is continuous base family in the next base interval, etc. Thus, in the base interval at the left end, there exists a subfamily whose points of intersection lie in base intervals with the appropriate distances, d_k, $-N \leqslant k \leqslant N$.

Now consider the set $S(N)$ of all solutions of Eq. (15.6) having points of intersection in each of the selected base intervals, $0 < \tau < \tau_1$, separated by distances of d_k, $-N \leqslant k \leqslant +N$, and such that at each point of intersection the inequality $|\dot{y} + \rho y + \rho b \cos t - b \sin t| < e^{-10/\rho}$ holds, while between the points of intersection the inequality $|y| < 4$ holds. We have just proved that the set $S(N)$ is nonempty.

Without loss of generality, we can assume that $t = \pi + \tau$ is one of the selected odd base intervals. Let $y(t)$ be a solution in the set $S(N)$. Its odd point of intersection with the odd base interval $t = \pi + \tau$, $0 < \tau < \tau_1$ is given in the (τ, v) plane by some point $\tau = t - \pi$, $\dot{y}(\pi + \tau) = v$. From the continuity of solutions with respect to initial data it follows that the set $S_1(N)$ of such points that corresponds to the set $S(N)$ of solutions is open. Moreover, it is nonempty, as we have just noted. Now consider the set $S(N+M)$, where M is a natural number, and consider the corresponding set $S_1(N+M)$ of points in the (τ, v) plane. It is clear that $S_1(N+M) \subset S_1(M)$.

It is not difficult to use the foregoing discussion to prove the more precise inclusion $S_1(N+M) \subset \bar{S}_1(M)$ (as usual, $\bar{S}_1$ denotes the closure of S_1). Thus, there exists a nonempty set $S_1(\infty)$ such that $S_1(\infty) \subset S_1(N)$ for any natural N, and it is clear that the set of solutions $S(\infty)$ corresponding to the point set $S_1(\infty)$ in the (τ, v) plane is the one required by Theorem 15.1. Q.E.D.

4. As we proved in Section 4 (see Theorem 4.1) system (15.4) is dissipative. Now we will study the structure of the set I of this system. At the same time, we will show that system (15.5) has an invariant set with the same structure as the set I of system (15.4) when certain additional conditions are imposed on the function $P(x)$ in the interval $|x| \leqslant 70$. It will be seen to follow from considerations given below that if $P(x)$ differs from $\Phi(x)$ by sufficiently little for all x, this invariant set will be the set I for system (15.5).

We define the transformation T of the (y, v) plane $(v = \dot{y})$ into itself, for Eq. (15.6), in the usual way. Let p be a point $(y_0, v_0 = \dot{y}_0)$ in this plane, and let $y(t, y_0, \dot{y}_0)$ be the solution of Eq. (15.6) with initial data $t = 0$, $y = y_0$, $\dot{y} = \dot{y}_0 = v_0$; then Tp is the point of the (y, v)

plane with coordinates $y = y(2\pi, y_0, \dot{y}_0)$, $v = \dot{y}(2\pi, y_0, \dot{y}_0)$. Let $\tilde{T}$ be the analogous transformation for Eq. (15.3).

It is not difficult to see that Eq. (15.3) has the 2π-periodic solution $x = b\cos(t)$. Solutions close to this periodic solution for $t=0$ are given by the formula

$$x = B_1 e^{t/\rho} + B_2 e^{t\rho} + b\cos t \tag{15.52}$$

where B_1 and B_2 are sufficiently small. Since both characteristic exponents are positive, it is clear that the solubion $x = b\cos(t)$ is asymptotically stable when $t \to -\infty$.

Consider the identity

$$\frac{d}{dt}[(x - b\cos t)^2 + (u + b\sin t)^2] = \frac{2}{\varepsilon}(u + b\sin t)^2 \tag{15.53}$$

where $u(t) = \dot{x}(t)$.

It follows from this identity that the distance between an arbitrary solution of Eq. (15.3) and the periodic solution $x = b\cos(t)$ increases as time increases as long as $|x| < 1$. Let Γ be a circle with sufficiently small radius and center at the point $(x = b\ u = 0)$ in the (x, u) plane, and let C_0 be the open disk with boundary Γ. It follows from (15.53) that $\bar{C}_0 = C_0 + \Gamma \subset \tilde{T}C_0$.

It is well known from the theory of perturbations of periodic solutions (see, for example, I. G. Malkin's monograph [67]) that if $P(x) - \Phi(x)$ and $P'(x) - 1$ are sufficiently small when $|x| < 0.95$, Eq. (15.6) has a periodic solution close to $y = b\cos(t)$. This solution is asymptotically stable as $t \to -\infty$, and the relation

$$\bar{C}_0 = C_0 + \Gamma \subset TC_0 \tag{15.54}$$

holds for it; this relation implies that

$$\overline{T^m C_0} \subset T^{m+1} C_0. \tag{15.55}$$

Consider the set

$$H = \sum_{m=0}^{\infty} T^m C_0. \tag{15.56}$$

It is not difficult to see that H is a simply connected region. This region is, for $t \to -\infty$, a region of asymptotic stability for a 2π-periodic solution of Eq. (15.6), i.e., if $y_1(t)$ is this periodic solution and (y_0, v_0) is a point of the plane (y, v), the relation

$$\lim_{t\to-\infty} |y_1(t) - y(t, y_0, v_0)| = \lim_{t\to-\infty} |\dot{y}_1(t) - \dot{y}(t, y_0, v_0)| = 0$$

holds if and only if the point (y_0, v_0) belongs to H.

Hereafter we will assume that $|P'(x)-1|$ is sufficiently small when $|x|\leqslant 0.95$ and $|\Phi(x)-P(x)|<\Delta$ when $|x|\leqslant 70$, where I is sufficiently small.

In order to study the set Δ, we will need the following lemma about the behavior of solutions of Eqs. (15.3) and (15.6).

Lemma 15.5. Let $x(t)$ *be the solution of Eq. (15.3) with initial data* $(t_0, x_0, \dot{x}_0)$ *subject to the conditions*

$$|x_0|<1, \quad |x_0-b\cos t_0|+\rho|\dot{x}_0+b\sin t_0|\geqslant h \tag{15.57}$$

with $0<h<1$; *then there exists a* t,

$$t_0<t<t_0+\frac{2}{\rho}\ln\frac{32}{h} \tag{15.58}$$

such that $|x(t)|>1$.

Proof. Since $|x(t)|<1$, we have

$$x=B_1e^{(t-t_0)/\rho}+B_2e^{(t-t_0)\rho}+b\cos t, \tag{15.59}$$

where

$$B_1+B_2=x_0-b\cos t_0, \quad \frac{1}{\rho}B_1+\rho B_2=\dot{x}_0+b\sin t_0 \tag{15.60}$$

as the initial conditions imply.

Thus,

$$|B_1|+|B_2|\geqslant|x_0-b\cos t_0|, \quad |B_1|+|B_2|>\rho|\dot{x}_0+b\sin t_0|$$

which yields

$$|B_1|+|B_2|\geqslant\frac{1}{2}(|x_0-b\cos t_0|+\rho|\dot{x}_0+b\sin t_0|)\geqslant\frac{1}{2}h. \tag{15.61}$$

Introduce the notation $s=(1/\rho)\ln(32/h)$ and assume, contrary to the assertion of the lemma, that $|x|\leqslant 1$ for $0\leqslant t-t_0\leqslant 2s$. By successively setting $t-t_0=0$, $t-t_0=s$, and $t-t_0=2s$ in Eq. (15.59), we find that

$$|B_1+B_2|\leqslant 1+b, \quad |B_1e^{s/\rho}+B_2e^{s\rho}|\leqslant 1+b$$
$$|B_1e^{2s/\rho}+B_2e^{2s\rho}|\leqslant 1+b. \tag{15.62}$$

From the first two inequalities in (15.62) we obtain

$$|B_1|(e^{s/\rho}-e^{s\rho})\leqslant(1+b)+|B_1+B_2|e^{s\rho}\leqslant(1+b)(1+e^{s\rho}).$$

It follows from the definition of s that $|B_1| < (1/4)\,h$; hence, (15.61) and (15.62) yield

$$\frac{1}{4}h < |B_2| < 1 + b + |B_1| < \frac{9}{4}. \tag{15.63}$$

We now use the third of inequalities (15.62) to obtain:

$$|B_1|\, e^{s/\rho} \leqslant (1 + b + |B_2|\, e^{2s\rho})\, e^{-s/\rho} \leqslant \frac{9}{4} e^{-s/\rho + 2s\rho}$$

which leads to

$$|B_1 e^{s/\rho} + B_2 e^{s\rho}| \geqslant |B_2|\, e^{s\rho} - |B_1|\, e^{s/\rho} \geqslant \frac{1}{4} h e^{s\rho} -$$
$$- \frac{9}{4} e^{-s/\rho + 2s\rho} \geqslant \frac{1}{8} h e^{s\rho} \geqslant 4 > 1 + b,$$

which contradicts (15.62). The contradiction proves the lemma.

Lemma 15.6. If inequalities (15.57) are satisfied and

$$|x_0| + \rho|\dot{x}_0| < 20 \tag{15.64}$$

then there exists a $t = t_1$ that satisfies the inequalities

$$t_0 \leqslant t_1 < t_0 + 5\pi + \frac{2}{\rho} \ln \frac{32}{h} + \frac{5}{(1-b)\,\varepsilon} \tag{15.65}$$

and is such that one of the following two cases holds: either

$$|t_1 (\mathrm{mod}\ 2\pi)| < 10\rho^{\frac{1}{2}}, \quad x_1 = 1, \ -10\rho^{\frac{1}{2}} < \dot{x}_1 \leqslant 0,$$

or

$$|t_1 (\mathrm{mod}\ 2\pi) - \pi| < 10\rho^{\frac{1}{2}}, \quad x_1 = -1, \quad 0 \leqslant \dot{x}_1 < 10\rho^{\frac{1}{2}}.$$

Here $|x(t)| \leqslant 60$ if $t_0 \leqslant t \leqslant t_1$.

Proof. We first assume that $|x_0| > 1$, or $x_0 = 1$ and $\dot{x}_0 > 0$ or $x_0 = -1$ and $\dot{x}_0 < 0$, then the solution of Eq. (15.3) can be written in the form

$$x = A_1 e^{-(t-t_0)/\rho} + A_2 e^{-(t-t_0)\rho} - b\cos t \tag{15.66}$$

where the initial conditions imply that $|A_i| < 22$ $(i = 1, 2)$. Moreover, we assume that $|x| > 1$, when $0 < t - t_0 < 4\pi$. Then as long as $|x| \geqslant 1$, we have, for $t > t_0 + \pi$,

$$|x - A_2 e^{-(t-t_0)\rho} + b\cos t| < e^{-2/\rho}$$

and, upon using Eq. (15.66) together with its derivative to eliminate A_2, we find that

$$|\dot{x} + \rho(x + b\cos t) - b\sin t| < \gamma e^{-2/\rho} \quad \text{for} \quad t > t_0 + \pi.$$

These inequalities imply the existence of a $t_1 < t_0 + (5/\rho)$ that satisfies the conditions of the lemma. Now assume that $|x| = 1$ for some $t = t_2$, $t_0 < t_2 < t_0 + 4\pi$. Then it is not difficult to see that, when $t = t_2$, we have either $x_2 = -1$, $0 \leqslant \dot{x}_2 < (28/\rho)$, or $x_2 = 1$ $(-28/\rho)\dot{x}_2 < \leqslant 0$.

If $x_0 = -1$, $\dot{x}_0 \geqslant 0$, then inequalities (15.64) imply that $\dot{x}_0 < (20/\rho)$, and, similarly, if $x_0 = 1$, $\dot{x}_0 \leqslant 0$, then $-20/\rho < \dot{x}_0$.

Finally, if we let $|x_0| < 1$, it follows from the preceding lemma that we will first have $|x| = 1$ when $t = t_3 < t_0 + (2/\rho)\ln(32/h)$. If $t_3 \leqslant t_0 + 1$, then, by integrating (15.3), we find that $|\dot{x}_3| < 25/\rho$. If, however, $t_3 > t_0 + 1$, it follows from Eq. (15.59) that if $|B_1 e^{(t_3 - t_0)/\rho}| > 10$, then

$$|B_2 e^{(t_3 - t_0)\rho}| > 2 + \frac{1}{2}|B_1 e^{(t_3 - t_0)/\rho}|$$

because $|x_3| = 1$. When $t = t_3 - 1/2$ we have

$$|x| > |B_2 e^{(t_3 - t_0)\rho}| e^{-\frac{1}{2}\rho} - |B_1 e^{(t_3 - t_0)/\rho}| e^{-\frac{1}{2\rho}} - b > 2e^{-\frac{\rho}{2}} - b > 1,$$

which is impossible. Thus, $|B_1 e^{(t_3 - t_0)/\rho}| < 10$. It follows then that $|\dot{x}_3| < 11/\rho$. If $|x| \geqslant 1$ when $t_3 \leqslant t \leqslant t_3 + 4\pi$, we can show, as we did at the beginning of the proof, that the lemma holds. If there exists a t_2, $t_3 \leqslant t_2 \leqslant t_3 + 4\pi$ such that $|x| = 1$ when $t = t_2$, we again have one of two situations: either $x_2 = -1$, $0 \leqslant \dot{x}_2 < 28/\rho$ or $x_2 = -1$ $-28/\rho < \dot{x}_2 \leqslant 0$.

In order to complete the proof of the lemma, therefore, there remains to be considered the case in which there exists a t_2, $t_0 < t_2 < t_0 + 4\pi + 2/\rho \ln 32/h$ such that $x_2 = -1$, $0 \leqslant \dot{x}_2 < 28/\rho$ (the case $x_2 = 1$ can be argued analogously).

By integrating Eq. (15.3) we find that

$$\varepsilon\dot{x} + \Phi(x) + b\cos t = \\ = \varepsilon\dot{x}_2 + \Phi(x_2) + b\cos t_2 - \varepsilon\int_{t_2}^{t} x\,dt. \tag{15.67}$$

This equation shows that of the two inequalities, $x > -3$ and

$$x < -\frac{1-b}{2} + b\cos t, \tag{15.68}$$

the first to break down will be (15.68). Indeed, when $x \leqslant -3$ we have $\dot{x} > 0$ as long as (15.68) is satisfied. Consequently, $x > -3$ as long as (15.68) is satisfied, and, when $t > t_2 + 1$, as long as (15.68) holds we have $\varepsilon\dot{x} < 7$. In fact, if we were to have $\varepsilon\dot{x} \geqslant 7$ when $t = t_6$, it would follow from (15.67) that, because $-3 \leqslant x \leqslant 1$, $\varepsilon\dot{x} > 2$ for $t_6 - 1 \leqslant t \leqslant t_6$. But then inequality (15.68) could not be satisfied for $t = t_6$, so that $\varepsilon\dot{x} < 7$.

It follows from (15.67) that in the interval in which inequality (15.68) is satisfied we have

$$\varepsilon\dot{x} > -2b + \frac{\varepsilon}{2}(1-b)\int_{t_2}^{t} dt - 2\varepsilon b. \qquad (15.69)$$

Consequently, if $t > t_2 + [5/(1-b)\varepsilon]$, inequality (15.68) is not satisfied. Assume that the inequality (15.68) is violated for the first time when $t = t_4$, and that $t_3 < t_4$ is the last value of t prior to $t = t_4$ at which $x = -1$. Then we have either $\varepsilon\dot{x}_3 < 7$ or $t_3 < t_2 + 1$; in the second case, (15.67) implies the inequality $\varepsilon\dot{x}_3 < 29$. In both cases because $x_3 = -1$, we have

$$x = B_1(e^{(t-t_3)/\rho} - e^{(t-t_3)\rho}) - (1 + b\cos t_3)e^{(t-t_3)\rho} + b\cos t \qquad (15.70)$$

when $t = t_3$. It follows from Eq. (15.20) that $|B_1| < 30$. When $t = t_4$ we have $x_4 = -(1 - b/2) + b\cos t_4$; consequently, in virtue of (15.70)

$$-\frac{1-b}{2} \leqslant B_1(e^{(t_4-t_3)/\rho} - e^{(t_4-t)\rho}) - (1-b)$$

or

$$\frac{1-b}{2} < B_1 e^{(t_4-t_3)/\rho}.$$

Differentiating (15.70) and using the last inequality, we obtain

$$\dot{x} < \frac{1-b}{4\rho} - 1.$$

Thus, for some $t_5 < t_4 + (10\rho/1-b)$, $x_5 = 1$ and $\dot{x}_5 > 0$. Because $|B_1| < 30$, it follows from (15.70) that $\dot{x}_5 < 31/\rho$, and then (15.11) implies that $|x(t)| < 60$ as long as $x > 1$. Using integral equation (15.67), with the lower and upper limits of integration, respectively, changed to t_3 and t_5, together with inequality (15.68), which is valid for $t_3 < t < t_4$, and noting that $t_4 > t_5 - (10\rho/1-b)$, we obtain

$$b\cos t_5 + \varepsilon\dot{x}_5 > 2 - b - 3b\varepsilon. \qquad (15.71)$$

Using this in the integrated form of Eq. (15.3), we find that $x(t)>1$ when $t_5<t<t_5+4\pi$; hence, as at the beginning of the proof, we can see that the lemma holds. Q.E.D.

Lemma 15.7. If $x(t)$ is a solution of Eq. (15.3) such that when $t=t_1$, $x_1=-1$, $0\leqslant \dot{x}_1<10\rho^{\frac{1}{2}}$ and $|t_1(\mathrm{mod}\,2\pi)-\pi|<10\rho^{\frac{1}{2}}$, then there exists a t_2, $t_1<t_2<t_1+2\pi+\varepsilon^{\frac{1}{4}}$ such that $x_2=1$ and $-3<x<1$ when $t_1<t<t_2$. x increases rapidly from $x_2=1$ to a maximum value which is close to three, and for $t>t_2$ we have

$$x=Ae^{-(t-t_2)\rho}-b\cos t+E(\rho,t) \tag{15.72}$$

as long as $x>1$ (this inequality is satisfied in a time interval of the order of $1/\rho\ \ln(3-b/1-b)$). Here

$$|A-(3-b)|<\gamma\varepsilon,\quad |E(\rho,t)|+\left|\frac{d}{dt}E(\rho,t)\right|<\frac{5}{\rho}e^{-\frac{t-t_2}{\rho}} \tag{15.73}$$

where, as usual, γ is a variable that is bounded for small ε. In the time interval $t_1<t<t_2$, $|x|<3$ and $\varepsilon|\dot{x}|<4$.

Proof. Without loss of generality, we can assume that $|t_1-\pi|<10\rho^{\frac{1}{2}}$. We will also assume that (15.68) is satisfied when $t_1<t<t_3=3\pi-\rho^{\frac{2}{3}}$ and that $x<-1$ when $t=t_3$. Integrating Eq. (15.3), we find that

$$\varepsilon\dot{x}_3+x_3+b\cos t_3\geqslant$$
$$\geqslant\varepsilon\dot{x}_1-1-b-\varepsilon\int_{t_1}^{t_3}x\,dt\geqslant-1-b+\frac{1}{2}(1-b)\pi\varepsilon. \tag{15.74}$$

As proved above, inequality (15.68) implies that $x_3>-3$. It follows then from (15.74) that

$$x=A_1e^{-\frac{t-t_3}{\rho}}+A_2e^{-(t-t_3)\rho}-b\cos t \tag{15.75}$$

where $|A_1|<4$ and $A_2>-1-b+(1/4)(1-b)\pi\varepsilon$. Consequently, formula (15.75) yields $x>-1$ when $t=3\pi$, which means that there exists a t_4, $t_3<t_4<3\pi$, such that $x_4=-1$ when $t=t_4$. Then (15.75) yields

$$1>\varepsilon\dot{x}_4>\frac{(1-b)\pi\varepsilon}{2}>0,$$

which, together with Eq. (15.20) and (15.21), implies that

$$B_1>\frac{1-b}{3}\pi\varepsilon,\quad |B_2|<2.$$

Differentiating the equation

$$x = B_1 e^{\frac{t-t_4}{\rho}} + B_2 e^{(t-t_4)\rho} + b\cos t$$

twice, we obtain

$$\ddot{x} = \frac{B_1}{\rho^2} e^{\frac{t-t_4}{\rho}} + B_2\rho^2 e^{(t-t_4)\rho} - b\cos t \geqslant \frac{1-b}{4\varepsilon}\pi.$$

as long as $t > t_4$ and $|x| \leqslant 1$. Since $\dot{x}_4 > 0$, then for $t > t_4$ we have

$$\dot{x} > \dot{x}_4 + \frac{(1-b)\pi}{4\varepsilon}(t-t_4) > \frac{(1-b)\pi}{4\varepsilon}(t-t_4)$$

Consequently, there exists a $t_5 < t_4 + \varepsilon^{\frac{1}{3}}$ such that $x_5 = 1$ and $\dot{x}_5 > 0$ when $t = t_5$.

If (15.68) is satisfied, then, when $-1 \leqslant x_3$, integration of (15.3) yields

$$\varepsilon\dot{x}_3 > \frac{(1-b)\pi\varepsilon}{20}$$

and, by the same argument as above, we find that there exists a $t_5 < t_3 + \varepsilon^{\frac{1}{3}}$ such that $x_5 = 1$ and $\dot{x}_5 > 0$.

We now assume that (15.68) is violated for the first time when $t = t_4$, $t_1 < t_4 < t_3$. In exactly the same way as in the proof of the preceding lemma, we find that here the relations $x = 1$ and $\dot{x} > 0$ are satisfied for some $t < t_4 + (10\rho/1-b)$. Thus, there always exists a $t < t_1 + 2\pi + \varepsilon^{\frac{1}{3}}$ such that $x = 1$ and $\dot{x} > 0$ for this t.

If we denote the first point after t_1 at which $x = 1$ by t_2, we obtain $t_2 < t_1 + 2\pi + \varepsilon^{\frac{1}{3}}$. Integrating (15.3), we find that

$$\varepsilon\dot{x}_2 - 1 + b\cos t_2 = \varepsilon\dot{x}_1 + 1 + b\cos t_1 - \varepsilon\int_{t_1}^{t_2} x\,dt. \tag{15.76}$$

Since $x > -3$ as long as (15.68) is satisfied, and since x increases to unity when (15.68) does not hold, it is clear that $x > -3$. Thus, (15.76) implies that

$$|\varepsilon\dot{x}_2 + b\cos t_2 + b - 2| < 200\varepsilon. \tag{15.77}$$

By using formulas (15.18) and (15.19) to find A_1 and A_2, we obtain (15.72) and (15.73). It follows from the integrated form of Eq. (15.3) in conjunction with Eq. (15.72) that when t increases, after passing t_2, x increases rapidly to its maximum, which is approximately equal to three. We have already shown that $|x| < 3$ when $t_1 < t < t_2$. It follows then from the integrated form of Eq. (15.3) that $\varepsilon|\dot{x}| < 4$, which proves the lemma.

The two last lemmas make it possible to prove the following important statement.

Lemma 15.8. Every solution of Eq. (15.6) that satisfies the conditions

$$|y_0| + \rho|\dot{y}_0| \leqslant 20, \tag{15.78}$$

$$(y_0 - b\cos t_0)^2 + (\dot{y}_0 + b\sin t_0)^2 \geqslant \alpha^2 \tag{15.79}$$

when $t = t_0$, *where* α *is a sufficiently small consonant, satisfies the inequality* $|y(t)| \leqslant 70$ *when* $t \geqslant t_0$. *Moreover, there exists an* L *that depends on* ε *and* α *and is such that*

$$|y(t)| < 3{,}2, \quad |\dot{y}(t)| < \frac{5}{\varepsilon} \tag{15.80}$$

for $t \geqslant t_0 + L$. *If a maximum occurs at* $t = t_M$, *then*

$$y = (3 - b)\, e^{-\rho(t - t_M)} - b\cos t + \gamma\rho$$

for $t > t_M > t_0 + L$ *as long as* $y > 1$. *After* y *reaches a value equal to unity,* $y(t)$ *attains a minimum, close to* -3, *at* $t > t_m$ *after a time interval which does not exceed* 7π. *When* $t = t_m$

$$y = -(3 - b)\, e^{-\rho(t - t_m)} - b\cos t + \gamma\rho$$

until y *reaches a value equal to* -1. *Then* y *attains a maximum, close to* 3, *after a time interval which does not exceed* 7π, *etc.*

Proof. First, we select a sufficiently small ε so that the preceding lemma holds; then we choose h sufficiently small so that (15.79) implies (15.57), and set $L = 9\pi + 2/\rho \ln 32/h + [5/(1-b)\varepsilon]$. Now, take Δ so small that the inequality

$$|x(t) - y(t)| + |\dot{x}(t) - \dot{y}(t)| < \varepsilon^2 \quad \text{for} \quad 0 \leqslant t - t_0 \leqslant L$$

holds for all solutions $x(t)$ and $y(t)$ that have the same initial data and satisfy inequalities (15.57) and (15.64).

Then Lemmas 15.6 and 15.7 imply that for $t_3 = t_1 + 4\pi$ (where t_1 is the point whose existence was established by Lemma 15.6) we have the inequalities

$$|y(t_3) - 3| < \varepsilon^{\frac{1}{2}}, \quad |\dot{y}(t_3)| < 20\varepsilon^{\frac{1}{2}}$$

or inequalities in which 3 is replaced by -3. The solution $x(t)$ of Eq. (15.3) that satisfies the same initial conditions as $y(t)$ at $t=t_3$ is given by formula (15.11) and, as shown in the proof of Lemma 15.6, intersects the line $x=1$ when $t=t_4$, $|t_4 (\mathrm{mod}\, 2\pi)| < 10\rho^{\frac{1}{2}}$, $0 \geqslant \dot{x} > -10\rho^{\frac{1}{2}}$. By Lemma 15.7, we have the inequalities $|y(t_5)+3| < \varepsilon^{\frac{1}{2}}$ and $|\dot{y}(t_5)| < 20\varepsilon^{\frac{1}{2}}$ for $t=t_5=t_4+4\pi$; moreover, $\left|t_4-t_3-(1/\rho)\ln(3-b/1+b)\right| < 10\pi$. Thus, $t_5-t_3<L$, and $y(t)$ and $\dot{y}(t)$ are close to $x(t)$ and $\dot{x}(t)$ on this interval. When $t=t_5$ the same conditions prevail as when $t=t_3$, and, consequently, we can use the same method to show that there exists a t_7 for which $y(t)$ is close to 3, etc.

$y(t)$ achieves a minimum value which is close to -3 for some t, $t_4<t<t_5$; between t_6 and t_7 it achieves a maximum; etc. Since $x(t) > 1+\varepsilon$ when $t<t_4-3\pi$, $y(t)>1$, and, consequently, $y(t)$ intersects the line $y=1$ when $t\in(t_4-3\pi,\ t_4+3\pi)$. Inequalities (15.80) follow from inequalities established for $x(t)$ and $\dot{x}(t)$ and from the fact that $y(t)$ and $\dot{y}(t)$ are very close to $x(t)$ and $\dot{x}(t)$. Q.E.D.

Remark. It follows from the results of Section 8 and the foregoing considerations that the inequality

$$|x|+\rho|\dot{x}| \leqslant 20 \tag{15.81}$$

holds for any solution of Eq. (15.3) when t is sufficiently large. Therefore, if t is sufficiently large, the last lemma is true for any solution of Eq. (15.3).

Let $C^{(0)}$ denote the region

$$|y|+\rho|v| < 20$$

in the (y, v) plane (where, as before, $\dot{y}=v$). It follows then from Lemma 15.8 that there exists an integer N such that $T^kC^{(0)} \subset C^{(0)}$ when $k \geqslant N$.

Consider the set

$$J=\prod_{k=0}^{\infty} T^{kN}C^{(0)}.$$

From the definition of J it follows that $T^NJ=J$; then by the procedure used in the proof that the set I of a dissipative system (see Section 2, Paragraph 3) is invariant, we can show that the set J is invariant under the transformation T, i.e.,

$$TJ=J.$$

It follows from the preceding remark that for Eq. (15.3) the set J coincides with the set I of this equation as a D-system.

We will now show that the set H [see (15.56)] belongs to J. Indeed, $C_0 \subset C^{(0)}$, so that $T^{kN}C_0 \subset T^{kN}C^{(0)}$ (for any natural k). From the definition of H it follows that $H = \sum_{k=1}^{\infty} T^{kN}C_0$ which implies that $H \subset J$.

Now consider the set $K = J - H$. It follows from the definition of H that $TH = H$, so that $TK = K$. We will show that the set K has zero area. It is not difficult to see that the annular region Λ bounded by the circle Γ (the boundary of the disk C_0) and the curve $|y| + \rho|v| = 20$ (the boundary of the region $C^{(0)}$) contains the set K. We will show that the area of the region $T^k\Lambda$ approaches zero as $k \to \infty$, and since the set K is invariant, this will imply that the area of K is zero. Let $y = y(t, y_0, v_0)$ be the solution of Eq. (15.6) with the initial data $t = 0$, $y = y_0$, $\dot{y} = v_0$, and consider the Jacobian

$$W = \frac{D(y, v)}{D(y_0, v_0)} = \begin{vmatrix} \frac{\partial y}{\partial y_0}, & \frac{\partial y}{\partial v_0} \\ \frac{\partial v}{\partial y_0}, & \frac{\partial v}{\partial v_0} \end{vmatrix}.$$

Differential equation (15.6) yields

$$\frac{dW}{dt} = -\frac{1}{\varepsilon} P'(y) W$$

or

$$W(t) = W(0)\, e^{-\frac{1}{\varepsilon}\int_0^t P'(y)\,dt}.$$

By Lemma 15.8, for each solution that is in Λ for $t = 0$, $|y(t)| > 1.1$ during a sufficiently long time interval $0 \leqslant t \leqslant t_1$ in the set of points t whose total measure is larger than 2/3 of the length of $(0, t_1)$. Choose $P(y)$ so that $P'(y) > 0.9$ for $|y| > 1.1$, and $P'(y) > -1.1$ when $|y| < 1.1$. Then, clearly, we have $W(t) \to 0$ as $t \to \infty$ uniformly for all solutions beginning in Λ at time $t = 0$. Hence, the area of $T^k\Lambda$ approaches zero as $k \to \infty$.

It also follows from the foregoing considerations that the invariant set Ω of solutions passing through the set K when $t = 0$ is asymptotically Lyapunov-stable, and that all solutions beginning in Λ at time $t = 0$ approach Ω as $t \to \infty$. Note also that in general all solutions of Eq. (15.3), except for the harmonic $x = b\cos t$, approach Ω as $t \to +\infty$.

5. We will now show that if b satisfies relations (15.39) and (15.40), then Eq. (15.6) has two systems of asymptotically stable subharmonics of order $2n - 1$ and $2n + 1$.

Set

$$\sigma_1 = \sqrt{\frac{(1+b)(3-b)}{2b}\delta\rho}, \tag{15.82}$$

and consider the solutions of Eq. (15.3) with initial data $(t_0, x_0, \dot{x}_0)$ satisfying the conditions $x_0 = -1$,

$$|t_0 - \pi + \sigma_1| \leqslant \rho^{\frac{3}{5}}, \quad |\dot{x}_0 - \rho + b\rho\cos t_0 - b\sin t_0| \leqslant e^{-\frac{10}{\rho}}. \tag{15.83}$$

Denote the region (15.83) of the plane $x = -1$ by D_0. By using formulas (15.11) and (15.12), we can show that

$$x = A_1 e^{-(t-\pi)/\rho} + A_2 e^{-(t-\pi)\rho} - b\cos t \tag{15.84}$$

for $t \geqslant \pi$ and $x \geqslant 1$, where

$$|A_1| < 1, \quad A_2 = 3 - b + \frac{1}{2}b\sigma_1^2 + \gamma\varepsilon^{\frac{3}{2}}. \tag{15.85}$$

If we set $t = 2n\pi - s$, it follows from (15.84), (15.85), and (15.40) that

$$x = 1 + b + (1+b)\rho(s - \delta) + \frac{b}{2}\frac{1+b}{3-b}\sigma_1^2 - b\cos s + \gamma\varepsilon^{\frac{3}{2}}.$$

Elementary operations now lead to the conclusion that $x = 1$ when

$$|s - \sigma_1| < \left[\frac{1+b}{3-b} + \rho^{\frac{1}{10}}\right]\rho^{\frac{3}{5}} < \frac{19}{20}\rho^{\frac{3}{5}}.$$

If we denote the time of the first intersection between the solution x and the line $x = 1$ by t_1 and write $\dot{x}(t_1) = \dot{x}_1$, then the last inequality and Eq. (15.17) yield

$$|t_1 - 2n\pi + \sigma_1| < \frac{19}{20}\rho^{\frac{3}{5}}, \quad |\dot{x}_1 + \rho + \rho b\cos t_1 - b\sin t_1| < \frac{1}{2}e^{-\frac{10}{\rho}}. \tag{15.86}$$

Denote the region (15.86) of the plane $x = 1$ by D_1, and construct the region D_2 in the following manner: Suppose the point (t, x) belong to D_1; then the point $(t - (2n-1)\pi, -\dot{x})$ belongs to D_2, and conversely. It is not difficult to see that $\bar{D}_2 \subset D_0$, and as we have just proved, any solution beginning in D_0 intersects D_1. This leads to a continuous transformation of the region D_0 into D_1. We now associate the points of D_2 with the points of D_1 in the manner indicated above, thus obtaining a transformation of the domain D_0 into D_2. Since $\bar{D}_2 \subset D_0$, it follows from Brouwer's theorem that there exists a stationary point, which means that there exists a solution $x = g(t)$ such that $g(t_0) = -1$, $g(t_0 + (2n-1)\pi) = 1$ and $\dot{g}(t_0) = -\dot{g}(t_0 + (2n-1)\pi)$. It follows then from the form of Eq. (15.3) that

$$g(t + (2n-1)\pi) = -g(t), \tag{15.87}$$

so that the solution $x = g(t)$ of Eq. (15.3) has period $2(2n-1)\pi$. Thus, system (15.4) has a $2(2n-1)\pi$-periodic solution.

In order to investigate the stability of this solution, consider a form of the equation which is associated with this solution:

$$\varepsilon \frac{d\xi_1}{dt} = \xi_2 - \varphi(g(t))\xi_1, \quad \frac{d\xi_2}{dt} = -\varepsilon\xi_1. \tag{15.88}$$

Since $\varphi(x)$ is an even function, it follows from (15.87) that $\varphi(g(t))$ has period $(2n-1)\pi$. We will now estimate the roots of the characteristic equation for system (15.88), corresponding to the period $(2n-1)\pi$. We will show that the magnitudes of both of these roots are less than unity and, consequently, a periodic solution of system (15.4) is asymptotically stable. Then it follows from the theory of perturbations of periodic systems that, if the function $P(y)$ is appropriately chosen, system (15.5) must also have an asymptotically stable solution with period $2(2n-1)\pi$.

Assume that t_0 satisfies the first of inequalities (15.83) and is such that $g(t_0) = -1$, and assume that t_1 is the first instant after $t = t_0$ at which $g(t_1) = 1$. Then it follows from formula (15.12) that $t_1 - t_0 < \varepsilon^{\frac{1}{2}}$. If we set $t_2 = t_0 + (2n-1)\pi$, we find that $g(t) > 1$ when $t_1 < t < t_2$. Denote the solution of system (15.88) with initial data $t = t_0$, $\xi_1 = 1$, and $\xi_2 = 0$ by $\xi_{11}(t)$, $\xi_{21}(t)$ and let $\xi_{12}(t)$, $\xi_{22}(t)$ denote the solution of this system with initial data $t = t_0$, $\xi_1 = 0$, and $\xi_2 = 1$. Consider the Wronskian

$$W(t) = \begin{vmatrix} \xi_{11}(t), & \xi_{12}(t) \\ \xi_{21}(t), & \xi_{22}(t) \end{vmatrix}.$$

By Liouville's formula,

$$W(t_2) = e^{-\frac{1}{\varepsilon}\int_{t_0}^{t_2} \varphi(g(t))\,dt} \leqslant e^{\frac{2}{\sqrt{\varepsilon}} - \frac{(2n-1)\pi}{\varepsilon}} < e^{-\frac{10}{\varepsilon}}$$

so that the roots of the characteristic equation satisfy the inequality $|\lambda_1\lambda_2| = W(t_2) < e^{-\frac{10}{\varepsilon}}$.

The sum of the roots of the characteristic equation is equal to $\xi_{11}(t_2) + \xi_{22}(t_2)$. It follows from formula (15.12) that

$$e^{(t_1-t_0)/\rho} \sim \frac{1}{b\varepsilon\sigma_1} \quad \text{for small } \varepsilon \tag{15.89}$$

and

$$e^{-\rho(t_2-t_1)} \sim \frac{1+b}{3-b} \quad \text{for small } \varepsilon. \tag{15.90}$$

Since $\varphi(g(t)) = -1$ when $t_0 < t < t_1$ and $\varphi(g(t)) = 1$ when $t_1 < t < t_2$, we can solve system (15.88) exactly. Using estimates (15.89) and (15.90), we can show that, when ε is sufficiently small, $\xi_{11}(t_2) + \xi_{22}(t_2)$ is arbitrarily close to $(1+b)/(3-b)$, from which it follows that one of the roots of the characteristic equation, say λ_1, is very small, and that the other is close to $(1+b)/(3-b) < 1$. This means that the magnitudes of both roots of the characteristic equation are less than unity.

The existence and asymptotic stability of the second system of subharmonics can be established in exactly the same way, except that σ_1 must be replaced by

$$\sigma_2 = \sqrt{\frac{(1+b)(3-b)(\delta+2\pi)}{2b}\rho}.$$

We note one more interesting fact: Both inside H and outside J there exist points through which solutions that approach stable periodic solutions of system (15.5) pass. We will prove this statement for system (15.4), but it is clear that the proof will also hold for system (15.5) if Δ is chosen sufficiently small.

Consider the following solution of Eq. (15.3):

$$x = (4 + b - c\rho)e^{-\rho t} - b\cos t, \quad |c| < 10.$$

When $t = 0$, this solution lies outside J, because $x(0) > 3.5$. It is not difficult, by appropriate selection of c, $|c| < 10$, to arrange for the solution $x(t)$ to intersect the line $x = 1$ when $|(t - \sigma_1)(\text{mod } 2\pi)| < \rho^{\frac{3}{5}}$, which yields the required result for a solution with period $2(2n-1)\pi$. In exactly the same way, the choice of c can be used to construct a solution that approaches a $2(2n+1)\pi$-periodic solution.

If m is a sufficiently large natural number, then the solution

$$x = (1 - b - c\rho)e^{\frac{t}{\rho} - \frac{2m\pi}{\rho}} + c\rho e^{\rho(t-2m\pi)} + b\cos t, \qquad |c| < 10$$

is inside H when $t = 0$. It is not difficult to see that $|x|$ becomes equal to unity for the first time when $t = 2m\pi$, at which time $x = 1$. When $t > (2m+1)\pi$ we have

$$x=(2-c\rho)e^{-\rho(t-2m\pi)}-b\cos t+\gamma\rho^2.$$

Appropriate selection of c, $|c|<10$, can be used to arrange for $x(t)$ to intersect the line $x=1$ in an interval of t corresponding to any of the stable subharmonics.

6. It follows from the very definition of the set K that the initial points of both families of subharmonics (those with period $2(2n-1)\pi$, as well as those with period $2(2n+1)\pi$) are in K, from which it follows that K has zero area, but can not be a closed Jordan curve. We will now prove this statement.

Assume that K is a closed Jordan curve, and that S is a topological mapping of this curve onto the circle C. Let p be the initial point of one of the subharmonics of the first family, and let q be the initial point of one of the subharmonics of the second family. Then we have $T^{2n-1}p=p$ and $T^lp\neq p$ for $l=1, 2, \ldots, 2n-2$; $T^{2n+1}q=q$ and $T^lq\neq q$ for $l=1, 2, \ldots, 2n$.

Now consider the transformation $P=STS^{-1}$ of the circle C onto itself. This transformation is a direction-preserving homeomorphism. If we let $a=Sp$, and $b=Sq$, it is clear that $P^{2n-1}a=a$ and $P^la\neq a$ for $l=1, 2, \ldots, 2n-2$; $P^{2n+1}b=b$ and $P^lb\neq b$ for $l=1, 2, \ldots, 2n$. But this is impossible in view of the results given at the end of Section 10.

The contradiction which we have obtained shows that the set K can not be a closed Jordan curve.

16. ON THE EXISTENCE OF HARMONIC OSCILLATIONS FOR A SYSTEM OF TWO DIFFERENTIAL EQUATIONS

In Section 12 we proved that if all solutions of a system of two equations extend to a period, existence of a bounded solution implies the existence of the harmonic oscillation. However, far from all solutions of a system prove to be continuable to a period. Systems in which polynomial terms "predominate" at infinity provide examples of systems for which solutions may become infinite prior to the end of a period. In this section we will study such systems.

Consider the system [75]

$$\left.\begin{aligned}\frac{dx}{dt}&=P(x, y)+X(x, y, t),\\ \frac{dy}{dt}&=Q(x, y)+Y(x, y, t)\end{aligned}\right\}\qquad(16.1)$$

where P and Q are homogeneous n-dimensional forms and X and Y are continuous, satisfy a Lipschitz condition with respect to the variables x and y in the neighborhood of each point (x, y), and have period ω in the variable t. Moreover, we will assume that, at infinity, these functions are "small" in comparison with P and Q. More precisely, we assume that the following relations are satisfied uniformly with respect to t:

$$\frac{X(x, y, t)}{(x^2+y^2)^{n/2}} \xrightarrow[x^2+y^2\to\infty]{} 0, \quad \frac{Y(x, y, t)}{(x^2+y^2)^{n/2}} \xrightarrow[x^2+y^2\to\infty]{} 0. \tag{16.2}$$

Together with system (16.1), we will also consider the "abbreviated" system

$$\frac{dx}{dt}=P(x, y), \quad \frac{dy}{dt}=Q(x, y). \tag{16.3}$$

1. Here we will study the behavior of solutions of systems (16.1) and (16.3) in the neighborhood of infinity. We use the formulas

$$x=r\cos\varphi, \quad y=r\sin\varphi, \tag{16.4}$$

to convert to polar coordinates, and introduce the notation

$$\begin{gathered}
Q(\cos\varphi, \sin\varphi)\cos\varphi-P(\cos\varphi, \sin\varphi)\sin\varphi=F(\varphi),\\
Y(r\cos\varphi, r\sin\varphi, t)\cos\varphi-X(r\cos\varphi, r\sin\varphi, t)\sin\varphi=f(r, \varphi, t),\\
P(\cos\varphi, \sin\varphi)\cos\varphi+Q(\cos\varphi, \sin\varphi)\sin\varphi=G(\varphi),\\
X(r\cos\varphi, r\sin\varphi, t)\cos\varphi+Y(r\cos\varphi, r\sin\varphi, t)\sin\varphi=g(r, \varphi, t),
\end{gathered}$$

so that systems (16.1) and (16.3) take the following forms:

$$\left.\begin{aligned}
\frac{dr}{dt}&=r^nG(\varphi)+g(r, \varphi, t),\\
r\frac{d\varphi}{dt}&=r^nF(\varphi)+f(r, \varphi, t)
\end{aligned}\right\} \tag{16.5}$$

and

$$\frac{dr}{dt}=r^nG(\varphi), \quad r\frac{d\varphi}{dt}=r^nF(\varphi). \tag{16.6}$$

Hereinafter, we will assume that the equation

$$F(\varphi)=0 \tag{16.7}$$

can have only simple roots, and that these roots do not coincide with the roots of the equation $G(\varphi)=0$.

First, consider the case in which Eq. (16.7) has real roots, and let $\varphi=\varphi_0$ be a root of Eq. (16.7). It is then clear that the ray $\varphi=\varphi_0$ is a trajectory of system (16.6). We will call the direction $\varphi=\varphi_0$ a critical direction for systems (16.5) and (16.6) [correspondingly for system (16.1) and (16.3)]. By hypothesis, $G(\varphi_0) \neq 0$ and $F'(\varphi_0) \neq 0$. If $G(\varphi_0) F'(\varphi_0) > 0$, we will call the direction $\varphi = \varphi_0$ a saddle direction, while if $G(\varphi_0) F'(\varphi_0) < 0$, we will call the direction $\varphi = \varphi_0$ a node direction.* If $G(\varphi_0) < 0$, we will call the direction negative, while if $G(\varphi_0) > 0$ we will call it positive.

Consider some critical direction $\varphi = \varphi_0$, and choose $\delta > 0$ so small that the inequalities

$$|G(\varphi) - G(\varphi_0)| < \frac{1}{2} |G(\varphi_0)| \tag{16.8}$$

and

$$|F(\varphi) - F'(\varphi_0)(\varphi - \varphi_0)| < \frac{1}{2} |F'(\varphi_0)| |\varphi - \varphi_0| \tag{16.9}$$

are satisfied when $|\varphi - \varphi_0| \leqslant \delta$. It follows from the first equation of system (16.5) and from relations (16.2) that if $R > 0$ is sufficiently large, then dr/dt does not change sign in the region $\{|\varphi - \varphi_0| \leqslant \delta, r \geqslant R\}$ and, in particular, the circular arc $\{r = R, |\varphi - \varphi_0| \leqslant \delta\}$ has no contact with the field vectors of system (16.5) for any t. From the second equation of system (16.5), it follows that when R is sufficiently large the rays $\{\varphi = \varphi_0 \pm \delta, r \geqslant R\}$ also have no contact with the field of system (16.5).

We introduce the following notation: We will denote the region $\{|\varphi - \varphi_0| \leqslant \delta, r \geqslant R\}$ by N_+ if the direction $\varphi = \varphi_0$ is a positive node direction; if the direction $\varphi = \varphi_0$ is a negative node direction, we will denote this region by N_-. We will denote the region $\{|\varphi - \varphi_0| \leqslant \delta, r \geqslant R\}$ by S_+ or S_- if the direction $\varphi = \varphi_0$ is a positive or negative saddle direction, respectively.

We will call the circular arc $\{r = R, |\varphi - \varphi_0| \leqslant \delta\}$ the bottom wall, and the rays $\{\varphi = \varphi_0 \pm \delta, r \geqslant R\}$ the side walls of the respective regions.

It is not difficult to see that, as time increases, all solutions beginning on the boundaries of a region N_+ enter this region, while solutions beginning on the boundaries of an N_- region, leave it. As time increases, solutions enter S_+ through the bottom wall, and leave through the side walls, while, for an S_- region, the solutions enter through the side walls and leave through the bottom wall.

2. We will now prove the following statement.

Theorem 16.1. Assume that the following conditions are satisfied:

a) Relations (16.2) hold.

*These names correspond to the types of singular (critical) points at infinity associated with the direction $\varphi = \varphi_0$.

b) Equation (16.7) has at least one real root, all of its real roots are simple, and none of its real roots coincides with a root of the equation $G(\varphi)=0$.

c) If $\varphi=\varphi_1$ *and* $\varphi=\varphi_2$ *are two adjacent exceptional directions* ($F(\varphi)\neq 0$) *for* $\varphi_1<\varphi<\varphi_2$), *one of them must be a node direction, i.e., two adjacent exceptional directions cannot be saddle directions.*

d) The index of the singular point $x=y=0$ *of system (16.3) is nonzero. Then system (16.1) has at least one* ω*-periodic solution.*

Proof. The function $F(\varphi)$ is a trigonometric polynomial; hence, it is clear that either Eq. (16.7) has a finite number of roots or it is an identity. Because we have assumed that the roots of Eq. (16.7) are simple, the second case is impossible.

We enclose each of the critical directions in a region $\{|\varphi-\varphi_0|\leqslant\delta, r\geqslant R\}$ of the above-described form, and we can assume that the quantities δ and R are the same for all such regions.

The most immediate problem is construction of a closed curve Γ such that, if the point (x_0, y_0) is on Γ, then the solution $x(t, x_0, y_0, t_0)$, $y(t, x_0, y_0, t_0)$ of system (16.1) does not coincide with this point for any $t>t_0$.

It is easy to see that the points of the boundaries of N_+ and N_- have this property, so that Γ can comprise any segments of these boundaries.

Consider a critical direction $\varphi=\varphi_1$ which is a node direction and for definiteness assume that this direction is positive. Let N_+ be the corresponding region; let $\varphi=\varphi_2$ be a critical direction adjacent to $\varphi=\varphi_1$, and assume, for definiteness, that $\varphi_2>\varphi_1$ and $F(\varphi)\neq 0$ for $\varphi_1<\varphi<\varphi_2$. Assume that $\varphi=\varphi_2$ is also a node direction; then it must be negative. Indeed, by the definition of a positive node direction we have $G(\varphi_1)>0$ and $F'(\varphi_1)<0$. Since $\varphi=\varphi_2$ is a root of Eq. (16.7) adjacent to $\varphi=\varphi_1$, it is clear that $F'(\varphi_2)>0$. The direction $\varphi=\varphi_2$ is a node direction, i.e., $F'(\varphi_2)G(\varphi_2)<0$, so that $G(\varphi_2)<0$, the direction $\varphi=\varphi_2$ is negative, and N_- is the corresponding region.

We will now construct a contactless curve γ connecting the adjacent side walls of the regions N_+ and N_-, i.e., the rays $\varphi=\varphi_1+\delta$ and $\varphi=\varphi_2-\delta$. Dividing the first equation of system (16.5) by the second, we find that

$$\frac{dr}{d\varphi}=r\frac{G(\varphi)+\dfrac{g(r,\varphi,t)}{r^n}}{F(\varphi)+\dfrac{f(r,\varphi,t)}{r^n}}. \tag{16.10}$$

Since $F(\varphi)\neq 0$ for $\varphi_1+\delta\leqslant\varphi\leqslant\varphi_2-\delta$, there exists an $a>0$, such that

$$\frac{dr}{d\varphi}<ar \tag{16.11}$$

for $r \geqslant R$, provided that R is sufficiently large. From inequality (16.11) it follows that, in the region $\{\varphi_1+\delta \leqslant \varphi \leqslant \varphi_2-\delta,\ r \geqslant R\}$, the solutions of the equation

$$\frac{dr}{d\varphi} = ar \tag{16.12}$$

are contactless curves. As a result, the curve

$$r = r_0 e^{a(\varphi-\varphi_1-\delta)} \tag{16.13}$$

where $r_0 \geqslant R$, also has no contact with the field of (16.5), and curve (16.13) is the desired curve γ when $\varphi_1+\delta \leqslant \varphi \leqslant \varphi_2-\delta$.

Consider the unbounded region K whose boundaries consist of the curve γ and the rays $\varphi=\varphi_1+\delta$ and $\varphi=\varphi_2-\delta$. It is not difficult to see that, as time increases, solutions of system (16.5) enter K through the curve γ. Let $(x_0,\ y_0)$ be a point on γ, and let $(x(t),\ y(t))$ be the solution with initial data $x(t_0)=x_0$ $y(t_0)=y_0$. As time increases, this solution enters the region K, and can leave it only through the wall $\varphi=\varphi_1+\delta$; but then our solution will enter the region N_+, and no solution can leave the region N_+ as time increases. Thus, the solution $(x(t),\ y(t))$ beginning at the point $(x_0,\ y_0)$ can not return to this point. As a result, the curve γ can be included in the desired contour Γ.

Now let φ_2 be a saddle direction. By hypothesis, the adjacent critical directions must be node directions. Let φ_1 and φ_3 be such directions $(\varphi_1 < \varphi_2 < \varphi_3)$, and, for definiteness, assume that the critical direction φ_2 is positive. Since φ_1 and φ_3 are node directions, $F'(\varphi_1)G(\varphi_1) < 0$ and $F'(\varphi_3)G(\varphi_3) < 0$ the direction φ_2 is a positive saddle direction, so that $F'(\varphi_2) > 0,\ G(\varphi_2) > 0$. Since all roots of Eq. (16.7) are simple, it is clear that $F'(\varphi_1) < 0$ and $F'(\varphi_3) < 0$. Consequently, $G(\varphi_1) > 0$, $G(\varphi_3) > 0$, and the directions φ_1 and φ_3 are positive. Now, enclose the directions φ_1, φ_2, and φ_3 in regions $N_+^{(1)}\{r \geqslant R,\ \varphi_1-\delta \leqslant \varphi \leqslant \varphi_1+\delta\}$, $S_+\{r \geqslant R,\ \varphi_2-\delta \leqslant \varphi \leqslant \varphi_2+\delta\}$ and $N_+^{(2)}\{r \geqslant R,\ \varphi_3-\delta \leqslant \varphi \leqslant \varphi_3+\delta\}$.

It is not difficult to see that inequality (16.11) holds in the region $\{\varphi_1+\delta \leqslant \varphi \leqslant \varphi_2-\delta,\ r \geqslant R\}$ and, therefore, the curve γ defined by Eq. (16.13) has no contact with the direction field of (16.5). Just as in the preceding case, it turns out that any solution beginning at some point of the curve γ cannot return to this point as time increases.

We now construct a contactless curve γ_1 connecting the adjacent side walls of the regions S_+ and $N_+^{(2)}$, i.e., the rays $\varphi=\varphi_2+\delta$ and $\varphi=\varphi_3-\delta$. As above, it follows from Eq. (16.10) that the inequality

$$\frac{dr}{d\varphi} > -ar \tag{16.14}$$

holds in the region $\{r \geqslant R, \varphi_2+\delta \leqslant \varphi \leqslant \varphi_3-\delta\}$, where, as before, a is some positive constant. But then it is clear that the curve

$$r = r_0 e^{-a(\varphi-\varphi_3+\delta)} \tag{16.15}$$

has no contact with the direction field of system (16.5), so that for $\varphi_2+\delta \leqslant \varphi \leqslant \varphi_3-\delta$ this curve is the desired curve γ_1. It is not difficult to prove that any solution beginning on γ_1 can not return to this curve as time increases.

Now draw a circle C with center at the coordinate origin and radius sufficiently large so that the curves γ and γ_1 are contained inside it. Let γ_2 denote the arc (of this circle) corresponding to the angles $\varphi_2-\delta \leqslant \varphi \leqslant \varphi_2+\delta$, i.e., the arc connecting the side walls of the region S_+, and let γ_3 and γ_4 denote the segments of the side walls of S_+ lying between the circle C and the curves γ and γ_1, respectively. Let λ denote the curve composed of the curvilinear segments $\gamma, \gamma_3, \gamma_2, \gamma_4$, and γ_1; the curve λ connects the adjacent side walls of the regions $N_+^{(1)}$ and $N_+^{(2)}$, i.e., the rays $\varphi=\varphi_1+\delta$ and $\varphi=\varphi_3-\delta$. Let K be the unbounded region whose boundaries are the curve λ and the infinite parts of the rays $\varphi=\varphi_1+\delta$ and $\varphi=\varphi_3-\delta$. By the very construction of the curve λ, solutions enter K through this curve. Now let (x_0, y_0) be a point on λ, and let $(x(t), y(t))$ be the solution with initial data $x(t_0)=x_0$, $y(t_0)=y_0$. As time increases, this solution enters K and can leave it only through one of the walls $\varphi=\varphi_1+\delta$ or $\varphi=\varphi_3-\delta$; but, in that event, the solution will enter one of the regions $N_+^{(1)}$ or $N_+^{(2)}$, and no solution having a point in N_+ may leave this region as time increases. Consequently, the solution $(x(t), y(t))$ can not reach the point (x_0, y_0) as time increases, and the curve λ can be included in the desired contour Γ.

Now take some node direction $\varphi=\varphi_0$, assuming, for definiteness, that it is positive, and let N_+ be the corresponding region. Let φ_1 be the node direction adjacent to φ_0 (of course, there may be one saddle direction between φ_0 and φ_1), and denote the region corresponding to the direction φ_1 by N' (this region can clearly be either of type N_+ or N_-). The regions N_+ and N' can be connected by curves of the same type as γ or of the same type as λ (depending on whether or not there is a saddle direction between φ_1 and φ_2). We connect all regions N_+ and N_- in this way. Consider the contour Γ consisting of the connecting curves and the appropriate parts of the boundaries of N_+ and N_-. The resultant contour will have the property that any solution beginning at one of its points can not return to this point as time increases.

It follows from Condition (b) of the theorem that system (16.3) has only one equilibrium state: the point $x=y=0$. The index of the curve Γ in the vector field $\{P(x, y), Q(x, y)\}$ is therefore nonzero. If the contour Γ is chosen so that it lies outside a circle with center at the coordinate origin and sufficiently large radius, it is clear that the vector fields $\{P(x, y), Q(x, y)\}$ and $\{P(x, y)+X(x, y, 0), Q(x, y)+Y(x, y, 0)\}$ neither vanish nor reverse directions anywhere on Γ. We will assume that the contour Γ has been selected in this way (this merely requires that the number R be sufficiently large), and, consequently, the indices of Γ in the fields $\{P(x, y), Q(x, y)\}$ and $\{P(x, y)+X(x, y, 0)\ Q(x, y)+Y(x, y, 0)\}$ are identical and nonzero.

Now consider the system of differential equations

$$\left.\begin{aligned} \frac{dx}{dt}&=[P(x, y)+X(x, y, t)]H(x, y), \\ \frac{dy}{dt}&=[Q(x, y)+Y(x, y, t)]H(x, y), \end{aligned}\right\} \tag{16.16}$$

where the function $H(x, y)$ is chosen in the following manner. Let D be a disk that has its center at the coordinate origin and contains the contour Γ; the function $H(x, y)$ is continuously differentiable and positive for all x and y; $H(x, y)=1$ if the point (x, y) is in D, and $(x^2+y^2)^{\frac{n}{2}} H(x, y)\to 0$ when $x^2+y^2\to\infty$. It is clear that the contour Γ has the same properties with respect to system (16.16) as it has with respect to system (16.1). But all solutions of system (16.16) can be extended to all times between $\infty-$ and $+\infty$. By Theorem 16.1, therefore, system (16.16) has a harmonic oscillation. Clearly, this ω-periodic solution lies inside the contour Γ. But, inside Γ, systems (16.1) and (16.16) coincide, which proves that system (16.1) has a harmonic oscillation. Q. E. D.

3. The last condition of the theorem in Paragraph 2 requires that the index of the stated singular point of system (16.3) be nonzero. This index can be computed by Poincare's integral formula (see, for example, [1, 76)]. In the case under consideration, however, the index may be determined by a simpler method.

Let $\varphi=\varphi_0$ be a critical direction, which means that $F(\varphi_0)=0$. But $F(\varphi)$ is an nth degree form in sin φ and cos φ; hence, it is clear that $F(\varphi_0+\pi)=0$ and, consequently, $\varphi_0+\pi$ is also a critical direction. The product $F'(\varphi)G(\varphi)$ is a $2n$th degree form in sin φ and cos φ, and therefore this product does not change when - sin φ is substituted for sin φ and - cos φ is substituted for cos φ. As a result, if $\varphi=\varphi_0$ is a saddle direction, then $\varphi=\varphi_0+\pi$ is a node direction, then so is $\varphi=\varphi_0+\pi$.

Thus, both node and saddle directions appear in pairs. Let the number of saddle directions be $2k$, and let the number of node directions be $2l$. It follows then from Condition (c) of the theorem, that $2l\geqslant 2k$.

Now draw a circle with center at the coordinate origin, and we will attempt to determine the rotation of the field vector as it traverses this circle in the positive direction.

Let $\varphi=\varphi_1$ and $\varphi=\varphi_2$ be two adjacent exceptional directions ($\varphi_1<\varphi_2$). It is not difficult to show that if both of these directions are node directions, then the field vector rotates through an angle of $\varphi_2-\varphi_1-\pi$ as it passes from φ_1 to φ_2, and if one of the directions is a node direction and the other is a saddle, the field vector rotates through an angle of $\varphi_2-\varphi_1$.

The total rotation of the field vector upon traversing the entire circle will therefore be equal to the sum of the angles between the critical directions (i.e., 2π) plus ($-\pi$) multiplied by the number of angles bounded from both sides by node directions. It is clear that there will be as many of these angles as there are "excessive" node directions, namely, $2l-2k$. We thus obtain the following formula for the index:

$$I=\frac{1}{2\pi}(2\pi-(2l-2k)\pi)=1+k-l. \tag{16.17}$$

Condition (d) of the theorem can therefore be formulated in the following manner: The number of node directions must not exceed the number of saddle directions by exactly 2.

4. Theorem 16.1 was concerned with the case in which Eq. (16.7) has real roots. Now we will consider the case in which the function $F(\varphi)$ does not vanish for real φ. We will prove the following statement.

Theorem 16.2. If $F(\varphi)$ does not vanish and the quantity

$$s=\frac{1}{2\pi}\int_0^{2\pi}\frac{G(\varphi)}{F(\varphi)}\,d\varphi \tag{16.18}$$

is nonzero, then system (16.2) has an ω-periodic solution.

Proof. For definiteness, assume that $F(\varphi)>0$ and $s<0$. If we set

$$\frac{G(\varphi)}{F(\varphi)}=h(\varphi)+s \tag{16.19}$$

it becomes clear that $\int_0^{\varphi}h(\varphi)\,d\varphi$ is a periodic function.

Dividing the first equation of system (16.6) by the second, we obtain

$$\frac{dr}{d\varphi}=r(h(\varphi)+s). \tag{16.20}$$

Now rewrite Eq. (16.10) in the following form:

$$\frac{dr}{d\varphi}=r(h(\varphi)+s+\alpha(r,\varphi,t)) \tag{16.21}$$

where

$$\alpha(r, \varphi, t)=\frac{F\frac{g}{r^n}-G\frac{f}{r^n}}{F\left(F+\frac{f}{r^n}\right)}.$$

It follows from relations (16.2) that there exists an R such that $|\alpha(r, \varphi, t)| < 1/2\,|s|$ when $r \geqslant R$.

Integration of Eq. (16.20) yields

$$r=r_0 e^{s\varphi} e^{\int_0^{\varphi} h(\varphi)\, d\varphi}.$$

Omitting the exponentially decreasing factor, we obtain the periodic function

$$r=r_0 e^{\int_0^{\varphi} h(\varphi)\, d\varphi}. \tag{16.22}$$

Now choose r_0 so large that $r > R$ for all φ on the curve (16.22). The closed curve (16.22) is a contactless curve for system (16.2). Indeed, along the curve (16.22) we have

$$\frac{dr}{d\varphi}=rh(\varphi).$$

In virtue of Eq. (16.21) and the relation $|\alpha| < 1/2\,|s|$, we have

$$\frac{dr}{d\varphi}=r(h(\varphi)+s+\alpha) < rh(\varphi) \tag{16.23}$$

on the solution curves of system (16.1), which proves that curve (16.22) is contactless.

By hypothesis, $F(\varphi)$ is positive, so that the second equation of system (16.5) and inequality (16.23) imply that the field vector are directed toward the inside of curve (16.22). As a result, in moving along solution curves of system (16.2) from $t=0$ to $t=\omega$, the plane region bounded by curve (16.22) is mapped into itself. From this and the Brouwer theorem, the theorem follows.

17. SUBHARMONIC OSCILLATIONS OF A NONDISSIPATIVE EQUATION

In this section we will consider the motion of a material point along a line under the influence of exciting and restoring forces in the absence of resistance. It is well known that such motion is described by the equation

$$\frac{d^2x}{dt^2}+g(x)=p(t). \tag{17.1}$$

We will assume that $g(x)$ satisfies a Lipschitz condition and that $p(t)$ is continuous and ω-periodic $p(t+\omega)=p(t)$.

Here we will establish sufficient conditions for Eq. (17.1) to have subharmonics (see [77, 78]).

1. Let us examine certain properties of solutions of Eq. (17.1) that satisfy particular boundary conditions.

Theorem 17.1. If the function $p(t)$ is even, i.e., $p(t)=p(-t)$, then the solution of (17.1) that satisfies the condition

$$\dot{x}(0)=\dot{x}\left(\frac{k}{2}\omega\right)=0 \tag{17.2}$$

where k is a natural number, has period $k\omega$.

Proof. Let $x=\varphi(t)$ be a solution of Eq. (17.1). We will show that the function $\psi(t)=\varphi(-t)$ is also a solution of (17.1). Indeed, $\ddot{\psi}(t)=\ddot{\varphi}(-t)$; $\varphi(t)$; is a solution of Eq. (17.1), so that

$$\ddot{\varphi}(-t)=-g(\varphi(-t))+p(-t)$$

or, because $p(t)$ is even,

$$\ddot{\varphi}(-t)=-g(\varphi(-t))+p(t),$$

which yields

$$\ddot{\psi}(t)=-g(\psi(t))+p(t).$$

This shows that the function $\psi(t)=\varphi(-t)$ is a solution of Eq. (17.1), from which it follows that any solution of Eq. (17.1) with the initial condition $\dot{x}(0)=0$ is an even function. Indeed, let $x=\varphi(t)$ be such a solution, and consider the solution $x=\psi(t)=\varphi(-t)$. When $t=0$, it turns out that $\psi(0)=\varphi(0)$ and $\dot{\psi}(0)=-\dot{\varphi}(0)=0$, i.e., the solution $x=\varphi(t)$ coincides with the solution $x=\psi(t)$, which proves that $\varphi(t)=\varphi(-t)$, i.e., $\varphi(t)$ is an even function.

Now consider a solution $x(t)$ of Eq. (17.1) that satisfies condition (17.2). It is an even function, and, therefore, $x(-k\omega/2) = x(k\omega/2)$, $\dot{x}(-k\omega/2) = -\dot{x}(k\omega/2) = 0$, which shows that the solution $x(t)$ has period $k\omega$ and proves the theorem.

Theorem 17.2. If the functions $p(t)$ and $g(x)$ are odd, i.e., $p(-t)=-p(t)$ and $g(-x)=-g(x)$, then a solution of Eq. (17.1) that satisfies the condition

$$x(0)=x\left(\frac{k}{2}\omega\right)=0, \tag{17.3}$$

where k is a natural number, has period $k\omega$.

Proof. Let $x=\varphi(t)$ be a solution of Eq. (17.1). We will show that then the function $\psi(t)=-\varphi(-t)$ is also a solution of this equation. We have $\ddot{\psi}(t)=-\ddot{\varphi}(-t)$. $\varphi(t)$ is a solution of Eq. (17.1), so that

$$-\ddot{\varphi}(-t)=g(\varphi(-t))-p(-t)$$

or, because the functions g and p are odd,

$$-\ddot{\varphi}(-t)=-g(-\varphi(-t))+p(t),$$

from which it follows that

$$\ddot{\psi}(t)=-g(\psi(t))+p(t),$$

which shows that the function $\psi(t)=-\varphi(-t)$ is a solution of Eq. (17.1).

Thus it follows that any solution of Eq. (17.1) with initial data $x(0)=0$ is an odd function. Indeed, let $x=\varphi(t)$ be such a solution, and consider the solution $x=\psi(t)=-\varphi(-t)$. When $t=0$, we have $\psi(0)=-\varphi(0)=0$ and $\dot{\psi}(0)=\dot{\varphi}(0)$. Thus, the solution $x=\varphi(t)$ coincides with the solution $x=\psi(t)$, and this shows that $\varphi(t)=-\varphi(-t)$, i.e., $\varphi(t)$ is an odd function.

Let $x(t)$ be a solution of Eq. (17.1) that satisfies condition (17.3). It is an odd function, so that $x(k\omega/2)=x(-k\omega/2)=0$, $\dot{x}(-k\omega/2)=\dot{x}(k\omega/2)$, which shows that the solution $x(t)$ has period $k\omega$. Q.E.D.

2. We now write Eq. (17.1) in the form of a system,

$$\frac{dx}{dt}=y, \quad \frac{dy}{dt}=-g(x)+p(t), \tag{17.4}$$

and we will prove the following theorem.

Theorem 17.3. If there exists an $a>0$ *such that* $xg(x)>0$ *when* $|x|\geqslant a$ *and*

$$\int_0^x g(x)\,dx\to\infty \quad \text{for} \quad |x|\to\infty, \tag{17.5}$$

then for any $R>0$ *and* $t_1>0$ *there exists an* $R_0\geqslant R$ *such that if* $x_0^2+y_0^2\geqslant R_0^2$ *the inequality*

$$x^2(t)+y^2(t)>R^2 \tag{17.6}$$

is satisfied for $t_0\leqslant t\leqslant t_0+t_1$ *on the solution* $(x(t), y(t))$ *of system (17.4) with initial* $x(t_0)=x_0$, $y(t_0)=y_0$.

Proof. Consider the function

$$v=\frac{1}{2}y^2+\int_0^x g(x)\,dx. \tag{17.7}$$

The hypothesis of the theorem implies that there exists an $\bar{R}$ such that $|y|<\sqrt{2v}$ when $x^2+y^2\geqslant\bar{R}^2$. Now take arbitrary positive t_1 and R, where, without loss of generality, we can assume that $R>\bar{R}$. Set

$$v_m=\max_{x^2+y^2\leqslant R^2} v \tag{17.8}$$

and

$$P=\max|p(t)| \tag{17.9}$$

and choose R_0 so that the inequality

$$\sqrt{v}>\sqrt{v_m}+\frac{\sqrt{2}}{2}Pt_1 \tag{17.10}$$

is satisfied when $x^2+y^2\geqslant R_0^2$. We will show that this R_0 is the one desired.

In virtue of the differential equations of system (17.4), differentiation of the function (17.7) with respect to time yields

$$\dot{v}=yp(t). \tag{17.11}$$

It follows then from (17.9) that

$$\dot{v}>-|y|P \tag{17.12}$$

and when $x^2+y^2\geqslant\bar{R}^2$ we have

$$\dot{v}>-\sqrt{2v}\,P \tag{17.13}$$

or

$$\frac{dv}{\sqrt{v}}>-P\sqrt{2}dt.$$

Integrating this inequality along the solution of system (17.4) with initial data $t=t_0$, $x=x_0$, $y=y_0$, $x_0^2+y_0^2\geqslant R_0^2$, we find that

$$\sqrt{v}>\sqrt{v_0}-\frac{\sqrt{2}}{2}P(t-t_0) \tag{17.14}$$

Inequality (17.14) is satisfied as long as the inequality $x^2+y^2 \geqslant \bar{R}^2$ holds for the chosen solution. For such t and for $t_0 \leqslant t \leqslant t_0+t_1$, it follows from (17.14) that

$$\sqrt{\bar{v}} > \sqrt{\bar{v}_0} - \frac{\sqrt{2}}{2} P t_1.$$

It follows then from this inequality and inequality (17.10) that

$$\sqrt{\bar{v}} > \sqrt{\bar{v}_m} \tag{17.15}$$

for the indicated time ranges, from which it follows that inequality (17.6) holds when $t_0 \leqslant t \leqslant t_0+t_1$. Q.E.D.

3. In order to examine additional properties of the solutions of Eq. (17.1), it is convenient to convert system (17.4) to polar form by means of the formulas

$$x = r\cos\varphi, \quad y = r\sin\varphi. \tag{17.16}$$

Thus,

$$\left.\begin{aligned} \frac{dr}{dt} &= r\cos\varphi\sin\varphi - g(r\cos\varphi)\sin\varphi + p(t)\sin\varphi, \\ \frac{d\varphi}{dt} &= -\frac{g(r\cos\varphi)}{r}\cos\varphi - \sin^2\varphi + \frac{p(t)}{r}\cos\varphi. \end{aligned}\right\} \tag{17.17}$$

Theorem 17.4. If

$$\lim_{|x|\to\infty} \frac{g(x)}{x} = \infty \tag{17.18}$$

then for any $t_1 > 0$ *and* $\Phi > 0$ *there exists an* $R_0 > 0$ *such that along the solution* $(x(t), y(t))$ *of system (17.4) with initial data* $t = t_0$, $x = x_0$, $y = y_0$, $x_0^2 + y_0^2 \geqslant R_0^2$ *the following statements are valid:*

a) The polar angle φ *monotonically decreases when* $t_0 \leqslant t \leqslant t_0+t_1$,

b) $\varphi(t_0+t_1) - \varphi(t_0) < -\Phi$.

Proof. Choose an arbitrary $\alpha > 0$. It follows from relation (17.18) and the second equation of system (17.17) that there exists an $R > 0$ such that the inequality

$$\frac{d\varphi}{dt} < -\left(\alpha^2\cos^2\varphi + \frac{1}{2}\sin^2\varphi\right) \tag{17.19}$$

holds when $r \geqslant R$.

Choose R_0 so that the inequality $r \geqslant R$ is satisfied when $t_0 \leqslant t \leqslant t_0 + t_1$ (the preceding theorem guarantees that such an R_0 exists). In such a case, inequality (17.19) will be satisfied in the interval $t_0 \leqslant t \leqslant t_0+t_1$, which proves statement (a) of the theorem.

In order to prove the second statement of the theorem, we integrate inequality (17.19) rewritten as

$$\frac{d\varphi}{\alpha^2\cos^2\varphi+\frac{1}{2}\sin^2\varphi}<-dt;$$

whence,

$$\int_{\varphi_0}^{\varphi}\frac{d\varphi}{\alpha^2\cos^2\varphi+\frac{1}{2}\sin^2\varphi}<t_0-t,$$

or

$$\frac{\sqrt{2}}{\alpha}\operatorname{Arctan}\frac{\tan\varphi}{\alpha\sqrt{2}}\Bigg|_{\varphi_0}^{\varphi}<t_0-t.$$

If we set

$$\frac{\sqrt{2}}{\alpha}\operatorname{Arctan}\frac{\tan\varphi_0}{\alpha\sqrt{2}}=\psi_0,$$

we obtain

$$\operatorname{Arctan}\frac{\tan\varphi}{\alpha\sqrt{2}}<\frac{\alpha}{\sqrt{2}}(t_0+\psi_0-t),$$

from which it follows that

$$\varphi<\operatorname{Arctan}\alpha\sqrt{2}\tan\left[\frac{\alpha}{\sqrt{2}}(t_0+\psi_0-t)\right].$$

It follows from the last inequality that the absolute value of the difference $\varphi-\varphi_0$ can be made arbitrarily large by choosing α sufficiently large. This proves statement (b) of the theorem, which completes the proof.

4. Now we will establish several fundamental statements concerning periodic solutions of Eq. (17.1).

Theorem 17.5. Assume that the function $p(t)$ *is even, i.e.,* $p(-t)=p(t)$, *and that condition (17.18) of the preceding theorem is satisfied. Then, for any natural* k, *there exist infinitely many solutions of Eq. (17.1) with periodic* $k\omega$, *and none of these solutions has a period of the form* $\bar{k}\omega$, *where* $\bar{k}$ *is a natural number less than* k.

Proof. Choose an arbitrary number $R>0$ and set $t_1=k\omega/2$, $\Phi=k\pi$. Using these quantities, choose $R_0>R$ so that the hypothesis of the preceding theorem is satisfied, and consider the solution of system (17.4) with initial data $t=0$, $x=x_0'>R_0$, $y=0$. By the preceding theorem, it turns out that the polar angle $\varphi(t, x_0')$ on this solution satisfies the inequality

$$\varphi\left(\frac{k}{2}\omega,\ x_0'\right) < -k\pi. \tag{17.20}$$

Let s be a natural number such that

$$-sk\pi < \varphi\left(\frac{k}{2}\omega,\ x_0'\right) \leqslant -(s-1)k\pi. \tag{17.21}$$

We now set $t_1 = k\omega/2$, $\Phi = -(sk+1)\pi$ and, using Theorem 17.4, we will find an $x_0'' > x_0'$ such that the inequality

$$\varphi\left(\frac{k}{2}\omega,\ x_0''\right) < -(sk+1)\pi \tag{17.22}$$

will be satisfied on the solution with initial data $x(0) = x_0''$, $y(0) = 0$.

Consider the family of solutions of system (17.4) with initial data $y(0) = 0$, $x_0' \leqslant x(0) \leqslant x_0''$. It is clear that, for these solutions, the polar angle $\varphi(k\omega/2,\ x(0))$ is a continuous function of $x(0)$ when $t = (k/2)\omega$. It follows then from inequalities (17.21) and (17.22) that there exists an $x_0 \in (x_0',\ x_0'')$ such that, for the appropriate solution,

$$\varphi\left(\frac{k}{2}\omega,\ x_0\right) = -(sk+1)\pi. \tag{17.23}$$

We will show that this solution satisfies the statement of the theorem. From Eq. (17.23) it follows that $y(k\omega/2) = 0$ on our solution. Since, by the choice of solution, $y(0) = 0$, this solution has, by Theorem 17.1, period $k\omega$.

We will now show that our solution can not have period $\bar{k}\omega$, where $\bar{k}$ is a natural number less than k. Assume to the contrary that the solution which we have constructed has such a period, and assume that $\bar{k}$ is the smallest natural number for which $\bar{k}\omega$ is a period of the solution under discussion, i.e., if $\bar{\bar{k}} < \bar{k}$, then $\bar{\bar{k}}$ is not a period of our solution. In that case, $\bar{k}$ must be a divisor of k. Indeed, the quantities $\omega^* = \omega(c_1\bar{k} + c_2 k)$, where c_1 and c_2 are positive or negative integers or zero are periods of our solution. But the set of numbers $c_1\bar{k} + c_2 k$ contains the greatest common divisor d of the numbers k and $\bar{k}$, so that $d\omega$ is also a period of the solution under discussion. It follows from the minimal properties of $\bar{k}$ that $\bar{k} = d$, so that $\bar{k}$ is a divisor of k, which means that $k = q\bar{k}$, where $q \geqslant 2$ is an integer.

As shown in the proof of Theorem 17.1, the constructed solution is an even function, so that the polar angle $\varphi(t)$ is an odd function:

$$\varphi(-t) = -\varphi(t)$$

this implies that

$$\varphi\left(-\frac{k}{2}\omega - t\right) = -\varphi\left(\frac{k}{2}\omega + t\right).$$

Since our solution has period $k\omega$, it follows from the last equation that

$$\varphi\left(\frac{k}{2}\omega - t\right) = -\varphi\left(\frac{k}{2}\omega + t\right). \tag{17.24}$$

From this equation it follows that the polar angle changes in the interval $k\omega/2 \leqslant t \leqslant k\omega$ by the same amount as in the interval $0 \leqslant t \leqslant k\omega/2$, i.e., by $-(sk+1)\pi$, which, together with (17.23), implies that

$$\varphi(k\omega, x_0) = -2(sk+1)\pi. \tag{17.25}$$

On the other hand, the quantity $\bar{k}\omega$ is a period of our solution, so that the polar angle changes by an integral multiple of 2π in the time interval $0 \leqslant t \leqslant \bar{k}\omega$, i.e., $\varphi(\bar{k}\omega, x_0) = -2r\pi$. But then it is clear that the polar angle changes by $-2r\pi$ in the time interval $\bar{k}m\omega \leqslant t \leqslant \bar{k}(m+1)\omega$, so that the polar angle changes by $-2qr\pi$ during the interval $0 \leqslant t \leqslant \bar{k}q\omega = k\omega$, i.e.,

$$\varphi(k\omega, x_0) = -2qr\pi \tag{17.26}$$

which, together with (17.25), implies that

$$-2(sk+1)\pi = -2qr\pi$$

or

$$sk+1 = qr$$

where s, k, q, and r are integers and $q \geqslant 2$ is a divisor of k. This is impossible.

The contradiction, which we have obtained, shows that the constructed solution can not have a period of the form $\bar{k}\omega$.

Thus, choosing an arbitrary $R > 0$, we have proved that a solution with initial data $y(0) = 0$, $x(0) > R$ and with the required properties exists, and because R is arbitrary, there are infinitely many such solutions, which proves the theorem.

Theorem 17.6. Assume that the functions $p(t)$ and $g(x)$ are odd, i.e., that $p(-t) = -p(t)$ and $g(-x) = -g(x)$, and that condition (17.18) holds. Then, for any natural k, there exist infinitely many solutions of Eq. (17.1) with period $k\omega$, and none of the solutions has a period of the form $\bar{k}\omega$, where $\bar{k}$ is a natural number less than k.

This theorem can be proved in the same way as the preceding theorem with the aid of Theorem 17.2; appropriate initial data for the solutions must be chosen on the Oy axis.

In concluding this section, we should note that Theorems 17.5 and 17.6 imply that the solutions constructed in their proofs may turn out not to be subharmonics only in the exceptional case in which, in addition to the period $k\omega$, they have a period of the form $(k/q)\omega$, where q is an integer which is prime relative to k.

3

Autonomous Systems

18. GENERAL THEOREMS ON EXISTENCE AND STABILITY OF PERIODIC SOLUTIONS OF AUTONOMOUS SYSTEMS

In this and the following sections we will consider systems of free oscillations

$$\frac{dX}{dt} = F(X). \tag{18.1}$$

As usual, we will assume that the n-dimensional vector function $F = \{f_1, f_2, \ldots, f_n\}$ is defined, continuous, and satisfies the uniqueness condition for all values of the n-dimensional vector $X = \{x_1, x_2, \ldots, x_n\}$.

Investigation of the problem concerning the existence of periodic solutions for system (18.1) involves certain additional difficulties which were not encountered in the same problem for system (1.1) for forced solutions. The complications arise because in dealing with autonomous systems it is, generally, impossible to state beforehand the period of the desired periodic solution, whereas in the case of a system of forced oscillations (1.1) the periodic solution usually has a period equal to or a multiple of the period of the right side. Furthermore, when system (1.1) has a solution whose period is incommensurable with the period of the right side, this solution, is a member of a set in which the right side is independent of time t, as indicated in Theorem 1.7, i.e., strictly speaking, in this case we are again dealing with a system of the form (18.1).

1. In this and subsequent sections, we will devote most of our attention to the problem concerning the existence of periodic solutions of autonomous systems.

Existence proofs for periodic solutions of system (18.1) usually proceed in the following manner. An $(n-1)$-dimensional hypersurface M that does not contact the direction field of system (18.1) is chosen in phase space. On this surface M, an $(n-1)$-dimensional simplex S is selected. It is assumed that if a point p lies in S, then, as time increases, the trajectory $\Phi(p, t)$ of system (18.1) that passes through the point p when $t=0$ intersects the surface M at the point $\Phi(p, \tau)$, $\tau > 0$. We thus obtain a transformation T of the simplex S into the hyperplane M that associates the point p with the point $\Phi(p, \tau)$. Usually there are no real difficulties in proving that this transformation is continuous, and, if the transformation T is such that there is a stationary point q on S, it is clear that the trajectory $\Phi(q, I_0)$ is closed, i.e., the solution $\Phi(q, t)$ is periodic.

This type of argument can also be used for proving the well-known principle of the torus. This principle states: Let R be a toroidal region bounded by an $(n-1)$-dimensional smooth surface Σ in phase space and such that all trajectories intersect this surface in passing into the region R as time increases. Let S be one of the cross sections of the torus R which are $(n-1)$-dimensional contactless simplexes. If any trajectory beginning in $\bar{S}$ intersects S as time increases, R contains a closed trajectory.

Indeed, let $p \in \bar{S}$, and let τ be the first time after $t=0$ at which the trajectory $\Phi(p, t)$ intersects S. Since the surface Σ bounding S has no contact with the direction field of system (18.1), it is clear that $\Phi(p, \tau)$ lies strictly within S (not on its boundary), which implies that the point $\Phi(p, \tau)$ is a continuous function of $p \in \bar{S}$. As above, we now associate the point $\Phi(p, \tau)$ with the point p, and the transformation T obtained in this way is a continuous transformation of the $(n-1)$-dimensional closed simplex into itself. By the Brouwer theorem, this transformation has a stationary point q, and then it is clear that the trajectory $\Phi(q, I_0)$ is closed.

In the next paragraph, in the course of investigating a concrete system, we will establish a method for constructing the region R and the cross section S.

2. In this paragraph we will establish a test for the existence of periodic solutions of an autonomous system [70].

Assume that the right sides of system (18.1) are continuously differentiable with respect to all of their arguments, and consider the Jacobian matrix of the right side of the system:

$$J(X)=\begin{pmatrix} \frac{\partial f_1}{\partial x_1}, & \frac{\partial f_1}{\partial x_2}, & \ldots, & \frac{\partial f_1}{\partial x_n} \\ \cdot & \cdot & \cdot & \cdot \\ \frac{\partial f_n}{\partial x_1}, & \frac{\partial f_n}{\partial x_2}, & \ldots, & \frac{\partial f_n}{\partial x_n} \end{pmatrix}. \tag{18.2}$$

As before, let $X \cdot Y$ denote the scalar product of the vectors X and Y, and let $\|X\|$ denote the Euclidean norm of the vector X.

Theorem 18.1. Assume that in a bounded region D of the phase space the relationship

$$J(Y)(X-Y)\cdot(X-Y)\leqslant-\Delta\|X-Y\|^2 \tag{18.3}$$

holds, where Δ *is a positive constant, and the vectors* $X\in D$ *and* $Y\in D$ *are such that their difference* $X-Y$ *is orthogonal to the direction field of system (18.1) at the point* Y, *i.e., assume that* $F(Y)\cdot(X-Y)=0$. *Moreover, assume that there is no equilibrium state in the region* $\bar{D}$. *Then any solution* $X=\Phi(p,t)$ *of system (18.1) that is located, when* $t\geqslant0$, *in some closed region embedded in D is Lyapunov-stable, and there exists a positive constant* λ *such that for any* $\varkappa>0$ *there exists an* $\varepsilon>0$ *such that if* $\rho(p,q)<\varepsilon$, *then there exists an* $h(q)$, $|h(q)|<\varkappa$, *such that*

$$\rho(\Phi(p,t+h(q)),\ \Phi(q,t))<e^{-\lambda t} \tag{18.4}$$

Proof. Let $\varphi_1(t),\ldots,\varphi_n(t)$ denote the components of the vector $\Phi(p,t)$. Since, by hypothesis, D does not contain an equilibrium state, there exists a constant $b>0$ such that the inequality

$$\sum_{k=1}^{n}[\varphi_k'(t)]^2>b \tag{18.5}$$

is satisfied for all $t\geqslant0$. Now assume that the functions $f_k(x_1,x_2,\ldots,x_n)(k=1,2,\ldots,n)$, i.e., the components of the vector $F(X)$, are continuously differentiable; consequently, the functions $\varphi_1(t)$, $\varphi_2(t),\ldots,\varphi_n(t)$ are twice continuously differentiable with respect to t and the second derivatives of these functions are bounded when $t\geqslant0$. Thus, when $t\geqslant0$ the curve $X=\Phi(p,t)$ has bounded curvature.

We now introduce new coordinates in the following manner: Through each point $X=\Phi(p,\theta)$ we draw an $(n-1)$-dimensional hyperplane normal to the curve $X=\Phi(p,t)$. In view of the fact that the curve $X=\Phi(p,t)$ has bounded curvature, if a sufficiently small neighborhood of the curve is taken, the hyperplanes corresponding to neighboring points on the curve will not intersect. In each of these hyperplanes we introduce orthogonal coordinates $y_1,y_2,\ldots,y_n$, so that the new coordinates are related to the old by the formulas

$$x_k=\varphi_k(\theta)+\sum_{i=1}^{n-1}\psi_{ki}(\theta)\,y_i\qquad(k=1,2,\ldots,n). \tag{18.6}$$

The coordinates y_i may be selected so that if the vector $X-\Phi(p,\theta)$ is normal to the curve $X=\Phi(p,t)$, i.e., to the vector $F(\Phi(p,\theta))$, then

$$\sum_{k=1}^{n}(x_k-\varphi_k(\theta))^2=\sum_{i=1}^{n-1}y_i^2. \tag{18.7}$$

The functions $\psi_{ki}(\theta)$ can be expressed in terms of $\varphi_s(\theta)$ and $\varphi_s'(\theta)$ by means of the usual rules. Thus, the functions ψ_{ki} are continuously differentiable when $\theta \geqslant 0$ and, together with their derivatives, are bounded when $\theta \geqslant 0$.

In such a manner, we have replaced the variables $x_1, x_2, \ldots, x_n$ by the variables $\theta, y_1, y_2, \ldots, y_{n-1}$. Differentiating (18.6) with respect to t and solving the system of equations thus obtained for $d\theta/dt$ and dy_k/dt, we obtain the following system of differential equations:

$$\left.\begin{aligned} \frac{d\theta}{dt} &= \bar{u}(Y, \theta), \\ \frac{dY}{dt} &= \bar{G}(Y, \theta), \end{aligned}\right\} \tag{18.8}$$

where Y is a vector with components $y_1, y_2, \ldots, y_{n-1}$ and $\bar{G}$ is a vector function with components $\bar{g}_1, \bar{g}_2, \ldots, \bar{g}_{n-1}$. It follows from formulas (18.6) that the solution $X = \Phi(p, t)$ of system (18.1) is transformed into the solution $\theta = t, Y = 0$ of system (18.8), so that $\bar{u}(\theta, 0) \equiv 1, \bar{G}(\theta, 0) \equiv 0$. We now make one more substitution. Setting $\theta = t + \tau$ leads to the system

$$\left.\begin{aligned} \frac{d\tau}{dt} &= u(Y, \tau, t), \\ \frac{dY}{dt} &= G(Y, \tau, t), \end{aligned}\right\} \tag{18.9}$$

where $u(Y, \tau, t) = \bar{u}(Y, t+\tau) - 1$, $G(Y, \tau, t) = \bar{G}(Y, t+\tau)$, and we denote the components of G by $g_1, g_2, \ldots, g_{n-1}$. The forms of the functions u and G imply the identities

$$u(0, \tau, t) \equiv 0, \quad G(0, \tau, t) \equiv 0. \tag{18.10}$$

It follows from the form of formulas (18.6) and the above-noted differentiability properties of the functions $\psi_{ki}(\theta)$ that the functions u and G are continuous when $t \geqslant 0$ and $\|Y\|$ and $|\tau|$ are sufficiently small and that they are bounded for these values of the arguments. Moreover, these functions are continuously differentiable with respect to y_i $(i = 1, 2, \ldots, n-1)$, and all derivatives of the form $\partial u/\partial y_i$ and $\partial g_k/\partial y_i$ are bounded when $t \geqslant 0$ and $\|Y\|$ and $|\tau|$ are sufficiently small.

It follows then from the first of identities (18.10) that there exists an $M > 0$ such that the inequality

$$|u(Y, \tau, t)| < M\|Y\| \tag{18.11}$$

is satisfied when $\|Y\|$ is sufficiently small.

From the second of identities (18.10), it follows that the functions $g_s(Y, \tau, t)$ can be represented in the form

$$g_s(y_1, y_2, \ldots, y_{n-1}, \tau, t) = a_{s1}(t)\, y_1 + \ldots + a_{sn-1}(t)\, y_{n-1} + \\ + A_s(y_1, \ldots, y_{n-1}, \tau, t)\,(s = 1, \ldots, n-1), \tag{18.12}$$

where the functions $a_{si}\,(s, i = 1, 2, \ldots, n-1)$ are continuous and bounded when $t \geqslant 0$ and the functions $A_s(y_1, y_2, \ldots, y_{n-1}, \tau, t)$ satisfy the inequalities

$$|A_s(y_1, y_2, \ldots, y_{n-1}, \tau, t)| < \gamma \|Y\| \; (s = 1, \ldots, n-1). \tag{18.13}$$

for sufficiently small $|\tau|$ and $\|Y\|$ for all $t \geqslant 0$, where the constant γ can be made arbitrarily small by the selection of sufficiently small $|\tau|$ and $\|Y\|$.

System (18.9) can be rewritten in the form

$$\left.\begin{aligned} \frac{d\tau}{dt} &= u(Y, \tau, t), \\ \frac{dy_s}{dt} &= a_{s1}(t)\, y_1 + \ldots + a_{sn-1}(t)\, y_{n-1} + \\ &\qquad + A_s(y_1, \ldots, y_{n-1}, \tau, t). \end{aligned}\right\} \tag{18.14}$$

Consider the function

$$V(y_1, \ldots, y_{n-1}) = \|Y\|^2 = \sum_{k=1}^{n-1} y_k^2. \tag{18.15}$$

In virtue of Eq. (18.7), we can write

$$V = \sum_{k=1}^{n} (x_k - \varphi_k(\theta))^2 = \|X - \Phi(p, \theta)\|^2 \tag{18.16}$$

where the vector $X - \Phi(p, \theta)$ is orthogonal to $F(\Phi(p, \theta))$.

We now use the differential equations of system (18.4) to take the total derivative of the function V with respect to t, thus obtaining the epxression

$$\dot{V} = 2 \sum_{s=1}^{n-1} y_s (a_{s1} y_1 + \ldots + a_{sn-1} y_{n-1}) + 2 \sum_{s=1}^{n-1} y_s A_s. \tag{18.17}$$

On the other hand, it follows from Eq. (18.16) and system (18.1) that

$$\dot{V} = 2 \sum_{k=1}^{n} (x_k - \varphi_k(\theta)) \Big[f_k(x_1, \ldots, x_n) - \\ - f_k(\varphi_1(\theta), \ldots, \varphi_n(\theta)) \frac{d\theta}{dt} \Big].$$

Since the vector $X-\Phi(p, \theta)$ is orthogonal to $F(\Phi(p, \theta))$, i.e.,

$$\sum_{k=1}^{n}(x_k-\varphi_k(\theta))f_k(\varphi_1(\theta), \ldots, \varphi_n(\theta))=$$
$$=[X-\Phi(p, \theta)]\cdot F(\Phi(p, \theta))=0$$

we can write, instead of the last equation,

$$\dot{V}=2\sum_{k=1}^{n}(x_k-\varphi_k(\theta))(f_k(x_1, \ldots, x_n)-$$
$$-f_k(\varphi_1(\theta), \ldots, \varphi_n(\theta))) \tag{18.18}$$

which, as in Paragraph 4 of Section 7, yields

$$\dot{V}=2\sum_{k=1}^{n}(x_k-\varphi_k(\theta))\sum_{i=1}^{n}\int_0^1\frac{\partial f_k}{\partial x_i}(x_i-\varphi_i(\theta))\,du, \tag{18.19}$$

where the derivatives $\partial f_k/\partial x_i$ are evaluated at the point $x_j^*=ux_j+(1-u)\varphi_j(\theta)$, and the vector X^* with components $x_1^*, \ldots, x_n^*$ is such that the difference $X^*-\Phi(p, \theta)$ has the same direction as $X-\Phi(p, \theta)$ but $\|X^*-\Phi(p, \theta)\|\leqslant\|X-\Phi(p, \theta)\|$. Equation (18.19) obviously means that

$$\dot{V}=2\int_0^1 J(X^*)(X-\Phi(p, \theta))\cdot(X-\Phi(p, \theta))\,du. \tag{18.20}$$

Now rewrite Eq. (18.20) in the form

$$\dot{V}=2\int_0^1 J(\Phi(p, \theta))(X-\Phi(p, \theta))\cdot(X-\Phi(p, \theta))\,du+$$
$$+2\int_0^1[J(X^*)-J(\Phi(p, \theta))](X-\Phi(p, \theta))\cdot(X-\Phi(p, \theta))\,du. \tag{18.21}$$

By hypothesis, the function $F(X)$ is continuously differentiable, so that the matrix $J(X)$ is uniformly continuous in D and, therefore, the difference $J(X^*)-J(\Phi(p, \theta))$ can be made arbitrarily small in norm by choosing $\|X-\Phi(p, \theta)\|=\|Y\|$ sufficiently small. Since the vector $X-\Phi(p, \theta)$ is orthogonal to $F(\Phi(p, \theta))$, we have, by the hypothesis of the theorem, the inequality

$$\dot{V}<-\frac{3}{2}\Delta\|Y\|^2 \tag{18.22}$$

for sufficiently small $\|Y\|$.

We now require that the quantities τ and Y satisfy the inequalities

$$|\tau| \leqslant \beta, \quad \|Y\| < \beta. \tag{18.23}$$

Assume that β is so small that inequalities (18.11), (18.13) and (18.22) are satisfied when inequalities (18.23) hold, with the constant γ in inequality (18.13) satisfying the inequality

$$\gamma < \frac{\Delta}{8(n-1)} \tag{18.24}$$

Then, by (18.17) and (18.22), we will have

$$2\sum_{s=1}^{n-1} y_s(a_{s1}y_1 + \ldots + a_{sn-1}y_{n-1}) < -\frac{5\Delta}{4}\|Y\|^2 \tag{18.25}$$

when (18.23) is satisfied. In virtue of this, we change variables by means of the formulas

$$\eta_s = e^{\lambda t} y_s \qquad (s = 1, 2, \ldots, n-1) \tag{18.26}$$

where λ is a sufficiently small positive constant.

In the new variables, the last $n-1$ equations of system (18.14) take the form

$$\frac{d\eta_s}{dt} = a_{s1}(t)\eta_1 + \ldots + (a_{ss}(t) + \lambda)\eta_s + \ldots$$
$$\ldots + a_{sn-1}(t)\eta_{n-1} + e^{\lambda t} A_s(e^{-\lambda t}\eta_1, \ldots, e^{-\lambda t}\eta_{n-1}, \tau, t). \tag{18.27}$$

We now use the differential equations of system (18.27) to find the total time derivative of the function $V(\eta_1, \eta_2, \ldots, \eta_{n-1})$:

$$\dot{V} = 2\sum_{s=1}^{n-1} \eta_s(a_{s1}\eta_1 + \ldots + a_{sn-1}\eta_{n-1}) + 2\lambda V(\eta_1, \ldots, \eta_{n-1}) +$$
$$+ 2e^{\lambda t}\sum_{s=1}^{n-1} \eta_s A_s(e^{-\lambda t}\eta_1, \ldots, e^{-\lambda t}\eta_{n-1}, \tau, t). \tag{18.28}$$

If the inequalities

$$|\tau| \leqslant \beta, \quad \sqrt{\eta_1^2 + \ldots + \eta_n^2} \leqslant \beta, \quad \text{and} \quad t \geqslant 0 \tag{18.29}$$

are satisfied, then (18.17), (18.24) and (18.25) imply that

$$\dot{V} < -\Delta V + 2\lambda V.$$

We now choose λ so that $0 < \lambda < \Delta/4$, which causes the last inequality to take the form

$$\dot{V} < -\frac{\Delta}{2} V \leqslant 0. \tag{18.30}$$

Now consider an arbitrary solution of system (18.14) with initial data $t=0$, $\tau=\tau_0$, $\eta_s=\eta_{s0}$ $(s=1, \ldots, n-1)$ that satisfy the inequalities

$$|\tau| < \delta, \quad \sqrt{\eta_{10}^2 + \ldots + \eta_{n-10}^2} < \delta \tag{18.31}$$

where δ is a positive constant less than β. The conditions

$$|\tau(t)| \leqslant \beta, \quad \sqrt{\eta_1^2(t) + \ldots + \eta_{n-1}^2(t)} \leqslant \beta \tag{18.32}$$

will be satisfied for this solution, at least for values of t sufficiently close to $t=0$. Let t be the end of the time interval for which conditions (18.32) are satisfied. Then dV/dt will be negative everywhere in the time interval $(0, t)$ along the selected solution, and we can write

$$V(\eta_1, \ldots, \eta_{n-1}) = V(\eta_{10}, \ldots, \eta_{n-10}) + \\ + \int_0^t \frac{dV}{dt} dt \leqslant V(\eta_{10}, \ldots, \eta_{n-10}). \tag{18.33}$$

Hence, it follows that the inequality

$$\sqrt{\eta_1^2(t) + \ldots + \eta_{n-1}^2(t)} < \delta \tag{18.34}$$

is satisfied in this time interval.

It follows then from (18.26) that along the solution under discussion the inequality

$$\|Y(t)\| < \delta e^{-\lambda t} \tag{18.35}$$

holds in such a time interval.

Whereupon, inequality (18.11) implies that the relationship

$$|u(Y(t), \tau, t)| < M\delta e^{-\lambda t} \tag{18.36}$$

holds in the indicated time interval. The first equation of system (18.9) yields the following integral equation:

$$\tau(t) = \tau_0 + \int_0^t u(Y(t), \tau, t)\, dt.$$

It follows then from (18.36) that in the time interval in which inequality (18.32) holds, the inequality

$$|\tau(t)| < |\tau_0| + M\delta \int_0^t e^{-\lambda t}\,dt = |\tau_0| + \\ + \frac{M\delta(1-e^{-\lambda t})}{\lambda} < |\tau_0| + \frac{M\delta}{\lambda} \tag{18.37}$$

also holds.

Choose an arbitrary positive number $E < \beta$ and, in inequalities (18.31), choose δ so that

$$\left(1 + \frac{M}{\lambda}\right)\delta < E. \tag{18.38}$$

It follows then from (18.37) that the inequality

$$|\tau(t)| < E \tag{18.39}$$

holds in the indicated time interval.

We will now show that inequalities (18.34) and (18.39) hold for all $t \geqslant 0$. When $t > 0$ and is sufficiently small, these inequalities hold because of (18.31). We assume, contrary to our assertion, that there exists a t^* such that inequalities (18.34) and (18.39) hold in the time interval $0 \leqslant t < t^*$, while at $t = t^*$, at least one of these inequalities becomes an equality. But the number E was chosen to be less than β, and $\delta < E$, in accord with (18.38), so that the continuity of the functions $\tau(t)$, $\eta_s(t)$ $(s = 1, 2, \ldots, n-1)$ implies the existence of a $t_1 > t^*$ such that inequality (18.32) is satisfied when $0 \leqslant t \leqslant t_1$; hence, it follows from the above argument that inequalities (18.34) and (18.39) also hold when $0 \leqslant t \leqslant t_1$. Consequently, these inequalities will also hold when $t = t^*$, which contradicts the definition of t^* and proves that inequalities (18.34) and (18.39) hold for all $t \geqslant 0$.

Thus, if the inequalities

$$|\tau_0| < \delta, \quad \|Y_0\| < \delta \tag{18.40}$$

hold, where τ_0 and Y_0 are the initial data corresponding to the solution of system (18.9) when $t = 0$, then inequalities (18.35) and (18.39) hold for all t.

We now take an arbitrary $\varkappa > 0$, and we will show that if δ is sufficiently small, then the relationship

$$\lim_{t \to +\infty} \tau(t) = h \tag{18.41}$$

where $|h| < \varkappa$, holds along the chosen solution.

Fix E in the interval $0 < E < \varkappa$ (of course we assume, in addition, that $E < \beta$). We have, as before

$$\tau(t) = \tau_0 + \int_0^t u(Y(t), \tau, t)\, dt.$$

It follows from (18.36) that the integral $\int_0^\infty u(Y(t), \tau, t)\, dt$ converges; if we set

$$\int_0^\infty u(Y(t), \tau, t)\, dt = h_1$$

then we obtain (18.41), where $h = \tau_0 + h_1$. It follows from (18.37) and inequality (18.38) that $|h| = |\tau_0 + h_1| < E < \varkappa$.

We will now estimate the difference $h - \tau(t)$. We have

$$h - \tau(t) = \int_t^\infty u(Y(t), \tau, t)\, dt$$

from which, with the aid of (18.36), we find that

$$|h - \tau(t)| < M\delta \int_t^\infty e^{-\lambda t}\, dt = \frac{M\delta}{\lambda} e^{-\lambda t}. \tag{18.42}$$

As already noted, the functions $\varphi_k(\theta)$ and $\psi_{ki}(\theta)$ in formulas (18.6) are, for $t \geqslant 0$, continuously differentiable and, together with their derivatives, bounded. Consequently, if the quantities $|\tau(t)|$ and $\|Y(t)\|$ are small, then $\|X - \Phi(p, t)\|$ is also small. Moreover, it is not difficult to use these formulas to prove that the quantities $|\tau_0|$ and $\|Y_0\|$ can be made arbitrarily small by choosing $\|X_0 - p\|$ sufficiently small. Thus it follows that the solution $X = \Phi(p, t)$ of system (18.1) is Lyapunov-stable, and it remains to be proved that inequality (18.4) holds.

We now choose a point q sufficiently close to the point p so that inequalities (18.31) hold, with δ subject to inequality (18.38) and $E \in (0, \varkappa)$. Since $\theta = t + \tau$, it follows from (18.6) that

$$x_k(t) = \varphi_k(t + \tau(t)) + \sum_{i=1}^{n-1} \psi_{ki}(t + \tau(t))\, y_i(t) \tag{18.43}$$

$$(k = 1, \ldots, n).$$

Subtract the function $\varphi_k(t + h)$, where h is as defined above, from both sides of these equations, thus obtaining

$$x_k(t)-\varphi_k(t+h)=\varphi_k(t+\tau(t))-\varphi_k(t+h)+$$
$$+\sum_{i=1}^{n-1}\psi_{ki}(t+\tau(t))\,y_i(t)\quad (k=1,2,\ldots,n). \tag{18.44}$$

The functions $\psi_{ki}(\theta)$ are bounded when $\theta \geqslant 0$, and the functions $\varphi_k(\theta)$ have bounded derivatives when $\theta \geqslant 0$; therefore, there exists an $L_1 > 0$ such that the inequalities

$$|x_k(t)-\varphi_k(t+h)| \leqslant$$
$$\leqslant L_1|h-\tau(t)|+L_1\|Y(t)\| \quad (k=1,2,\ldots,n) \tag{18.45}$$

hold when $t \geqslant 0$. But the $x_k(t)$ are the components of the vector $\Phi(q, t)$, and the $\varphi_k(t+h)$ are the components of the vector $\Phi(p, t+h)$. It follows from (18.35) and (18.42) that there exists an L such that

$$\|\Phi(q,t)-\Phi(p,t+h)\| \leqslant L\delta e^{-\lambda t}$$

If we choose $\delta \leqslant 1/L$, we obtain inequality (18.4), where, as we have already proved, $|h| < \varkappa$. Q.E.D.

Theorem 18.2. If the conditions of the preceding theorem are satisfied and there exists a solution $X=\Phi(q,t)$ of system (18.1) that is located, when $t \geqslant 0$, in some closed domain embedded in D, then D contains a closed trajectory of system (18.1).

Proof. Let Ω be the limit set of the half-trajectory $\Phi(q,t)$ for $t \geqslant 0$. It is clear that $\Omega \subset D$. It follows from Corollary 1.2 that Ω contains a point p through which a recurrent trajectory $\Phi(p,t)$ passes. $\Phi(p,t) \in \Omega$ for all t, and because the set Ω is closed, there exists a closed region embedded in D that contains $\Phi(p, I_0)$. As noted in Section 1, any recurrent motion is Poisson-stable. The solution $\Phi(p,t)$ is, therefore, Poisson-stable and, by the preceding theorem, is subject to relation (18.4). If we set $\alpha(t)=e^{-\lambda t}$, then all conditions of Theorem 1.6 will be satisfied for the motion $\Phi(p,t)$, and it will follow that the motion $\Phi(p,t)$ is periodic. Q.E.D.

Note that Theorem 18.1 implies that this periodic motion is Lyapunov-stable, and any solution beginning in a sufficiently small neighborhood of its trajectory approaches this trajectory set as $t \to +\infty$, i.e., this periodic solution is orbitally asymptotically stable.

We will now prove a uniqueness theorem for periodic solutions in certain regions.

Theorem 18.3. Assume that the conditions of Theorem 18.1 are satisfied in a region D, and assume that D has the property that for any $p \in \bar{D}$ the solution $\Phi(p,t)$ lies in D for $t > 0$. Then D contains a unique periodic solution which is Lyapunov-stable, and every solution approaches its trajectory as $t \to +\infty$.

Proof. Consider an arbitrary point $p \in \bar{D}$ and the solution $\Phi(p,t)$ passing through this point when $t=0$. Let Ω be the limit set of the positive half-trajectory of $\Phi(p, t)$. It is clear that $\Omega \subset D$, but we will prove the more precise relation $\Omega \in D$. Assume to the contrary that there exists a point $q \in \Omega$ on the boundary of D, and consider the point $\Phi(q, t_1)$, where $t_1 < 0$. The set Ω is the limit set for $\Phi(p, t)$ and it is therefore invariant, so that $\Phi(q, t_1) \in \Omega \subset D$. By hypothesis, we have $\Phi(\Phi(q, t_1), -t_1) = q \in D$, which contradicts the assumptions we have made about the point q and shows that $\Omega \subset D$. It follows then from Theorem 18.2 that there exists a point $r \in \Omega$ through which a periodic solution $\Phi(r, t)$ of system (18.1) passes.

As proved above, the solution $\Phi(r, t)$ is Lyapunov-stable and any solution beginning in a sufficiently small neighborhood of the trajectory $\Phi(r, I_0)$ approaches $\Phi(r, I_0)$ as $t \to +\infty$.

Now consider the set A of points of the region D through which trajectories approaching $\Phi(r, I_0)$ pass. The set A is open. Indeed, if $p \in A$, then $\Phi(p, t) \to \Phi(r, I_0)$ as $t \to +\infty$, so that, by the theorem on integral continuity, all solutions beginning sufficiently close to the point p enter an arbitrarily small neighborhood of $\Phi(r, I_0)$, and, therefore, approach $\Phi(r, I_0)$ as $t \to \infty$, which shows that the set A is open.

If the set A coincides with D, the theorem is proved. Assume that A does not coincide with D. Let Σ be the boundary of the set A. By the definition of A, if $p \in \Sigma$, then $\Phi(p, t) \in \Sigma$ for all t. Moreover, it is clear that Σ is a closed set. As above, we will show that Σ contains a point s through which a periodic solution $\Phi(s, t)$ passes. It is clear that the trajectories $\Phi(r, I_0)$ and $\Phi(s, I_0)$ do not intersect, and, by Theorem 18.1, all solutions beginning in a sufficiently small neighborhood of the trajectory $\Phi(s, I_0)$ approach $\Phi(s, I_0)$ as $t \to \infty$. But then the point s can not be a boundary point for A, and the contradiction proves that $A = D$. Q.E.D.

19. THE EXISTENCE OF PERIODIC SOLUTIONS FOR AN AUTONOMOUS SYSTEM OF THREE DIFFERENTIAL EQUATIONS

In this section we will use the above-noted principle of the torus [81] to study a concrete system encountered in applications.

Consider the system of three equations

$$\left.\begin{aligned} \frac{dx}{dt} &= a[f(x) - (1+b)x - z], \\ \frac{dy}{dt} &= -c[f(x) - x - z], \\ \frac{dz}{dt} &= -d(y+z). \end{aligned}\right\} \qquad (19.1)$$

This system is encountered in the study of oscillatory phenomena in electrical circuits.

In this system, a, b, c, and d are positive constants and the function $f(x)$ is defined, continuous, and satisfies the condition required for uniqueness of solutions in the neighborhood of each point x. We will also assume that $f(x)$ is twice continuously differentiable in the neighborhood of the point $x=0$.

Hereinafter we will assume that the following conditions hold:

$$xf(x)>0 \quad \text{for} \quad x\neq 0, \tag{19.2}$$

$$|f(x)|<M \quad \text{for all } x \tag{19.3}$$

where M is a positive constant;

$$g>\frac{c}{2a}+\frac{d}{2a}+(1+b)-\sqrt{\left(\frac{c}{2a}-\frac{d}{2a}\right)^2+\frac{bc}{a}}, \tag{19.4}$$

where $g=f'(0)$; and

$$d>4.6c \sup_{-\infty<x<+\infty} \frac{f(x)}{x}+9.7c+5a+2.4ab. \tag{19.5}$$

Under these conditions, will prove that system (19.1) has a periodic solution.

If the function $f(x)$ is twice continuously differentiable, then system (19.1) can be represented in the form of one third-order equation. To accomplish this, it is necessary to differentiate the first equation of the system twice with respect to t and to use the usual rules to eliminate y, $\dot{y}$, z, and $\dot{z}$; we then obtain the following equation:

$$\dddot{x}+[d+a(1+b)-af'(x)]\ddot{x}-af''(x)\dot{x}^2+ \\ +[cd+ad(1+b)-adf'(x)]\dot{x}+abcdx=0. \tag{19.6}$$

1. The equilibrium states of system (19.6) are points at which the following equations are simultaneously satisfied:

$$f(x)-(1+b)x-z=0;$$
$$f(x)-x-z=0;$$
$$y+z=0.$$

Subtracting the second equation from the first, we find that $x=0$. From (19.2) and the continuity of $f(x)$, it follows that $f(0)=0$, from which it follows that $y=z=0$. Thus, system (19.1) has a unique equilibrium state, the coordinate origin.

Let us examine the behavior of solutions in the neighborhood of this equilibrium state. Set $f(x)=gx+S(x)$. Since $f(x)$ is continuously differentiable in the neighborhood of $x=0$, it is clear that $S(x)/x \to 0$ as $x \to 0$. System (19.1) can be rewritten in the form

$$\left.\begin{aligned}\frac{dx}{dt} &= a[(g-1-b)x - z] + aS(x),\\ \frac{dy}{dt} &= -c[(g-1)x - z] + cS(x),\\ \frac{dz}{dt} &= -d(y+z).\end{aligned}\right\} \tag{19.7}$$

In conjunction with this system, we will consider the "linearized" system

$$\left.\begin{aligned}\frac{dx}{dt} &= a[(g-1-b)x - z],\\ \frac{dy}{dt} &= -c[(g-1)x - z],\\ \frac{dz}{dt} &= -d(y+z).\end{aligned}\right\} \tag{19.8}$$

The linearized third-order equation takes the form

$$\begin{aligned}\dddot{x} + [d + a(1+b) - ag]\ddot{x} &+ \\ + [cd + ad(1+b) - adg]\dot{x} &+ abcdx = 0.\end{aligned} \tag{19.9}$$

Now write the characteristic equation:

$$\begin{aligned}\lambda^3 + [d + a(1+b) - ag]\lambda^2 &+ \\ + [cd + ad(1+b) - adg]\lambda &+ abcd = 0.\end{aligned} \tag{19.10}$$

Let λ_1, λ_2, and λ_3 be the roots of this equation. It is then clear that

$$\lambda_1\lambda_2\lambda_3 = -abcd < 0 \tag{19.11}$$

from which it follows that the characteristic equation has at least one negative root, which, for definiteness, we will assume to be λ_1.

The conditions of the Hurwitz criterion for the real parts of all roots of Eq. (19.10) to be negative take the form

$$abcd > 0, \tag{19.12}$$

$$d + a(1+b) - ag > 0, \tag{19.13}$$

$$[d + a(1+b) - ag][cd + ad(1+b) - adg] - abcd > 0. \tag{19.14}$$

The last inequality can be rewritten in the form

$$\begin{aligned}g^2 - \left[\frac{c}{a} + 2(1+b) + \frac{d}{a}\right]g &+ \\ + \frac{c}{a} + \frac{cd}{a^2} + \frac{d}{a}(1+b) + (1+b)^2 &> 0.\end{aligned} \tag{19.15}$$

This inequality holds if one of the following two inequalities holds:

$$g < \frac{c}{2a} + \frac{d}{2a} + (1+b) - \sqrt{\left(\frac{c}{2a} - \frac{d}{2a}\right)^2 + \frac{bc}{a}}; \tag{19.16}$$

$$g > \frac{c}{2a} + \frac{d}{2a} + (1+b) + \sqrt{\left(\frac{c}{2a} - \frac{d}{2a}\right)^2 + \frac{bc}{a}}. \tag{19.17}$$

Inequality (19.13) yields

$$g < \frac{d}{a} + 1 + b \tag{19.18}$$

Since

$$\frac{c}{2a} + \frac{d}{2a} + (1+b) - \sqrt{\left(\frac{c}{2a} - \frac{d}{2a}\right)^2 + \frac{bc}{a}} < \frac{d}{a} + 1 + b <$$
$$< \frac{c}{2a} + \frac{d}{2a} + (1+b) + \sqrt{\left(\frac{c}{2a} - \frac{d}{2a}\right)^2 + \frac{bc}{a}}, \tag{19.19}$$

it is clear that the Hurwitz conditions (19.12)-(19.14) hold if and only if inequality (19.16) holds. It follows from condition (19.4) that the Hurwitz conditions do not hold in the case under consideration, i.e., characteristic equation (19.10) has at least one root with a positive real part. It follows from (19.11) that there are exactly two such roots, so that

$$\operatorname{Re}\lambda_2 > 0, \quad \operatorname{Re}\lambda_3 > 0. \tag{19.20}$$

It is clear that, under our conditions, the linearized system has two trajectories that approach the coordinate origin as $t \to +\infty$. Both of these trajectories are rays of the same line. We will call the direction of this line the principal direction.

System (19.1) also has exactly two trajectories that approach the coordinate origin as $t \to +\infty$. These trajectories are tangent to the principal direction at the coordinate origin. All of the remaining trajectories of system (19.1) that begin in an arbitrarily small neighborhood of the coordinate origin leave some fixed neighborhood of the origin as time t increases.

We will now locate more precisely the position of the principal direction in phase space. Equation (19.9) has the particular solution

$$x = e^{\lambda_1 t}. \tag{19.21}$$

If we substitute this solution into the first equation of system (19.8), we find that

$$z = \left[g - (1 + b) - \frac{\lambda_1}{a} \right] x. \tag{19.22}$$

Substituting this into the third equation of system (19.8) and using (19.21), we obtain

$$y = -\left(1 + \frac{\lambda_1}{d}\right) z. \tag{19.23}$$

Equations (19.22) and (19.23) also determine the principal direction. If we set

$$\alpha = g - (1 + b) - \frac{\lambda_1}{a} \tag{19.24}$$

$$\beta = 1 + \frac{\lambda_1}{d} \tag{19.25}$$

then the equations of the principal direction take the form

$$z = \alpha x \tag{19.26}$$

$$y = -\beta z. \tag{19.27}$$

The direction cosines of this direction are

$$X = \frac{1}{\sqrt{1 + \alpha^2 (1 + \beta^2)}}, \quad Y = \frac{-\alpha\beta}{\sqrt{1 + \alpha^2 (1 + \beta^2)}}$$
$$Z = \frac{\alpha}{\sqrt{1 + \alpha^2 (1 + \beta^2)}}. \tag{19.28}$$

In what follows we will need an estimate of the angle between the principal direction and the line $x = 0$, $y = z$. The direction cosines of this line are $X = 0$, $Y = 1/\sqrt{2}$, $Z = 1/\sqrt{2}$. Consequently, η, the cosine of the angle between the indicated lines, is equal to

$$\eta = \frac{1}{\sqrt{2}} \cdot \frac{\alpha (1 - \beta)}{\sqrt{1 + \alpha^2 (1 + \beta^2)}}. \tag{19.29}$$

Let $P(\lambda)$ denote the left side of Eq. (19.10). Then

$$P(-d) = -cd^2 + abcd. \tag{19.30}$$

It follows from condition (19.25) that

$$P(-d) < 0. \tag{19.31}$$

Since λ_1 is the only negative root of Eq. (19.10), it is clear that

$$\lambda_1 > -d. \tag{19.32}$$

Let k be some number in the interval (0, 1); then

$$P(-kd) = k^2(1-k)d^3 + \\ + k(1-k)ad^2[g-(1+b)] - kcd^2 + abcd. \tag{19.33}$$

Condition (19.4) yields

$$g-(1+b) > \frac{c}{2a} + \frac{d}{2a} - \sqrt{\left(\frac{c}{2a} - \frac{d}{2a}\right)^2 + \frac{bc}{a}}. \tag{19.34}$$

It follows then from condition (19.5) that

$$g-(1+b) > 0. \tag{19.35}$$

We will now find a condition under which the inequality

$$k^2(1-k)d^3 > kcd^2 \tag{19.36}$$

holds. Since $k > 0$, this inequality is equivalent to

$$k(1-k)d > c.$$

Inequality (19.5) implies the inequality

$$d > 9.7c.$$

Thus, the preceding inequality will hold if

$$k(1-k) \geqslant \frac{1}{9.7}$$

so that if $k = 0.876$, inequality (19.36) holds. It follows from inequality (19.36) and from (19.33) that

$$P(-0{,}876d) > 0.$$

Hence, it follows from (19.32) that

$$-d < \lambda_1 < 0.876d. \tag{19.37}$$

These inequalities combined with condition (19.5) yield

$$\alpha > 4.38 \tag{19.38}$$

$$\beta < 0.124. \tag{19.39}$$

Finally, then, it follows from (19.29) that

$$\eta > 0.60. \tag{19.40}$$

2. We now proceed directly to the construction of the toroidal contactless surface. For the side boundaries, we choose two right circular conical surfaces with common vertex at the coordinate origin. The axis of these surfaces is the line $x=0,\ y=z$, while the generatrix is inclined at an angle ξ to the plane $y+z=0$. The equations of these surfaces are clearly of the form

$$\frac{y+z}{\sqrt{2}\sqrt{x^2+y^2+z^2}} = \pm\sin\xi \tag{19.41}$$

We will show that, if $\sin\xi = 1/2$, the vectors of the direction field of system (19.1) intersect surfaces (19.41) in the direction toward the plane $y+z=0$, i.e., we will show that the trajectories of the system (19.1) intersect surfaces (19.41) as they pass into a region bounded by both of these surfaces. For definiteness, we will consider the one surface

$$\frac{y+z}{\sqrt{2}\sqrt{x^2+y^2+z^2}} = \frac{1}{2}. \tag{19.42}$$

Let

$$v = \frac{y+z}{\sqrt{2}\sqrt{x^2+y^2+z^2}}. \tag{19.43}$$

Our assertion will be proved if we can show that the derivative of v with respect to time, obtained with the aid of the differential equations of system (19.1), is negative when $v=1/2$. To prove this, set

$$\rho = \sqrt{x^2+y^2+z^2} \tag{19.44}$$

so that

$$\dot{v} = \frac{1}{\sqrt{2}}\left(\frac{\dot{y}+\dot{z}}{\rho} - \frac{v\sqrt{2}\,(x\dot{x}+y\dot{y}+z\dot{z})}{\rho^2}\right). \tag{19.45}$$

Substituting the expressions given for the derivatives in system (19.1), we find that

$$\dot{v}\sqrt{2}=-\frac{c}{\rho}f(x)+\frac{c}{\rho}x+\frac{c}{\rho}z-\frac{d}{\rho}y-\frac{d}{\rho}z-$$
$$-\frac{av\sqrt{2}}{\rho^2}xf(x)+\frac{av\sqrt{2}}{\rho^2}(1+b)x^2+\frac{av\sqrt{2}}{\rho^2}xz+$$
$$+\frac{cv\sqrt{2}}{\rho^2}yf(x)-\frac{cv\sqrt{2}}{\rho^2}yx-\frac{cv\sqrt{2}}{\rho^2}yz+$$
$$+\frac{dv\sqrt{2}}{\rho^2}yz+\frac{dv\sqrt{2}}{\rho^2}z^2. \tag{19.46}$$

It follows from Eqs. (19.43) and (19.44) that

$$z=\frac{v\rho\pm\rho\sqrt{1-v^2-\frac{x^2}{\rho^2}}}{\sqrt{2}} \tag{19.47}$$

$$y=\frac{v\rho\mp\rho\sqrt{1-v^2-\frac{x^2}{\rho^2}}}{\sqrt{2}}. \tag{19.48}$$

Here the radicals in Eqs. (19.47) and (19.48) must be of opposite sign when these relations are considered simultaneously.

Using (19.47), (19.48), and introducing the notation $x=\rho w$, we obtain

$$\dot{v}\sqrt{2}=\frac{c(v^2-1)}{\rho}f(\rho w)\mp\frac{cv}{\rho}f(\rho w)\sqrt{1-v^2-w^2}-$$
$$-\frac{av\sqrt{2}}{\rho}wf(\rho w)-v(1-v^2)\sqrt{2}(d-c)+$$
$$+[av^2+c(1-v^2)]w\pm(av+cv)w\sqrt{1-v^2-w^2}\pm$$
$$\pm\left(dv^2\sqrt{2}+\frac{c}{\sqrt{2}}\right)\sqrt{1-a^2-w^2}-$$
$$-\left(\frac{cv}{\sqrt{2}}-av\sqrt{2}-abv\sqrt{2}\right)w^2, \tag{19.49}$$

where $w^2\leqslant 1-v^2$. We will now obtain an upper bound for the right side of the last equation for $v=1/2$:

$$\dot{v}\sqrt{2}\leqslant-\left(\frac{3\sqrt{2}}{8}-\frac{\sqrt{6}}{8}\right)d+$$
$$+c\left(\frac{3}{4}+\frac{\sqrt{3}}{4}\right)\frac{\sqrt{3}}{2}\sup_{-\infty<x<+\infty}\frac{f(x)}{x}+$$
$$+\left(\frac{3\sqrt{2}}{8}+\frac{3\sqrt{3}}{8}+\frac{3}{8}+\frac{\sqrt{3}}{2\sqrt{2}}\right)c+$$
$$+\left(\frac{\sqrt{3}}{8}+\frac{3}{8}+\frac{3\sqrt{2}}{8}\right)a+\frac{3\sqrt{2}}{8}ab. \tag{19.50}$$

When we evaluate the radicals in the above estimate and use condition (19.5), we find that

$$\dot{v}<0 \tag{19.51}$$

when $v=1/2$.

The proof that $\dot{v} > 0$ when $v = -1/2$ is completely analogous. Thus, the trajectories of system (19.1) intersect the surfaces $v = \pm 1/2$ and enter the region $|v| < 1/2$.

We will now construct the outer boundary of our toroidal surface, and begin by studying the function

$$u = \frac{1}{c^2} y^2 + \frac{1}{b}\left(\frac{y}{c} + \frac{x}{a}\right)^2 + \frac{z^2}{cd}. \tag{19.52}$$

The time derivative of this function, as evaluated by means of the differential equations of system (19.1), can easily be shown to be equal to

$$\dot{u} = -\frac{2}{c} y f(x) - \frac{2x^2}{a} - \frac{2z^2}{c}. \tag{19.53}$$

It immediately follows from the form of this derivative and condition (19.3) that, if u is sufficiently large and $|v| \leqslant 1/2$, then $\dot{u} < 0$. For the upper boundary of our region, therefore, we can choose the elliptical surface $u = L$, if L is sufficiently large and positive.

The region bounded by the surfaces $v = \pm 1/2$ and $u = L$ is homeomorphic to a torus. Nevertheless, it can not be used to prove the existence of periodic solutions by means of the principle of the torus, because there is an equilibrium state on its boundary, and it is possible that use of the Brouwer theorem will prove the existence of the stationary point at the coordinate origin. In connection with this, we will now introduce the inner boundary surface which will separate the torus from the coordinate origin.

In virtue of inequality (19.40), proved above, the principal direction lies outside the region $|v| \leqslant 1/2$. On the other hand, since inequalities (19.20) hold, we can surround the principal direction by a family of cylinders intersected by the trajectories of linear system (19.8) from inside outward. In order to do so, we reduce system (19.8) to canonical form:

$$\left.\begin{aligned} \dot{q}_1 &= \lambda_1 q_1, \\ \dot{q}_2 &= \mu_1 q_2 - \varkappa q_3, \\ \dot{q}_3 &= \varkappa q_2 + \mu_2 q_3. \end{aligned}\right\} \tag{19.54}$$

The q_1 axis will lie along the principal direction, while the q_2 and q_3 axes will depend on the roots λ_2 and λ_3. If λ_2 and λ_3 are real, then $\varkappa = 0$ and $\mu_1 = \lambda_2$, $\mu_2 = \lambda_3$, while if λ_2 and λ_3 are complex conjugates, $\mu_1 = \mu_2 = \operatorname{Re}\lambda_2$. In both cases, as (19.20) implies, $\mu_1 > 0$ and $\mu_2 > 0$.

If we transform system (19.7) into the coordinates q_1, q_2, and q_3, we obtain the system

$$\left.\begin{aligned}\dot{q}_1&=+\lambda_1 q_1+c_1 S(x),\\ \dot{q}_2&=\mu_1 q_2-\varkappa q_3+c_2 S(x),\\ \dot{q}_3&=\varkappa q_2+\mu_2 q_3+c_3 S(x),\end{aligned}\right\} \tag{19.55}$$

where c_1, c_2, and c_3 are constants.

Consider the function

$$\varphi=q_2^2+q_3^2. \tag{19.56}$$

Its time derivative, which can be evaluated by means of the differential equations of system (19.7), is

$$\frac{1}{2}\dot{\varphi}=\mu_1 q_2^2+\mu_2 q_3^2+(c_2 q_2+c_3 q_3)\,S(x). \tag{19.57}$$

Since $S(x)/x\to 0$ as $x\to 0$ and the principal direction lies outside the region $|v|\leqslant 1/2$, the surface

$$q_2^2+q_3^2=K \tag{19.58}$$

will, for sufficiently small K and $|v|\leqslant 1/2$, be intersected by the trajectories as φ increases, i.e., from inside outward. We take surface (19.58) for the inner boundary.

The region R bounded by the surfaces $v=\pm 1/2$, $u=L$ and $\varphi=K$ is, as we can see with little difficulty, homeomorphic to a torus, while its boundary Σ, as we have proved, is intersected by the trajectories of system (19.1) from outside inward. Thus, in order to prove the existence of a periodic solution, it remains to be shown that the torus R has a contactless profile such that any trajectory beginning on this profile intersects it once more as time increases. We will now prove this.

Let D_1 be the profile of the region R in the half-plane $x=0$, $z<0$, and let D_2 be the profile in the half-plane $x=0,\ z>0$. These profiles are clearly simply connected regions, and the closed region $\overline{D}_1$ lies with the region $x=0,\ y>0,\ z<0$, while $\overline{D}_2$ lies within the region $x=0,\ y<0,\ z>0$.

The profiles $\overline{D}_1$ and $\overline{D}_2$ have no contact with the direction field of system (19.1); indeed, when $x=0$ we have

$$\dot{x}=-az \tag{19.59}$$

from which our assertion follows. The trajectories of system (19.1) intersect the profile $\overline{D}_1$ in passing from the half-space $x<0$ into the half-space $x>0$; the profile D_2, on the other hand, is intersected by trajectories in the opposite direction. It is clear that if a trajectory begins at a point that lies in $\overline{R}$ sufficiently close to $\overline{D}_2$ in the half-space $x>0$, this trajectory will intersect D_2 as t increases. Similarly, if a trajectory begins at a point that lies in $\overline{R}$ sufficiently close to $\overline{D_1}$ in the half-space $x < 0$, this trajectory will intersect D_1 as t increases.

Consider the solution $(x(t), y(t), z(t))$ of system (19.1) beginning at $t=0$ in $\overline{D_1}$. This solution lies in R for all $t > 0$, and $x(t) > 0$ for all sufficiently small $t > 0$. As t increases further, our solution can not reach the profile D_1 from the half-space $x(t) > 0$, because trajectories intersect this profile in the opposite direction. Consequently, one of two cases must occur: Either $x(t) > 0$ for all t, or the solution under discussion intersects D_2 when t is positive.

We will show that the second case is the one that takes place. Assume that this is not so, i.e., assume that $x(t) > 0$ for all $t > 0$. Then there exists a $\delta > 0$ such that $x(t) > \delta$ for $t \geqslant 1$; indeed, if such a δ did not exist, it would follow from the above-noted properties of the profiles $\overline{D_1}$ and $\overline{D_2}$ that there exists a $t^* > 1/2$ such that when $t=t^*$ our solution lies either on D_1 or D_2, i.e., $x(t^*)=0$, which would contradict the hypothesis.

If we multiply the first equation in system (19.1) by c, the second by a, and add, we obtain the equation

$$c\frac{dx}{dt} + a\frac{dy}{dt} = -abcx. \tag{19.60}$$

Integrating this equation along the solution under discussion from 1 to t, we find that

$$cx + ay - cx(1) - ay(1) = -abc\int_1^t x(t)\,dt. \tag{19.61}$$

But $x(t) > \delta$ for $t \geqslant 1$, so that Eq. (19.61) yields

$$cx + ay - cx(1) - ay(1) < -abc\delta(t-1). \tag{19.62}$$

Now, if we let $t \to +\infty$, we obtain the relationship

$$cx(t) + ay(t) \to -\infty \quad \text{for} \quad t \to \infty. \tag{19.63}$$

This relationship contradicts the fact that the solution under discussion lies in the bounded domain R for all $t > 0$, which shows that the solution under discussion intersects D_2 as t increases.

Similarly, we can show that our solution again intersects D_1 upon further increase in t.

Let $t = \tau > 0$ be the first point after $t=0$ at which our solution intersects D_1. We associate the point $x = x(0) = 0$, $y = y(0)$, $z = z(0)$ with the point $x = x(\tau) = 0$, $y = y(\tau)$, $z = z(\tau)$. Since the point $y = y(0)$, $z = z(0)$ is an arbitrary point in $\overline{D_1}$, we obtain in this manner a transformation T of $\overline{D_1}$ into itself. It is not difficult to show that this transformation is continuous, so that, by the Brouwer theorem, this transformation has a stationary point in D_1. A closed trajectory of system (19.1) passes through this point, which proves:

Theorem 19.1. When conditions (19.2)-(19.5) are satisfied, system (19.1) has a periodic solution distinct from the equilibrium state.

3. Under the conditions we have formulated, it is extremely difficult (if at all possible) to prove stability in the small and uniqueness of the periodic solution whose existence we have just proved. It is, however, possible to prove that any solution of system (19.1) is not very far from a periodic solution. More precisely, it can be shown that every trajectory (except for the two approaching the coordinate origin) enters the region R as time increases, and then remains there.

We will prove this by considering an arbitrary point p in phase space and showing that the trajectory $\Phi(p, t)$ either approaches the coordinate origin as $t \to +\infty$ or intersects the plane $y+z=0$ when $t \geqslant 0$. Assume that the point p has coordinates x_0, y_0 and z_0, and for definiteness, assume that $y_0+z_0>0$. Also, assume that the inequality

$$y(t)+z(t)>0 \tag{19.64}$$

is satisfied on $\Phi(p, t)$ when $t \geqslant 0$.

We will show then that the trajectory $\Phi(p, t)$ is bounded for $t \geqslant 0$. From inequality (19.64), it follows that z decreases along $\Phi(p, t)$.

Initially, assume that $z(t)$ is bounded when $t \geqslant 0$. It follows from the first equation of system (19.1) and condition (19.3) that x is also bounded on $\Phi(p, t)$, since $\operatorname{sign} \dot{x} = -\operatorname{sign} x$ for sufficiently large $|x|$. Dividing the second equation of system (19.1) by the third, we obtain

$$\frac{dy}{dz}=\frac{c}{d}\,\frac{f(x)-x-z}{y+z} \tag{19.65}$$

It follows from this equation that the inequality

$$\left|\frac{dy}{dz}\right|<1$$

is satisfied when $|y|$ is sufficiently large, and then it follows from the boundedness of z and that y is bounded. When z is bounded, therefore, the half-trajectory $\Phi(p, t)$, $t \geqslant 0$, is also bounded.

We now assume that $z(t)$ is not bounded when $t \geqslant 0$. Since $\dot{z}(t)<0$ when $t \geqslant 0$ because of inequlity (19.64), $z(t) \to -\infty$ when $t \to +\infty$. Consequently, there exists a t_1 such that

$$\dot{z}(t)\,\frac{b}{2+b}<-M \tag{19.66}$$

where $t \geqslant t_1$, where M is the number appearing in condition (19.3).

It follows from the first equation of system (19.1) that there exists a $t_2 \geqslant t_1$ such that the inequality

$$x(t) < -\frac{2z(t)}{2+b} \tag{19.67}$$

holds when $t \geqslant t_2$.

Indeed, when

$$x \geqslant -\frac{2z}{2+b}$$

x decreases along $\Phi(p, t)$, and since $z(t)$ decreases for all $t \geqslant 0$, inequality (19.67) follows. This inequality and the second equation of system (19.1) imply that

$$\frac{dy}{dt} < -c\left[f(x) + \frac{2z}{2+b} - z\right]$$

or

$$\frac{dy}{dt} < -c\left[f(x) - \frac{bz}{2+b}\right].$$

It follows then from (19.66) that $dy/dt < 0$ when $t \geqslant t_2$; thus, as $t \to +\infty$, y is bounded from above on $\Phi(p, t)$. This contradicts inequality (19.64) and the fact that $z(t) \to -\infty$ as $t \to +\infty$.

The contradiction which we have obtained shows that the half-trajectory $\Phi(p, t)$, $t \geqslant 0$, is bounded.

Since the trajectory $\Phi(p, t)$ is bounded when $t \geqslant 0$, it has an ω-limit point q. Assume that the coordinates of the point q are x_1, y_1 and z_1. z is bounded on the trajectory $\Phi(p, t)$, and it follows from inequality (19.64) and the last equation of system (19.3) that $\dot{z}(t) < 0$, so that

$$\lim_{t \to +\infty} z(t) = z_1.$$

Since $\Phi(t)$ is bounded when $t \geqslant 0$, it follows that its limit trajectory $\Phi(q, I_0)$ is also bounded.

From the last equation, it follows that $z = z_1$ on $\Phi(q, t)$ for all t. Thus, $\dot{z} = 0$ on this trajectory and, therefore, $y + z = 0$, i.e.,

$$y = -z_1. \tag{19.68}$$

Hence, the second equation of system (19.1) implies that

$$z_1 = f(x) - x \tag{19.69}$$

on $\Phi(q, t)$ for all t. It follows then from the first equation of the system that, on the trajectory $\Phi(q, t)$,

$$\frac{dx}{dt} = -abx \tag{19.70}$$

for all t. This equation implies that $x=0$ on $\Phi(q, t)$ for all t, since, if we have $x=x_0 \neq 0$ for $t=t_0$, it would follow from (19.70) that $x=x_0 e^{-ab(t-t_0)}$ on $\Phi(q, t)$ and x would not be bounded for $t \to -\infty$, which is impossible, because $\Phi(q, I_0)$ is bounded. But then

$$x=0, \ z=z_1=0, \ y=y_1=0 \tag{19.71}$$

on $\Phi(q, t)$ for all t, i.e., the point q coincides with the equilibrium state at the coordinate origin.

Thus, if a trajectory $\Phi(p, t)$ does not intersect the plane $y+z=0$, it approaches the coordinate origin.

We will now prove the following statement:

Theorem 19.2. If a trajectory $\Phi(p, t)$ *of system (19.1) does not approach the coordinate origin as* $t \to +\infty$, *this trajectory enters the region* R *upon increase in time and does not leave this region upon further increase in* t.

Proof. Assume that $\Phi(p, t)$ does not approach the coordinate origin as $t \to +\infty$. Then, as we have just proved, $\Phi(p, t)$ intersects the plane $y+z=0$ when $t \geqslant 0$. Thus, without loss of generality, we can assume that the point p lies on this plane.

As shown at the beginning of the preceding Paragraph, for all $t \geqslant 0$, the trajectory $\Phi(p, t)$ lies in the region $|v| < 1/2$, where v is the function introduced by formula (19.43).

If the point p lies in the closed region $\bar{R}$, the theorem is proved, since the trajectories of system (19.1) intersect the boundary of R from the outside inward. Therefore, assume that p is not contained in $\bar{R}$. Then one of two cases can occur at p: Either $u > L$ or $\varphi < K$.

Consider the first case. It follows from the selection of the constant L and Eq. (19.53) that $u \geqslant L$ when $\dot{u} < 0$ and $|v| \leqslant 1/2$.

Assume, contrary to our assertion, that $\Phi(p, t)$ lies outside R for all t. It is then clear that, for $t \geqslant 0$, the inequalities $|v| \leqslant 1/2$, $L \leqslant u \leqslant u_0$ hold on $\Phi(p, t)$, where u_0 is the value of u at p. The set $\{|v| \leqslant 1/2, \ L \leqslant u \leqslant u_0\}$ is clearly bounded, so that the trajectory $\Phi(p, t)$ has an ω-limit point q in this set. Let u_1 be the value of u at q. It is clear that

$$\lim_{t \to +\infty} u(t) = u_1 \tag{19.72}$$

on $\Phi(p, t)$.

Consider the trajectory $\Phi(q, t)$. This trajectory is an ω-limit trajectory for $\Phi(p, t)$, and, therefore, lies within $\{|v| \leqslant 1/2, \ L \leqslant u \leqslant u_0\}$. It follows then that along the trajectory $\Phi(q, t)$ the function u

decreases, and therefore, $u < u_1$ at the point $\Phi(q, t_1)$ if $t_1 > 0$. But the point $\Phi(q, t_1)$ is an ω-limit point for $\Phi(p, t)$, so that it follows from the continuity of u that there exists a t^* such that $u < u_1$ on $\Phi(p, t)$ when $t = t^*$. This contradicts (19.72) and the fact that the function u decreases on $\Phi(p, t)$ when $t \geqslant 0$. The contradiction proves that the trajectory $\Phi(p, t)$ enters the region R.

Similarly, if $\varphi < K$ at p, we can show that $\Phi(p, t)$ enters R as time increases, which proves the theorem.

4. We now turn our attention to the following situation: As proved at the beginning of the present section, the characteristic equation of linearized system (19.8) has one negative root and two roots with positive real parts, i.e., for sufficiently small x, system (19.1) is very close to a linear system with two positive characteristic exponents. This made it possible for us to construct the interior, cylindrical part of the boundary Σ of the region R.

When x is sufficiently large, on the other hand, system (19.1) is very close to a linear system with negative characteristic exponents. Indeed, rewrite system (19.1) in the form

$$\left.\begin{aligned} \frac{dx}{dt} &= a\left\{\left[\frac{f(x)}{x} - (1+b)\right]x - z\right\}, \\ \frac{dy}{dt} &= -c\left\{\left[\frac{f(x)}{x} - 1\right]x - z\right\}, \\ \frac{dz}{dt} &= -d(y+z). \end{aligned}\right\} \tag{19.73}$$

It is clear that, in virtue of condition (19.3), our system is, for sufficiently large x, arbitrarily close to the system

$$\left.\begin{aligned} \frac{dx}{dt} &= -a[(1+b)x + z], \\ \frac{dy}{dt} &= c(x+z), \\ \frac{dz}{dt} &= -d(y+z). \end{aligned}\right\} \tag{19.74}$$

The characteristic equation of this system is of the form

$$\lambda^3 + [d + a(1+b)]\lambda^2 + d[c + a(1+b)]\lambda + abcd = 0. \tag{19.75}$$

The conditions resulting from the Hurwitz criterion for Eq. (19.75) take the following form:

$$abcd > 0, \quad d + a(1+b) > 0,$$
$$[d + a(1+b)][cd + ad(1+b)] - abcd > 0.$$

These conditions are satisfied when a, b, c, and d are positive. Thus, the roots of the characteristic equation of system (19.74) have negative real parts.

Because system (19.1) is close to system (19.74), it was possible for us to construct the outer, ellipsoidal part of the boundary of R.

Thus, system (19.1) is such that for small x the "majority" of solutions are "repelled" from the coordinate origin, while, on the other hand, for large x the solutions are "attracted" to the origin. This makes it possible to construct a toroidal region R bounded by a contactless surface.

Similar considerations make it possible to establish the existence of periodic solutions for multidimensional systems in a whole series of very interesting cases (see [82-88]).

It turns out, however, that when the system satisfies a so-called generalized Hurwitz criterion, periodic solutions may appear. A separate section of the book is devoted to the study of such systems.

20. INVESTIGATION OF A DIFFERENTIAL EQUATION WITH A NONLINEARITY SATISFYING A GENERALIZED HURWITZ CRITERION

In this and subsequent paragraphs we will study the equation

$$\frac{d^3\xi}{dt_1^3}+f_1\left(\frac{d^2\xi}{dt_1^2}\right)+a_1\frac{d\xi}{dt_1}+b_1\xi=0, \tag{20.1}$$

where a_1 and b_1 are positive constants, while the function $f_1(\eta)$ satisfies a Lipschitz condition in the neighborhood of each point η.

Equation (20.1) can be converted into a system of equations by setting

$$x=\frac{d^2\xi}{dt_1^2}, \quad y_1=-\left(a_1\frac{d\xi}{dt_1}+b_1\xi\right), \quad z_1=-b_1\frac{d\xi}{dt_1} \tag{20.2}$$

thus, we obtain

$$\frac{dx}{dt_1}=y_1-f_1(x), \quad \frac{dy_1}{dt_1}=z_1-a_1x, \quad \frac{dz_1}{dt_1}=-b_1x. \tag{20.3}$$

If, in this system, we make the substitutions

$$y_1=\sqrt{a_1}y, \quad z=a_1z, \quad t_1=\frac{1}{\sqrt{a_1}}t \tag{20.4}$$

we obtain

$$\frac{dx}{dt}=y-f(x), \quad \frac{dy}{dt}=z-x, \quad \frac{dz}{dt}=-ax \tag{20.5}$$

where

$$a=\frac{b_1}{a_1\sqrt{a_1}}, \quad f(x)=\frac{1}{\sqrt{a_1}}f_1(x).$$

In what follows we will study system (20.5). Together with system (20.5), we will consider the following linear system with constant coefficients:

$$\frac{dx}{dt} = y - hx, \quad \frac{dy}{dt} = z - x, \quad \frac{dz}{dt} = -ax. \tag{20.6}$$

It is easily verified that the characteristic equation of this system is of the form

$$\lambda^3 + h\lambda^2 + \lambda + a = 0. \tag{20.7}$$

The Hurwitz criterion for the real parts of all roots of this equation to be negative takes the form $h > a$.

As a result, we will frequently call the inequality

$$\frac{f(x)}{x} > a \quad \text{for} \quad x \neq 0 \tag{20.8}$$

the generalized Hurwitz criterion for system (20.5).

Hereinafter, we will assume that the nonlinearity $f(x)$ satisfies the generalized Hurwitz criterion.*

1. In this paragraph we will study the general behavior of the trajectories of system (20.5).

We will denote the trajectory of system (20.5) that passes through the point p of phase space at $t = 0$ by $\varphi(p, t)$. Let E be some set of points in phase space, and denote the set of trajectories of system (20.5) that pass through the points of the set E when $t = 0$ by $\varphi(E, t)$.

We will now discuss the direction field defined by system (20.5). It is immediately clear from system (20.5) that x increases along all solutions of the system when $y > f(x)$, but decreases with increase in time t when $y < f(x)$. Also, along all solutions of system (20.5), y increases when $z > x$, but when $z < x$ it decreases as time increases. Since $a > 0$, the sign of the derivation dz/dt is opposite to the sign of x. Thus, z decreases along all solutions of system (20.5) when $x > 0$, but increases with increasing time when $x < 0$.

The trajectories of system (20.5) intersect the plane $x = 0$ when $y > 0$ by passing from the half-space $x < 0$ into the half-space $x > 0$; but when $y < 0$ the trajectories of system (20.5) intersect the plane $x = 0$ by passing from the half-space $x > 0$ into the half-space $x < 0$ as time increases. When $y = 0$ the trajectories of system (20.5) are tangent to the plane $x = 0$. Assume that p is on the Oz axis, and that its z-coordinate is positive; then the trajectory $\varphi(p, t)$ of system (20.5) is tangent to the plane $x = 0$ at $t = 0$. When $t \neq 0$ but

*A more detailed study of third-order systems satisfying the generalized Hurwitz criterion can be found in [89].

sufficiently small, the trajectory $\varphi(p, t)$ lies in the half-space $x > 0$. If the point p is on the z axis but is negative, the trajectory $\varphi(p, t)$ is tangent to the plane $x = 0$ at the point p, so that, when $t \neq 0$ but sufficiently small, $\varphi(p, t)$ is the half-space $x < 0$. Thus, the z-coordinate on the plane $x = 0$ attains a maximum along all trajectories of (20.5) when $y > 0$, and a minimum when $y < 0$. When $y = 0$, the z-coordinate has no extrema in the plane $x = 0$ on the trajectories of the system.

We will now describe the behavior of the trajectories of system (20.5) in the neighborhood of the plane $z - x = 0$. Here we will assume that $x \geqslant 0$, since the pattern for $x < 0$ will obviously be symmetrical to it. Assume that the point p is in the plane $z - x = 0$. If $y \geqslant f(x)$ at p, the trajectory $\varphi(p, t)$ will intersect the plane $z - x = 0$ at $t = 0$ by passing from the half-space $z - x > 0$ into the half-space $z - x < 0$. If $y - f(x) < 0$ at the point p but

$$\frac{dz}{dx} = \frac{-ax}{y - f(x)} > 1, \tag{20.9}$$

the trajectory $\varphi(p, t)$ will intersect the plane $z - x = 0$ at the point p by passing from the half-space $z - x > 0$ into the half-space $z - x < 0$. In both cases, the y-coordinate of the trajectory $\varphi(p, t)$ achieves a maximum at the point p.

Now assume that we have

$$\frac{dz}{dx} = \frac{-ax}{y - f(x)} < 1 \tag{20.10}$$

at the point p; then the trajectory $\varphi(p\ t)$ intersect the plane $z - x = 0$ by passing from the half-space $z - x < 0$ into the half-space $z - x > 0$. In this case, the y-coordinate of the trajectory $\varphi(p, t)$ has a minimum at the point p. If, however, we have

$$y < f(x), \quad \frac{-ax}{y - f(x)} = 1 \tag{20.11}$$

at p, the trajectory $\varphi(p, t)$ is tangent to the plane $z - x = 0$ at the point p.

Now assume that the point p lies on the cylindrical surface $y - f(x) = 0$; here, as before, we will assume that $x \geqslant 0$ at p. If $z > x$ at p, the trajectory $\varphi(p, t)$ intersects the surface $y = f(x)$ at p by passing from the region $\{y - f(x) < 0\}$ into the region $\{y - f(x) > 0\}$ (here and henceforth inequalities in braces denote the regions of phase space where these inequalities hold). In this case, the x-coordinate of the trajectory $\varphi(p, t)$ has a minimum at p. If $z < x$ at p, the trajectory $\varphi(p, t)$ intersects the surface $y - f(x) = 0$ by passing from the region $\{y - f(x) > 0\}$ into the region $\{y - f(x) < 0\}$. In this case, the x-coordinate of the trajectory $\varphi(p, t)$ has a maximum at the point p.

2. In this paragraph we will establish a theorem on the behavior of the trajectories of system (20.5). In order to prove this theorem, we will need several lemmas.

Lemma 20.1. If $p \in \{x > 0,\ z < 0\}$, *then the trajectory* $\varphi(p, t)$ *intersects the plane* $x = 0$ *when* $t > 0$.

Proof. Assume that $p \in \{x > 0,\ y - f(x) > 0,\ z < 0\}$. We will show that then the trajectory $\varphi(p, t)$ of system (20.5) intersects the surface $y - f(x) = 0$ as time increases, and enters the region $\{x > 0, y - f(x) < 0,\ z < 0\}$. Indeed, in the region $\{x > 0,\ y - f(x) > 0,\ z < 0\}$ the x-coordinate increases along all solutions of system (20.5), while the y-coordinate and z-coordinate decrease as time increases. In the region under discussion, y is bounded on the trajectory $\varphi(p, t)$, because it decreases in this region and is positive. But then x is also bounded in this region of the trajectory $\varphi(p, t)$. Indeed, dividing the first equation of system (20.5) by the second, we find that

$$\frac{dx}{dy} = \frac{y - f(x)}{z - x}. \tag{20.12}$$

It is clear that $z - x < 0$ on $\varphi(p, t)$ for $t > 0$ such that $\varphi(p, t) \in \{x > 0, y - f(x) > 0,\ z < 0\}$. It then follows from the fact that y is bounded in the region under consideration that x is also bounded.

We will now show that the z-coordinate is also bounded on $\varphi(p, t)$ in the region $\{x > 0,\ y - f(x) > 0,\ z < 0\}$. In order to do so, we divide the third equation of system (20.5) by the second, thus obtaining the equation

$$\frac{dz}{dy} = \frac{-ax}{z - x}. \tag{20.13}$$

Since x is bounded on $\varphi(p, t)$ in the region under discussion, and z decreases as time increases in this region, the right side of Eq. (20.13) is bounded, which, together with the fact that y is bounded, implies that z is bounded. We now assume that the trajectory $\varphi(p, t)$ remains in the region $\{x > 0,\ y - f(x),\ z > 0\}$ for all $t \geqslant 0$. Then $\varphi(p, t)$ is bounded when $t \geqslant 0$. But in the region under discussion all coordinates are monotonic functions of time, so that the trajectory $\varphi(p, t)$ approaches some point distinct from the origin of phase space as $t \to +\infty$. It is well known that such a point can only be an equilibrium state for our system. But system (20.5) has only one equilibrium state, the point $x = y = z = 0$. Thus, the assumption that the trajectory $\varphi(p, t)$ remains in the region $\{x > 0,\ y - f(x) > 0,\ z < 0\}$ for $t \geqslant 0$ leads to a contradiction; hence, $\varphi(p, t)$ intersects the surface $y - f(x) = 0$ and enters the region $\{x > 0,\ y - f(x) < 0,\ z < 0\}$.

We will now show that the trajectory $\varphi(p, t)$ can not lie in the region $\{x > 0,\ y - f(x) < 0,\ z < 0\}$ for all $t > t_1$. Assume to the contrary that $\varphi(p, t)$ lies in this region for all $t > t_1$, and we will show that then $\varphi(p, t)$ is bounded for $t > t_1$. Indeed, in this region x is positive and decreases, so that it is bounded. Assume that the z-coordinate of the trajectory $\varphi(p, t)$ decreases without bound as time increases. Divide the third equation of system (20.5) by the first, obtaining

$$\frac{dz}{dx} = \frac{-ax}{y - f(x)}. \tag{20.14}$$

It follows from this equation that the z-coordinate of $\varphi(p, t)$ can be unbounded only when y is bounded on $\varphi(p, t)$ for $t > t_1$. But then, as we can see from Eq. (20.13), z is also bounded on $\varphi(p, t)$ when $t > t_1$. As a result, the assumption that the z-coordinate of the trajectory $\varphi(p, t)$ is unbounded for $t > t_1$ leads to a contradiction, and, therefore, the z-coordinate of the trajectory $\varphi(p, t)$ is bounded for $t > t_1$. From the equation

$$\frac{dy}{dx} = \frac{z - x}{y - f(x)} \tag{20.15}$$

and the fact that y monotonically decreases and x and z are unbounded for $t > t_1$ on the trajectory $\varphi(p, t)$, it follows that the y-coordinate of $\varphi(p, t)$ can not be unbounded for $t > t_1$.

Thus, if the trajectory $\varphi(p, t)$ remains in the region $\{x > 0, y - f(x) < 0, z < 0\}$ when $t > t_1$, then $\varphi(p, t)$ is bounded for $t > t_1$. But all coordinates of the trajectory $\varphi(p, t)$ vary monotonically in the region $\{x > 0, y - f(x) < 0, z < 0\}$. Since the z-coordinate of the trajectory $\varphi(p, t)$ decreases in this region as time increases, it follows that system (20.5) has an equilibrium state other than $x = y = z = 0$, and this, as previously noted, is not true. Neither can this trajectory intersect the plane $z = 0$, because as time increases, z decreases in the region $\{x > 0\}$ along all solutions of (20.5); nor can the trajectory $\varphi(p, t)$ intersect the surface $y - f(x) = 0$, because, as noted above, when $z < x$ the trajectories of system (20.5) intersect the surface $y = f(x)$ by passing from the region $\{y - f(x) > 0\}$ into the region $\{y - f(x) < 0\}$, and not in the opposite direction.

Consequently, the trajectory $\varphi(p, t)$ must intersect the plane $x = 0$ when $t = T_p > t_1$, which proves the lemma.

Remark. The lemma is also clearly true when $p \in \{x > 0, \ z = 0\}$ and when $p \in \{x = 0, z \leqslant 0, y > 0\}$.

The proof of the following lemma is absolutely analogous.

Lemma 20.2. If $p \in \{x < 0, z > 0\}$, *then* $\varphi(p, t)$ *intersects the plane* $x = 0$ *when* $t > 0$.

Lemma 20.3. If $p \in \{x > 0, y - f(x) > 0\}$, *then the trajectory* $\varphi(p, t)$ *of system (20.5) intersects the surface* $y - f(x) = 0$ *when* $t > 0$, *and enters the region* $\{x > 0, y - f(x) < 0\}$.

Proof. Initially, assume that $p \in \{x > 0, y - f(x) > 0, z > x\}$. In this region, x and y increase and z decreases as t increases.

Contrary to the lemma, assume that $\varphi(p, t) \in \{x > 0, y - f(x) > 0\}$ for all $t > 0$. We will show that then $\varphi(p, t)$ intersects the plane $z - x = 0$ when $t > 0$.

Indeed, the x- and z-coordinates of the trajectory $\varphi(p, t)$ are bounded in the region $\{x > 0,\ y - f(x) > 0,\ z - x > 0\}$, because here z decreases as time increases. We will show that, in this region, y is also bounded on $\varphi(p, t)$. In order to do so, we use the equation

$$\frac{dy}{dz} = \frac{z - x}{-ax}. \qquad (20.16)$$

The denominator of the fraction on the right side of this equation can vanish only when $x = 0$. Since $x \geqslant x(p)$ on $\varphi(p, t)$ in the region $\{x > 0,\ y - f(x) > 0,\ z - x > 0\}$ when $t \geqslant 0$ and, as noted above, the x-coordinate of $\varphi(p, t)$ is bounded in this region when $t \geqslant 0$, there exists an $l > 0$ such that $ax > l$ for $t \geqslant 0$ and such that the trajectory $\varphi(p, t)$ remains in the region $\{x > 0,\ y - f(x) > 0,\ z > x\}$. Thus, because z is bounded, y is also bounded in this region, and the trajectory $\varphi(p, t)$ is bounded for $t > 0$ in the region $\{x > 0,\ y - f(x) > 0,\ z - x > 0\}$.

Hence, it follows that $\varphi(p, t)$ leaves this region as time increases. Indeed, assume to the contrary that $\varphi(p, t) \in \{x > 0,\ y - f(x) > 0,\ z - x > 0\}$ for all $t \geqslant 0$. Then, because of boundedness, the trajectory $\varphi(p, t)$ has an ω-limit point q. Since, in the region under discussion, x increases along $\varphi(p, t)$, it is clear that $x(q) > 0$. Moreover, it follows from the fact that z increases along $\varphi(p, t)$ that $\lim_{t \to \infty} z(\varphi(p, t)) = z(q)$. But $x(q) > 0$ implies that for sufficiently small $t > 0$ we have $z(\varphi(q, t)) < z(q)$, and then it follows from the properties of ω-limit sets that there exists a $\tau > 0$ such that $z(\varphi(p, \tau)) < z(q)$. This last inequality contradicts the fact that the function $z(\varphi(p, t))$ is monotonic and the relationship $z(\varphi(p, t)) \to z(q)$ as $t \to \infty$. The contradiction obtained shows that $\varphi(p, t)$ leaves the region $\{x > 0,\ y - f(x) > 0,\ z > x\}$ when $t > 0$.

By hypothesis, the trajectory $\varphi(p, t)$ does not intersect the surface $y - f(x) = 0$; consequently, $\varphi(p, t)$ intersects the plane $z - x = 0$ when $t = t_1$ and enters the region $\{x > 0,\ y - f(x) > 0,\ z - x < 0,\ z > 0\}$. In this region, y and z are bounded along the trajectory $\varphi(p, t)$, because they are positive and decrease. We will now show that, in this region, x is also bounded on $\varphi(p, t)$. Indeed, because z decreases and x increases, we have in this region the inequality

$$z - x < l_1 < 0, \qquad (20.17)$$

where l_1 is some constant. It follows then from Eq. (20.12) and the fact that y is bounded in the region $\{x > 0,\ y - f(x) > 0,\ z - x < 0\}$, that x is bounded in the region under consideration. Thus, all coordinates of the trajectory $\varphi(p, t)$ are bounded and vary monotonically with time in the region under discussion, so that the trajectory $\varphi(p, t)$ can not lie in this region for all $t > t_1$, and so, as time increases, it leaves it.

The trajectory $\varphi(p, t)$ can not intersect the plane $z - x = 0$, because x increases and z decreases along $\varphi(p, t)$ in the region $\{x > 0, y > f(x), z < x, z > 0\}$ as time increases. Also, $\varphi(p, t)$ cannot intersect the plane $x = 0$, because x increases when $y > f(x)$. As a result, when $t = t_2 > t_1$ the trajectory $\varphi(p, t)$ intersects either the plane $z = 0$ or the surface $y - f(x) = 0$. In the second case, the lemma is proved. If, however, $\varphi(p, t)$ intersects the plane $t = t_2$ when $z = 0$, it enters the region $\{x > 0, y - f(x) > 0\ z < 0\}$. But then, as we can see from the proof of Lemma 20.1, the trajectory $\varphi(p, t)$ intersects the surface $y - f(x) = 0$ when $t = t_3 > t_2$ and enters the region $\{x > 0, y - f(x) < 0\}$, which completes the proof of Lemma 20.3.

Remark. Obviously, the lemma is also true when $p \in \{x \geqslant 0, y - f(x) \geqslant 0, z - x > 0\}$.

Lemma 20.4. If $p \in \{x < 0, y - f(x) < 0\}$, then the trajectory $\varphi(p, t)$ intersects the surface $y - f(x) = 0$ when $t > 0$ and enters the region $\{x < 0, y - f(x) > 0\}$.

The proof of this lemma is analogous to the proof of Lemma 20.3.

Lemma 20.5. If $\varphi(p, t) \in \{x > 0, y - f(x) \leqslant 0, z > 0\}$ for all $t \geqslant 0$, then $\varphi(p, t)$ approaches the coordinate origin as $t \to +\infty$.

Proof. Since the x- and z-coordinates of $\varphi(p, t)$ decrease as time increases, they are also bounded on this trajectory for $t \geqslant 0$.

Set

$$g_1 = \max f(x) \quad \text{for} \quad 0 \leqslant x \leqslant x(p). \tag{20.18}$$

Then, since the trajectory $\varphi(p, t)$ is contained in the region $\{x > 0, y - f(x) \leqslant 0, z > 0\}$ when $t \geqslant 0$, the y-coordinate is bounded from above by some number g_1. Moreover, from Eq. (20.15), the boundedness of x and z, and the fact that x monotonically decreases along the trajectory $\varphi(p, t)$ as time increases, it follows that the y-coordinate of $\varphi(p, t)$ is also bounded from below for $t \geqslant 0$. Thus, the trajectory $\varphi(p, t)$ is positive Lagrange-stable, and, consequently, has an ω-limit point q with coordinates x_0, y_0, and z_0. We will show that $x_0 = y_0 = z_0 = 0$. Indeed, because z monotonically decreases as time increases along the trajectory $\varphi(p, t)$ when $t \geqslant 0$, we must have

$$z(\varphi(p, t)) > z_0 \quad \text{for} \quad t \geqslant 0 \tag{20.19}$$

and

$$\lim_{t \to +\infty} z(\varphi(p, t)) = z_0. \tag{20.20}$$

Since the point q is an ω-limit point for the trajectory $\varphi(p, t)$, it lies inside or on the boundary of the region containing the trajectory

$\varphi(p, t)$ for $t \geqslant 0$; as a result, $q \in \{x \geqslant 0\ \ y - f(x) \leqslant 0,\ z \geqslant 0\}$. Since the trajectory $\varphi(q, t)$ is an ω-limit trajectory for $\varphi(p, t)$, we have $\varphi(q, t) \in \{x \geqslant 0,\ y - f(x) \leqslant 0,\ z \geqslant 0\}$. Now assume that the point q does not coincide with the equilibrium state (0, 0, 0) of system (20.5). But then it is easy to see from the foregoing discussion that for any $t_1 > 0$ we have

$$z(\varphi(q, t_1)) < z_0. \tag{20.21}$$

Since the trajectory $\varphi(q, t)$ is an ω-limit trajectory for $\varphi(p, t)$, it follows from inequality (20.21) that there exists a $\tau > 0$ such that the inequality

$$z(\varphi(p, \tau)) < z_0 \tag{20.22}$$

holds.

This last inequality contradicts inequality (20.19), which shows that the point q coincides with the coordinate origin. Thus, the trajectory $\varphi(p, t)$ has the point $x = y = z = 0$ as its only ω-limit point, which proves the lemma.

A similar proof holds for:

Lemma 20.6. If $\varphi(p, t) \in \{x < 0,\ y - f(x) \geqslant 0,\ z < 0\}$ *for* $t \geqslant 0$, *then* $\varphi(p, t)$ *approaches the coordinate origin as* $t \to +\infty$.

Theorem 20.1. Any positive half-trajectory of system (20.5) that lies entirely either within the half-space $x \geqslant 0$ *or within the half-space* $x \leqslant 0$ *approaches the coordinate origin.*

Proof. For definiteness, assume that $\varphi(p, t) \in \{x \geqslant 0\}$ for $t \geqslant 0$. Then it follows from Lemma 20.1 that $\varphi(p, t) \in \{x \geqslant 0,\ z > 0\}$ (provided that p does not coincide with the point (0, 0, 0), a condition which we will assume to be satisfied in the proof that follows). Two cases are possible: either there exists a T such that $\varphi(p, t) \in \{x > 0,\ y - f(x) \leqslant 0,\ z > 0\}$ for $t > T$, or no such T exists. In the first case, the proof can be completed by reference to Lemma 20.5; we will, therefore, consider the second case: Because of Lemma 20.3, there exists a $\theta_1 > 0$ such that $\varphi(p, \theta_1) \in \{x > 0,\ y - f(x) < 0,\ z > 0\}$. Since, by hypothesis, we do not have $\varphi(p, t) \in \{x > 0,\ y - f(x) < 0,\ z > 0\}$ for all $t \geqslant \theta_1$, there exists a $\tau_1 > \theta_1$ such that, on the trajectory $\varphi(p, t)$, we have

$$y(\tau_1) = f(x(\tau_1)). \tag{20.23}$$

In that case, it is clear from the considerations given in the first Paragraph of the present chapter that

$$z(\tau_1) - x(\tau_1) \geqslant 0 \tag{20.24}$$

on the trajectory $\varphi(p, t)$.

By Lemma 20.3, there exists a $\theta_2 > \tau_1 + 1$ such that $\varphi(p, \theta_2) \in \{x > 0,\ y - f(x) < 0,\ z > 0\}$, and for this θ_2 in turn, there exists a $\tau_2 > \theta_2$ such that

$$y(\tau_2) = f(x(\tau_2)), \quad z(\tau_2) - x(\tau_2) = 0. \tag{20.25}$$

Continuing this process, we can find a sequence of times τ_1, τ_2, τ_3, ... such that $\tau_k > \tau_{k-1} + 1$,

$$y(\tau_k) - f(x(\tau_k)) = 0, \tag{20.26}$$

and

$$z(\tau_k) - x(\tau_k) \geqslant 0 \tag{20.27}$$

on the trajectory $\varphi(p, t)$.

Since the trajectory $\varphi(p, t)$ is contained in the half-space $t \geqslant 0$ when $x \geqslant 0$, the z-coordinate of this trajectory decreases as time increases with $t \geqslant 0$, so that we can write

$$z(\tau_k) \leqslant z(p) \tag{20.28}$$

for the trajectory $\varphi(p, t)$. It follows then from (20.27) that

$$x(\tau_k) \leqslant z(p) \tag{20.29}$$

along $\varphi(p, t)$. Now set

$$g_2 = \max f(x) \qquad \text{for} \qquad 0 \leqslant x \leqslant z(p). \tag{20.30}$$

The following inequalities are a consequence of (20.26), (20.18), (20.29) and (20.30):

$$0 \leqslant y(\varphi(p, \tau_k)) \leqslant g_2. \tag{20.31}$$

Inequalities (20.29)-(20.31) imply that the sequence of points $\{\varphi(p, \tau_k)\}$ is bounded, so that it has a limit point q with coordinates x_0, y_0, and z_0.

Since $\tau_k > \tau_{k-1} + 1$, we have $\lim\limits_{k\to\infty} \tau_k = \infty$ as a result, the point q is an ω-limit point for the trajectory $\varphi(p, t)$. We will show that the point q coincides with the coordinate origin. Indeed, because the z-coordinate of the trajectory $\varphi(p, t)$ decreases monotonically as time increases, we must have

$$z(\varphi(p, t)) > z_0 \quad \text{for} \quad t \geqslant 0 \tag{20.32}$$

and

$$\lim_{t\to+\infty} z(\varphi(p, t)) = z_0. \tag{20.33}$$

The trajectory $\varphi(q, t)$ is an ω-limit trajectory for $\varphi(p, t)$, so that we have $\varphi(q, t) \in \{x \geqslant 0, z \geqslant 0\}$ for all t. Now assume that q does not coincide with the coordinate origin. Then there obviously exists a $t_1 > 0$ such that

$$z(\varphi(q, t_1)) < z_0. \tag{20.34}$$

Since the point $\varphi(q, t_1)$ is an ω-limit point for the trajectory $\varphi(p, t)$, there exists a $t_2 > 0$ such that

$$z(\varphi(p, t_2)) < z_0. \tag{20.35}$$

This inequality contradicts inequality (20.32), which shows that the point q coincides with the coordinate origin. Similarly, we can show that any other ω-limit point of the trajectory $\varphi(p, t)$ coincides with the coordinate origin. Consequently, $\varphi(p, t)$ approaches this equilibrium state as $t \to +\infty$. Q.E.D.

3. Here we will discuss the case $a \geqslant 1$. Set

$$f(x) = ax + \alpha(x); \tag{20.36}$$

then inequality (20.8) takes the form

$$\frac{\alpha(x)}{x} > 0 \quad \text{for} \quad x \neq 0. \tag{20.37}$$

We will prove the following:

Lemma 20.7. If $a \geqslant 1$ *and* $p \in \{x \geqslant 0,\ y - f(x) > 0\}$ *the trajectory* $\varphi(p, t)$ *intersects the plane* $x = 0$ *at some* $t \geqslant 0$.

Proof. If $z(p) \leqslant 0$, this lemma follows directly from Lemma 20.1. Now let $z(p) > 0$ and assume initially that $p \in \{x \geqslant 0,\ y - f(x) > 0,\ z - x > 0\}$. As was shown in the proof of Lemma 20.3, the trajectory $\varphi(p, t)$ intersects the plane $z - x = 0$ when $t = t_1 > 0$ and, in that case, inequality (20.17) is satisfied on this trajectory. Thus, if $p \in \{x \geqslant 0,\ y - f(x) > 0,\ z - x > 0\}$ there exists a $t_1 \geqslant 0$ for which the following relationships hold on $\varphi(p, t)$:

$$z(t_1) - x(t_1) \leqslant 0; \tag{20.38}$$

$$y(t_1) - f(x(t_1)) \geqslant 0. \tag{20.39}$$

If, however, $p \in \{x > 0,\ y > f(x),\ z - x \leqslant 0\}$, we set $t_1 = 0$; then (20.38) and (20.39) will also hold on the trajectory $\varphi(p, t_1)$. Inequality (20.8) implies the following inequality holds on $\varphi(p, t)$:

$$y(t_1) \geqslant f(x(t_1)) > ax(t_1). \tag{20.40}$$

If we set

$$f(x(t_1)) - ax(t_1) = h,$$

it follows from (20.40) that

$$y(t_1) \geqslant ax(t_1) + h \tag{20.41}$$

on the trajectory $\varphi(p, t)$. We now turn to Eq. (20.16), rewriting it in the form

$$\frac{dy}{dz} = \frac{x}{ax} - \frac{z}{ax}.$$

Since, by hypothesis, $a \geqslant 1$, it follows from the last equation that, when $x > 0$ and $z > 0$, we have the inequality

$$\frac{dy}{dz} < 1. \tag{20.42}$$

Let $T > t_1$ be an artibrary number such that, when $t \in (t_1, T)$, $x > 0$ and $z > 0$ on the trajectory $\varphi(p, t)$. Then inequality (20.42) will be satisfied on the trajectory $\varphi(p, t)$ for $t \in (t_1, T)$. If we integrate this inequality along the trajectory $\varphi(p, t)$ between t_1 and T, we obtain

$$y(\varphi(p, T)) - y(\varphi(p, t_1)) > z(\varphi(p, T)) - z(\varphi(p, t_1))$$

or

$$y(\varphi(p, T)) > z(\varphi(p, T)) + y(\varphi(p, t_1)) - z(\varphi(p, t_1)).$$

Then it follows from (20.38), (20.41), and from the fact that $a \geqslant 1$ that

$$y(\varphi(p, T)) > z(\varphi(p, T)) + h. \tag{20.43}$$

This relationship implies the inequality

$$x(\varphi(p, T)) > 0 \tag{20.44}$$

since, when $y > 0$, the trajectories of system (20.5) intersect the plane $x = 0$ by passing from the half-space $x < 0$ into the half-space $x > 0$.

We will now show that $\varphi(p, t)$ intersects the plane $z = 0$ at some $t > t_1$. Indeed, assume the contrary, i.e., assume that $z(\varphi(p, t)) > 0$ for $t > t_1$. But then it follows from (20.44) that $x(\varphi(p, t)) > 0$ for all $t > t_1$ (since T can be any number larger than t_1). It now follows from Theorem 20.1 that the trajectory $\varphi(p, t)$ approaches the coordinate origin as $t \to +\infty$, which is impossible in view of (20.43) and in view of the fact that $z(\varphi(p, t)) > 0$ for $t > t_1$. The contradiction which we have obtained shows that $\varphi(p, t)$ intersects the plane $z = 0$ at $t = t_2 > t_1$. It is also clear that $x(\varphi(p, t)) > 0$ for $t \in [t_1, t_2]$.

By Lemma 20.1, the trajectory $\varphi(p, t)$ intersects the plane $x = 0$. Q.E.D.

If we again assume that $a \geqslant 1$ and $p \in \{x \geqslant 0, y - f(x) > 0\}$, then, by Lemma 20.7, the trajectory $\varphi(p, t)$ will intersect the plane $t > 0$ at some $x=0$. Let t_p be the first point after $t=0$ at which the trajectory $\varphi(p, t)$ intersects the plane $x=0$. Then it follows from the proof of Lemma 20.7 that the inequalities

$$y(t_p)<0, \quad z(t_p)<0 \tag{20.45}$$

hold on the trajectory $\varphi(p, t)$.

Similarly, we can prove:

Lemma 20.8. If $a \geqslant 1$ *and* $p \in \{x \leqslant 0,\ y-f(x)<0\}$ *the trajectory* $\varphi(p, t)$ *intersects the plane* $x=0$ *at some* $t>0$.

The following theorems are corollaries of Lemmas 20.7 and 20.8.

Theorem 20.2. If $a \geqslant 1$ *and* p *lies in the plane* $x=0$, *then the trajectory* $\varphi(p, t)$ *of system (20.5) intersects the plane* $x=0$ *at some* $t>0$.

Theorem 20.3. Assume that: $a \geqslant 1$; p *is a point distinct from* $x=y=z=0$ *and lies in the plane* $x=0$; $t_1>0$ *is the first point after* $t=0$ *at which the trajectory* $\varphi(p, t)$ *intersects the plane* $x=0$; $t_2>t_1$ *is the first point after* t_1 *at which* $\varphi(p, t)$ *intersects the plane* $x=0$. *Then one of the following two cases must hold: Either* $y(t_1)>0$ *and* $z(t_1)>0$, *whereupon* $y(t_2)<0$ *and* $z(t_2)<0$; *or* $y(t_1)<0$ *and* $z(t_1)<0$, *whereupon* $y(t_2)>0$ *and* $z(t_2)>0$.

21. ON THE BOUNDEDNESS OF SOLUTIONS

As above, consider system (20.5), assuming that the function $f(x)$ satisfies condition (20.8), is continuously differentiable for all x and has the additional property that there exist $\varepsilon>0$ and $x_0>0$ such that

$$\alpha'=f'(x)-a>\varepsilon \quad \text{for} \quad |x| \geqslant x_0. \tag{21.1}$$

We will now show that, under these conditions, all solutions of system (20.5) are bounded when $t \to +\infty$, and we will present a more detailed discussion with regard to the behavior of the trajectories of this system.

1. Consider the function

$$v=\frac{1}{2}(z-x)^2+\frac{1}{2}y^2-y\alpha(x)+ax\alpha(x)+ \\ +\frac{1}{2}\alpha^2(x)-a\int_0^x \alpha(x)\,dx. \tag{21.2}$$

The derivative of this function with respect to t, obtained with the aid of the differential equations of system (20.5), is, as we can easily show, equal to

$$\dot{v} = -\alpha'(x)(y - f(x))^2. \tag{21.3}$$

When $|x| \geqslant x_0$, this derivative is nonpositive, i.e., for such x the function v does not increase along the solutions of system (20.5).

We introduce the following notation: Let $D \geqslant 0$ be such that

$$D \geqslant -\min \alpha'(x) \quad \text{for} \quad |x| \leqslant x_0. \tag{21.4}$$

In addition, let

$$x_1 = \frac{10D + 2\varepsilon}{\varepsilon} x_0, \quad x_2 = 10x_1, \tag{21.5}$$

$$m = \max_{|x| \leqslant x_2} |f(x) + x|, \quad R = \frac{200m^2}{x_0}. \tag{21.6}$$

We will prove the following lemma:

Lemma 21.1. Assume that: Condition (21.1) is satisfied; p is a point in the region $\{0 \leqslant x < x_0,\ z \geqslant -x_0,\ y \geqslant f(x)\}$; *and*

$$v(p) \geqslant \frac{1}{2} R^2, \tag{21.7}$$

where v is the function of the phase-space coordinates which was defined by Eq. (21.2). Then the trajectory $\varphi(p, t)$ of system (20.5) intersects the plane $x = x_1$ at $t = t_1 > 0$ (by t_1 we mean the first point after $t = 0$ at which $\varphi(p, t)$ intersects the plane $x = x_1$), and the following inequalities hold on the trajectory $\varphi(p, t)$:

$$y - f(x) > 0 \quad \text{for} \quad t \in (0, t_1] \tag{21.8}$$

and

$$v(\varphi(p, 0)) = v(p) > v(\varphi(p, t_1)). \tag{21.9}$$

Proof. In proving this lemma, we will consider only one trajectory of system (20.5), $\varphi(p, t)$. In this connection, we will sometimes treat the various functions of the phase-space coordinates simply as functions of time t. Thus, for example, $v(t)$ is the value of the function v at the point $\varphi(p, t)$. In proving the lemma, we will consider two different cases:

$$\text{I.} \ \frac{y(p)}{z(p)} \geqslant 1, \qquad \text{II.} \ \frac{y(p)}{z(p)} < 1.$$

Case I. From inequality (21.7) together with the form of the function v [Eq. (21.2)], the generalized Hurwitz criterion (20.8), and Eq. (20.36), it follows that

$$y(p) > 100m. \tag{21.10}$$

Thus, it follows that for sufficiently small $t > 0$ we have the inequality

$$y(t) > f(x(t)). \tag{21.11}$$

The first equation of system (20.5) implies that x increases for such values of t. We will now show that, as long as $x \leqslant x_1$, the inequality

$$y > 0.9y(p) \tag{21.12}$$

holds on $\varphi(p, t)$.

From inequality (21.10) and the notation (21.6), it follows that inequality (21.12) implies inequality (21.11). Thus, if we can prove inequality (21.12), we will have proved that $\varphi(p, t)$ intersects the plane $x = x_1$ at $t = t_1$, as well as relationship (21.8). Let us prove inequality (21.12). If $z(p) > x(p)$ and if the trajectory $\varphi(p, t)$, prior to its intersection of the plane $x = x_1$, does not intersect the plane $z - x = 0$, inequality (21.12) will follow immediately from the fact that y increases along all trajectories of system (20.5) when $z - x > 0$. We now assume that $z(p) - x(p) \leqslant 0$, or that $z(p) - x(p) > 0$, but the trajectory $\varphi(p, t)$ intersects the plane $z - x = 0$ prior to its intersection the plane $x = x_1$. We will prove inequality (21.12) by contradiction. Assume that there exists a $t^* > 0$ such that

$$y(t^*) = 0.9y(p) \tag{21.13}$$

$$x(t^*) \leqslant x_1 \tag{21.14}$$

and such that inequality (21.12) is satisfied when $t \in [0, t^*)$, i.e., we assume that t^* is the first point at which inequality (21.12) does not hold.

Consider the equation

$$\frac{dz}{dx} = -\frac{ax}{y - f(x)}. \tag{21.15}$$

This, in combination with inequalities (21.10) and (21.12), implies that

$$\frac{dz}{dx} = -\frac{ax}{89m}$$

on $\varphi(p, t)$ when $t \in [0, t^*)$, so that

$$\frac{dz}{dx} > -\frac{1}{89}. \tag{21.16}$$

We now integrate the last inequality along the trajectory $\varphi(p, t)$ from 0 to t^*, thus obtaining, in virtue of (21.14), the inequality

$$z(0) - z(t^*) < \frac{x_1}{89}. \tag{21.17}$$

Now consider Eq. (20.15); from this, together with inequalities (21.12) and (21.17) and the fact that, by hypothesis, $z(p) = z(0) \geqslant -x_0$, it follows that

$$\frac{dy}{dx} > -\frac{x_0 + \frac{1}{89}x_1 + x_1}{89m} > \frac{1}{20}.$$

Integrating this inequality along $\varphi(p, t)$ over the interval $0 < t < t^*$, we find that

$$y(p) - y(t^*) < \frac{x_1}{20}. \tag{21.18}$$

Since $x_1 < m$, this last inequality contradicts Eq. (21.13), which proves inequality (21.12).

We will now prove inequality (21.9). We have

$$v(t_1) - v(0) = \int_{x(p)}^{x_0} \frac{dv}{dx}\,dx + \int_{x_0}^{x_1} \frac{dv}{dx}\,dx,$$

from which, together with (21.3), it follows that

$$v(t_1) - v(0) = -\int_{x(p)}^{x_0} \alpha'(x)(y - f(x))\,dx - \\ - \int_{x_0}^{x_1} \alpha'(x)(y - f(x))\,dx. \tag{21.19}$$

We will now estimate the integrals in the right side of this equation. In order to do so, we first estimate $y(t)$ in the interval $0 \leqslant t \leqslant t_1$. From Eq. (20.15) it follows that

$$\frac{dy}{dx} < \frac{|z - x|}{y - m}.$$

Since, for $t \in [0, t_1]$, z decreases along $\varphi(p, t)$ when time increases, and inequality (21.12) is satisfied on $\varphi(p, t)$, it follows from the last inequality and from the hypothesis of case I that

$$\frac{dy}{dx} < 2.$$

Integrating this inequality and utilizing inequality (21.10), we find that

$$y(t) < 2y(p) \quad \text{for} \quad t \in [0,\ t_1].$$

Using this inequality, we can write

$$\int_{x(p)}^{x_0} \alpha'(x)(y - f(x))\,dx > -2Dy(p)\,x_0. \tag{21.20}$$

Moreover, inequalities (21.10) and (21.12) yield

$$\int_{x_0}^{x_1} \alpha'(x)(y - f(x))\,dx > \frac{1}{2}\varepsilon y(p)(x_1 - x_0),$$

which, together with (21.5), leads to

$$\int_{x_0}^{x_1} \alpha'(x)(y - f(x))\,dx > 5Dy(p)\,x_0. \tag{21.21}$$

Inequality (21.9) is a consequence of Eq. (21.19) and inequalities (21.20) and (21.21).

Case II. As in case I, it is easy to establish the inequality

$$z(p) > 105\,\frac{m^2}{x_0}. \tag{21.22}$$

We will show that, in the case under discussion, the trajectory $\varphi(p,\ t)$ first intersects the plane $x = x_1$, and only then intersects the plane $z - x = 0$. This will clearly prove the existence of a time t_1 and inequality (21.8). We assume, contrary to our assertion, that there exists a $t^* > 0$ such that

$$z(t^*) - x(t^*) = 0, \tag{21.23}$$

$$x(t^*) \leqslant x_1 \tag{21.24}$$

and that the inequality

$$z(t) - x(t) > 0 \tag{21.25}$$

holds when $t \in [0,\ t^*)$.

Thus, t^* is the first time after $t = 0$ at which inequality (21.25) is violated; (when $t = 0$ inequality (21.25) holds, as (21.22) implies). It follows from Eq. (21.23) and inequality (21.22) that there exists a $t^{**} \in (0, t^*)$ such that

$$z(0) - z(t^{**}) = m. \tag{21.26}$$

Consider the equation

$$\frac{dy}{dz} = -\frac{z-x}{ax}. \tag{21.27}$$

From (21.26), (21.27) and (21.22), it follows that the inequality

$$\frac{dy}{dz} < -100$$

holds on the trajectory $\varphi(p, t)$ for $t \in (0, t^{**})$. Integrating this inequality along the trajectory $\varphi(p, t)$ from $t=0$ to $t=t^{**}$, we find, in virtue of (21.26), that

$$y(t^{**}) > 100m. \tag{21.28}$$

Since inequality (21.25) holds in the interval $t^{**} < t < t^{*}$, $y(t)$ increases in this interval, and, consequently, the last inequality yields

$$y(t) > 100m \quad \text{for} \quad t \in [t^{**}, t^{*}]. \tag{21.29}$$

Equation (21.15) and inequality (21.27) imply the following inequality on the trajectory $\varphi(p, t)$ for $t \in [t^{**}, t^{*}]$:

$$\frac{dy}{dx} > \frac{10m}{x_0}.$$

Integrating this inequality along $\varphi(p, t)$ over the interval $t^{**} < t < t^{*}$ and utilizing (21.24), we find that

$$y(t') - y(0) > 10m$$

which, together with (21.26), shows that

$$z(0) - z(t^{*}) < m + \frac{1}{99}x_1.$$

The last inequality contradicts Eq. (21.23), as well as inequalities (21.22) and (21.24), which shows that, in the case under discussion, the trajectory $\varphi(p, t)$ first intersects the plane $x = x_1$, and only then intersects the plane $z - x = 0$.

We introduce the following notation: As before, let t_0 and t_1 be the times of intersection of $\varphi(p, t)$ with the planes $x = x_0$ and $x = x_1$, respectively, and let $t = t'$ be the time at which $\varphi(p, t)$ intersects the plane $x = 2x_0$. It is clear that $0 \leqslant t_0 < t' < t_1$. We will show that, when $t \in [t', t_1]$, we have the inequality

$$y(t) > 10m. \tag{21.30}$$

Indeed, if there exists a $t^{**} \in [0, t']$ such that Eq. (21.26) holds when $t = t^{**}$, then, as above, we can prove the inequality (21.28), whereupon (21.30) will follow, since $y(t)$ increases with time when $t \in [0, t_1]$. If, however, such a t^{**} does not exist, the inequality

$$z(0) - z(t) < m \tag{21.31}$$

holds when $t \in [0, t']$.

In this case, we prove inequality (21.30) by contradiction. Assume that the inequality

$$y(t) \leqslant 10m \tag{21.32}$$

holds when $t \in [0, t']$. Then Eq. (21.15) and inequalities (21.22) and (21.31) imply that

$$\frac{dy}{dx} > \frac{100m^2}{yx_0},$$

from which, together with (21.32), it follows that

$$\frac{dy}{dx} > \frac{10m}{x_0}$$

on the trajectory $\varphi(p, t)$ when $t \in [0, t']$. Integrating the last inequality along $\varphi(p, t)$ from $t = 0$ to $t = t'$, we find that

$$y(t') - y(0) > 10m.$$

Since, by hypothesis $y(0) > 0$, the last inequality contradicts inequality (21.32), which proves inequality (21.30).

We will now prove inequality (21.9), using Eq. (21.19) for the proof. We first estimate the integrals in the right side of this equation:

$$\int_{x(p)}^{x_0} \alpha'(x)(y - f(x))\,dx > -Dy(t')\,x_0; \tag{21.33}$$

since $y(t)$ increases when $t \in [0, t_1]$;

$$\int_{x_0}^{x_1} \alpha'(x)(y - f(x))\,dx > \varepsilon(y(t') - m)(x_1 - 2x_0).$$

It now follows from (21.30) and (21.5) that

$$\int_{x_0}^{x_1} \alpha'(x)(y - f(x))\,dx > 5Dy(t')\,x_0. \tag{21.34}$$

Inequality (21.9) follows from (21.19), (21.33) and (21.34). Q.E.D.

Lemma 21.2. Assume that condition (21.1) is satisfied and that the point p lies in one of the regions $\{0 \leqslant x \leqslant x_0,\ z \geqslant 0,\ y = f(x),\ v \geqslant 1/2\,R^2\}$ *or* $\{x = 0,\ y \leqslant 0,\ z > 0,\ y/z \geqslant -1,\ v \geqslant 1/2\,R^2\}$, *where, as in Lemma 21.1, v is the function defined by Eq. (21.2). Then the trajectory* $\varphi(p, t)$ *of system (20.5) intersects the plane* $x = x_1$ *at* $t = t_1 < 0$ *(*t_1 *is the first time after* $t = 0$ *at which* $\varphi(p, t)$ *intersects the plane* $x = x_1$ *in the direction of decreasing time), and the following relationships hold on the trajectory* $\varphi(p, t)$

$$y < f(x) \quad \text{for} \quad t \in [t_1, 0), \tag{21.35}$$

$$v(p) < v(\varphi(p, t_1)). \tag{21.36}$$

Proof In proving this lemma we will consider only one trajectory of system (20.5), $\varphi(p, t)$. Thus, as in the proof of Lemma 21.1, the various functions of the coordinates of phase space will be considered as functions of time.

Again, as in the proof of Lemma 21.1, it is easy to prove the inequality

$$z(p) > 105\,\frac{m^2}{x_0}. \tag{21.37}$$

We will show that the trajectory $\varphi(p, t)$ intersects the plane $x = x_1$ at $t = t_1 < 0$. When $t < 0$ and is sufficiently close to zero, the trajectory $\varphi(p, t)$, as we can easily show, lies in the region $\{x > 0,\ y < f(x),\ z > x\}$. The trajectory $\varphi(p, t)$ can leave this region only through the plane $z - x = 0$. But $z(t)$ increases with decreasing time in the region $\{x > 0\}$. It follows then from inequality (21.37) that $\varphi(p, t)$ can intersect the plane $z - x = 0$ only after (in the direction of decreasing time) its intersection of the plane $x = x_1$.

We now assume that the trajectory $\varphi(p, t)$ does not intersect the plane $x = x_1$ when $t < 0$. It is then clear that, for all $t < 0$, the trajectory $\varphi(p, t)$ lies in the region $\{0 < x < x_1,\ y < f(x),\ z - x > 0\}$.

Consider the following function of the phase-space coordinates:

$$w = \frac{1}{2}\,y^2 + \frac{1}{2}\,(z - x)^2. \tag{21.38}$$

The time derivative of this function is easily obtained with the aid of the differential equations of system (20.5):

$$\dot{w} = (z - x)\,\alpha(x). \tag{21.39}$$

From Eq. (21.39) it follows that, in the region $\{x > 0,\ z - x > 0\}$, the function w decreases with time along all trajectories of system (20.5). This implies that, in the region $\{0 < x < x_1,\ y - f(x),\ z - x > 0\}$, the trajectory $\varphi(p, t)$ is bounded when $t < 0$, so that it must approach an equilibrium state other than the coordinate origin as $t \to -\infty$. But system (20.5) has only one equilibrium state, the point $x = y = z = 0$. The contradiction thus obtained shows that the trajectory $\varphi(p, t)$ intersects the plane $x = x_1$ at $t = t_1 < 0$. Inequality (21.35) has also been proved, incidentally.

We now turn to the proof of inequality (21.36). Let t_0 and t' be the times at which the trajectory $\varphi(p, t)$ intersects the planes $x = x_0$ and $x = 2x_0$, respectively. It is clear that $0 \geqslant t_0 > t' > t_1$. We will show that

$$y(t') < -9m. \tag{21.40}$$

Assume to the contrary that

$$y(t') \geqslant -9m.$$

Since $y(t)$ decreases with a decrease in time, it follows from the last inequality that

$$y(t) \geqslant -9m \quad \text{for} \quad t' \leqslant t \leqslant 0. \tag{21.41}$$

From (20.15), (21.37), and (21.41), it follows that, when $0 \leqslant t \leqslant t'$,

$$\frac{dy}{dx} < -10\frac{m}{x_0}$$

on the trajectory $\varphi(p, t)$.

Integrating the last inequality along the trajectory $\varphi(p, t)$ from $t = 0$ to $t = t'$, we find that

$$y(t') - y(0) < -10m. \tag{21.42}$$

But, by hypothesis, $y(0) = y(p) \leqslant f(x(p)) < m$; from this, together with (21.42), it follows that

$$y(t') < -9m.$$

The last inequality contradicts (21.41), which proves inequality (21.40).

We will now prove inequality (21.36). In order to do so, consider Eq. (21.19). First, we estimate the integrals in the right side of this equation:

$$\int_{x(p)}^{x_0} \alpha'(x)(y - f(x))\,dx < D(y(t') - m)\,x_0, \tag{21.43}$$

since $y(t)$ increases with time when $t \in [t_1, 0]$;

$$\int_{x_0}^{x_1} \alpha'(x)(y - f(x))\,dx < \varepsilon y(t')(x_1 - 2x_0).$$

It follows then from (21.5) that

$$\int_{x_0}^{x_1} \alpha'(x)(y-f(x))\,dx < 10Dy(t')\,x_0. \qquad (21.44)$$

From inequalities (21.39), (21.43), and (21.44), it follows that

$$\int_{x(p)}^{x_1} \alpha'(x)(y-f(x))\,dx < 0, \qquad (21.45)$$

which, together with (21.19), implies (21.36). Q.E.D.

Lemma 21.3. Assume that condition (21.1) is satisfied that p *is a point in the region* $\{x=0,\ y<0\,|\,|z|/|y|\leqslant 1,\ v\geqslant 1/2\ R^2\}$, *where, as above,* v *is the function defined by Eq. (21.2).*

Then the trajectory $\varphi(p,t)$ *of system (20.5) intersects the plane* $x=x_1$ *at* $t=t_1<0$ *(*t_1 *is the first point after* $t=0$ *at which* $\varphi(p,t)$ *intercepts the plane* $x=x_1$ *in the direction of decreasing time), and the following relationships hold on the trajectory* $\varphi(p,t)$:

$$y<f(x) \quad \text{for} \quad t\in[t_1,0) \qquad (21.46)$$

and

$$v(p)<v(\varphi(p,t_1)). \qquad (21.47)$$

Proof. As above, in proving this lemma we will consider only one trajectory of system (20.5), $\varphi(p,t)$; we assume, as before, that the various functions of the phase-space coordinates are functions of time.

As in the proofs of the preceding lemmas, here again it is not difficult to prove the inequality

$$y(p)<-100m. \qquad (21.48)$$

We begin by following the motion along the trajectory $\varphi(p,t)$ from the point p in the direction of decreasing time, and we will show that, as long as $x\leqslant x_1$,

$$y<0.9y(p) \qquad (21.49)$$

on $\varphi(p,t)$.

The proof is by contradiction. Assume that, on the trajectory $\varphi(p,t)$, in the direction of decreasing time from the point p, inequality (21.49) does not hold for some $x\leqslant x_1$. Since inequality (21.49) does hold for $t=0$, there exists a $t^*<0$ such that

$$y(t^*)=0\,9y(p) \qquad (21.50)$$

$$x(t^*) \leqslant x_1 \tag{21.51}$$

and

$$y(t) < 0.9y(p) \quad \text{for} \quad t \in (t^*, 0], \tag{21.52}$$

$$x(t) \leqslant x_1 \quad \text{for} \quad t \in [t^*, 0]. \tag{21.53}$$

Consider Eq. (20.15). From this equation, inequalities (21.59) and (21.48), and the fact that $z(t)$ increases as time decreases with $t \in [t^*, 0]$, it follows that, when $t \in [t^*, 0]$, the inequality

$$\frac{dy}{dx} < 2$$

holds on the trajectory $\varphi(p, t)$. Integrating this inequality along $\varphi(p, t)$ from $t=0$ to $t=t^*$ and using inequalities (21.51) and (21.53), we find that

$$y(t^*) - y(0) < 2x_1. \tag{21.54}$$

Inequalities (21.48) and (21.54) contradict Eq. (21.50), which proves inequality (21.49).

We will now show that the trajectory $\varphi(p, t)$ intersects the plane $x = x_1$ at $t = t_1 < 0$. Assume that this is not so. Then $\varphi(p, t)$ will be contained in the region $\{0 < x < x_1, \ y < 0.9y(p)\}$ for all $t < 0$. We will show that $\varphi(p, t)$ is then bounded for $t < 0$. If $\varphi(p, t)$ is contained in the region $\{z - x > 0\}$ for all $t < 0$, then the boundedness of the trajectory $\varphi(p, t)$ for $t < 0$ can be proved, as in the proof of Lemma 21.2, by considering the function w defined by Eq. (21.38).

Assume that there exists at least one time $t' < 0$ such that the point $\varphi(p, t')$ is contained in the region $\{0 < x \leqslant x_1, \ y < 0.9y(p), \ z - x \leqslant 0\}$. Then the trajectory $\varphi(p, t)$ will lie in this region for all $t < t'$. Indeed, it can leave this region only through the plane $z - x = 0$, but, as inequality (20.10) shows, for $x > 0$ and $y < 0$ all trajectories of system (20.5) intersect the plane $z - x = 0$ by passing, as time decreases, from the region $\{z - x > 0\}$ into the region $\{z - x < 0\}$. Thus, for $t < t'$, the trajectory $\varphi(p, t)$ lies in the region $\{0 < x \leqslant x_1, \ y < 0.9y(p), \ z - x < 0\}$. In this region, $z(t)$ increases with a decrease in time, and is bounded above by x_1, while $y(t)$ increases and is negative. Thus, for $t < 0$, the trajectory $\varphi(p, t)$ is bounded, and, for sufficiently small t, lies entirely either in region $\{0 < x \leqslant x_1, \ y - f(x) < 0, \ z - x > 0\}$ or in region $\{0 < x \leqslant x_1, \ y - f(x) < 0, \ z - x < 0\}$. Consequently, as $t \to -\infty$, the trajectory $\varphi(p, t)$ approaches an equilibrium state of system (20.5) other than the point $x = y = z = 0$. This contradicts the fact that system (20.5) has only one equilibrium state, and shows that, when $t = t_1 < 0$, the trajectory $\varphi(p, t)$ intersects the plane $x = x_1$. Inequality (21.46) follows from inequality (21.49).

We will now obtain a lower bound for $y(t)$ on the interval $t_1 \leqslant t \leqslant 0$. From Eq. (21.15) and inequalities (21.48) and (21.49), it follows that, when $t \in [t_1, 0]$,

$$\frac{dz}{dx} < \frac{1}{90}$$

on the trajectory $\varphi(p, t)$. Integrating this inequality along $\varphi(p, t)$ from $t=0$ to $t=t_1$, we find that

$$z(t_1) - z(0) < \frac{1}{90} x_1. \tag{21.55}$$

From Eq. (20.15), inequalities (21.48), (21.49), and (21.55), and the condition $|z(p)|/|y(p)| \leqslant 1$, it follows that the inequality

$$\frac{dy}{dx} > -2$$

holds on $\varphi(p, t)$ when $t \in [t_1, 0]$. Integrating this inequality $\varphi(p, t)$ from $t=0$ to $t=t_1$, we obtain

$$y(t_1) - y(0) > -2x_1,$$

from which it is clear that

$$y(t_1) > -2y(0). \tag{21.56}$$

We will now prove inequality (21.47), and begin by estimating the integrals in the right side of Eq. (21.19). We have

$$\int_0^{x_0} \alpha'(x)(y - f(x))\,dx < -D(2y(p) - m)\,x_0 \tag{21.57}$$

which follows from inequality (21.56).

Inequality (21.49) implies that

$$\int_{x_0}^{x_1} \alpha'(x)(y - f(x))\,dx < 0{,}9\varepsilon y(p)(x_1 - x_0),$$

from which, in combination with (21.5), we find that

$$\int_{x_0}^{x_1} \alpha'(x)(y - f(x))\,dx < 9Dy(p)\,x_0. \tag{21.58}$$

From (21.48), (21.57), and (21.58), it follows that

$$\int_0^{x_1} \alpha'(x)(y - f(x))\,dx < 0, \tag{21.59}$$

and inequality (21.47) follows from inequality (21.59) and Eq. (21.19). Q.E.D.

Lemma 21.4. Assume that condition (21.1) is satisfied and that p *is a point in the region* $\{x=0,\ y<0,\ z<0,\ y/z \leqslant 1,\ v \geqslant 1/2\, R^2\}$, *where, as above,* v *is the function (of the phase-space coordinates) defined by Eq. (21.2). Moreover, assume that there exists a* $t_2 < 0$ *such that the following relationships hold on the trajectory* $\varphi(p, t)$:

$$x(t_2) = x_2; \tag{21.60}$$

$$y - f(x) < 0 \quad \text{for} \quad t \in [t_2, 0]. \tag{21.61}$$

Then the trajectory $\varphi(p, t)$ *intersects the plane* $x = x_1$ *at* $t = t_1 \in (t_2, 0)$ *and the following inequality holds:*

$$v(p) < v(\varphi(p, t_1)). \tag{21.62}$$

Proof. In the proof, we will confine our interest to only one trajectory of system (20.5), the trajectory $\varphi(p, t)$, and, as above, we will consider the functions of the phase-space coordinates simply as functions of time. Set $\xi = 9x_1$. In virtue of conditions (21.60) and (21.61), we can assert that there exist times t_0, t_1, and t' such that

$$x(t_0) = x_0,\ x(t_1) = x_1,\ x(t') = \xi, \tag{21.63}$$

and that these times are unique in the time interval $(t_2, 0)$. It is clear that $t_2 < t' < t_1 < t_0 < 0$. It follows from the conditions $v \geqslant 1/2\, R^2$ and $y(p)/z(p) \leqslant 1$, combined with the notation (21.6) that

$$z(p) < -100\frac{m^2}{x_0}. \tag{21.64}$$

We will now show that the following inequality holds in the interval $t \in [t_2, 0]$

$$z(t) < 0.9z(0). \tag{21.65}$$

We will prove this inequality by contradiction. Assume that there exists a $t^* \in [t_2, 0]$ such that

$$z(t^*) = 0.9z(0), \tag{21.66}$$

and that inequality (21.65) is satisfied when $t \in (t^*, 0]$. It follows from inequality (21.65) that $z(t) < 0$ when $t \in [t^*, 0]$ and, as the second equation of system (20.5) and Eq. (21.39) show, both $y(t)$ and $w(t)$ increase as time decreases when $t \in [t^*, 0]$. We, therefore, have

$$w(0) \leqslant w(t^*).$$

It follows from the very form of the function w that

$$z^2(0) + y^2(0) \leqslant [z(t^*) - x(t^*)]^2 + y^2(t^*). \qquad (21.67)$$

But $y(t)$ increases with decreasing time when $t \in [t^*, 0]$; moreover, it follows from condition (21.61) that $y(t) < m$ when $t \in [t^*, 0]$. Hence, it follows from inequality (21.67) that

$$z^2(0) \leqslant [z(t^*) - m]^2 + m^2,$$

which, together with Eq. (21.66), implies that

$$z^2(0) \leqslant 0{,}81 z^2(0) - 1{,}8\, z(0)m + 2m^2. \qquad (21.68)$$

This inequality contradicts inequality (21.64), which proves inequality (21.65).

We will now show that when $t \in [t', 0]$

$$y(t) < -8m. \qquad (21.69)$$

Since $y(t)$ decreases as time increases when $t \in [t_2, 0]$, inequality (21.69) will be proved if we establish the inequality

$$y(t') < -8m, \qquad (21.70)$$

which we will now proceed to prove.

If we assume that the preceding inequality is not satisfied, we have, for $t \in [t_2, t']$, the inequality

$$y(t) \geqslant -8m. \qquad (21.71)$$

From (20.15), (21.64), (21.65), and (21.71), it follows that the inequality

$$\frac{dy}{dx} > \frac{90\,\frac{m^2}{x_0}}{9m} = 10\,\frac{m}{x_0}$$

holds on the trajectory $\varphi(p, t)$ when $t \in [t_2, t']$.

Integrating this inequality along $\varphi(p, t)$ from $t = t'$ to $t = t_2$, we find that

$$y(t_2) - y(t') > 10\frac{m}{x_0}(x_2 - \xi) > 10m.$$

Since, by hypothesis, $y(t_2) \leqslant f(x(t_2)) \leqslant m$, it follows from the last inequality that

$$y(t') < -9m.$$

This inequality contradicts inequality (21.71), which proves inequality (21.70), and therefore (21.69) as well.

From (20.15), (21.64), (21.65), and (21.69), it follows that the inequality

$$\frac{dy}{dx} > \frac{z(p)}{2y}$$

holds on the trajectory $\varphi(p, t)$ when $t \in [t', 0]$. Multiplying this inequality by $2y < 0$ and integrating the inequality thus obtained along the trajectory $\varphi(p, t)$ from $t = 0$ to $t = t'$, we obtain

$$y^2(0) - y^2(t') > -z(p)\xi,$$

which, in turn, yields

$$y(0) < -\sqrt{-z(p)}\sqrt{\xi}. \tag{21.72}$$

On the other hand, (20.15), (21.64), (21.65), and (21.69) imply that the inequality

$$\frac{dy}{dx} < \frac{2z(p)}{y}$$

holds on the trajectory $\varphi(p, t)$ when $t \in [t', 0]$.

Multiplying this inequality by $y < 0$ and integrating from t_1 to 0, we find that

$$y^2(0) - y^2(t_1) < -4z(p)x_1$$

or

$$[y(0) - y(t_1)][y(0) + y(t_1)] < -4z(p)x_1.$$

It follows then from (21.72) and (21.69) that

$$y(t_1) - y(0) < \frac{4\sqrt{-z(p)x_1}}{\sqrt{\xi}},$$

which, together with (21.72), implies that

$$y(t_1) - y(0) < -\frac{4y(0)}{\xi} x_1.$$

Since $\xi = 9x_1$, the last inequality yields

$$y(t_1) < \frac{1}{2} y(0). \quad (21.73)$$

We will now prove inequality (21.62); for this purpose, we will use Eq. (21.19) and estimate the integrals in the right side of this equation. We have

$$\int_0^{x_0} \alpha'(x)(y - f(x))\,dx < D(y(0) - m)\,x_0. \quad (21.74)$$

On the other hand,

$$\int_{x_0}^{x_1} \alpha'(x)(y - f(x))\,dx < \varepsilon y(t_1)(x_1 - x_0).$$

It follows then from (21.73) and (21.5) that

$$\int_{x_0}^{x_1} \alpha'(x)(y - f(x))\,dx < 5Dy(0)\,x_0. \quad (21.75)$$

Inequalities (21.74), (21.75), and (21.69) yield the inequality

$$\int_0^{x_1} \alpha'(x)(y - f(x))\,dx < 0. \quad (21.76)$$

Inequality (21.62) follows from Eq. (21.19) and inequality (21.76). Q.E.D.

Lemma 21.5. Assume that: Condition (21.1) is satisfied; p is a point in the region $\{x = 0,\ y < 0,\ z < 0,\ y/z \leqslant 1,\ v \geqslant 1/2\ R^2\}$, where, as before, v is the function defined by Eq. (21.2); there does not exist a $t_2 < 0$ for which relationships (21.60) and (21.61) are satisfied on the trajectory $\varphi(p, t)$ of system (20.5). Then there exists a $T < 0$, such that

$$x(T) = 0, \quad (21.77)$$

$$x(t) > 0, \quad z(t) < 0 \quad \text{for} \quad t \in (T, 0) \quad (21.78)$$

on the trajectory $\varphi(p, t)$.

Proof. We begin by considering motion along the trajectory $\varphi(p, t)$ from the point p in the direction of decreasing time. We will show that as long as the trajectory $\varphi(p, t)$ lies in the region $\{0 \leqslant x \leqslant x_2,\ y \leqslant 10m\}$, the inequality

$$z(t) < 0.9z(p) \tag{21.79}$$

is satisfied on it. Note that under the conditions of the lemma, inequality (21.64) is satisfied. We will prove inequality (21.79) by contradiction. Assume that there exists a $t^* < 0$ such that

$$z(t^*) = 0.9z(p) \tag{21.80}$$

and $\varphi(p, t) \in \{0 \leqslant x \leqslant x_2,\ y \leqslant 10m,\ z \leqslant 0.9z(p)\}$ when $t \in [t^*, 0]$. It is clear that z and w increase along $\varphi(p, t)$ as time decreases when $t \in [t^*, 0]$, so that we have

$$w(0) \leqslant w(t^*).$$

From the form of the function w, it follows that

$$z^2(p) + y^2(p) \leqslant [z(t^*) - x(t^*)]^2 + y^2(t^*). \tag{21.81}$$

But y increases with decreasing time on $\varphi(p, t)$ when $t \in [t^*, 0]$; moreover, by hypothesis, $y \leqslant 10m$, so that inequality (21.81) yields the inequality

$$z^2(p) \leqslant [z(t^*) - m]^2 + 100m^2.$$

It now follows from (21.80) that

$$z^2(p) \leqslant 0.81z^2(p) - 1.8z(p)m + 101m^2.$$

This inequality contradicts inequality (21.64), which proves inequality (21.79).

We will now show that there exists a $t = t_1 < 0$ such that, on $\varphi(p, t)$,

$$y(t_1) = f(x(t_1)), \tag{21.82}$$

and $\varphi(p, t) \in \{0 \leqslant x \leqslant x_2,\ y < f(x)\}$ when $t \in (t_1, 0]$. Indeed, because of (21.79), y increases as time decreases along $\varphi(p, t)$ in the region $\{0 \leqslant x \leqslant x_2,\ y < f(x)\}$; moreover, z increases, and, because of (21.79), is bounded. Thus, the trajectory $\varphi(p, t)$ leaves the region $\{0 \leqslant x \leqslant x_2,\ y < f(x)\}$ as time decreases. But $\varphi(p, t)$ can not intersect the plane $x = x_2$ when $y < f(x)$ since the time of intersection, $t = t_2$, would then have to satisfy (21.60) and (21.61), so that the trajectory $\varphi(p, t)$ intersects the surface $y - f(x) = 0$ when $t = t_1$, and $\varphi(p, t) \in \{0 \leqslant x \leqslant x_2,\ y < f(x)\}$ when $t \in (t_1, 0)$.

It is easily seen that the trajectory $\varphi(p, t)$ leaves the region $\{0 \leqslant x \leqslant x_2, \ f(x) < y \leqslant 10m\}$ when $t < t_1$. If $\varphi(p, t)$ intersects the plane $x = 0$, then, in virtue of inequality (21.79), the intersection time $t = T < t_1$ satisfies relationships (21.77) and (21.78). Assume that $\varphi(p, t)$ intersects the plane $y = 10m$ at $t = \tau < t_1$ and that $x(\tau) \in [0, x_2)$ in this case. It follows from Eq. (21.15) that as long as the trajectory $\varphi(p, t)$ lies within the region $\{0 \leqslant x \leqslant x_2, \ y \geqslant 10m\}$ the inequality

$$\frac{dz}{dx} > -0.2$$

holds on it. Therefore, for those $t < \tau$ for which $\varphi(p, t)$ lies in $\{x \geqslant 0\}$, the inequality

$$z(t) \leqslant 0.8z(p) \tag{21.83}$$

is satisfied on this trajectory. It follows from Eq. (20.15) that for those $t < \tau$ for which the trajectory $\varphi(p, t)$ lies within the region $\{x \geqslant 0\}$, the points of this trajectory satisfy the inequality

$$\frac{dy}{dx} > \frac{z(p) - m}{9m}.$$

It now follows that for such t the trajectory $\varphi(p, t)$ is bounded. Consequently, it leaves the region $\{x > 0\}$ when $t < \tau$, so that there exists a time $T < 0$ satisfying (21.77) and (21.78). Q.E.D.

Theorem 21.1. Assume that: Condition (21.1) is satisfied; p *is a point in the plane* $x = 0$; *the inequality*

$$z^2(p) + y^2(p) < R^2 \tag{21.84}$$

is satisfied; and, finally, the point $\varphi(p, T)$, *where* $T > 0$, *lies in the plane* $x = 0$. *Then the following inequality holds:*

$$y^2(\varphi(p, T)) + z^2(\varphi(p, T)) < R^2. \tag{21.85}$$

Proof. In proving this theorem we will consider only one trajectory of system (20.5), $\varphi(p, t)$. As above then, we will sometimes consider the various functions of the points in phase space as functions of time.

For definiteness, we assume that $y(p) \geqslant 0$ and, in case $z(p) \leqslant 0$, we assume that $y(p) > 0$. Without loss of generality, we can assume that T is the first time after $t = 0$ at which the trajectory $\varphi(p, t)$ intersects the plane $x = 0$, i.e., that $x(t) > 0$ when $t \in (0, T)$.

We will first consider the case $z(p) \leqslant 0$. It follows from the third equation of system (20.5) that $dz/dt < 0$ when $t \in (0, T)$; therefore, $z(t) < 0$ when $t \in (0, T]$ and, consequently, the function w defined by Eq. (21.38) decreases along $\varphi(p, t)$ for all $t \in (0, T)$, so that

$$w(T) < w(0). \tag{21.86}$$

Inequality (21.85) follows from the definition of the function w and inequality (21.86).

Now assume that $z(p) > 0$. Initially assume that, in the time interval $0 < t < T$, the trajectory $\varphi(p, t)$ does not intersect the surface $\{y = f(x), 0 < x \leqslant x_0, z - x \geqslant 0\}$ by passing from the region $\{y - f(x) < 0\}$ into the region $\{y - f(x) > 0\}$. As Lemma 20.3 implies, when $t = \tau \in (0, T)$, the trajectory $\varphi(p, t)$ intersects the surface $y - f(x) = 0$ at $t = \tau$ by passing from the region $\{y - f(x) > 0\}$ into the region $\{y - f(x) < 0\}$. If we assume that $x(\tau) \leqslant x_0$, the trajectory $\varphi(p, t)$ will, at some $t \in (0, T)$, intersect the surface $y - f(x) = 0$, passing from the region $\{y - f(x) > 0\}$ into the region $\{y - f(x) < 0\}$ only once at $t = \tau$. Indeed, the trajectory $\varphi(p, t)$ can pass from the region $\{y - f(x) < 0\}$ into the region $\{y - f(x) > 0\}$ only by intersecting the surface $\{y = f(x), 0 < x \leqslant x_0, z - x \geqslant 0\}$, and this is impossible by hypothesis. For $t \in (0, T)$, therefore, $x(t)$ has only one maximum (at $t = \tau$) and, consequently, $x(t) \leqslant x_0$ when $t \in [0, T]$.

We will now show that inequality (21.85) is satisfied in the case under discussion. Assume that inequality (21.85) is not satisfied; then the inequality

$$v(T) \geqslant \frac{1}{2} R^2, \tag{21.87}$$

is satisfied, where v is the point function in phase space defined by Eq. (21.2). If $z(T) \geqslant 0$, or if $z(T) < 0$ and $z(T)/y(T) \leqslant 1$, it follows from inequality (21.87) and Lemmas 21.2 and 21.3 that the trajectory $\varphi(p, t)$ intersects the plane $x = x_1$ at some $t \in (0, T)$, which contradicts the inequality $x(t) \leqslant x_0$ for $0 \leqslant t \leqslant T$. If, on the other hand, $z(T) < 0$ $y(T)/z(T) \leqslant 1$, and the trajectory $\varphi(p, T)$ does not intersect the plane $x = x_2$ when $t \in (0, T)$, then, by Lemma 21.5, $z(0) = z(p) \leqslant 0$, which contradicts the assumption that $z(p) > 0$. This contradiction proves inequality (21.85) for the case under discussion.

Now let $x(\tau) > x_0$. Then the trajectory $\varphi(p, t)$ will intersect the plane $x = x_0$ at $t = t_0 \in (0, T)$. By $t = t_0$ we mean the first time after $t = 0$ at which $\varphi(p, t)$ intersects the plane $x = x_0$. Let $t = t_3$ be the last point prior to $t = T$ at which the trajectory $\varphi(p, t)$ intersects the plane $x = x_0$. From the condition that the trajectory $\varphi(p, t)$ does not intersect the surface $\{y = f(x), 0 < x \leqslant x_0, z - x \geqslant 0\}$ by passing from the region $\{y - f(x) < 0\}$ into the region $\{y - f(x) > 0\}$, it follows that in this case $\varphi(p, t)$ lies entirely in the half-space $\{x \geqslant x_0\}$ when $t \in [t_0, t_3]$, while when $t \in [0, t_0]$ and $t \in [t_3, T]$ it lies in the strip $\{0 \leqslant x \leqslant x_0\}$. We will now prove inequality (21.85) for the case under discussion. If $v(t) < 1/2\, R^2$ when $t \in [0, T]$, inequality (21.85) is an immediate consequence of the form of the function v. We now assume that there exists a time $t = \theta \in [0, T]$ such that $v(\theta) = R^2/2$ and that θ is the first such moment, i.e., we assume that $v(t) < R^2/2$

when $t \in [0, \theta)$. Since $dv/dt \leqslant 0$ when $x \geqslant x_0$, it follows from (21.3) and condition (21.1) of the theorem that the point $\varphi(p, \theta)$ must lie in the strip $\{0 \leqslant x \leqslant x_0\}$.

Thus, one of the following two cases must occur: either $\theta \in [0, t_0]$ or $\theta \in [t_3, T]$, and we will prove inequality (21.85) by contradiction. Assume that it is not satisfied, i.e., assume that

$$v(T) \geqslant \frac{1}{2} R^2. \tag{21.88}$$

Because $z(p) > 0$, this inequality and Lemmas 21.2–21.5 imply that $\varphi(p, t)$ intersects the plane $x = x_1$ at $t = t_2 \in (t_0, t_3)$, and we have the inequality

$$v(t_1) > \frac{1}{2} R^2. \tag{21.89}$$

But $t_1 < t_3 \leqslant \theta$, and, by the definition of θ, $v(t) < R^2/2$ for all $t \in [0, \theta)$. This proves that inequality (21.88) can not hold in the case under discussion, and inequality (21.85) must be satisfied. Now let $\theta \in [0, t_0]$. We will show that now

$$z(\theta) > -x_0. \tag{21.90}$$

Assume that

$$z(\theta) \leqslant -x_0. \tag{21.91}$$

We will show that

$$z(0) \leqslant 0. \tag{21.92}$$

If we first consider the case $|z(\theta)|/y(\theta) \leqslant 1$, it follows from the definition of θ and the form of the function v that

$$y(\theta) > 100m. \tag{21.93}$$

Assume that there exists a $t^* \in [0, \theta)$ such that

$$z(t^*) = 0 \tag{21.94}$$

and

$$z(t) < 0 \quad \text{for} \quad t \in (t^*, \theta]. \tag{21.95}$$

Then $y(t)$ will increase as time decreases, with $t \in (t^*, \theta]$. It now follows from inequality (21.93) and Eq. (21.15) that the following inequality is satisfied on $\varphi(p, t)$ for all $t \in [t^*, \theta]$:

$$\frac{dz}{dx} > -\frac{1}{99}.$$

If we integrate this inequality along the trajectory $\varphi(p, t)$ from $t=t^*$ and to $t=\theta$ and use inequality (21.91), we can see that Eq. (21.94) can not hold, so that inequality (21.92) must hold. We now assume that $y(\theta)/|z(\theta)| \leqslant 1$. In this case, inequality (21.92) can be proved in the same way as in the proof of Lemma 21.5. But inequality (21.92) contradicts the fact that $z(p) > 0$, which proves inequality (21.90). It follows from inequality (21.90) and Lemma 21.1 that the trajectory $\varphi(p, t)$ intersects the plane $x = x_1$ at $t = t_1 \in (t_0, t_3)$, and we have the inequality

$$v(t_1) < v(\theta) = \frac{1}{2} R^2. \tag{21.96}$$

We will now prove inequality (21.85) by contradiction. Assume that inequality (21.88) is satisfied. Then from Lemmas 21.2-21.5 and the fact that $z(p) > 0$, it follows that the trajectory $\varphi(p, t)$ intersects the plane $x = x_1$ at $t = t_2 \in (t_1, t_3)$ and the following inequality holds:

$$v(t_2) > v(T) \geqslant \frac{1}{2} R^2. \tag{21.97}$$

For $t \in [t_1, t_2] \subset [t_0, t_3]$ the trajectory $\varphi(p, t)$ lies in the half-space $\{x \geqslant x_0\}$, as proved above. But, as Eq. (21.2) and condition (21.1) of the theorem show, the function $v(t)$ decreases when $x \geqslant x_0$, from which it follows that

$$v(t_1) \geqslant v(t_2).$$

The last inequality contradicts inequalities (21.96) and (21.97), which proves inequality (21.85).

We now consider the case in which the trajectory $\varphi(p, t)$ intersects the surface $\{y = f(x),\ 0 < x \leqslant x_0,\ z - x \geqslant 0\}$ when $t \in (0, T)$ by passing from the region $\{y - f(x) < 0\}$ into the region $\{y - f(x) > 0\}$. It is not difficult to see that there is a finite number of such intersections. Let $\tau_1, \tau_2, \tau_3, \ldots, \tau_k$ be the sequence of times at which such intersections occur. We have

$$0 < \tau_1 < \tau_2 < \ldots < \tau_k < T. \tag{21.98}$$

In the time intervals $0 < t < \tau_1$, $\tau_1 < t < \tau_2, \ldots, \tau_{k-1} < t < \tau_k$, $\tau_k < t < T$ the trajectory $\varphi(p, t)$ does not intersect the surface $\{y - f(x) = 0,\ 0 < x \leqslant x_0\ z - x \geqslant 0\}$ by passing from the region $\{y - f(x) < 0\}$ into the region $\{y - f(x) > 0\}$. Thus, by means of considerations similar to those presented in the proof of inequality (21.85), we can successively prove the inequalities

$$v(\tau_i) < \frac{1}{2} R^2 \quad (i = 1, 2, \ldots, k), \tag{21.99}$$

and we can use the inequalities $v(\tau_k) < R^2/2$ to derive the inequality $v(T) < R^2/2$, which coincides with (21.85). Q.E.D.

Similarly, we can prove:

Theorem 21.2. Assume that: Condition (21.1) is satisfied; p *is a point in the plane* $x = 0$*; the inequality*

$$y^2(p) + z^2(p) \geqslant R^2 \tag{21.100}$$

is satisfied; the point $\varphi(p, T)$*, where* $T > 0$*, lies in the plane* $x = 0$*. Then*

$$y^2(\varphi(p, T)) + z^2(\varphi(p, T)) < y^2(p) + z^2(p). \tag{21.101}$$

Theorem 21.3. If condition (21.1) is satisfied, then any trajectory of system (20.5) that does not approach the coordinate origin as $t \to +\infty$ *has a point in the region* $\{x = 0,\ y^2 + z^2 < R^2\}$.

Proof. From Theorem 20.1, it follows that there exists a sequence of times

$$t_1 < t_2 < t_3 < \ldots \to +\infty \tag{21.102}$$

such that

$$x(\varphi(p, t_k)) = 0. \tag{21.103}$$

If we assume, contrary to the assertion of the theorem, that the trajectory $\varphi(p, t)$ has no points in the region $\{x = 0,\ y^2 + z^2 < R^2\}$, then

$$y^2(t_k) + z^2(t_k) \geqslant R^2 \tag{21.104}$$

on $\varphi(p, t)$ for all natural k. Then it follows from Theorem 21.2 that

$$\begin{gathered} y^2(t_{k+1}) + z^2(t_{k+1}) < y^2(t_k) + z^2(t_k) < \\ < y^2(t_1) + z^2(t_1) \quad \text{for} \quad k > 1. \end{gathered} \tag{21.105}$$

In virtue of inequality (21.105) and the Bolzano-Weierstrass theorem, we can assume that the sequence $\varphi(p, t_k)$ converges. Set

$$\lim_{k \to +\infty} \varphi(p, t_k) = q. \tag{21.106}$$

It follows from inequality (21.104 that

$$y^2(q) + z^2(q) \geqslant R^2. \tag{21.107}$$

On the other hand, from (21.105) and (21.106), it follows that the inequality

$$y^2(t_k)+z^2(t_k)>y^2(q)+z^2(q) \tag{21.108}$$

holds on $\varphi(p, t)$ for all natural k.

Let t^* be a time such that $\varphi(p, t^*)$ lies in the plane $x=0$. Then, in virtue of Theorem 21.2 and relationships (21.103), (21.104), and (21.108), the inequality

$$y^2(t^*)+z^2(t^*)>y^2(q)+z^2(q) \tag{21.109}$$

holds on $\varphi(p, t)$.

We now consider the trajectory $\varphi(q, t)$ of system (20.5). This trajectory will clearly be an ω-limit trajectory for $\varphi(p, t)$. Assume first that for all $t\geqslant 0$ the trajectory $\varphi(q, t)$ lies in one of the half-spaces $\{x\geqslant 0\}$ or $\{x\leqslant 0\}$; in that case, by Theorem 20.1, the trajectory $\varphi(q, t)$ approaches the coordinate origin. Then the trajectory $\varphi(p, t)$ has points in any neighborhood of the coordinate origin, and it is not difficult to see that this trajectory has points of intersection with the plane $x=0$ arbitrarily close to the coordinate origin.

We will now find a $t'>0$ such that the trajectory $\varphi(q, t)$ will pass from one of the half-spaces, $\{x\geqslant 0\}$ or $\{x\leqslant 0\}$, into the other at $t=t'$. By Theorem 21.2,

$$\varphi(q, t')\in\{x=0,\ y^2+z^2<y^2(q)+z^2(q)\}. \tag{21.110}$$

By the theorem on integral continuity, there exists a t^* such that

$$\varphi(p, t^*)\in\{x=0,\ y^2+z^2<y^2(q)+z^2(q)\}, \tag{21.111}$$

which contradicts inequality (21.109), proving the theorem.

Theorem 21.4. Assume that condition (21.1) is satisfied. Then there exists an $M>0$ *such that for any point* p *in phase space there exists a* T_p *such that when* $t\geqslant T_p$ *the inequalities*

$$|x|<M,\quad |y|<M,\quad |z|<M \tag{21.112}$$

are satisfied on the trajectory $\varphi(p, t)$ of system (20.5).

Proof. Consider an arbitrary trajectory $\varphi(p, t)$ of system (20.5). If $\varphi(p, t)$ approaches the coordinate origin as $t\to+\infty$, the theorem obviously follows. Assume that $\varphi(p, t)$ does not approach the coordinate origin. Then, by Theorem 21.3, the trajectory $\varphi(p, t)$ intersects the disk $\{x=0,\ y^2+z^2<R^2\}$ at $t=T_p$. We set

$$N=\max|f(x)+x|\quad\text{for}\quad |x|\leqslant R, \tag{21.113}$$

and we will show that the inequality

$$|y| < 3N \tag{21.114}$$

is satisfied on the trajectory $\varphi(p, t)$ when $t \geqslant T_p$.

Let $t_1 > T_p$ be the first point after T_p at which the trajectory $\varphi(p, t)$ intersects the plane $x = 0$. We will now show that inequality (21.114) is satisfied on $\varphi(p, t)$ in the interval $T_p \leqslant t \leqslant t_1$. For definiteness, assume that $y(\varphi(p, T_p)) \geqslant 0$, and, if $z(\varphi(p, T_p)) \leqslant 0$, then $y(\varphi(p, T_p)) > 0$. If $z(\varphi(p, T_p)) \leqslant 0$, then, as noted above, y decreases along $\varphi(p, t)$ when $t \in [T_p, t_1]$ and, consequently,

$$|y(\varphi(p, t))| \leqslant \max\{y(\varphi(p, T_p)), |y(\varphi(p, t_1))|\}$$

holds for such t.

From the last inequality and Theorem 21,1, it follows that $|y| < R$ on $\varphi(p, t)$ when $t \in [T_p, t_1]$, and (21.114) follows.

Now assume that $z(\varphi(p, T_p)) > 0$. Since $y^2(\varphi(p, T_p)) + z^2(\varphi(p, T_p)) < R^2$, we have $z(\varphi(p, T_p)) < R$. The maxima of y, as noted in Section 20, lie in the plane $z - x = 0$. But z decreases along $\varphi(p, t)$ when $t \in [T_p, t_1]$, so that intersections of $\varphi(p, t)$ with the plane $z - x = 0$ in the interval $t \in [T_p, t_1]$ have abscissas less than R. We will show that the inequality

$$y < 3N \tag{21.115}$$

holds on $\varphi(p, t)$ when $t \in [T_p, t_1]$.

Indeed, if the inequality $y \leqslant 2N$ holds, then inequality (21.115) is an immediate corollary. If, however, this inequality does not hold, we can easily see that there exists a $t = t^* \in (T_p, t_1)$ such that

$$y(t^*) = 2N, \quad z(t^*) - x(t^*) > 0 \tag{21.116}$$

on the trajectory $\varphi(p, t)$. Then, prior to intersection of the trajectory with the plane $z - x = 0$, the inequality $y \geqslant 2N$ will hold on $\varphi(p, t)$. From this inequality, the fact that $z(\varphi(p, t)) < R$ for $t \in (T_p, t_1)$, and Eq. (20.15), it follows that the inequality

$$\frac{dy}{dx} = \frac{z - x}{y - f(x)} < 1$$

holds for such $t \geqslant t^*$ that $z(\varphi(p, t)) - x(\varphi(p, t)) \geqslant 0$.

Integrating this inequality along $\varphi(p, t)$ from $t = t^*$ to the point of intersection of $\varphi(p, t)$ with the plane $z - x = 0$ and using Eq. (21.116) together with the fact that $x(\varphi(p, t)) < R$ on the plane $z - x = 0$, we obtain inequality (21.115).

We will now show that, when $t \in (T_p, t_1)$, the inequality

$$y > -3N \tag{21.117}$$

holds on the trajectory $\varphi(p, t)$. Since the minima of y are located in the plane $z-x=0$ and since these minima alternate with maxima, it follows from (21.38) and (21.39) that between a maximum and a minimum of y the function w decreases as time increases along $\varphi(p, t)$. It now follows from the form of the function w that the absolute value of y at a minimum is less than its value at the preceding maximum; from this we obtain (21.117), which together with (21.115) yields (21.114).

Since x decreases along the trajectory $\varphi(p, t)$ when $y-f(x)\leqslant 0$, it follows from the generalized Hurwitz criterion, $f(x)>ax$ when $x>0$, that the inequality

$$x<\frac{1}{a}\max y$$

holds on the trajectory $\varphi(p, t)$ when $t\in[T_p, t_1]$. It now follows from (21.114) that, when $t\in[T_p, t_1]$, we have the following inequality on the trajectory $\varphi(p, t)$:

$$|x|<\frac{3}{a}N. \tag{21.118}$$

Since z decreases along $\varphi(p, t)$ in the interval $T_p\leqslant t\leqslant t_1$, it follows from Theorem 21.1 that, in this interval, the following inequality holds on $\varphi(p, t)$:

$$|z|<R. \tag{21.119}$$

Inequalities (21.114), (21.118), and (21.119) have been proved only for the time interval $[T_p, t_1]$, but, in virtue of Theorem 21.1, they are clearly valid for all $t\geqslant T_p$, which proves the theorem.

2. In this paragraph we will consider the case in which $a\geqslant 1$ and condition (21.1) is satisfied, and we will prove a theorem about the distribution of trajectories of (20.5) in this case. Let P denote the region $\{x=0,\ y>0,\ z>0,\ y^2+z^2<R^2\}$.

Consider a periodic motion of system (20.5). As Theorems 20.2, 20.3, and 21.3 imply, this trajectory intersects the region P. We will call a periodic motion of system (20.5) regular if its trajectory has only one point in common with the region P.

Theorem 21.5. Assume that: The inequality $a\geqslant 1$ *holds; the function* $f(x)$ *is continuously differentiable for all real* x, *and there exist positive* ε *and* x_0 *such that condition (21.1) is satisfied. Then, all solutions of system (20.5) will approach the coordinate origin as* $t\to+\infty$ *if and only if system (20.5) has no regular periodic motion.*

Proof. Necessity is obvious; we will prove sufficiency.

Assume that system (20.5) has no regular periodic motion. It is necessary to prove that, in such a case, all trajectories of this system approach the coordinate origin as $t \to +\infty$. Assume, contrary to the theorem, that there exists a point q in phase space such that the trajectory $\varphi(q, t)$ does not approach the coordinate origin as $t \to +\infty$. In virtue of Theorems 20.2, 20.3, and 21.3, we can, without loss of generality, assume that $q \in P$.

Now consider an arbitrary point $p \in P$, $p \neq (0, 0, 0)$, and the trajectory $\varphi(p, t)$ of system (20.5). By Theorems 20.2, 20.3, and 21.1, there exists a $t_p > 0$ such that $\varphi(p, t_p) \in P$. Here t_p denotes the first time after $t = 0$ at which $\varphi(p, t)$ intersects the region P. With each point $p \in \bar{P}$, $p \neq (0, 0, 0)$, we associate the point $\varphi(p, t_p)$, while the point $(0, 0, 0)$ is associated with itself. We denote this transformation of the closed region $\bar{P}$ into itself by T. From the theorem on uniqueness, the theorem on integral continuity, and Theorems 20.2, 20.3, and 21.1, it follows that the transformation T is one-to-one and continuous in both directions. Moreover, it is a direction-preserving mapping. Indeed, consider an arbitrary closed contour l in P, and orient it in some manner. We extend the surface $\varphi(l, t)$ until it intersects $\bar{P}$ after $t = 0$. This intersection will clearly give us the contour Tl. The orientation of the contour Tl will fail to coincide with the orientation of l only if trajectories intersect on the surface $\varphi(l, t)$, which, by the uniqueness theorem, is impossible.

Consider the sequence $T^n q$. For any natural n we have $T^n q \in P$. Since the region P is bounded, the sequence $T^n q$ has limit points in the closed region $\bar{P}$. Assume that q_0 is some limit point of the sequence $T^n q$. It follows from Theorems 20.3 and 21.1 that, if q_0 is on the boundary of P, then it must coincide with the coordinate origin.

The limit set of the sequence $T^n q$ can not consist of the coordinate origin alone, since here, as in the proof of Theorem 21.4, we would be able to show that $\varphi(q, t)$ lies in an arbitrarily small neighborhood of the coordinate origin if t is sufficiently large, i.e., we would be able to show that it approaches the coordinate origin as $t \to +\infty$, but this is impossible, by the choice of q. Thus, the sequence of $T^n q$ has a limit point q_1 other than the coordinate origin, and, consequently, it has a limit point not on the boundary of P, i.e., the sequence of $T^n q$ has a subsequence $T^{n_k} q$ for which

$$\lim_{k \to \infty} T^{n_k} q = q_1 \in P. \tag{21.120}$$

Thus, we have a homeomorphic and direction-preserving mapping T of the plane region P into itself. This transformation is such that there exists a point $q \in P$ for which relationship (21.120) holds. But, by Theorem 12.5, this transformation T has a stationary point p_0 in P (and, consequently, a stationary point other than the coordinate origin). By the definition of T, the trajectory $\varphi(p_0, t)$ is a regular trajectory of system (20.5), which contradicts the hypothesis of the theorem, and completes the proof of sufficiency.

22. PERIODIC SOLUTIONS

In this section we will show that system (20.5) may have periodic solutions even if condition (20.8) is satisfied.

As before [see Eq. (20.36)], we denote by $\alpha(x)$ the function $\alpha(x) = f(x) - ax$. We assume that the function $\alpha(x)$ satisfies the following conditions:

$$hx^2 \leqslant \alpha(x)\,x \leqslant Hx^2 \quad \text{for} \quad 0 \leqslant |x| \leqslant \delta; \tag{22.1}$$

$$0 < \alpha(x)\,x \leqslant Hx^2 \quad \text{for} \quad \delta \leqslant |x| \leqslant \varepsilon; \tag{22.2}$$

$$0 < \alpha(x)\operatorname{sign} x \leqslant \delta^4 \quad \text{for} \quad |x| \geqslant \varepsilon. \tag{22.3}$$

Hereinafter, we will call these conditions the $E(h, H, \delta)$ conditions or, more simply, the E conditions. In the E conditions, ω is subject to the inequalities

$$0 < \varepsilon - \delta < \delta^2, \tag{22.4}$$

while h and H satisfy the inequalities

$$H \geqslant h > \frac{1}{a}. \tag{22.5}$$

The quantity δ is sufficiently small. The last statement is meant in the sense that for fixed h and H there exists a $\delta_0 > 0$ such that for $\delta \leqslant \delta_0$ the corresponding statements are true.

Hereinafter, we will use the symbol $O(\delta^r)$, which, as usual, denotes a quantity for which there exists constants N and δ_0 such that the inequality

$$|O(\delta^r)| \leqslant N\delta^r \quad \text{for} \quad \delta \leqslant \delta_0 \tag{22.6}$$

holds.

Using notation (20.36), system (20.5) can now be rewritten in the form

$$\frac{dx}{dt} = y - ax - \alpha(x), \quad \frac{dy}{dt} = z - x, \quad \frac{dz}{dt} = -ax. \tag{22.7}$$

We carry out the following substitutions in system (22.7):

$$x_1 = a^2x - ay + z; \quad y_1 = z - x, \quad z_1 = y; \tag{22.8}$$

$$x = \frac{x_1 - y_1 + az_1}{a^2 + 1}; \quad y = z_1; \quad z = \frac{x_1 + a^2y_1 + az_1}{a^2 + 1}. \tag{22.9}$$

Thus, we obtain

$$\frac{dx_1}{dt} = -ax_1 - a^2\alpha(x), \quad \frac{dy_1}{dt} = -z_1 + \alpha(x), \quad \frac{dz_1}{dt} = y_1. \tag{22.10}$$

In what follows, we will frequently compare the solutions of system (20.5) with the solutions of the system obtained by setting $\alpha(x)=f(x)-ax=0$ in (20.5), i.e., with the solutions of the system

$$\frac{dx}{dt}=y-ax, \quad \frac{dy}{dt}=z-x, \quad \frac{dz}{dt}=-ax. \tag{22.11}$$

In terms of the variables x_1, y_1, and z_1, this system takes the canonical form

$$\frac{dx_1}{dt}=-ax_1, \quad \frac{dy_1}{dt}=-z_1, \quad \frac{dz_1}{dt}=z_1. \tag{22.12}$$

Hereinafter, $\psi(p, t)$ will denote that trajectory of system (22.11) which, at $t=0$, passes through the point p in phase space. It is easy to see that the general solution of system (22.12) is of the form

$$x_1=x_{10}e^{-at}, \quad y_1=y_{10}\cos t-z_{10}\sin t,$$
$$z_1=y_{10}\sin t+z_{10}\cos t, \tag{22.13}$$

where x_{10}, y_{10}, and z_{10} are the values of the functions x_1, y_1, and z_1 at $t=0$.

Let a and q be two points in phase space, and denote the distance between them by $\rho(p, q)$. Let $\varphi(p, t)$ and $\psi(p, t)$ be trajectories of systems (22.7) and (22.11), respectively. We will study these trajectories over the time interval $0\leqslant t\leqslant T$, where T is fixed. It is well known that

$$\rho(\varphi(p, t), \psi(q, t))=O(\delta)\cdot t+O(\rho(p, q)). \tag{22.14}$$

Owing to the special form of the $E(h, H, \delta)$ conditions, estimate (22.14) can be improved. We will prove:

Lemma 22.1. Assume that: The function $\alpha(x)$ *satisfies the* $E(h, H, \delta)$ *conditions; p and q are points in the region* $\{x=0, |x_1|\leqslant\delta, y=z_1\geqslant 1/2\}$ *and* $\rho(p, q)=O(\delta^2)$. *Then, for sufficiently small* δ,

$$\rho(\varphi(p, t), \psi(q, t))=O(\delta^2) \tag{22.15}$$

for $t\in[0, 5\pi/2]$.

Proof. From formulas (22.13), it follows immediately that the trajectory $\psi(q, t)$ of system (22.12) intersects the plane $x=0$ three times during the time interval $0\leqslant t\leqslant 5\pi/2$: At $t=0$, $t=t_1'$ and $t=t_2'$. It is easily seen that here $t_1'=\pi+O(\delta)$ and $t_2'=2\pi+O(\delta)$. But then it follows from (22.14) and the discussion of Section 20 that, for sufficiently small δ, the trajectory $\varphi(p, t)$ also intersects the plane $x=0$ three times in the time interval $[0, 5\pi/2]$: At $t=0$, $t=t_1$, and $t=t_2$. It is clear that here

$$t_1=\pi+O(\delta), \quad t_2=2\pi+O(\delta).$$

It also follows from formulas (22.13) that, in the time interval $[0, t_1']$, the trajectory $\psi(q, t)$ intersects the plane $x=\varepsilon$ twice (at $t=\tau_1'$ and $t=\theta_1$) and the plane $x=2\varepsilon$ (at $t=\tau_2'$ and $t=\theta_2$). It is clear that $\tau_1'<\theta_1<\theta_2<\tau_2'$.

Using (22.14), is not difficult to show that the trajectory $\varphi(p, t)$ of system (22.7) also intersects the plane $x=\varepsilon$ twice in the interval $[0, t_1]$, at $t=\tau_1$ and $t=\tau_2$. Moreover, it follows from formulas (22.13) that $\theta_1=O(\delta)$. But then (22.14) implies that (22.15) is satisfied when $t\in[0, \theta_1]$.

It follows from this estimate that $\tau_1\in(0, \theta_1)$, so that the point $\varphi(p, \theta_1)$ lies in the region $\{x>\varepsilon\}$. From the $E(h, H, \delta)$ conditions and estimate (22.15), it follows that as long as both trajectories $\varphi(p, t)$ and $\psi(q, t)$ lie in the region $\{x>\varepsilon\}$ relationship (22.15) holds. From this relationship it is clear that, in the time interval $\theta_1\leqslant t\leqslant\theta_2$, both of these trajectories lie in the half-space $x>\varepsilon$. If we denote the time after θ_3 at which the trajectory $\psi(q, t)$ intersects the plane $x=-2\varepsilon$ by θ_2, we can prove, as above, that

$$\theta_3-\theta_2=O(\delta).$$

It now follows that (22.15) also holds when $0\leqslant t\leqslant\theta_3$. The lemma follows from a continuation of the same argument. The following equations are consequences of Lemma 22.1:

$$\rho\left(\varphi(p, t_1), \psi(q, t_1')\right)=O(\delta^2); \tag{22.16}$$

$$\rho\left(\varphi(p, t_2), \psi(q, t_2')\right)=O(\delta^2). \tag{22.17}$$

Lemma 22.2. Assume that: The function $\alpha(x)$ *satisfies the* $E(h, H, \delta)$ *conditions with sufficiently small* δ; p *is a point in the region*

$$\left\{x=0,\ |x_1|\leqslant\delta^{\frac{3}{2}},\ y=z_1\geqslant\frac{1}{2}\right\}.$$

Then

$$|x_1(\varphi(p, t_2))|<\delta^{\frac{3}{2}} \tag{22.18}$$

where, as above, t_2 *is the first time after* $t=0$ *at which the trajectory* $\varphi(p, t)$ *intersects the half-space* $\{x=0, y>0\}$.

Proof. It is an immediate consequence of formulas (22.13) and (22.14) that for sufficiently small δ the trajectory $\varphi(p, t)$ intersects the half-plane $\{x=0, y>0\}$ when $t=t_2\in(0, 2\pi/2)$. Now, as above, assume that t_2' is the first time after $t=0$ at which the trajectory $\psi(p, t)$ of system (22.11) intersects the half-plane $\{x=0, y>0\}$. Then it follows from the first of formulas (22.13) that there exists a positive constant $r<1$ such that

$$|x_1(\psi(p,\ t_2'))| < r\delta^{\frac{3}{2}}.$$

The lemma now follows from (22.17).

Consider the following function of the phase-space coordinates:

$$w = \frac{1}{2}(z - x)^2 + \frac{1}{2}y^2. \tag{22.19}$$

The time derivative of this function, obtained with the aid of the differential equations of system (22.7), is

$$\dot{w} = (z - x)\,\alpha(x). \tag{22.20}$$

Consider the following region in the plane $x=0$: $P=\{x=0,\ |x_1|<\delta^{\frac{3}{2}},\ w>(a^2+1)/2,\ y>0\}$. We will denote its close by $\bar{P}$. Now, consider an arbitrary point $p\in\bar{P}$, and let us examine the trajectory $\varphi(p,\ t)$ of system (22.7). If the E conditions are satisfied, then, as the foregoing arguments show, there exist times $0<t_1<t_2$ such that the points $\varphi(p,\ t_1)$ and $\varphi(p,\ t_2)$ lie in the plane $x=0$, and x does not change sign on the trajectory $\varphi(p,\ t)$ in the intervals $0<t<t_1$ and $t_1<t<t_2$. We associate the point $\varphi(p.\ t_2)$ in the half-plane $\{x=0,\ y>0\}$ with the point $p\in\bar{P}$, and denote by T the transformation of the plane region $\bar{P}$ into the half-plane $\{x=0,\ y>0\}$ thus defined. It follows from uniqueness theorem and the theorem on integral continuity that T is one-to-one and continuous in both directions.

Lemma 22.3. If $\alpha(x)$ satisfies the $E(h,\ H,\ \delta)$ conditions with sufficiently small δ, then

$$T\bar{P}\subset P. \tag{22.21}$$

Proof: From Lemmas 22.1 and 22.2 it follows that in order to prove (22.21) it will be sufficient to prove the inequality

$$w(p) < w(\varphi(p,\ t_2)), \tag{22.22}$$

provided that $p\in\{x=0,\ |x_1|\leqslant\delta^{\frac{3}{2}},\ (a^2+1)/2\leqslant w\leqslant 2(a^2+1),\ y>0\}$. We will first show that the inequality

$$w(p) < w(\varphi(p,\ t_1)) \tag{22.23}$$

is satisfied $p\in\{x=0,\ |x_1|\leqslant\delta^{\frac{3}{2}},\ (a^2+1)/2\leqslant w\leqslant 2(a^2+1),\ y>0\}$. As before, t_1 and t_2 in equalities (22.22) and (22.23) denote successive times of intersection of the trajectory $\varphi(p,\ t)$ with the plane $x=0$.

As we have already noted, the trajectory $\varphi(p,\ t)$ intersects the plane $x=\varepsilon$ twice in the time interval $[0,\ t_1]$, at $t=\tau_1$ and $t=\tau_2$, $\tau_1<\tau_2$. Additionally, it is clear that $\varphi(p,\ t)$ intersects the plane $x=\delta$ twice in the interval $0 \leqslant t \leqslant t_1$. Let $t = T_1$ and $t = T_2$ be successive points of intersection of the trajectory $\varphi(p, t)$ with the plane $x = \delta$. Clearly, $0 < T_1 < \tau_1 < \tau_2 < T_2 < t_1$.

We will now compute the increment in w along the trajectory $\varphi(p, t)$ as t varies from $t = 0$ to $t = t_1$. Let y_0 and z_0 be the y- and z-coordinates of the point p, and let $y^{(1)}$ and $z^{(1)}$ be the corresponding coordinates of $\varphi(p, t_1)$. It follows from the definition of the point p that

$$z_0 = ay_0 + O\left(\delta^{\frac{3}{2}}\right). \tag{22.24}$$

Using Lemmas 22.1 and 22.2 and formulas (22.13), it is easy to show that

$$y^{(1)} = -y_0 + O\left(\delta^{\frac{3}{2}}\right), \quad z^{(1)} = -z_0 + O\left(\delta^{\frac{3}{2}}\right). \tag{22.25}$$

We will now estimate, with an accuracy to higher orders of δ, the values of y and z on the trajectory $\varphi(p, t)$ for $t \in [0, \tau_1]$. We have

$$\frac{dy}{dx} = \frac{z - x}{y - f(x)}. \tag{22.26}$$

Since the function $\alpha(x) = f(x) - ax$ satisfies the $E(h, H, \delta)$ conditions, the last equation and Eq. (22.24) imply that the following equation holds on the trajectory $\varphi(p, t)$ when $t \in [0, \tau_1]$:

$$\frac{dy}{dx} = a + O(\delta). \tag{22.27}$$

Integrating this equation along the trajectory $\varphi(p, t)$ from $t = 0$ to $t = \tau_1$, we find that

$$y = y_0 + ax + O(\delta^2). \tag{22.28}$$

Similarly, we can use the equation

$$\frac{dz}{dx} = \frac{-ax}{y - f(x)} \tag{22.29}$$

to show that the following estimate holds on the trajectory $\varphi(p, t)$ for $t \in [0, \tau_2]$:

$$\frac{dz}{dx} = O(\delta). \tag{22.30}$$

Integrating this relationship along $\varphi(p, t)$ for $t \in [0, \tau_1]$ and utilizing (22.24), we obtain the following expression:

$$z = ay_0 + O\left(\delta^{\frac{3}{2}}\right). \tag{22.31}$$

We will now use the same technique to estimate y and z on $\varphi(p, t)$ for $t \in [\tau_2, t_1]$. We obtain (22.27) from (22.26) with the aid of (22.24) and (22.25), and then we use (22.25) to conclude that

$$y = -y_0 + ax + O\left(\delta^{\frac{3}{2}}\right) \tag{22.32}$$

on the trajectory $\varphi(p, t)$ for $t \in [\tau_2, t_1]$. Similarly, we obtain (22.31) from (22.30), and then show that

$$z = -ay_0 + O\left(\delta^{\frac{3}{2}}\right) \tag{22.33}$$

on $\varphi(p, t)$ for $t \in [\tau_2, t_1]$.

We will now estimate the increment of the function w along the trajectory $\varphi(p, t)$ as this trajectory passes through the strip $0 \leqslant x \leqslant \varepsilon$. In order to do so, we consider the function w on the trajectory $\varphi(p, t)$ for $t \in [0, \tau_1]$ and $t \in [\tau_2, t_1]$ as a function of x. Here a nonuniqueness appears, since the trajectory $\varphi(p, t)$ passes through the strip $0 \leqslant x \leqslant \varepsilon$ twice in the interval $[0, t_1]$. In order to eliminate this nonuniquenesss, we identify the function w by a "plus" sign for the time interval $[0, \tau_1]$, and a "minus" sign for the time interval $[\tau_2, t_1]$.

Dividing Eq. (22.20) by the first of the equations of system (22.7), we obtain

$$\frac{dw}{dx} = \frac{z - x}{y - ax - \alpha(x)}\,\alpha(x). \tag{22.34}$$

From this equation and estimates (22.28) and (22.31), it follows that

$$\frac{dw_+}{dx} = \frac{ay_0 - x + O\left(\delta^{\frac{3}{2}}\right)}{y_0 - \alpha(x) + O(\delta^2)}\,\alpha(x). \tag{22.35}$$

Similarly, Eq. (22.34) and estimates (22.32) and (22.33) show that

$$\frac{dw_-}{dx} = \frac{-ay_0 - x + O\left(\delta^{\frac{3}{2}}\right)}{-y_0 - \alpha(x) + O\left(\delta^{\frac{3}{2}}\right)}\,\alpha(x). \tag{22.36}$$

We will now find the difference $(dw_+/dx) - (dw_-/dx)$. Direct computation shows that the following equation holds:

$$\frac{dw_+}{dx} - \frac{dw_-}{dx} = 2\,\frac{a\alpha(x) - x + O\left(\delta^{\frac{3}{2}}\right)}{\left(y_0 - \alpha(x) + O\left(\delta^{\frac{3}{2}}\right)\right)\left(y_0 + \alpha(x) + O\left(\delta^{\frac{3}{2}}\right)\right)}\,y_0\alpha(x). \tag{22.37}$$

This estimate is valid on the trajectory $\varphi(p, t)$ for $0 \leqslant x \leqslant \varepsilon$.

We will now estimate the increment of the function w along the trajectory $\varphi(p, t)$ as it passes across the strip $0 \leqslant x \leqslant \delta$. By hypothesis, we have $p \in \{x=0, |x_1| \leqslant \delta^{\frac{3}{2}}, (a^2+1)/2 \leqslant w \leqslant 2(a^2+1)\}$; but then, by the definition of w, it follows that

$$1 + O(\delta) \leqslant y_0 \leqslant 2 + O(\delta). \tag{22.38}$$

Hence, (22.37) and the $E(h, H, \delta)$ conditions imply that for sufficiently small δ

$$\frac{dw_+}{dx} - \frac{dw_-}{dx} > \frac{1}{2}[a\alpha(x) - x]\alpha(x) + O\left(\delta^{\frac{3}{2}}\right)\alpha(x). \tag{22.39}$$

Therefore, since $hx \leqslant \alpha(x) \leqslant Hx$ for $0 < x \leqslant \delta$ by the E conditions, we find that

$$\frac{dw_+}{dx} - \frac{dw_-}{dx} > \frac{1}{2}(ah-1)hx^2 + O\left(\delta^{\frac{5}{2}}\right) \tag{22.40}$$

for $x \in [0, \delta]$. Integrating this inequality from $x=0$ to $x=\delta$, we obtain

$$\Delta_1 w > \frac{1}{6}(ah-1)h\delta^3 + O\left(\delta^{\frac{7}{2}}\right), \tag{22.41}$$

where $\Delta_1 w$ is the increment in the function w along the trajectory $\varphi(p, t)$ in the strip $0 \leqslant x \leqslant \delta$.

We will now estimate the increment of the function w along the trajectory $\varphi(p, t)$ in the strip, $\delta \leqslant x \leqslant \varepsilon$. From (22.37), (22.38), and the $E(h, H, \delta)$ conditions, it follows that

$$\frac{dw_+}{dx} - \frac{dw_-}{dx} > -4x\alpha(x) + O\left(\delta^{\frac{5}{2}}\right). \tag{22.42}$$

This inequality is valid on the trajectory $\varphi(p, t)$ for $x \in [\delta, \varepsilon]$. Integrating inequality (22.42) from $x=\delta$ to $x=\varepsilon$, we obtain

$$\Delta_2 w > -\frac{4}{3}H(\varepsilon^3 - \delta^3) + O\left(\delta^{\frac{5}{2}}\right)(\varepsilon - \delta); \tag{22.43}$$

here $\Delta_2 w$ denotes the increment of the function w as the trajectory $\varphi(p, t)$ passes through the strip $\delta \leqslant x \leqslant \varepsilon$. From inequality (22.43) and condition (22.4), it follows that

$$\Delta_2 w > O(\delta^4). \tag{22.44}$$

Finally, we will estimate the increment of the function w along the trajectory $\varphi(p, t)$ for $t \in [\tau_1, \tau_2]$. From (22.13), (22.14), and the definition of p, it follows that, in the interval $[0, t_1]$, that the absolute values of all coordinates of the trajectory $\varphi(p, t)$ are bounded by the same number which depends only on the parameter a of system (22.7). By the definition of τ_1 and τ_2, $x \geqslant \varepsilon$ on the trajectory $\varphi(p, t)$ when $t \in [\tau_1, \tau_2]$; but then it follows from condition (22.3) that $0 < \alpha(x) \leqslant \delta^4$ on $\varphi(p, t)$ when $t \in [\tau_1, \tau_2]$. Therefore, it follows from (22.20) that the following equation is satisfied on the trajectory $\varphi(p, t)$ when $t \in [\tau_1, \tau_2]$:

$$w = O(\delta^4). \tag{22.45}$$

Moreover, it follows from (22.13) and (22.14) that $\tau_2 - \tau_1 < 2\pi$, and therefore, it follows from (22.45) that

$$\Delta_3 w = O(\delta^4), \tag{22.46}$$

where $\Delta_3 w$ denotes the increment of the function w along the trajectory $\varphi(p, t)$ in the time interval $\tau_1 \leqslant t \leqslant \tau_2$. Combining (22.41), (22.44), and (22.46), we find that

$$\Delta w > \frac{1}{6}(ah - 1) h\delta^3 + O\left(\delta^{\frac{7}{2}}\right), \tag{22.47}$$

where Δw is the increment of the function w along the trajectory $\varphi(p, t)$ for $t \in [0, t_1]$. It now follows from condition (22.5) that inequality (22.23) holds for sufficiently small δ.

Inequality (22.22) can be proved by the extension of this argument to $t > t_1$, and, as noted above, the lemma follows from this inequality. Q.E.D.

We will now prove a theorem on the existence of periodic solutions for system (20.5).

Theorem 22.1. Assume that: $\alpha(x) = f(x)$ *satisfies the* $E(h, H, \delta)$ *conditions with sufficiently small* δ; *there exists a positive* λ *such that*

$$\alpha(x)\, x \geqslant \lambda \quad \textit{for} \quad |x| \geqslant \varepsilon, \tag{22.48}$$

where the ε *is the same as that appearing in the* E *conditions. Then system (22.7) has periodic solutions other than equilibrium states.*

Proof. As above, let P denote the region

$$\left\{x = 0,\ |x_1| < \delta^{\frac{3}{2}},\ w > \frac{1}{2}(a^2 + 1),\ y > 0\right\},$$

where w is the function defined by Eq. (22.19). Now, consider the function v defined by the formula

$$v = \frac{1}{2} x_1^2 + \frac{1}{2} a^2 y_1^2 + \frac{1}{2} a^2 z_1^2 - a^3 \int_0^x \alpha(x)\,dx. \tag{22.49}$$

In virtue of the differential equations of system (22.7), the time derivative of the function v is

$$\dot{v} = -ax_1^2 - a^2(x - a\alpha(x))\,\alpha(x). \tag{22.50}$$

Consider an arbitrary point $p \in \bar{P}$, and let $0, t_1, t_2$ denote the points at which the trajectory $\varphi(p, t)$ intersects the plane $x = 0$. As proved above, there exists within the time interval $0 < t < t_1$ two and only two points at which the trajectory $\varphi(p, t)$ intersects the plane $x = \varepsilon$. Let τ_1 and τ_2 be these points, and assume that $\tau_1 < \tau_2$.

It follows from formulas (22.13) and estimate (22.14) that, if we choose a sufficiently large $v_0 > 2(a^2 + 1)$, the inequality

$$aH^2\varepsilon^2(\tau_1 + t_1 - \tau_2) < \frac{\lambda}{2}(\tau_2 - \tau_1) \tag{22.51}$$

will be satisfied on the trajectory $\varphi(p, t)$, provided that the point p is located on that part of the curve $\{x = 0, v = v_0\}$ which lies in the closed region $\bar{P}$. Denote this curve by l, and let p be an arbitrary point on it. We will now compute the increment Δv of the function v along the trajectory $\varphi(p, t)$ from 0 to t_1. It follows from formula (22.50) and the E conditions that the inequality

$$\dot{v} < a^3H^2\varepsilon^2 \tag{22.52}$$

is satisfied on $\varphi(p, t)$ for $t \in [0, \tau_1]$ and $t \in [\tau_2, t_1]$. If we denote the total increment of the function v along the trajectory $\varphi(p, t)$ over the time intervals $[0, \tau_1]$ and $[\tau_2, t_1]$ by $\Delta_1 v$, inequality (22.52) yields the inequality

$$\Delta_1 v > a^3H^2\varepsilon^2(\tau_1 + t_1 - \tau_2). \tag{22.53}$$

It follows from Eq. (22.50) and the $E(h, H, \delta)$ conditions that for sufficiently small δ

$$\dot{v} < -\frac{a^2}{2} x\alpha(x) \tag{22.54}$$

on the trajectory $\varphi(p, t)$ when $t \in [\tau_1, \tau_2]$; this, together with condition (22.48), proves that

$$\dot{v} < -\frac{a^2}{2}\lambda \tag{22.55}$$

on $\varphi(p, t)$ and $t \in [\tau_1, \tau_2]$.

Let $\Delta_2 v$ be the increment of the function v along the trajectory $\varphi(p, t)$ in the time interval $[\tau_1, \tau_2]$. Integrating inequality (22.55) along $\varphi(p, t)$ from $t=\tau_1$ to $t=\tau_2$, we find that

$$\Delta_2 v < -\frac{a^2\lambda}{2}(\tau_2-\tau_1). \tag{22.56}$$

Combining (22.53) with (22.56), we find, in virtue of (22.51),

$$\Delta v < 0. \tag{22.57}$$

The last inequality implies that

$$v(p) > v(\varphi(p, t_1)). \tag{22.58}$$

Application of the same argument to the time interval between t_1 and t_2 shows that

$$v(p) > v(\varphi(p, t_2)). \tag{22.59}$$

Let Q denote the region $\{x=0, |x_1| < \delta^{\frac{3}{2}}, v < v_0, w > (a^2+1)/2, y > 0\}$, and, as above, let T denote the transformation of the closed region $\bar{P}$ into itself, which occurs during motion along the trajectories of system (20.5). It follows from Lemma 22.3 and inequality (22.59) that

$$T\bar{Q} \subset Q. \tag{22.60}$$

It now follows from the Brouwer theorem that the region Q contains a point q that is stationary under T. But then, by the definition of T, the trajectory $\varphi(q, t)$ is the trajectory of a periodic motion of system (20.5). Q.E.D.

References

1. V. V. Nemytskiy and V. V. Stepanov, Qualitative Theory of Differential Equations, Princeton Univ. Press, 1960.
2. G. D. Birkhoff, Dynamical Systems, Pub. Amer. Math. Soc., N. Y., 1927.
3. E. A. Coddington and N. Levinson, Theory of Ordinary Differential Equations, McGraw-Hill, N. Y., 1955.
4. F. Hausdorff, Set Theory (German) Dover Pub., 1944; (English translation) Chelsea Pub. Co., 1962.
5. J. Massera, Boletin de la Facultad de Ingenieria, IV, 1 mayo, 1950.
6. J. Massera, Publ. Inst. mat. Fac. ingr., 2, 7, 1954.
7. N. P. Erugin, Appl. Math. Mech. Vol. XX, No. 1, 1956.
8. Ya. Kurtsveyl' and O. Veyvoda, Czechoslovakian Mathematics Journal, Vol. 5, No. 3, 1955, pp. 362-370.
9. N. P. Erugin, Dokl. Acad. Sci., BSSR, Vol. VI, No. 7, 1962.
10. N. Levinson, Annals of Math., 45, 4, 1944, pp. 723-737.
11. B. P. Demidovich, Vest. Moscow State Univ., Vol. I, No. 6, 1961.
12. E. A. Barbashin, Matem. Sb., Vol. 29(71), 1951.
13. T. Yoshizawa, Mem. Coll. Sci. Univ. Kyoto, No. 3, 1955.
14. Ya. Kurtsveyl', Czechoslovakian Mathematical Journal, Vol. 5, No. 3, 1955.
15. I. G. Malkin, The Theory of Stability of Motion (in Russian), Gostekhizdat, 1952.
16. J. Massera, Annals of Math., 50, 3, 1949, pp. 705-721.
17. J. Whithey, Trans. of American Math. Soc., 36, 1934.
18. V. V. Nemytskiy, "On certain methods for qualitative investigation 'in the large' of multidimensional autonomous systems," Tr. Mosk. matem. o-va, Vol. 5, 1956.
19. P. V. Atrashenok, Vestn. Leningrad State Univ., No. 8, (3), 1954.
20. P. Bol', On Certain Differential Equations of a General Nature, Applicable to Mechanics (in Russian), Yur'yev, 1900.
21. K. Corduneanu, C. r. Acad. sci., 245, No. 1, 1957.
22. K. Corduneanu, An stünt. Univ. Iasi. Sec., 1, 3, No. 1-2, 1957.
23. K. Corduneanu, Dokl. Acad. Sci. USSR, Vol. 131, No. 4, 1960.
24. K. Corduneanu, Acad. RPR, Fil. Iasi. Mat., 8, No. 2, 1957, 107-126.

25. B. Manfredi, Boll. Unione mat. ital., No. 1, 1956, 64-71.
26. D. Craffi, Atti IV congr. Unione mat. ital., 1, 1953, 218-231.
27. A. Castro, Rend. Seminar mat. Univ. Padova, 22, No. 2, 1953.
28. V. A. Pliss, Dokl. Acad. Sci. BSSR, Vol. 5, No. 6, 1961.
29. I. O. C. Ezeilo, Proc. Lond. Math. Soc., 9, No. 13, 1959, 74-114.
30. V. A. Pliss, Dokl. Acad. Sci. USSR, Vol. 139, No. 2, 1961.
31. M. A. Krasnosel'skiy and A. I. Perov, Dokl. Acad. Sci. USSR, Vol. 123, No. 2, 1962.
32. M. A. Krasnosel'skiy, Positive Solutions of Operator Equations (in Russian), Stechert, N. Y., 1965.
33. I. Barbalat and A. Halanay, Rev. Math. pures at appl. (RPR), 3, 1958, 395-411.
34. V. A. Pliss, Dokl. Acad. Sci. USSR, Vol. 137, No. 5, 1961.
35. V. A. Pliss, Vestn. Leningrad State Univ., No. 11, 1954.
36. N. N. Krasovskiy, Prikl. Mat. Mekh., Vol. 21, No. 3, 1957, pp. 309-319.
37. V. A. Pliss, Dokl. Acad. Sci. USSR, Vol. 138, No. 2, 1961.
38. T. Yoshizawa, Mem. Coll. Sci. Univ. Kyoto, A28, No. 2, 1954, 43-151.
39. V. I. Zubov, Oscillations in Nonlinear and Controlled Systems (in Russian), Sudpromgiz, 1962.
40. N. Ya. Lyashchenko, Dokl. Acad. Sci. USSR, Vol. 104, No. 2, 1955, pp. 177-179.
41. A. M. Lyapunov, The General Problem of Stability of Motion (in Russian), Acad. Sci. USSR, 1956.
42. B. P. Demidovich, Uch. zap. Moscow State Univ., Vol. 8, 1956, p. 181.
43. A. I. Lur'ye, Certain Nonlinear Problems in the Theory of Automatic Controls (in Russian), Gostekhizdat, 1951.
44. M. L. Cartwright, Contrib. to the theory of nonlinear oscillations, 1, 1950.
45. S. Lefschetz, Differential Equations; Geometric Theory (English edition, Interscience Publishers, N. Y., 1957).
46. Z. Opial, Ann. Polon. math., 7, No. 3, 1960, 309-319.
47. V. A. Pliss, Dokl. Acad. Sci. USSR, Vol. 127, No. 5, 1959.
48. A. Denjoy, J. de Mathematiques, 11, 1932, 333-375.
49. V. A. Pliss, Vestn. Leningrad State Univ., No. 13, 1960.
50. Chin Yuan-shun, Science Record, 1, No. 3, 7-11, 1957.
51. A. A. Andronov and L. S. Pontryagin, Dokl. Acad. Sci. USSR, Vol. 14, No. 5, 1937.
52. G. F. DeBaggis, "Coarse systems of two differential equations," Usp. Matemat. Nauk, Vol. 10, No. 4, 1955, pp. 101-126 (Translation from "Contributions to the Theory of Nonlinear Oscillations," Princeton Univ. Press, Vol. II, 1952, Annals of Math. Studies No. 29; Translator's preface by M. I. Minkeirch.)

53. J. Massera, Duke Math. J., 17, 4, 1950, pp. 457-475.
54. L. E. J. Brouwer, Math. Annalen, 72, 1912.
55. A. A. Andronov and A. G. Mayer, Avtomat. i Telemekh., Vol. 14, No. 5, 1953.
56. N. N. Krasovskiy, Problems in the Theory of Stability of Motion (in Russian), Fizmatgiz, 1959 (English edition: Stanford Univ. Press, 1963).
57. C. Caratheodory, Math. Annalen, 73, 1913, 305-320.
58. A. I. Markushevich, Theory of Analytic Functions (in Russian), Gostekhizdat, 1950 (English edition: Prentice-Hall, N. J., 1964).
59. M. L. Cartwright and J. E. Littlewood, Annals of Math., 54, 1951, 1-37.
60. E. R. Reifenberger, Annals of Math., 61, 1, 1955, pp. 137-139.
61. N. N. Bogolyubov and Yu. A. Mitropol'skiy, Asymptotic Methods in the Theory of Nonlinear Oscillations (in Russian), Fizmatgiz, 1958 (English edition: Gordon and Breach, N. Y., 1962).
62. N, M. Krylov and N. N. Bogolyubov, Application of Methods from Nonlinear Mechanics to the Theory of Stationary Oscillations (in Russian), Kiev, 1934 (English edition: Introduction to Nonlinear Mechanics, Princeton Univ. Press, 1943).
63. M. D. Marcus, Ann. math. studies, No. 36, Ed. S. Lefschetz, Princeton Univ. Press, 1956.
64. S. P. Diliberto and G. Hufford, Ann. Math. studies, No. 36, Ed. S. Lefschetz, Princeton Univ. Press, 1956.
65. P. Koosis, Ann. math. studies, No. 36, Ed. S. Lefschetz, Princeton Univ. Press, 1956.
66. N. Levinson, Annals of Math., 52, 1958, 727-738.
67. I. G. Malkin, Problems in the Theory of Nonlinear Oscillations (in Russian), Gostekhizdat, 1956.
68. N. P. Erugin, Reducible Systems (in Russian), Acad. Sci. USSR, 1946.
69. V. A. Pliss, Dokl. Acad. Sci. USSR, Vol. 131, No. 5, 1960.
70. Borg Göran, Kingl. Tekn. Hogskol. handl., No. 153, 1960, 12 pp.
71. J. E. Littlewood, Acta math., 97, 3-4, 1957, pp. 267-308.
72. J. E. Littlewood, Acta math., 98, 1-2, 1957, pp. 1-110.
73. J. E. Littlewood, IRE Trans. circuit theory, 7, 4, 535-542, 1960.
74. N. Levinson, Annals of Math., 50, 1949, No. 36, 126-153.
75. R. E. Gomory, Ann. math. studies, 36, Ed. S. Lefschetz, Princeton Univ. Press, 1956.
76. H. Poincaré, On Curves Defined by Differential Equations (Russian translation), Gostekhizdat, 1947.

77. H. Ehrman, Zs. angew. Math. und Mech., 35, 1955, 9-10, 326-327.
78. H. Ehrman, Arch. Ration. Mech. and Analysis, 1, 2, 1957, 124-137.
79. G. R. Morris, Proc. Cambridge Phil. soc., 51, 2, 1955, pp. 297-312.
80. G. R. Morris, Proc. Cambridge Phil. soc., 54, 4, 1958, pp. 424-438.
81. L. L. Rauch, Ann. Math. studies, No. 20, Ed. S. Lefschetz, Princeton Univ. Press, 1950, pp. 39-88.
82. K. O. Friedrichs, pp. 65-103 of Studies in Nonlinear Vibration Theory, Lecture Notes, New York University, 1946.
83. G. Colombo, Rend. Sem. mat. univ. Padova, XIX, 1950.
84. B. V. Shirokorad, Avtomat. i Telemekh., Vol. 19, No. 10, 1958.
85. E. M. Vaysbord, Izvestiya vyssh. uch. zaved., Matematika, No. 4, 1959, pp. 38-49.
86. E. M. Vaysbord, Nauchn. dokl. shkoly, Fiz.-matem. nauki, No. 3, 1958, pp. 10-13.
87. V. S. Blinchevskiy, Matem. sb., Vol. 50(92), No. 1, 1960.
88. E. M. Vaysbord, Matem. sb., Vol. 56(98), No. 1, 1962.
89. V. A. Pliss, Problems in the Theory of Stability of Motion in the Large (in Russian), Leningrad State Univ. Press, 1958.
90. A. A. Andronov, A. A. Vitt and S. E. Khaykin, Theory of Oscillations (in Russian), Fizmatgiz, 1959.
91. M. L. Cartwright, Proc. Int. Congr. Math., Vol. 3, 1954, pp. 71-76.
92. V. A. Pliss, Vestn. Leningrad State Univ., No. 13, 1962.

Index